2 Grammar in Context

4TH EDITION

SANDRA N. ELBAUM

Australia • Brazil • Japan • Korea • Mexico • Singapore • Spain • United Kingdom • United States

Grammar in Context 2, Fourth Edition

SANDRA N. ELBAUM

JUDI PEMÁN

Publisher, Adult & Academic, ESL: James W. Brown

Senior Acquisitions Editor, Adult & Academic, ESL: Sherrise Roehr

Director of Product Development: Anita Raducanu

Associate Development Editors: Yeny Kim, Tom Jefferies

Production Manager: Sally Giangrande

Director of Marketing: Amy Mabley

Marketing Manager: Laura Needham

Senior Print Buyer: Mary Beth Hennebury

Development Editor: Charlotte Sturdy

Compositor: Nesbitt Graphics, Inc.

Project Manager: Julie DeSilva

Photo Researcher: Connie Gardner

Illustrators: Ralph Canaday, James Edwards, Larry Frederick, and Brock Nichol

Interior Designer: Jerilyn Bockorick

Cover Designer: Joseph Sherman

Photo credits appear at the end of the book, which constitutes an extension of this copyright page.

Copyright © 2006 by Sandra N. Elbaum

Cover Image: © Jerry Emmons

ALL RIGHTS RESERVED. No part of this work covered by the copyright herein may be reproduced, transmitted, stored or used in any form or by any means graphic, electronic, or mechanical, including but not limited to photocopying, recording, scanning, digitizing, taping, Web distribution, information networks, or information storage and retrieval systems, except as permitted under Section 107 or 108 of the 1976 United States Copyright Act, without the prior written permission of the publisher.

> For product information and technology assistance, contact us at
> **Cengage Learning Customer & Sales Support, 1-800-354-9706**
> For permission to use material from this text or product, submit all requests online at **cengage.com/permissions**
> Further permissions questions can be emailed to
> **permissionrequest@cengage.com**

Library of Congress Control Number: 2006900241

ISBN-13: 978-1-4130-0742-8

ISBN-10: 1-4130-0742-2

ISE ISBN-13: 978-1-4130-1395-5

ISE ISBN-10: 1-4130-1395-3

Heinle
25 Thomson Place
Boston, MA 02210
USA

Cengage Learning is a leading provider of customized learning solutions with office locations around the globe, including Singapore, the United Kingdom, Australia, Mexico, Brazil, and Japan. Locate your local office at:
international.cengage.com/region

Cengage Learning products are represented in Canada by Nelson Education, Ltd.

Visit **elt.heinle.com**

Visit our corporate website at **cengage.com**

Printed in the United States of America
8 9 10   09 08

In loving memory of
Roberto Garrido Alfaro

Acknowledgments

Many thanks to Dennis Hogan, Jim Brown, Sherrise Roehr, Yeny Kim, and Sally Giangrande from Thomson Heinle for their ongoing support of the *Grammar in Context* series. I would especially like to thank my editor, Charlotte Sturdy, for her keen eye to detail and invaluable suggestions.

And many thanks to my students at Truman College, who have increased my understanding of my own language and taught me to see life from another point of view. By sharing their observations, questions, and life stories, they have enriched my life enormously—*Sandra N. Elbaum*

Thomson Heinle would like to thank the following people for their contributions:

Marki Alexander
Oklahoma State University
Stillwater, OK

Joan M. Amore
Triton College
River Grove, IL

Edina Pingleton Bagley
Nassau Community College
Garden City, NY

Judith A. G. Benka
Normandale Community College
Bloomington, MN

Judith Book-Ehrlichman
Bergen Community College
Paramus, NJ

Lyn Buchheit
Community College of Philadelphia
Philadelphia, PA

Charlotte M. Calobrisi
Northern Virginia Community College
Annandale, VA

Sarah A. Carpenter
Normandale Community College
Bloomington, MN

Jeanette Clement
Duquesne University
Pittsburgh, PA

Allis Cole
Shoreline Community College
Shoreline, WA

Jacqueline M. Cunningham
Triton College
River Grove, IL

Lisa DePaoli
Sierra College
Rocklin, CA

Maha Edlbi
Sierra College
Rocklin, CA

Rhonda J. Farley
Cosumnes River College
Sacramento, CA

Jennifer Farnell
University of Connecticut
American Language Program
Stamford, CT

Abigail-Marie Fiattarone
Mesa Community College
Mesa, AZ

Marcia Gethin-Jones
University of Connecticut
American Language Program
Storrs, CT

Linda Harlow
Santa Rosa Junior College
Santa Rosa, CA

Suha R. Hattab
Triton College
River Grove, IL

Bill Keniston
Normandale Community College
Bloomington, MN

Walton King
Arkansas State University
Jonesboro, AR

Kathleen Krokar
Truman College
Chicago, IL

John Larkin
NVCC-Community and Workforce Development
Annandale, VA

Michael Larsen
American River College
Sacramento, CA

Bea C. Lawn
Gavilan College
Gilroy, CA

Rob Lee
Pasadena City College
Pasadena, CA

Oranit Limmaneeprasert
American River College
Sacramento, CA

Gennell Lockwood
Shoreline Community College
Shoreline, WA

Linda Louie
Highline Community College
Des Moines, WA

Melanie A. Majeski
Naugatuck Valley Community College
Waterbury, CT

Maria Marin
De Anza College
Cupertino, CA

Karen Miceli
Cosumnes River College
Sacramento, CA

Jeanie Pavichevich
Triton College
River Grove, IL

Herbert Pierson
St. John's University
New York City, NY

Dina Poggi
De Anza College
Cupertino, CA

Mark Rau
American River College
Sacramento, CA

John W. Roberts
Shoreline Community College
Shoreline, WA

Azize R. Ruttler
Bergen Community College
Paramus, NJ

Ann Salzmann
University of Illinois,
Urbana, IL

Eva Teagarden
Yuba College
Marysville, CA

Susan Wilson
San Jose City College
San Jose, CA

Martha Yeager-Tobar
Cerritos College
Norwalk, CA

Contents

Lesson 1   1

GRAMMAR   The Simple Present Tense; Frequency Words
CONTEXT   Pets and Other Animals
READING   Americans and Their Pets   2
    1.1   *Be*—Forms and Uses   3
    1.2   Contractions with *Be*   5
READING   Dog Walkers   7
    1.3   Questions with *Be*   8
READING   Guide Dogs   14
    1.4   The Simple Present Tense—Affirmative Statements   15
    1.5   Negative Statements with the Simple Present Tense 17
READING   Search and Rescue Dogs   18
    1.6   Questions with the Simple Present Tense   19
    1.7   *Wh-* Questions with a Preposition   21
    1.8   Questions About Meaning, Spelling, and Cost   23
READING   Marianne and Sparky   26
    1.9   Simple Present Tense with Frequency Words   27
    1.10   Position of Frequency Words and Expressions   29
    1.11   Questions with *Ever*   31
    1.12   Questions with *How Often* and Answers with Frequency Expressions   32

Summary   33
Editing Advice   33
Test/Review   36
Expansion Activities 39

Lesson 2   43

GRAMMAR	The Present Continuous Tense; Action and Nonaction Verbs; The Future Tense	
CONTEXT	Getting Older	
READING	Retirement Living	44
2.1	Present Continuous Tense	46
READING	Life After Retirement	48
2.2	Using the Present Continuous for Longer Actions	49
2.3	Questions with the Present Continuous Tense	51
2.4	Contrasting the Simple Present and the Present Continuous	56
2.5	Action and Nonaction Verbs	59
READING	The Graying of America	64
2.6	The Future Tense with *Will*	66
2.7	The Future Tense with *Be Going To*	69
2.8	*Will* vs. *Be Going To*	72
2.9	Future Tense + Time / *If* Clause	75
	Summary	79
	Editing Advice	80
	Test/Review	81
	Expansion Activities	85

Lesson 3   87

GRAMMAR	Habitual Past with *Used To*; The Simple Past Tense	
CONTEXT	Working Towards a Better Life	
READING	Equal Rights for All	88
3.1	Habitual Past with *Used To*	90
READING	George Dawson—Life Is So Good	92
3.2	Past Tense of *Be*	94
3.3	The Simple Past Tense of Regular Verbs	96
3.4	The Simple Past Tense of Irregular Verbs	98
3.5	Negative Statements	101
3.6	Questions with the Simple Past Tense	103
	Summary	106
	Editing Advice	106
	Test/Review	108
	Expansion Activities	111

Lesson 4   **115**

GRAMMAR	Possessive Forms; Object Pronouns; Reflexive Pronouns; Questions	
CONTEXT	Weddings	
READING	A Traditional American Wedding	116
4.1	Possessive Forms of Nouns	117
4.2	Possessive Adjectives	119
4.3	Possessive Pronouns	120
4.4	Questions with *Whose*	123
4.5	Object Pronouns	124
READING	New Wedding Trends	126
4.6	Direct and Indirect Objects	127
4.7	*Say* and *Tell*	128
READING	Economizing on a Wedding	129
4.8	Reflexive Pronouns	131
READING	Questions and Answers About an American Wedding	133
4.9	Questions About the Subject or Complement	135
	Summary	140
	Editing Advice	141
	Test/Review	143
	Expansion Activities	147

Lesson 5   **149**

GRAMMAR	Singular and Plural; Count and Noncount Nouns; *There* + *Be*; Quantity Words	
CONTEXT	Thanksgiving, Pilgrims, and American Indians	
READING	A Typical Thanksgiving	150
5.1	Noun Plurals	151
5.2	Using the Singular and Plural for Generalizations	154
5.3	Special Cases of Singular and Plural	155
READING	The Origin of Thanksgiving	156
5.4	Noncount Nouns	158
5.5	Count and Noncount Nouns	159
READING	Recipe for Turkey Stuffing	161
5.6	Quantities with Count and Noncount Nouns	162

READING	Taking the Land from the Native Americans	163
5.7	*There* + a Form of *Be*	164
5.8	Using *There*	165
READING	Code Talkers	166
5.9	Quantity Expressions— An Overview	167
5.10	*Some, Any, A, No*	169
5.11	*A Lot Of, Much, Many*	171
5.12	*A Lot Of* vs. *Too Much / Too Many*	172
5.13	*A Few, Several, A Little*	174
5.14	*A Few* vs. *Few*; *A Little* vs. *Little*	175
	Summary	179
	Editing Advice	180
	Test/Review	181
	Expansion Activities	185

Lesson 6   187

GRAMMAR	Adjectives; Noun Modifiers; Adverbs; *Too / Enough / Very / A Lot Of*	
CONTEXT	Health	
READING	Obesity: A National Problem	188
6.1	Adjectives	190
6.2	Noun Modifiers	192
READING	Obesity: The Solution	194
6.3	Adverbs of Manner	196
6.4	Adjective vs. Adverb	198
READING	Sleep	200
6.5	*Too* and *Enough*	201
6.6	*Too* and *Very* and *A Lot Of*	203
	Summary	204
	Editing Advice	205
	Test/Review	206
	Expansion Activities	208

Lesson 7   211

GRAMMAR	Time Words and Time Clauses; The Past Continuous Tense	
CONTEXT	Immigrants	
READING	Ellis Island	212
7.1	*When, Until, While*	213
7.2	*When* and *Whenever*	215

	7.3	Time Words	216
	7.4	The Past Continuous Tense—An Overview	218
READING		Albert Einstein—Immigrant from Germany	218
	7.5	The Past Continuous Tense—Forms	220
	7.6	The Past Continuous Tense—Uses	221
	7.7	***Was / Were Going To***	226
READING		Gloria Estefan—Cuban Immigrant	227
	7.8	Simple Past vs. Past Continuous with ***When***	228
	7.9	Simple Past vs. Past Continuous	229
	7.10	Using the *–ing* Form After Time Words	230
		Summary	231
		Editing Advice	232
		Test/Review	232
		Expansion Activities	235

Lesson 8   237

GRAMMAR		Modals; Related Expressions	
CONTEXT		Renting an Apartment	
	8.1	Modals and Related Expressions—An Overview	238
READING		An Apartment Lease	238
	8.2	Negatives with Modals	240
	8.3	Statements and Questions with Modals	241
	8.4	***Must, Have To, Have Got To***	242
	8.5	Obligation with ***Must*** or ***Be Supposed To***	244
	8.6	***Can, May, Could,*** and Alternate Expressions	246
READING		Tenants' Rights	249
	8.7	***Should; Had Better***	250
	8.8	Negatives of Modals	253
READING		The New Neighbors	258
	8.9	***Must*** for Conclusions	259
	8.10	***Will*** and ***May / Might***	261
READING		At a Garage Sale	264
	8.9	Using Modals and Questions for Politeness	265
		Summary	269
		Editing Advice	270
		Test/Review	272
		Expansion Activities	274

Lesson 9   277

GRAMMAR   The Present Perfect; The Present Perfect Continuous
CONTEXT   Searching the Web

9.1	The Present Perfect Tense—An Overview	278

READING   Google   278

9.2	The Past Participle	280
9.3	Irregular Past Participle Forms of Verbs	281
9.4	The Present Perfect—Contractions, Negatives	282
9.5	Adding an Adverb	283
9.6	The Present Perfect—Statements and Questions	284
9.7	Continuation from Past to Present	285
9.8	The Simple Present vs. the Present Perfect	288
9.9	The Present Perfect vs. the Simple Past	290
9.10	The Present Perfect Continuous—An Overview	292

READING   Genealogy   292

9.11	The Present Perfect Continuous—Forms	293
9.12	The Present Perfect Continuous—Statements and Questions	294
9.13	The Present Perfect Continuous—Use	295
9.14	The Present Perfect with Repetition from Past to Present	299
9.15	The Simple Past vs. the Present Perfect with Repetition	301
9.16	The Present Perfect with Indefinite Past Time	302
9.17	Answering a Present Perfect Question	304

Summary   308
Editing Advice   309
Test/Review   310
Expansion Activities   313

Lesson 10   315

GRAMMAR   Gerunds; Infinitives
CONTEXT   Finding a Job

10.1	Gerunds—An Overview	316

READING   Finding a Job   316

10.2	Gerund as Subject	318
10.3	Gerund After Verb	320
10.4	Gerund After Preposition	322
10.5	Gerund in Adverbial Phrase	325
10.6	Infinitives—An Overview	327

READING   Tips on Writing a Résumé   327

10.7	Infinitive as Subject	329
10.8	Infinitive After Adjective	331

10.9	Infinitive After Verb	333
10.10	Gerund or Infinitive After Verb	335
10.11	Object Before Infinitive	336
10.12	Infinitive to Show Purpose	338

READING Rita's Story — 339

10.13 ***Used To*** vs. ***Be Used To*** — 341

Summary — 345
Editing Advice — 346
Test/Review — 347
Expansion Activities — 350

Lesson 11 — 353

GRAMMAR Adjective Clauses

CONTEXT Making Connections—Old Friends and New

11.1 Adjective Clauses—An Overview — 354

READING Finding Old Friends — 354

11.2 Relative Pronoun as Subject — 356
11.3 Relative Pronoun as Object — 358
11.4 ***Where*** and ***When*** — 362
11.5 Formal vs. Informal — 363

READING Internet Matchmaking — 364

11.6 ***Whose*** + Noun — 365

Summary — 369
Editing Advice — 370
Test/Review — 371
Expansion Activities — 373

Lesson 12 — 375

GRAMMAR Superlatives; Comparatives

CONTEXT Sports and Athletes

12.1 Superlatives and Comparatives—An Overview — 376

READING Michael Jordan — 376

12.2 The Superlative Form — 378
12.3 Comparative and Superlative Forms of Adjectives and Adverbs — 379
12.4 Superlatives and Word Order — 384

READING Americans' Attitude Toward Soccer — 385

12.5 Comparatives — 386
12.6 Comparatives and Word Order — 388

READING	An Amazing Athlete	390
	12.7 *As . . . As*	391
	12.8 *As Many / Much . . . As*	393
	12.9 *The Same . . . As*	395
	12.10 Equality with Nouns or Adjectives	396
READING	Football and Soccer	397
	12.11 Similarity with *Like* and *Alike*	398
	12.12 *Be Like*	400
	12.13 Same or Different	401
	Summary	404
	Editing Advice	405
	Test/Review	406
	Expansion Activities	408

Lesson 13   413

GRAMMAR	Passive Voice and Active Voice	
CONTEXT	The Law	
	13.1 The Passive Voice and the Active Voice—An Overview	414
READING	Jury Duty	414
	13.2 The Passive Voice	415
	13.3 Passive Voice—Form and Use	416
	13.4 Negatives and Questions with Passive Voice	421
READING	Unusual Lawsuits	422
	13.5 Choosing Active Voice or Passive Voice	424
	Summary	429
	Editing Advice	431
	Test/Review	431
	Expansion Activities	434

Lesson 14   437

GRAMMAR	Articles; *Other / Another;* Indefinite Pronouns	
CONTEXT	Money	
	14.1 Articles—An Overview	438
READING	Kids and Money	438
	14.2 The Indefinite Article—Classifying or Identifying the Subject	439
	14.3 The Indefinite Article—Introducing a Noun	440
	14.4 The Definite Article	443
	14.5 Making Generalizations	445
	14.6 General or Specific with Quantity Words	449

READING	Changing the American Dollar	451
	14.7 *Another* and *Other*	452
	14.8 More About *Another* and *Other*	453
READING	The High Cost of a College Education	456
	14.9 Definite and Indefinite Pronouns	458
	Summary	462
	Editing Advice	463
	Test/Review	464
	Expansion Activities	467

Appendices

A.	Spelling and Pronunciation of Verbs	AP1
B.	Irregular Noun Plurals	AP4
C.	Spelling Rules for Adverbs Ending in *-ly*	AP5
D.	Metric Conversion Chart	AP6
E.	The Verb *Get*	AP8
F.	*Make* and *Do*	AP10
G.	Nouns That Can Be Both Count or Noncount	AP11
H.	Verbs and Adjectives Followed by a Preposition	AP12
I.	Direct and Indirect Objects	AP13
J.	Capitalization Rules	AP15
K.	Glossary of Grammatical Terms	AP15
L.	Special Uses of Articles	AP20
M.	Alphabetical List of Irregular Verb Forms	AP22
N.	Maps of the United States of America and North America	AP25

Index   I1

A word from the author

It seems that I was born to be an ESL teacher. My parents immigrated to the U.S. from Poland as adults and were confused not only by the English language but by American culture as well. Born in the U.S., I often had the task as a child to explain the intricacies of the language and allay my parents' fears about the culture. It is no wonder to me that I became an ESL teacher, and later, an ESL writer who focuses on explanations of American culture in order to illustrate grammar. My life growing up in an immigrant neighborhood was very similar to the lives of my students, so I have a feel for what confuses them and what they need to know about American life.

ESL teachers often find themselves explaining confusing customs and providing practical information about life in the U.S. Often, teachers are a student's only source of information about American life. With **Grammar in Context, Fourth Edition,** I enjoy sharing my experiences with you.

Grammar in Context, Fourth Edition connects grammar with American cultural context, providing learners of English with a useful and meaningful skill and knowledge base. Students learn the grammar necessary to communicate verbally and in writing, and learn how American culture plays a role in language, beliefs, and everyday situations.

Enjoy the new edition of **Grammar in Context!**

Sandra N. Elbaum

Grammar in Context

Students learn more, remember more, and use language more effectively when they learn grammar in context.

Learning a language through meaningful themes and practicing it in a contextualized setting promote both linguistic and cognitive development. In **Grammar in Context**, grammar is presented in interesting and culturally informative readings, and the language and context are subsequently practiced throughout the chapter.

New to this edition

- **New and updated readings** on current American topics such as Instant Messaging and eBay.
- **Updated grammar charts** that now include essential language notes.
- **Updated exercises and activities** that provide contextualized practice using a variety of exercise types, as well as additional practice for more difficult structures.
- **New lower-level *Grammar in Context Basic*** for beginning level students.
- **New wrap-around Teacher's Annotated Edition** with page-by-page, point-of-use teaching suggestions.
- **Expanded Assessment CD-ROM** with ExamView® Pro Test Generator now contains more question types and assessment options to easily allow teachers to create tests and quizzes.

Distinctive Features of *Grammar in Context*

Students prepare for academic assignments and everyday language tasks.

Discussions, readings, compositions, and exercises involving higher-level critical thinking skills develop overall language and communication skills.

Students expand their knowledge of American topics and culture.

The readings in **Grammar in Context** help students gain insight into and enrich their knowledge of American culture and history. Students gain ample exposure to the practicalities of American life, such as writing a résumé, dealing with telemarketers and junk mail, and getting student internships. Their new knowledge helps them adapt to everyday life in the U.S.

Students learn to use their new skills to communicate.

The exercises and Expansion Activities in **Grammar in Context** help students learn English while practicing their writing and speaking skills. Students work together in pairs and groups to find more information about topics, to make presentations, to play games, and to role-play. Their confidence in using English increases, as does their ability to communicate effectively.

Welcome to Grammar in Context, Fourth Edition

Students learn more, remember more, and use language more effectively when they learn grammar in context.

Grammar in Context, Fourth Edition connects grammar with rich, American cultural context, providing learners of English with a useful and meaningful skill and knowledge base.

An **Audio Program** allows students to hear the readings and dialogs, and provides an opportunity to practice their listening skills.

Readings on American topics such as Google, Internet Matchmaking, and Jury Duty present and illustrate the grammatical structure in an informative and meaningful context.

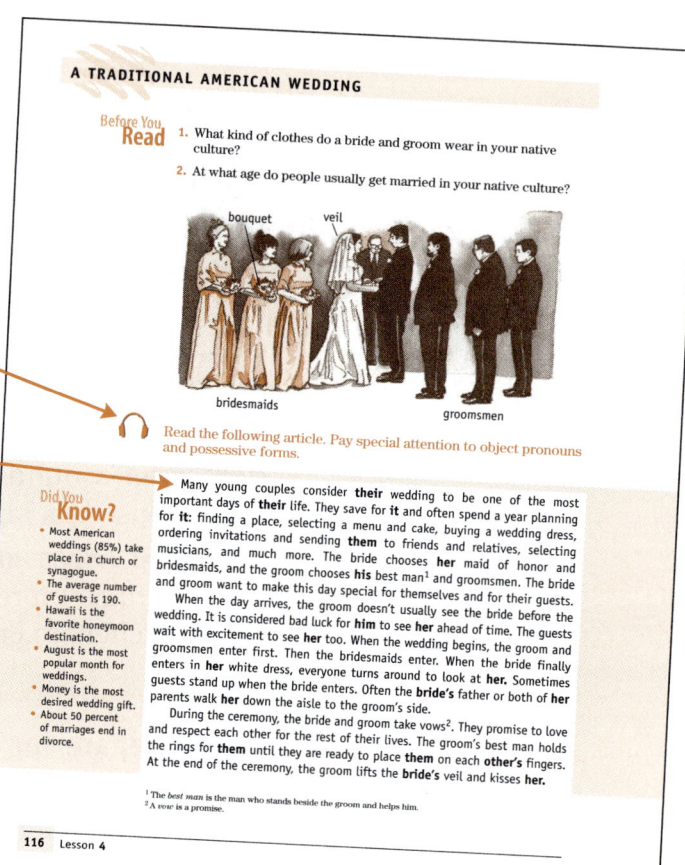

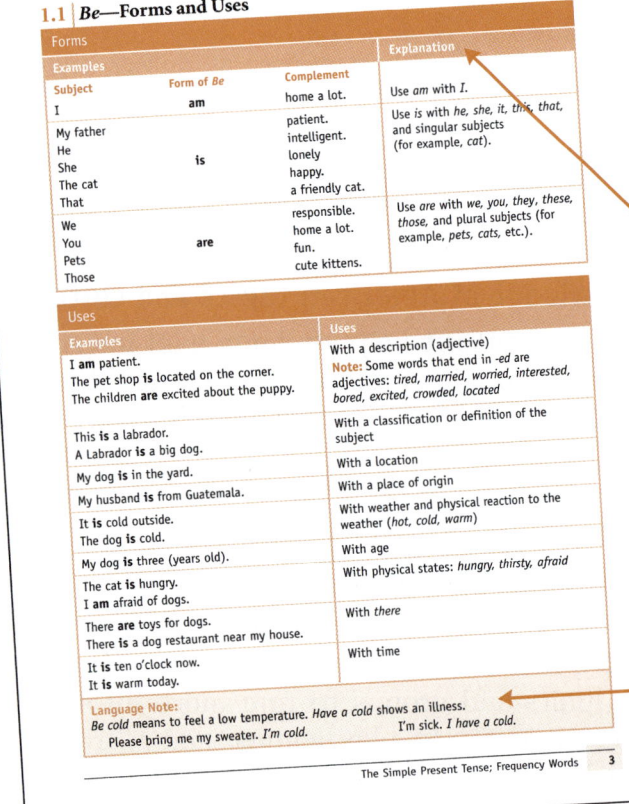

Grammar charts offer clear explanations and provide contextualized examples of the structure.

Language Notes refine students' understanding of the target structure.

xvi   Welcome to *Grammar in Context*

EXERCISE 15 ABOUT YOU Check (✓) the things you did this past week. Exchange books with another student. Ask the other student about the items he or she checked.

EXAMPLE ✓ I made a long-distance phone call.
A: I made a long-distance phone call.
B: Who(m) did you call?
A: I called my father in Mexico.
B: How long did you talk?
A: We talked for about 15 minutes.

1. ___ I made a long-distance phone call.
2. ___ I shopped for groceries.
3. ___ I met someone new.
4. ___ I got together with a friend.
5. ___ I wrote a letter.
6. ___ I bought some new clothes.
7. ___ I went to the bank.
8. ___ I read something interesting (a book, an article).
9. ___ I went to the post office.
10. ___ I did exercises.
11. ___ I received a letter.
12. ___ I went to an interesting place.

EXERCISE 16 Decide which is better: the simple past tense or *used to* + base form. Fill in the blanks.

EXAMPLES Martin Luther King, Jr. __went__ (go) to Alabama in 1955.

Oprah Winfrey __used to be__ (be) poor.

1. There _____ (be) a lot more discrimination in the past than there is today.
2. President Lincoln _____ (end) slavery in 1865.
3. African-Americans _____ (have) a hard time getting into certain professions.
4. Black children _____ (go) to separate schools in the South.
5. In 1964, Congress _____ (pass) a law that gave equality to all.
6. Colin Powell _____ (become) secretary of state in 2001.

Habitual Past with *Used To*; The Simple Past Tense **105**

A variety of contextualized activities keeps the classroom lively and targets different learning styles.

A **Summary** provides the lesson's essential grammar in an easy-to-reference format.

SUMMARY OF LESSON 4

1. Pronouns and Possessive Forms

Subject Pronoun	Object Pronoun	Possessive Adjective	Possessive Pronoun	Reflexive Pronoun
I	me	my	mine	myself
you	you	your	yours	yourself
he	him	his	his	himself
she	her	her	hers	herself
it	it	its	—	itself
we	us	our	ours	ourselves
you	you	your	yours	yourselves
they	them	their	theirs	themselves
who	whom	whose	whose	—

EXAMPLES Robert and Lisa are my friends.
They come from Canada.
I like **them**.
Their wedding was beautiful.
My wedding was small.
Theirs was big.
They paid for the wedding **themselves**.

Who has a new car?
With **whom** do you live? (FORMAL)
Who do you live with? (INFORMAL)
Whose book is that?
This is my dictionary.
Whose is that?

2. Possessive Form of Nouns

Singular Nouns
the **bride's** dress
my **father's** house
the **child's** toy
the **man's** hat
Charles' wife / **Charles's** wife

Plural Nouns
the **bridesmaids'** dresses
my **parents'** house
the **children's** toys
the **men's** hats

3. *Say* and *Tell*
He **said** his name.
He **told** me his name.

He **said** good-bye to his friends.
He **told** them to write often.

4. Questions About the Subject
Simple Present:
Who has the rings?
How many bridesmaids have a pink dress?
Which bridesmaid has a red dress?
Which bridesmaids have pink flowers?

Simple Past:
Who kissed the bride?
Which man kissed the bride?
What happened next?

140 Lesson 4

Welcome to *Grammar in Context* **xvii**

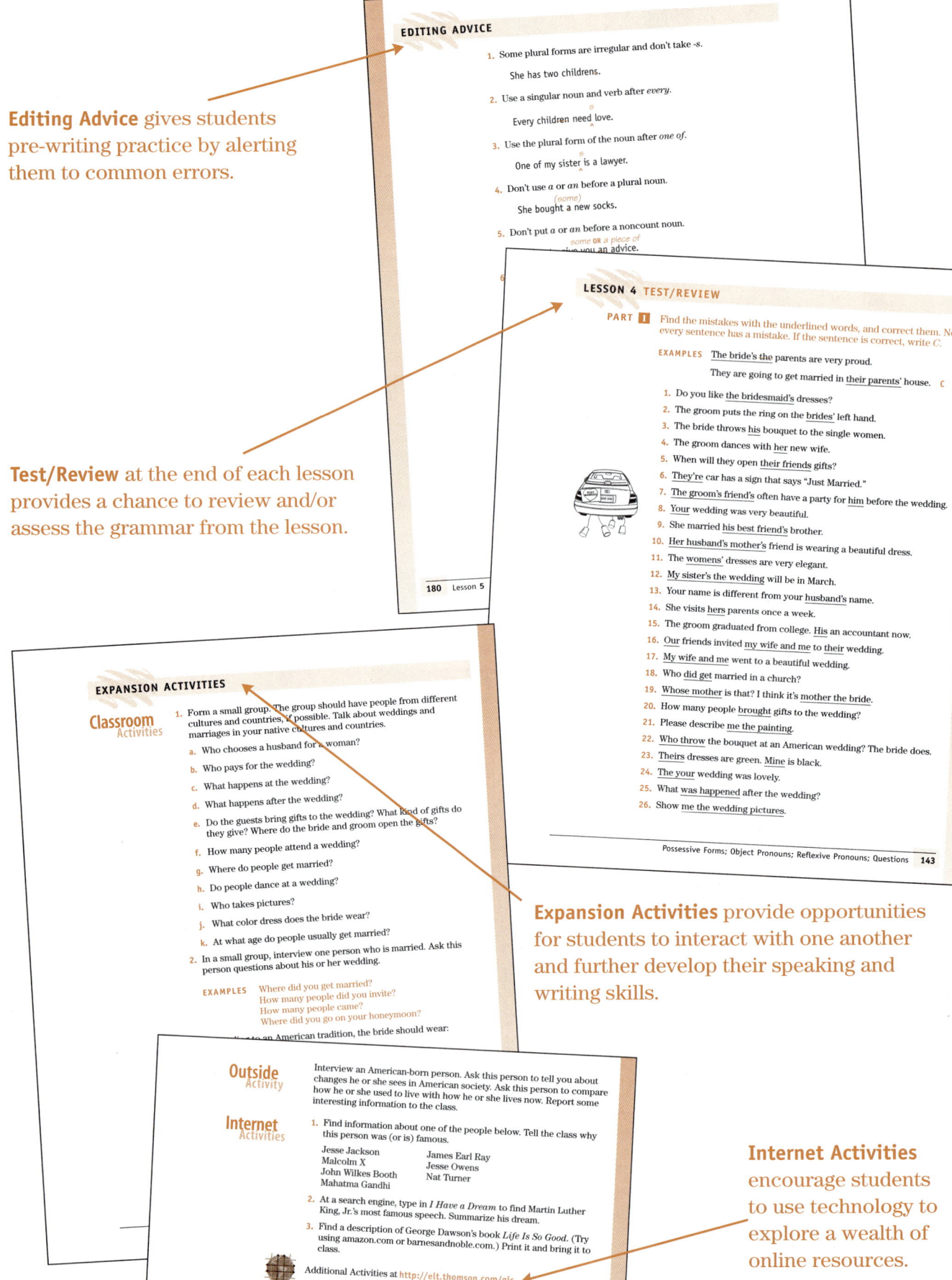

Grammar in Context Student Book Supplements

Audio Program
- Audio CDs and Audio Tapes allow students to listen to every reading in the book as well as selected dialogs.

More Grammar Practice Workbooks
- Can be used with *Grammar in Context* or any skills text to learn and review the essential grammar
- Great for in-class practice or homework
- Includes practice on all grammar points in *Grammar in Context*

Teacher's Annotated Edition
- New component offers page-by-page answers and teaching suggestions.

Assessment CD-ROM with ExamView® Pro Test Generator
- Test Generator allows teachers to create tests and quizzes quickly and easily.

Interactive CD-ROM
- CD-ROM allows for supplemental interactive practice on grammar points from *Grammar in Context*.

Split Editions
- Split editions provide options for short courses.

Instructional Video/DVD
- Video/DVD offers teaching suggestions and advice on how to use *Grammar in Context*.

Web Site
- Web site gives access to additional activities and promotes the use of the Internet.

LESSON 1

GRAMMAR
The Simple Present Tense
Frequency Words

CONTEXT: Pets and Other Animals
Americans and Their Pets
Dog Walkers
Guide Dogs
Search and Rescue Dogs
Marianne and Sparky

AMERICANS AND THEIR PETS

Before You Read

1. Do you like animals?
2. Do you have a pet?

Read the following article. Pay special attention to the verb *be* and other verbs in the simple present tense.

Did You Know?

The most common registered breed of dog in the U.S. is the Labrador retriever.

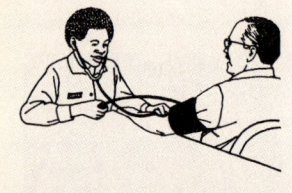

Most Americans **love** pets. About 64% of Americans **live** with one or more animals. About 36% of households **have** at least one dog. Three in ten households **own** at least one cat.

Americans **think** of their pets as part of the family. Seventy-nine percent of pet owners **give** their pets holiday or birthday presents. Thirty-three percent of pet owners **talk** to their pets on the phone or through the answering machine. Many pet owners **sleep** with their dogs or cats. Many people **travel** with their pets. (It **costs** about $50 to fly with a pet.) Some hotels **allow** guests to bring their pets.

Americans **pay** a lot of money to keep pets. They **spend** $12 billion a year in vet[1] bills and pet supplies. There **are** schools, toys, hotels, restaurants, clothes, perfumes, and cemeteries for pets. There **are** magazines for pet owners. There **are** hundreds of Web sites for pet owners.

Pets **are** a lot of fun. They **are** affectionate[2] too. People who **are** lonely **get** a lot of love from their animals. Medical research **shows** that contact with a dog or a cat can lower a person's blood pressure.

Pets **need** a lot of attention. Before you **buy** a pet, it **is** important to answer these questions:

- **Are** you patient?
- **Are** you home a lot?
- If you **have** children, **are** they responsible?
- **Are** pets allowed where you live?
- **Do** you **have** money for medical bills for your pet?

Unfortunately, some people **don't realize** that pets need a lot of care. Some people **see** a cute puppy or kitten, **buy** it, and later **abandon**[3] it because they **don't want** to take care of it. It **is** important to understand that a pet is a long-term responsibility.

---

[1] *Vet* is short for *veterinarian*. This is an animal doctor.
[2] *Affectionate* means loving.
[3] *To abandon* means to leave something. When people abandon a pet, they leave it on the street.

1.1 *Be*—Forms and Uses

Forms

Examples			Explanation
Subject	**Form of *Be***	**Complement**	
I	**am**	home a lot.	Use *am* with *I*.
My father He She The cat That	**is**	patient. intelligent. lonely happy. a friendly cat.	Use *is* with *he, she, it, this, that,* and singular subjects (for example, *cat*).
We You Pets Those	**are**	responsible. home a lot. fun. cute kittens.	Use *are* with *we, you, they, these, those,* and plural subjects (for example, *pets, cats,* etc.).

Uses

Examples	Uses
I **am** patient. The pet shop **is** located on the corner. The children **are** excited about the puppy.	With a description (adjective) **Note:** Some words that end in *-ed* are adjectives: *tired, married, worried, interested, bored, excited, crowded, located.*
This **is** a Labrador. A Labrador **is** a big dog.	With a classification or definition of the subject
My dog **is** in the yard.	With a location
My husband **is** from Guatemala.	With a place of origin
It **is** cold outside. The dog **is** cold.	With weather and physical reaction to the weather (*hot, cold, warm*)
My dog **is** three (years old).	With age
The cat **is** hungry. I **am** afraid of dogs.	With physical states: *hungry, thirsty, afraid*
There **are** toys for dogs. There **is** a dog restaurant near my house.	With *there*
It **is** ten o'clock now. It **is** warm today.	With time

Language Note:
Be cold means to feel a low temperature. *Have a cold* shows an illness.
    Please bring me my sweater. *I'm cold.*   I'm sick. *I have a cold.*

EXERCISE 1 Fill in the blanks with the correct form of *be*.

EXAMPLE My dog ___is___ very small.

1. You take care of your dog. You _____ responsible.
2. Pet ownership _____ a big responsibility.
3. My cat _____ soft.
4. Dogs _____ great pets because they _____ affectionate. They _____ also good protection for a house.
5. My dog _____ a member of my family.
6. Some cats _____ very affectionate. Other cats _____ very independent.
7. It _____ a big responsibility to own a pet.
8. Kittens and puppies _____ cute.
9. We _____ ready to get a pet.
10. Some people _____ lonely.
11. My kitten _____ very sweet.
12. The dog _____ cold.

1.2 Contractions with *Be*

A *contraction* combines two words. We put an apostrophe (') in place of the missing letter.

Examples		Explanation
I am	**I'm** responsible.	We can make a contraction with the subject pronoun (*I, you, she,* etc.) and *am, is, are*.
You are	**You're** patient.	
She is	**She's** happy.	
He is	**He's** kind.	
It is	**It's** necessary to walk a dog.	
We are	**We're** busy.	
They are	**They're** cute.	
There is	**There's** a cat on the computer.	We can make a contraction with *there is*.
That is	**That's** a friendly cat.	We can make a contraction with *that is*.
My **grandmother's** lonely.		We can make a contraction with most nouns and *is*.
Your **dog's** cute.		
A fo<u>x</u> is a relative of a dog.	fox	We don't make a contraction with *is* if the noun ends in *s, se, ce, ze, sh, ch,* or *x*.
A mou<u>se</u> is a small animal.		
Thi<u>s</u> is a cute cat.		
Pet **products are** expensive.		In writing, don't make a contraction with a plural noun and *are* or with *there are*.
Dogs are popular pets.		
There are hotels for pets.		
The owner **is not** home now.		To make a negative with *be*, put *not* after a form of *be*. The negative contractions are *isn't* and *aren't*. There is no contraction for *am not*.
She **isn't** home in the day.		
You **are not** ready for a pet.		
You **aren't** patient.		

EXERCISE 2 Which of the sentences in Exercise 1 can use a contraction?

EXERCISE 3 Fill in the blank with the correct form of *be*. Then fill in the second blank with a negative form. Use contractions wherever possible.

EXAMPLE Today <u>'s</u> my daughter's birthday. It <u>isn't</u> a holiday.

1. My daughter and I _____ at the pet shop. We _____ at home.

2. My husband _____ at work now. He _____ with me.

3. I _____ patient. My husband _____ patient.

4. This puppy _____ for my daughter. It _____ for my son.

The Simple Present Tense; Frequency Words

5. My daughter _____ responsible. My son _____ responsible.
6. Dogs _____ good for protection. Cats _____ good for protection.
7. My daughter _____ excited. She _____ bored.
8. I _____ afraid of big dogs. I _____ afraid of small dogs.
9. This _____ a Chihuahua. It _____ a big dog.

EXERCISE 4 Fill in the blanks.

EXAMPLE My dog **'s** _____ hungry. He wants to eat.

1. My cat _____ near the window.
2. My aunt _____ married. Her dog _____ her only companion.
   (not)
3. In the U.S., there _____ cemeteries for pets.
4. Some cats _____ very affectionate.
5. My dog _____ thirsty. Put water in his dish.
6. This _____ a kitten. It _____ only two weeks _____.
7. Don't leave your dog in the car. _____ hot today.
8. My dog _____ cold in the winter. She needs a sweater.
9. My vet's office _____ located about two miles from my house.
10. _____ is a picture of my dog.
11. I _____ worried about my dog because she _____ sick.
12. Your son _____ responsible because
    (not)
    he _____ only four years _____.

DOG WALKERS

Before You Read

1. Do working people have problems taking care of their pets?
2. Are some animals easier to take care of than others?

Read the following conversation. Pay special attention to questions with the verb *be*.

A: Your dog is beautiful. What kind of a dog **is it?**
B: It's a Dalmatian.
A: How old **is he?**
B: It's a *she*. She's two years old.
A: What**'s her name?**
B: Her name is Missy.
A: **Are we** neighbors? **Are you** new in the neighborhood?
B: I don't live here. Missy isn't my dog. I'm a dog walker.
A: A dog walker? What**'s that?**
B: I walk other people's dogs when they're at work or on vacation.
A: **Are you** a friend of the family?
B: No. I'm from an agency.
A: What agency **are you** from?
B: It's a professional dog-walking service.
A: **Are you** serious?
B: Of course, I'm serious.
A: **Is the pay** good?
B: It's OK. But I love my job for other reasons. My "customers" are always happy to see me. Also, I'm outside all day.
A: Cool! **Are the owners** happy too?
B: Yes, they are. When they go to work, they're worried that their dogs can be lonely or bored. Some people even leave the TV on for their pets. But when they use a dog-walking service, they are happy because their dogs are happy too.
A: **Are there** jobs at your agency?
B: Yes, there are. **Are you** interested in becoming a dog walker too?
A: Yes. It sounds like fun.
B: Here's my card. The agency's phone number is on the card.
A: Thanks!

The Simple Present Tense; Frequency Words

1.3 Questions with *Be*

Compare statement word order and word order in *yes/no* questions.

Statement Word Order	Yes/No Question	Short Answer	Explanation
I am responsible.	**Am I** responsible with pets?	Yes, you are.	In a *yes/no* question, we put *am, is, are* before the subject.
You are a dog walker.	**Are you** a friend of the family?	No, I'm not.	
The owner is busy.	**Is the owner** at home?	No, she isn't.	
The pay is important.	**Is the pay** good?	No, it isn't.	We usually answer a *yes/no* question with a short answer. A short answer contains a pronoun (*he, it, we, they,* etc.).
The dog is a female.	**Is the dog** young?	Yes, she is.	
It is a big dog.	**Is it** a Labrador?	No, it isn't.	
We are new here.	**Are we** neighbors?	No, we aren't.	
The owners are at work.	**Are the owners** happy?	Yes, they are.	
They are out.	**Are they** at work?	Yes, they are.	We don't use a contraction for a short *yes* answer. We usually use a contraction for a short *no* answer.
There are interesting jobs.	**Are there** jobs at your agency?	Yes, there are.	
That is a cute dog.	**Is that** your dog?	No, it isn't.	
It isn't a big dog.	**Isn't it** a puppy?	No, it isn't.	

Pronunciation Note:
We usually end a *yes/no* question with rising intonation. Listen to your teacher pronounce the questions above.

Compare statement word order and word order in *wh-* questions.

Statement Word Order	Wh- Question	Explanation
I am lost. **You are** from an agency. **That is** a nice dog. **The dog is** old. **That is** a strange pet. **Her name is** long. **You are** here. **There are** a lot of dog walkers.	Where **am I**? What agency **are you** from? What kind of dog **is that**? How old **is the dog**? What **is that**? What **is her name**? Why **are you** here? How many dog walkers **are there** in your agency?	We put *am, is, are* before the subject.
The owner isn't home. **The dogs aren't** bored. **You aren't** at work.	Why **isn't the owner** at home? Why **aren't the dogs** bored? Why **aren't you** at work?	Notice the word order in negative *wh-* questions.

Lesson 1

Language Notes:
1. Most question words can contract with *is*.
   (EXCEPTIONS: *which is; how much is*)
   Who's that?
   What's a Dalmatian?
   Where's your cat?
   Which is bigger, a collie or a Labrador?

2. Study these common questions and answers with *be*.
   What's your name? My name is Linda.
   What time is it? It's 4:32.
   What color is the dog? It's brown and white.
   What kind of dog is this? It's a collie.
   What's a collie? It's a dog.
   What's this? It's a leash.
   How are you? I'm fine.
   How's the weather? It's sunny and warm.
   How old is your daughter? She's 10 (years old).[4]
   How tall are you? I'm five feet, three inches tall (or 5'3").[5]
   Where are you from? I'm from Mexico.
   What's wrong? I'm sick.

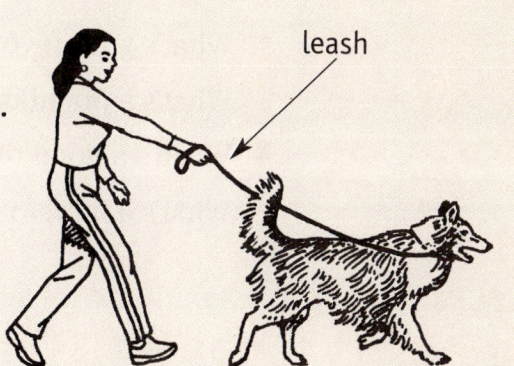
leash

EXERCISE 5 Read each question. Answer with a short answer. Do not make a contraction for a short answer after *yes*.

EXAMPLES Is the teacher a native speaker of English?
Yes, she is.

Is the teacher near the door?
No, she isn't.

1. Are you an immigrant?
2. Are you from Africa?
3. Is the teacher from your native country?
4. Is this lesson hard for you?
5. Are the students bored?
6. Are you tired?
7. Are the windows of the classroom open?
8. Is the door open?
9. Is it warm in the classroom?
10. Is there a map in the classroom?
11. Is the school located near your house?

[4] It is not polite to ask an adult American about his or her age.
[5] For conversion to the metric system, see Appendix D.

The Simple Present Tense; Frequency Words

EXERCISE 6 Answer the questions.

1. What pets are good for children?
2. What kind of pets are popular in your native country (or with people in your native culture)?
3. What's your favorite animal in the zoo?
4. What's a popular name for dogs in your native culture?
5. When's a good time to get a pet?
6. What's a better pet—a dog or a cat?

EXERCISE 7 Fill in the blanks to complete this conversation. Use contractions wherever possible.

A: __Is this__ your dog?
    (example)

B: Yes, it _____.
        (1)

A: He _____ beautiful.
      (2)

B: Thanks. But it's a "she."

A: _____ friendly?
   (3)

B: Yes, she _____.
         (4)

A: What kind of dog _____?
                  (5)

B: She _____ a collie.
       (6)

A: What _____?
        (7)

B: Her name is Samantha.

A: _____?
  (8)

B: She _____ three years old now.
        (9)

A: _____ hard to take care of a dog?
  (10)

B: Not for me. I _____ home a lot. And when
                (11)

I _____ home, my brother or parents _____ home.
  (12 not)   (13)

A: I love dogs, but I _____ (14 not) home very much, so that's a problem.

B: Why _____ (15) a lot?

A: Because I'm a nurse. I work eight hours a day. I want to get a dog for my grandmother.

B: Why?

A: Because _____ (16) lonely.

B: Why _____ (17) lonely?

A: Because nobody _____ (18) home all day. We _____ (19) all at work.

B: I think that _____ (20) a good idea.

EXERCISE 8 Fill in the blanks in the following cell phone conversation.

A: Hello?

B: Hi. This __is__ (example) Betty.

A: Hi, Betty. How _____ (1)?

B: I'm fine. How _____ (2)?

A: I'm fine. But the cat _____ (3) sick. I _____ (4 not) home now. I _____ (5) at the animal hospital.

B: _____ (6) wrong?

A: Fluffy _____ (7 not) hungry or thirsty. He _____ (8) tired all the time.

B: _____ (9) so hot today. Maybe the heat _____ (10) the problem.

A: I don't think so. The house _____ (11) air-conditioned.

B: _____ (12)?

A: He _____ (13) only four years _____ (14).

B: _____ (15) alone?

A: No, I'm not.

The Simple Present Tense; Frequency Words   11

B: _____ with you?
(16)

A: My daughter _____ with me. We _____ in the waiting room.
(17) (18)

B: Why _____ at school?
(19)

A: She _____ on spring break now. I think the doctor _____
(20) (21)
ready to see us now.

B: Call me when you get home. Let me know if I can help.

A: Thanks. _____ a good friend.
(22)

EXERCISE 9 Fill in the blanks in the following conversation.

A: Look at the dog. What kind of dog __is it__?
(example)

B: I think it _____ a mutt.
(1)

A: What _____ a mutt?
(2)

B: It _____ a mixed breed dog. Look, it _____
(3) (4)
so friendly with those children.

A: My daughter's birthday is next week. She wants a dog. But dogs
_____ so expensive.
(5)

B: A purebred[6] dog, like a Labrador, is expensive, but a mutt
_____ so expensive. In fact, there _____ animal shelters
(6 not) (7)
that can give you a dog for free or for a very low price.

A: What _____ an animal shelter?
(8)

B: It's an organization that takes unwanted pets and tries to find homes for them.

A: But _____ healthy?
(9)

B: Yes, they are. The shelter's doctors check an animal's health before giving it to a family.

A: Why _____ so many unwanted pets?
(10)

[6] A *purebred* dog is one breed (race) only. It is not mixed with other breeds.

B: There are unwanted pets because some people get a pet and then realize it _____(11)_____ too much trouble to take care of it.

A: That _____(12)_____ terrible.

B: Yes, it is. What about your daughter? _____(13)_____ responsible?

A: Yes, she _____(14)_____.

B: How old _____(15)_____?

A: She _____(16)_____ ten years old.

B: My son has a dog. But he _____(17 not)_____ responsible. He says it's *his* dog, but I _____(18)_____ the one who feeds it and takes it out three times a day.

A: Why _____(19)_____ responsible?

B: He says he _____(20)_____ too busy with school and sports. I _____(21)_____ busy too. But I find the time to take care of the dog. What about you? _____(22)_____ home a lot?

A: No, I _____(23)_____. My work day _____(24)_____ very long. And my daughter _____(25)_____ at school all day.

B: Then you should find a dog-walking service.

A: _____(26)_____ expensive?

B: Yes, it _____(27)_____. But _____(28)_____ the only way to have a happy dog.

A: Maybe a fish would be a better pet!

The Simple Present Tense; Frequency Words   13

GUIDE DOGS

Before You Read

1. Do you think most dogs are intelligent? Are some dogs more intelligent than others?
2. Do you ever see blind people walking with dogs?

 Read the following article. Pay special attention to simple present tense verbs.

harness

obstacle

curb

Most dogs **have** an easy life in the U.S. They **eat, play, get** attention from their owners, and **sleep.** But some dogs **work** hard. They **are** called guide dogs. Guide dogs **help** blind people move from place to place safely.

Guide dogs and their owners **are** a team. Guide dogs **don't lead** the owners, and their owners **don't** completely **control** the guide dogs. They **work** together. The guide dogs **don't know** where the owners want to go, so they **follow** the owner's instructions. The owners **can't see** the obstacles[7] along the way, so the dogs **make** decisions for the safety of the owners. Guide dogs **stop** at all curbs and intersections before crossing a street. They **don't see** color, so they **don't know** if the light **is** red or green. The owners **decide** if it **is** time to cross the street by listening to the sound of traffic. The dogs **help** the owners get on a bus or train. They **learn** to obey many verbal commands.

Most guide dogs **are** golden retrievers, Labrador retrievers, or German shepherds. These three breeds **are** very intelligent, obedient[8], and friendly. A guide dog **needs** to work without distraction in noisy places, bad weather, crowds of people, and difficult situations. When you **see** a guide dog, it **is** important that you **recognize** that the dog **needs** to concentrate on its job. **Don't pet** or **talk** to the dog. Guiding **is** very complicated, and it **requires** a dog's full attention.

Guide dog training **lasts** about five months. Only about 72 percent of dogs that **enter** the training program "**graduate**." Those that **graduate bring** their owners valuable help and love. In other dog training programs, trainers **use** food as a reward. In guide dog training, the trainer **does not use** food. He or she **uses** physical and verbal affection. This **is** because a guide dog sometimes **takes** the owner to a restaurant. It must **lie** patiently at the owner's feet without wanting to eat.

Guide dogs **like** to play too, but only after the work **is** finished. How **do** dogs **know** when their work is finished? When the harness **is** on, they **know** they have to work. When it **is** off, they **can play.** Like all dogs, they **love** to play.

---

[7] An *obstacle* is something that blocks your way. An obstacle creates an unsafe situation.
[8] An *obedient* animal is one that obeys.

1.4 The Simple Present Tense—Affirmative Statements

Form
A simple present tense verb has two forms: the base form and the -s form.[9]

Examples	Explanation
Subject — **Base Form** — **Complement** I You We **work** hard. They Guide dogs	We use the base form when the subject is *I, you, we, they,* or a plural noun.
Subject — **-s Form** — **Complement** He She It **works** hard. The dog	We use the -s form when the subject is *he, she, it,* or a singular noun.
My family **has** three cats. Everyone in the shelter **likes** animals. No one **wants** the new kittens.	We use the -s form with *family, everyone, everybody, no one, nobody,* and *nothing*.

I **have** a pet dog. My friend **has** a guide dog.
I **go** out without my dog. My friend **goes** everywhere with his dog.
I **do** a lot of work. A guide dog **does** a lot of work too.
	Three verbs have an irregular -s form:
	   have → has (pronunciation /hæz/)
	   go → goes
	   do → does (pronunciation /dəz/)

Use

Examples	Uses
Dogs **give** people love. Guide dogs **help** people. Most dogs **have** an easy life. Americans **love** pets.	With general truths, to show that something is consistently true
Many pet owners **sleep** with their dogs or cats. Some pet owners **buy** presents for their pets. Owners **walk** dogs on a leash.	With customs
He **walks** his dog three times a day. He **feeds** his cat every morning and every night.	To show regular activity (a habit) or repeated action
I **come** from Bosnia. He **comes** from Pakistan.	To show place of origin

[9] For the spelling of the -s form, see Appendix A.

EXERCISE 10 Fill in the blanks with the base form or the -s form.

EXAMPLES Americans __love__ pets.
(love)

My son __loves__ his new kitten.
(love)

1. Most dogs _____ an easy life.
(have)

2. My dog _____ all day.
(sleep)

3. Guide dogs _____ to obey many commands.
(learn)

4. A guide dog _____ safety decisions.
(make)

5. Trainers _____ with a dog for five months.
(work)

6. Most guide dogs _____ from the training program.
(graduate)

7. My girlfriend _____ her dog a present on his birthday.
(give)

8. People _____ affection from animals.
(get)

9. Everyone _____ affection.
(need)

10. It _____ a lot of money to have a pet.
(cost)

11. Some pet owners _____ to their pets on the phone.
(talk)

12. My daughter _____ a puppy for her birthday.
(want)

13. My neighbor's dog _____ all the time.
(bark)

14. Some people _____ with their dogs.
(travel)

15. Forty percent of Americans _____ at least one dog.
(have)

16. My brother _____ three dogs.
(have)

17. Dogs _____ their owners.
(protect)

18. My family _____ animals.
(love)

19. Nobody _____ the dog's age.
(know)

20. Everybody _____ that puppies and kittens are cute.
(think)

Lesson 1

1.5 Negative Statements with the Simple Present Tense

Examples	Explanation
The owner **knows** the destination. The dog **doesn't know** the destination. The dog **stops** at a curb. It **doesn't stop** because of a red light.	Use *doesn't* + the base form with *he, she, it,* or a singular noun. **Compare:** knows → doesn't **know** stops → doesn't **stop** *Doesn't* is the contraction for *does not*.
Some trainers **use** food to reward a dog. Guide dog trainers **don't use** food. Guide dogs **work** when the harness is on. They **don't work** when the harness is off. You **have** a cat. You **don't have** a dog.	Use *don't* + the base form with *I, you, we, they,* or a plural noun. **Compare:** use → don't **use** work → don't **work** *Don't* is the contraction for *do not*.

Usage Note:
American English and British English use different grammar to form the negative of *have*.
Compare:
   American: He *doesn't have* a dog.
   British: He *hasn't* a dog. OR He *hasn't got* a dog.

EXERCISE 11 Fill in the blanks with the negative form of the underlined verb.

EXAMPLE A guide dog <u>needs</u> a lot of training. A pet dog __doesn't need__ a lot of training.

1. Most dogs <u>play</u> a lot. Guide dogs _____ a lot.
2. Obedience trainers <u>use</u> food to teach dogs. Guide dog trainers _____ food.
3. A guide dog <u>works</u> hard. A pet dog _____ hard.
4. People <u>see</u> colors. Dogs _____ colors.
5. A guide dog <u>goes</u> on public transportation. A pet dog _____ on public transportation.
6. My cats <u>eat</u> special food. They _____ food from our table.
7. My cats <u>like</u> fish. They _____ chicken.
8. One cat <u>sleeps</u> on my bed. She _____ alone.
9. My landlord <u>allows</u> cats. He _____ dogs.
10. My cats <u>need</u> attention. They _____ a lot of my time.
11. We <u>have</u> cats. We _____ fish.
12. I <u>like</u> cats. My sister _____ cats.

SEARCH AND RESCUE DOGS

Before You Read

1. Besides helping blind people, do you know of any other ways that dogs work?
2. Do dogs have some qualities that humans don't have?

 Read the following conversation. Pay special attention to questions with the simple present tense.

A: There's a program on TV tonight about search and rescue dogs. **Do** you **want** to watch it with me?

B: I know about guide dogs. But I don't know anything about search and rescue dogs. What **does** "search" **mean**? What **does** "rescue" **mean**?

A: Search means "look for." Rescue means "to help someone in a dangerous situation."

B: What **do** these dogs **do**?

A: When there is a disaster, like an earthquake or a flood, they help the workers find missing people. They save people's lives.

B: How **do** they **do** that?

A: They have a great sense of smell. They can find things that people can't.

B: Do they **need** a lot of training?

A: I think they need at least one year of training.

B: What kind of dogs **do** they **use** as search and rescue dogs?

A: They usually use large, strong dogs. Labrador retrievers or golden retrievers are often SAR dogs. Let's watch the program together tonight.

B: What time **does** it **begin**?

A: At 9 p.m.

B: Does your dog **want** to watch the program with us?

A: My dog is a lazy, spoiled Chihuahua. She just wants to eat, play, and sleep.

1.6 | Questions with the Simple Present Tense

Compare statements and *yes/no* questions

Do	Subject	Verb	Complement	Short Answer	Explanation
	Guide dogs	need	training.		For questions with *I, we, you, they*, or a plural noun, use:
Do	rescue dogs	need	training?	Yes, they do.	
	You	like	dogs.		Do + subject + base form + complement
Do	you	like	cats?	No, I don't.	

Does	Subject	Verb	Complement	Short Answer	Explanation
	Jamie	trains	rescue dogs.		For questions with *he, she, it*, or a singular subject, use:
Does	Jamie	train	guide dogs?	No, she doesn't.	
	My dog	plays	a lot.		Does + subject + base form + complement
Does	a rescue dog	play	a lot?	No, it doesn't.	

Compare statements and *wh-* questions

Wh- Word	do	Subject	Verb	Complement	Explanation
		Rescue dogs	need	training.	For questions with *I, we, you, they*, or a plural noun, use:
How much training	do	they	need?		
		You	prefer	cats.	Wh- word + do + subject + base form + complement
Why	do	you	prefer	cats?	

Wh- Word	does	Subject	Verb	Complement	Explanation
		The program	begins	soon.	For questions with *he, she, it*, or a singular noun, use:
What time	does	the program	begin?		
		My dog	sleeps	a lot.	Wh- word + does + subject + base form + complement
Where	does	your dog	sleep?		

Compare negative statements and *why* questions

Why	don't/doesn't	Subject	Negative Verb	Complement
		I	don't like	cats.
Why	don't	you	like	cats?
		My dog	doesn't sleep	in his bed.
Why	doesn't	he	sleep	in his bed?

Language Note:
Compare questions with *be* to other simple present tense questions:

Is the dog friendly? Yes, it **is**.

Does the dog **have** a sweater? Yes, it **does**.

Where **is** your dog?

What kind of dog **do** you **have**?

The Simple Present Tense; Frequency Words

EXERCISE 12 Fill in the blanks to complete this conversation.

A: Do you ____like____ animals?
  (example)

B: Yes, I _____. In fact, I love animals very much. I especially
       (1)
   like dogs.

A: _____ you have a dog?
      (2)

B: No, I _____.
        (3)

A: If you love dogs, why _____ a dog?
                           (4 not/have)

B: Because my landlord _____ dogs.
                         (5 not/permit)

A: _____ he permit cats?
        (6)

B: Yes, he _____.
            (7)

A: _____ a cat?
      (8 have)

B: Yes, I do, but I _____ to find a new home for my cat.
                    (9 need)

   _____ you know anyone who wants a cat?
    (10)

A: Why _____ your cat?
         (11 not/have)

B: I'm getting married in three months, and my girlfriend

   _____ to live with cats.
      (12 not/want)

A: Why _____ to live with cats? Doesn't she
         (13 not/want)

   _____ them?
    (14 like)

B: She _____ them, but she's allergic to them. When she
        (15 like)

   _____ over, she _____ and
    (16 come)   (17 sneeze)

   _____. She _____ to come over any more.
   (18 cough)   (19 not/want)

A: That's a big problem.

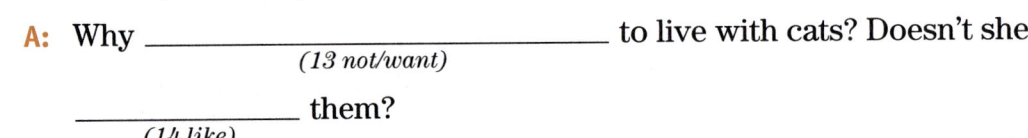

EXERCISE 13 Part 1: Use the words below to interview a student with a dog.

EXAMPLES
your dog / big
A: Is your dog big?
B: Yes, she is.

your dog / sleep a lot (how many hours)
A: Does your dog sleep a lot?
B: Yes, she does.
A: How many hours does she sleep?
B: She sleeps about 15 hours a day.

1. how old / your dog
2. what / your dog's name
3. it / a male or a female
4. what / your dog / eat
5. how often / you / take your dog out
6. your dog / do tricks (what kind)
7. your dog / have toys (what kind)
8. your dog / friendly
9. your dog / bark a lot
10. why / you / like dogs

Part 2: Use the words below to interview a student with a cat.

1. how old / your cat
2. what / your cat's name
3. it / a male or a female
4. your cat / catch mice
5. your cat / friendly
6. your cat / sit on your lap a lot
7. your cat / have toys (what kind)
8. why / you / like cats

lap

1.7 | *Wh-* Questions with a Preposition

Examples	Explanation
What does she talk **about**? 　She talks about her cats. What does your cat sleep **on**? 　She sleeps on a pillow.	In conversation, most people put the preposition at the end of the sentence.
Formal: **With whom** does the dog sleep? **Informal:** **Who** does the dog sleep **with**?	Putting the preposition before a question word is very formal. When the preposition comes at the beginning, we use *whom*, not *who*.
Where do you come **from**? 　I come from Mexico. Where are you **from**? 　I'm from Mexico.	For country of origin, you can use *be from* or *come from*.
What time does the program begin? 　It begins **at** 9 p.m.	Omit *at* in a question about time.

The Simple Present Tense; Frequency Words

EXERCISE 14 ABOUT YOU Ask a *yes / no* question using the words given. Then use the words in parentheses ( ) to ask a *wh-* question whenever possible. Another student will answer.

EXAMPLE you / eat in the cafeteria (with whom) OR (who . . . with)

A: Do you eat in the cafeteria?
B: Yes, I do.
A: Who do you eat with? OR With whom do you eat?
B: I eat with my friends.

1. you / live alone (with whom) OR (who . . . with)
2. you / go to bed early (what time)
3. your teacher / come to class on time (what time)
4. your teacher / come from this city (where . . . from)
5. you / practice English outside of class (with whom) OR (who . . . with)
6. you / think about your future (what else)
7. you / complain about English grammar (what else)
8. you / listen to the radio (what station)
9. your teacher / talk about spelling (what else)
10. you / interested in animals (what animals)
11. you / come from Mexico (where)
12. you / go to sleep at midnight (what time)

EXERCISE 15 Circle the correct words to complete this conversation.

A: We're late. Hurry. The train is ready to leave.

B: Let's go . . . (*on the train*) . . . Why (*that dog is* / *is that dog*) on the
                                                              (example)
train? (*Are* / *Do*) they allow dogs on trains?
        (1)

A: That's not an ordinary dog. That's a guide dog.

B: What's a guide dog?

A: It's a dog that helps people with disabilities.

B: How (*do they help* / *they help*) people?
        (2)

A: They (*help* / *helps*) blind people move from place to place, on foot
         (3)
and by public transportation.

B: (*Are* / *Do*) they need special training?
    (4)

A: Yes, they (*are* / *do*).
              (5)

B: Where (*do* / *are*) they get their training?
          (6)

A: They get their training at special schools.

B: Are they only for blind people?

A: No. Guide dogs help people with other disabilities too. There are guide dogs for the deaf[10] and for people in wheelchairs.

B: Why (*are you / you are*) such an expert on guide dogs?
(7)

A: My cousin is blind. He has a guide dog.

B: Let's play with the dog.

A: No. (*It's not / It doesn't*) good to distract a guide dog. A guide dog
(8)
(*need / needs*) to concentrate.
(9)

B: When (*are / do*) they play?
(10)

A: They (*play / plays*) when the owner (*takes / take*) off the dog's
(11)   (12)
harness.

B: What (*do / does*) they eat?
(13)

A: They eat the same thing other dogs eat.

B: It's amazing what a dog can do.

1.8 Questions About Meaning, Spelling, and Cost

Wh-Word	Do/Does	Subject	Verb (Base form)	Complement	Explanation
What	does	"kitten"	mean?		*Mean, spell, say,* and *cost* are verbs and should be in the verb position of a question. Use the base form in the question.
How	do	you	spell	"kitten"?	
How	do	you	say	"kitten" in your language?	
How much	does	a kitten	cost?		

EXERCISE 16 Fill in the blanks to complete the conversation.

A: ___Do you have___ a pet?
       (example)

B: Yes. I have a new kitten.

A: I don't know the word "kitten." What _____?
                                                  (1)

B: Kitten means baby cat.

A: Oh. What's his name?

B: Romeo.

A: How _____?
           (2)

[10] A *deaf* person cannot hear.

B: R-O-M-E-O.

A: Where _____(3)_____?

B: He sleeps with me, of course. _____(4)_____ any pets?

A: Yes, I do.

B: What kind of pet _____(5)_____?

A: I have a bird that talks. I don't know the word in English. How _____(6)_____ "perico" in English?

B: Parrot. So you have a parrot. What _____(7)_____?

A: His name is Chico.

B: How old _____(8)_____?

A: He's almost 20 years old.

B: Wow! How long _____(9)_____?

A: They live a long time. Some live up to 80 years.

B: Are parrots expensive? How much _____(10)_____?

A: It depends on what kind you get. But they usually cost between $175 and $1,000.

B: _____(11)_____ parrots affectionate?

A: Oh, yes. They're very affectionate. Chico sits on my shoulder all the time.

B: What _____(12)_____?

A: He eats fruit, vegetables, rice, nuts, and seeds.

B: _____(13)_____?

A: Yes. He talks a lot.

B: What _____(14)_____?

A: He says, "Good-bye," "Hello," "I love you," and many more things. He speaks Spanish and English.

B: Maybe he speaks English better than we do!

EXERCISE 17 Fill in the blanks to complete the conversation.

A: I know you love dogs. ___Do you have___ a dog now?
(example)

B: No, I _____(1)_____. But I have two cats. I don't have time for a dog.

A: Why _____(2)_____ a dog?

B: Because I'm not at home very much.

A: Why _____(3)_____?

B: Because I work eight hours a day, and at night, I take classes. Dogs need a lot of attention. I _____(4)_____ have enough time right now.

A: What about your cats? _____(5)_____ need attention too?

B: Not as much as dogs. What about you? _____(6)_____ any pets?

A: I have several tropical fish.[11]

B: _____(7)_____ expensive?

A: Some of them are very expensive.

B: How much _____(8)_____?

A: Some of them cost over $100.

B: Wow! That's a lot of money for a boring pet.

A: Fish _____(9)_____ boring. It _____(10)_____ fun to look at them. And when I go to work, they _____(11)_____ get lonely, like dogs and cats.

B: Yes, but they _____(12)_____ affectionate like dogs and cats.

A: They _____(13)_____ make noise like dogs do, so neighbors never complain about fish.

B: How many fish _____(14)_____?

A: I have about 14 or 15. My favorite is my Oranda.

B: How _____(15)_____ "Oranda"?

A: O-R-A-N-D-A. It's a kind of a goldfish. When you have time, come and see my fish tank.

---

[11] *Fish* can be singular or plural. In this case, *fish* is plural.

MARIANNE AND SPARKY

Before You Read

1. Do people in your native culture treat pets the same way Americans do?

2. What kinds of animals or pets do people prefer in your native culture?

Read the following letter from Elena in the U.S. to her friend Sofia in Russia. Pay special attention to frequency words.

Dear Sofia,

I want to tell you about one aspect of American life that seems strange to me—how Americans treat their pets. I have a new American friend, Marianne. She lives alone, but she has a dog, Sparky. Marianne treats him like a child. She **always** carries a picture of Sparky in her wallet. She **often** buys toys for him, especially on his birthday. She **often** calls him on the telephone when she's not home and talks into the answering machine. Sparky **always** sleeps in bed with her.

When she goes to work, she uses a dog walking service. **Twice a day,** someone comes to her house to play with Sparky and take him for a walk. She says that he gets lonely if he's home alone all day. She **always** leaves the TV on when she goes to work to keep Sparky entertained.

Once a month, she takes him to a dog groomer. The groomer gives him a bath and cuts and paints his nails. When she travels, she **usually** takes him with her, but **sometimes** she puts him in a kennel[12] or pet hotel. All of these dog services cost a lot of money. But Marianne doesn't care. Nothing is too expensive when it comes to Sparky.

There's a small beach near her house that is just for dogs and their owners. She takes Sparky there **whenever** the weather is nice so that he can play with other dogs. While the dogs play together, the dog owners talk to each other. She **always** cleans up after her dog.

In winter, she **always** puts a coat on Sparky. In fact, Sparky has about four different winter coats. **Whenever** it rains, Sparky wears his bright yellow raincoat.

Sometimes I think American dogs live better than most people in the world.

Your good friend,
Elena

---

[12] A *kennel* is a place where pets are kept while their owners are away.

Lesson 1

1.9 Simple Present Tense with Frequency Words

Examples	Explanation
Marianne **often** calls her dog on the phone. Sparky **always** sleeps in bed with her. When she travels, she **usually** takes Sparky with her.	We use the simple present tense with frequency words to show a regular activity. Frequency words are: *always, usually, often, sometimes, rarely, seldom,* and *never*.
Whenever the weather is nice, she takes her dog to the beach. Sparky wears a raincoat **whenever** it rains.	*Whenever* shows a regular activity. It means "any time."
Once a month, she takes her dog to a groomer. Someone comes to her house to walk the dog **twice a day.**	Expressions that show frequency are: • every day (week, month, year) • every other day (week, month, year) • once a day (week, month, year) • from time to time • once in a while
Frequency Words	always — 100% usually/generally often/frequently sometimes/occasionally rarely/seldom/hardly ever never/not ever — 0%

EXERCISE 18 Fill in the blanks with an appropriate verb.

EXAMPLE Marianne always __*puts*__ a coat on Sparky when the weather is cold.

1. Elena sometimes _____ a letter to her friend Sofia.
2. Marianne _____ always worried about her dog.
3. The dog _____ always happy to see Marianne when she comes home.
4. Marianne often _____ toys for her dog.
5. The TV _____ always on when Marianne is at work.
6. Sparky always _____ in bed with Marianne.
7. Marianne usually _____ with her dog when she goes on vacation.

EXERCISE 19 ABOUT YOU Fill in the blanks with an appropriate frequency word.

EXAMPLE I __*rarely*__ use a public telephone.

1. I _____ say, "How are you?" when I meet a friend.
2. I'm _____ confused about American customs.

3. I _____ smile when I pass someone I know.
4. I _____ shake hands when I get together with a friend.
5. Americans _____ ask me, "What country are you from?"
6. I _____ celebrate my birthday in a restaurant.
7. I _____ buy birthday presents for my good friends.
8. If I invite a friend to a restaurant, I _____ pay for both of us.
9. I _____ use a cell phone.
10. I _____ eat in fast-food restaurants.
11. I _____ leave my computer on overnight.

EXERCISE 20 Fill in the blanks with an appropriate frequency word. You may find a partner and compare your answers.

EXAMPLE People in my native culture ___*rarely*___ ask, "How are you?"

1. Dogs in my native culture _____ sleep with their owners.
2. Dogs in my native culture are _____ part of the family.
3. Cats in my native culture are _____ part of the family.
4. People in my native culture _____ feed pet food to cats and dogs.
5. People in my native culture _____ travel with their pets.
6. Women in my native culture _____ kiss their friends when they get together.
7. People in my native culture _____ visit each other without calling first.
8. Men in my native culture _____ do housework.
9. Married women in my native culture _____ wear a wedding ring.
10. Married men in my native culture _____ wear a wedding ring.
11. Women in my native culture _____ wear shorts in the summer.
12. People in my native culture _____ eat in restaurants.

EXERCISE 21 In the sentences in Exercise 20, notice if the frequency word comes before or after the verb. Write **B** for *before* or **A** for *after*.

EXAMPLE People in my native culture ___rarely___ ask, "How are you?" **B**

1.10 | Position of Frequency Words and Expressions

Examples	Explanation
Verb Sparky *is* **always** happy to see Marianne. **Verb** The TV *is* **always** on in the day. **Verb** Marianne *is* **rarely** home during the day.	The frequency word comes **after** the verb *be*.
Verb Marianne **often** *calls* Sparky on the phone. **Verb** She **usually** *travels* with Sparky. **Verb** She **always** *carries* a picture of Sparky.	The frequency word comes **before** other verbs.
Sometimes she puts Sparky in a kennel. **Usually** she feeds Sparky dog food. **Often** Elena writes to her friend about American customs.	*Sometimes, usually,* and *often* can come at the beginning of the sentence too. Do not put *always, never, rarely,* and *seldom* at the beginning of the sentence. *Wrong:* Always she carries a picture of her dog.
Once a month, she travels. She travels **once a month.** **Every week,** she goes to the beach. She goes to the beach **every week.**	A frequency expression can come at the beginning or at the end of a sentence. When it comes at the beginning of the sentence, we sometimes separate it from the sentence with a comma.

EXERCISE 22 **ABOUT YOU** Add a frequency word to each sentence to make a **true** statement about yourself.

EXAMPLE I drink coffee at night.
I never drink coffee at night.

1. I talk to my neighbors.
2. I pay my rent on time.
3. I'm busy on Saturdays.
4. I receive e-mail from my friends.

The Simple Present Tense; Frequency Words 29

5. I call my family in my native country.
6. I travel in the summer.
7. I speak English at home with my family.
8. I eat meat for dinner.
9. I go out of town.
10. I study in the library.
11. I eat cereal for breakfast.
12. I bring my dictionary to class.

EXERCISE 23 ABOUT YOU Add a verb (phrase) to make a **true** statement about yourself.

EXAMPLE I / usually

I usually drink coffee in the morning. OR

I'm usually afraid to go out at night.

1. I / rarely / on Sunday

2. I / usually / on the weekend

3. I / hardly ever

4. I / sometimes / at night

5. people from my native culture / often

6. people from my native culture / seldom

7. My family / sometimes

8. My family / rarely

9. women from my native culture / hardly ever

10. men from my native culture / hardly ever

1.11 Questions with *Ever*

We use *ever* in a question when we want an answer that has a frequency word.

Do/Does	Subject	Ever	Verb	Complement	Short Answer
Do	you	**ever**	sleep	with your cat?	Yes, I **sometimes** do.
Does	the teacher	**ever**	bring	her dog to school?	No, she **never** does.

Be	Subject	Ever		Complement	Short Answer
Are	dogs	**ever**		unhappy?	Yes, they **sometimes** are.
Is	Marianne	**ever**		home during the day?	No, she **never** is.

Language Notes:
1. In a short answer, the frequency word comes between the subject and the verb.
2. The verb after *never* is affirmative.
   Does your cat ever drink milk?
   No, she never **does**.

EXERCISE 24 ABOUT YOU Fill in the blanks with a frequency word to make a **true** statement about yourself. Then ask a question with *ever*. Another student will answer.

EXAMPLE I ___rarely___ eat breakfast in a restaurant.

  A: Do you ever eat breakfast in a restaurant?
  B: No, I never do.

1. I _____ sleep with the light on.
2. I _____ watch TV in the morning.
3. I _____ take a bubble bath.
4. I _____ spend money on foolish things.
5. I'm _____ afraid to go out at night.
6. I'm _____ tired while I'm in class.
7. I _____ cry during a sad movie.
8. I _____ dream in English.
9. I _____ take off my shoes when I enter my house.
10. I _____ babysit for a member of my family.
11. I _____ eat fast food.
12. I _____ wear a watch.
13. I _____ use cologne or perfume.
14. I _____ fall asleep with the TV on.

The Simple Present Tense; Frequency Words

15. I _____ fall asleep in class.
16. I _____ write personal letters to my friends and family.
17. I _____ sit in the sun to get a suntan.
18. I _____ carry a personal stereo.
19. I _____ wear running shoes.
20. I _____ discuss politics with my friends.
21. I _____ wear sandals in warm weather.
22. I'm _____ friendly with my neighbors.

1.12 Questions with *How Often* and Answers with Frequency Expressions

Examples	Explanation

How often do you take your dog out?
    I take her out **three times a day.**
How often does Marianne travel?
    She travels **every other month.**
How often do you take your cat to the doctor?
    I take my cat to the doctor **twice a year.**
	We use *how often* when we want to ask about the frequency of an activity.

Once a month, she takes her dog to a groomer. She takes her dog to a groomer **once a month.**	Frequency expressions can come at the beginning or the end of the sentence.

EXERCISE 25 ABOUT YOU Ask a question with *"How often do you . . . ?"* and the words given. Another student will answer.

EXAMPLE eat in a restaurant

A: How often do you eat in a restaurant?
B: I eat in a restaurant once a week.

1. check your e-mail
2. shop for groceries
3. exercise
4. get a haircut
5. use your dictionary
6. use public transportation
7. use the Internet
8. go to the dentist
9. watch the news on TV
10. go to the teacher's office

SUMMARY OF LESSON 1

1. Observe the simple present tense with the verb *be*.
   Your dog **is** beautiful.
   It **isn't** big.
   Is it a collie? No, it **isn't**.
   What kind of dog **is** it?

   You **are** young.
   You **aren't** ready for a dog.
   Are you responsible? Yes, I **am**.
   Why **aren't** you ready for a dog?

2. Observe the simple present tense with other verbs.

Base Form	**-s Form**
They **have** a dog.	She **likes** birds.
They **don't have** a cat.	She **doesn't like** cats.
Do they **have** a bird?	**Does** she **like** small birds?
No, they **don't**.	Yes, she **does**.
What kind of dog **do** they **have**?	Why **does** she **like** birds?
Why **don't** they **have** a cat?	Why **doesn't** she **like** cats?

3. Frequency words:

always	100%
usually / generally	↑
often / frequently	
sometimes / occasionally	
rarely / seldom / hardly ever	↓
never / not ever	0%

4. Questions with frequency words:
   Does he **ever** take his dog to the park? Yes, he **often** does.
   How often does he feed his dog? Twice a day.

EDITING ADVICE

1. Don't use a contraction in a short affirmative answer.

   Are you happy in the U.S. Yes, ~~I'm~~ *I am*.

2. Don't make a contraction with a word that ends with *s, se, ce, ze, sh, ch,* or *x*.

   English~~'s~~ *is* a difficult language.

3. Don't use *have* with age. Do not use *years* without *old*.

   My daughter ~~has~~ *is* 10 years *old*.

The Simple Present Tense; Frequency Words   33

4. Don't use *have* with *hungry, thirsty, hot, cold,* or *afraid.*

   Please open the window. I ~~have~~ *am* hot.

5. Don't forget the subject *it* with time, weather, and impersonal expressions.

   It i
   ~~Is~~ cold today.

   It i
   ~~Is~~ important to know English.

6. Don't forget the verb *be.* Remember that some words that end in *-ed* are adjectives, not verbs.

   The college ^*is* located downtown.

   I ^*am* very tired.

7. Don't confuse *your* (possession) and *you're* (you are).

   You're
   ~~Your~~ a very good student.

8. Use correct word order in questions.

   are you
   Why ~~you are~~ late?

   doesn't your sister
   Why ~~your sister doesn't~~ drive?

9. In a contraction, be careful to put the apostrophe in place of the missing letter. Put the apostrophe above the line.

   isn't
   The teacher ~~is'nt~~ here today.

   doesn't
   He ~~doesn,t~~ know the answer.

10. There's no contraction for *am not.*

    I'm not
    ~~I amn't~~ sick today.

11. Don't repeat the subject with a pronoun.

    My brother ~~he~~ lives in Puerto Rico.

12. Don't use *be* with another present tense verb.

    I~~'m~~ come from Poland.

    We~~'re~~ have a new computer.

Lesson 1

13. Use the -s form when the subject is *he, she, it, everyone,* or *family.*

    My father live˄ in New York. *(s)*

    Everyone know˄ the answer. *(s)*

    My family live˄ in Egypt. *(s)*

14. Use *doesn't* when the subject is *he, she, it,* or *family.*

    He ~~don't~~ have a car. *doesn't*

    My family ~~don't~~ live here. *doesn't*

15. Use the base form after *does.*

    He doesn't speaks English.

    Where does he lives?

16. Don't forget to use *do* or *does* and the base form in the question.

    Where˄ your father works? *does*

17. Use normal question formation for *spell, mean,* and *cost.*

    What ~~means "custom"~~? *does "custom" mean?*

    How˄ spell "responsible"? *do you*

    How much ~~costs~~ the newspaper˄? *does* ... *cost*

18. Use the correct word order with frequency words.

    He ~~goes sometimes~~ to the zoo. *sometimes goes*

    ~~Never I~~ eat in a restaurant. *I never*

    I ~~never am~~ late to class. *am never*

19. Don't put a frequency phrase between the subject and the verb.

    She ~~all the time~~ talks on the phone˄. *all the time*

The Simple Present Tense; Frequency Words   35

20. She ~~all the time~~ *always* talks on her cell phone.

    OR

    She talks on her cell phone all the time.

LESSON 1 TEST/REVIEW

PART 1 Find the mistakes with the underlined words and correct them. Not every sentence has a mistake. If the sentence is correct, write *C*.

EXAMPLES Does your mother <u>speaks</u> Polish?

Where <u>do</u> they live?   *C*

1. How often <u>does</u> they go shopping?
2. I <u>don't need</u> help.
3. Why <u>you don't</u> answer my question?
4. How many languages <u>speaks your brother</u>?
5. My brother <u>don't</u> like American food.
6. Who does your sister <u>lives</u> with?
7. She <u>doesn't understand</u> your question.
8. <u>How you spell</u> "occasion"?
9. What <u>means</u> "occasion"?
10. How much <u>costs the textbook</u>?
11. I <u>never am</u> bored in class.
12. I <u>never go</u> out at night.
13. <u>Do you ever</u> rent a movie? Yes, we often do.
14. <u>Sometimes I don't understand</u> Americans.
15. <u>What often</u> do you get a haircut?
16. <u>She every other day</u> writes a letter.
17. Everyone <u>need</u> love.
18. My family <u>live</u> in Colombia.
19. Is your father an engineer? Yes, <u>he's</u>.
20. <u>France's</u> a beautiful country.
21. I want to eat. I <u>am</u> hungry.
22. <u>Is</u> very hot today.

23. The college <u>located</u> on Main and Green.
24. <u>You're</u> my favorite teacher.
25. Why <u>the teacher isn't</u> here today?
26. My little brother <u>has 10 years</u>.
27. I <u>don't interested</u> in sports.
28. She <u>doesn't have</u> a cell phone.
29. I have my sweater, so I <u>amn't</u> cold.
30. <u>I'm have</u> a new TV.
31. <u>She's comes</u> from Mexico.

PART 2 Fill in the blanks with the affirmative form of the verb in parentheses ( ). Then write the negative form of the verb.

EXAMPLES Elena ___*wants*___ to write about strange American customs.
(want)

She ___*doesn't want*___ to write about the weather.

1. Marianne _____ Elena.
(know)

   She _____ Sofia.

2. Marianne _____ a dog.
(have)

   Elena _____ a dog.

3. Elena _____ in the U.S.
(live)

   Sofia _____ in the U.S.

4. Marianne _____ American.
(be)

   Elena _____ American.

5. You _____ some American customs.
(understand)

   You _____ all American customs.

6. American customs _____ strange for Elena.
(be)

   American customs _____ strange for Marianne.

7. I _____ cats.
(like)

   I _____ dogs.

8. Dogs _____ a lot of attention.
   (need)

   Cats _____ so much attention.

9. Almost everyone _____ kittens
   (love)
   and puppies.

   Most people _____ snakes.

PART 3 Read each statement. Then write a *yes / no* question about the words in parentheses ( ). Write a short answer.

EXAMPLE Elena lives in the U.S. (Marianne)
Does Marianne live in the U.S.? Yes, she does.

1. Marianne has a dog. (Elena) (no)
   _____

2. Elena and Marianne live in the U.S. (Sofia) (no)
   _____

3. Elena has an American friend. (Sofia) (no)
   _____

4. Elena often writes letters. (you / ever) [Give a true answer about yourself.]
   _____

5. You like animals. (you / ever / go to the zoo)
   _____

6. American customs are strange for Elena. (for Marianne) (no)
   _____

PART 4 Fill in the blanks to complete the question.

EXAMPLE Dogs like people.
Why *do dogs like people?*

1. Marianne sometimes travels with her dog.
   How _____ with her dog?

2. Sofia doesn't understand American customs.
   Why _____ American customs?

3. Elena writes to Sofia once a week.
   How often _____ to Elena?

Lesson **1**

4. A dog service costs a lot of money.

   How much _____?

5. Elena doesn't have a dog.

   Why _____ a dog?

6. Marianne carries a picture of Sparky in her wallet.

   Why _____ in her wallet?

7. Marianne walks her dog several times a day.

   How often _____?

8. She takes her dog to the animal hospital.

   How often _____ to the animal hospital?

9. Guide dogs need a lot of training.

   Why _____ a lot of training?

10. Rescue dogs save people's lives.

    How _____ people's lives?

11. A purebred dog costs a lot of money.

    How much _____?

PART 5 Write a question with the words given.

EXAMPLE What / a dog / eat

What does a dog eat?

1. How / spell / "kitten"

   _____

2. What / mean / "puppy"

   _____

3. How / say / "cat" in Spanish

   _____

4. How much / cost / a parrot

   _____

EXPANSION ACTIVITIES

Classroom Activity

Customs Put a check (✓) to indicate which of the following are typical customs in the U.S. and which are typical customs in your native culture. Discuss your answers in a small group or with the entire class.

Customs	In the U.S.	In my native culture
People walk their dogs on a leash.	✓	
Dogs have jackets and other clothes.		
Supermarkets sell a lot of pet food.		
Students wear jeans to class.		
Students call their teachers by their first names.		
Students write in their textbooks.		
Teachers stand in class.		
People talk a lot about politics.		
People drink a lot of soft drinks.		
Children watch TV a lot.		
Friends get together in coffee houses.		
Women wear makeup.		
People eat some foods with their hands.		
People are friendly with their neighbors.		
People say, "How are you?"		
People use credit cards.		
Men open doors for women.		
People eat with chopsticks.		
People have a car.		
People wear gym shoes.		
People travel in the summer.		
People take off their shoes when they enter a house.		
Young adults live separately from their parents.		
People usually leave a tip in a restaurant.		
People know how to use a computer.		
People pay attention to the weather report.		
Students study a foreign language.		

Talk About it

1. Do a lot of people you know have a pet? Do they treat their pet like a member of the family? Do you have a pet now? What kind?

2. Work with a partner or in a small group. Tell if you think each animal is a good pet. Why or why not?

   a. a snake

   b. a parakeet

   c. a rabbit

   d. a lizard

   e. a turtle

   f. a hamster

   g. a cat

   h. a dog

   i. tropical fish (**Note:** *Fish* can be singular or plural)

3. **Proverbs** The following proverbs mention animals. Discuss the meaning of each proverb. Do you have a similar proverb in your native language?

   a. You can't teach an old dog new tricks.

   b. While the cat's away, the mice will play.

   c. Man's best friend is his dog.

   d. Curiosity killed the cat.

   e. The dog's bark is worse than his bite.

4. **Joke** A woman is outside of her house. A dog is near her. A man walks by and is interested in the dog. He wants to pet the dog. He asks the woman, "Does your dog bite?" The woman answers no. The man pets the dog and the dog bites him. He says, "You told me that your dog doesn't bite." The woman answers, "This is not my dog. My dog is in the house."

Write About it

1. Write about three American customs that seem strange to you. Compare these customs to how people behave in your country or native culture.

2. Write about differences in how people treat pets in the U.S. and in another country you know about.

Outside Activities

1. Take a notebook and a pen / pencil and go to a park. Observe people with dogs. Write your observations. Bring your notebook to class and discuss your observations with your classmates.

2. Interview a friend or neighbor who has a pet. Find out five interesting things about this pet. Bring the results of your interview to the class.

3. Rent the movie *Best in Show*. Write a summary of the movie.

Internet Activities

1. At a search engine type in *pet*. Find a Web site that advertises pet supplies. Make a list of all the unusual things people buy for their pets.

2. Find information about a breed of dog that you like. (Try the Web site of the American Kennel Club or AKC.)

3. At a search engine, type in *animal shelter* and the name of the city where you live (or the nearest big city). Find information about what this shelter does.

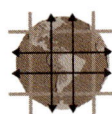
Additional Activities at **http://elt.heinle.com/gic**

LESSON 2

GRAMMAR

The Present Continuous Tense[1]
Action and Nonaction Verbs
The Future Tense

CONTEXT: Getting Older

Retirement Living
Life After Retirement
The Graying of America

[1] Some textbooks refer to this tense as the *present progressive tense*.

RETIREMENT LIVING

Before You Read

1. What observations do you make about older people in the U.S.?
2. What is the retirement age in other countries? Do older people usually have a good life?

As the U.S. population ages, many building developers **are building** homes for people over 55. Read the following conversation of a sixty-two-year-old man, Jack (J), taking a tour of a retirement village, and the manager of the retirement village (M). Pay special attention to present continuous tense verbs.

J: **I'm thinking** about moving to this retirement village. Can you give me some information?

M: This is a village for people over 55 years old. The people here are retired, but most are very active. There are different types of housing: single family homes, townhouses[2], and apartments. For those who need more help, we also have an assisted living section. Let me give you a tour. This is our fitness center. It has state-of-the-art equipment[3].

J: What **are** these people **doing**?

M: They**'re doing** yoga. And that group over there **is lifting** weights. Another group **is doing** aerobics. Let's move on to the game room. Those people **are playing** chess. And that group **is playing** cards. Now let me take you to the pool area. In this area, people **are swimming** laps[4].

J: What **are** those people **doing**?

M: Those people **are taking** a water aerobics class. Let's go to the computer room now. That's the computer teacher. He**'s teaching** that group how to design Web pages. Jerry, over there, **is putting** all his family pictures on his Web site. Marge, in the corner, **is designing** a Web site with her vacation pictures and stories about her interesting trips. She likes to travel all over the world. . . . Now let's look at the dance area.

[2] A *townhouse* is one of a series of houses attached to each other in a row.
[3] *State-of-the-art* equipment is the latest equipment.
[4] Swimming *laps* means swimming from one end of the pool to the other and back again, over and over.

Did You Know?

In 2000, there were 20.6 million older women and 14.4 million older men, or a ratio of 143 women for every 100 men. The female-to-male ratio increases with age, with 245 women for every 100 men in the 85 and over age group.

J: The band **is playing** a great song, and many of the people **are dancing.** This place is beautiful and certainly offers a lot of activities. But I don't know if it's right for me. I don't know how to dance, play chess, or design Web pages.

M: Don't worry. There are instructors here who will help you.

J: Is everybody **doing** something?

M: No. My wife is at home now. I think she**'s reading** or **watching** TV. Or maybe she**'s playing** with our grandchildren.

J: I notice that there are more women than men here.

M: Well, as you know, women live longer than men.

J: I'm a widower, you know. Maybe I can meet a woman here.

M: That's entirely possible. We have a singles group that meets once a week in the game room. Mary Dodge can give you information about the singles group. She**'s standing** over there. She**'s wearing** blue jeans and a red T-shirt.

J: How much does it cost to live here?

M: That depends on what kind of a house you choose. Come to my office and we'll look at the costs.

2.1 Present Continuous Tense

To form the present continuous tense, use a form of *be* (*is, am, are*) + verb *-ing*[5].

Examples	Explanation
Subj. *Be* Verb + *-ing* Complement I **am putting** my pictures on a Web site. Jack **is visiting** a retirement village. She **is teaching** Web design. They **are doing** yoga.	I → am He/She/It → is Singular Subject → is } + verb *-ing* We/You/They → are Plural Subject → are
a. Some people **are dancing** now. b. My wife **is watching** TV now.	In sentences (a) and (b), we use the present continuous tense to describe an action in progress at this moment.
c. Mary Dodge **is standing** over there. d. She **is wearing** blue jeans. e. A man **is sitting** in front of a computer.	In sentences (c), (d), and (e), we use the present continuous tense to describe a state or condition, using the following verbs: *sit, stand, wear,* and *sleep*. We can observe these things now.
They**'re playing** cards. Jack**'s taking** a tour of the retirement village. He**'s asking** questions. The **manager's answering** his questions.	We can make a contraction with the subject pronoun and a form of *be*. Most nouns can also contract with *is*.[6]

Jack **isn't** doing yoga.
Most people **aren't** watching TV.
I**'m not** playing tennis.
	To form the negative, put *not* after the verb *am/is/are*.
	Negative contractions:
	   is not = isn't
	   are not = aren't
	There is no contraction for *am not*.

Jerry **is designing** a Web site *and* **putting** his family pictures on it.
They **are playing** cards *and* **laughing.**
She**'s reading** *or* **watching** TV.
	Do not repeat the *be* verb after these connectors:
	   and
	   or

[5] For a review of the spelling of the *-ing* form of the verb, see Appendix A.
[6] See Lesson 1, page 5 for exceptions.

EXERCISE 1 Fill in the blanks with the present continuous form of the verb in parentheses ( ). Use correct spelling.

EXAMPLE Jack __is visiting__ a retirement village.
(visit)

1. He _____ a tour.
   (take)

2. He _____ at the different activities.
   (look)

3. The manager of the village _____ him information.
   (give)

4. Some people _____.
   (dance)

5. Some people _____ the exercise equipment.
   (use)

6. One woman _____ weights.
   (lift)

7. Those people _____ chess.
   (play)

8. Some people _____.
   (swim)

9. Jerry _____. He _____
   (not/read)   (put)
   his family pictures on his Web site.

10. The manager's wife is at home. She _____ or
    (read)
    _____ TV. She _____ an
    (watch)   (not/take)
    aerobics class.

11. Some people _____ anything.
    (not/do)

EXERCISE 2 Fill in the blanks with an affirmative or negative verb to make a **true** statement about what is happening now.

EXAMPLES I __'m wearing__ jeans now.
(wear)
The teacher __isn't writing__ on the blackboard now.
(write)

1. The sun _____ now.
   (shine)

2. It _____ now.
   (rain)

The Present Continuous Tense; Action and Nonaction Verbs; the Future Tense

3. I _____ my answers in my book.
       (write)

4. I _____ a pencil to write this exercise.
       (use)

5. We _____ this exercise together.
       (do)

6. The teacher _____ the students with this exercise.
       (help)

7. The teacher _____ a watch.
       (wear)

8. I _____ my dictionary now.
       (use)

9. We _____ possessive forms now.
       (practice)

10. I _____ jeans.
       (wear)

11. The teacher _____.
       (stand)

12. I _____ near the door.
       (sit)

LIFE AFTER RETIREMENT

Before You Read

1. Is anyone in your family retired? How does that person keep busy?
2. What observations do you make about older Americans?

Read the following article. Pay special attention to present continuous tense verbs and simple present tense verbs.

The U.S. population **is aging.** More and more Americans **are thinking** about retirement. But today, many people **are retiring** younger and healthier than ever before. People **are living** longer. But they **are not leaving** their jobs to spend their days at the beach or babysitting for their grandchildren. Most older people **prefer** to keep busy. Many healthy seniors **are starting** new careers. They **want** to explore new avenues in their lives.

Judy Pearlman is a 62-year-old retired school teacher from Chicago. After 35 years in education, she **is starting** a new career—making dolls. "Now I **have** time to do what I always dreamed about," she says. "I'**m having** more fun than ever before. I'**m meeting** new people, **traveling** in my new job, and **earning** money all at the same time. And I'm still **getting** my teacher pension. I'**m enjoying** every minute of it. I **think** this is the best time of my life."

Lesson 2

Did You Know?
Today 28 percent of retired people **are working**.

"After 33 years as an accountant, I'**m** now **taking** art classes," says Charles Haskell of Cleveland. "I'**m discovering** a new talent."

Some senior citizens **decide** not to retire at all. Frank Babbit of Milwaukee **is** a carpenter. He **has** his own business and **works** 50 hours a week. And he'**s** almost 88 years old.

Many older women **are returning** to work after raising their children. "My kids **are** grown and **don't need** me now," says Miriam Orland of San Francisco. "So I **have** time for myself now. I'**m taking** courses at a community college. I'**m thinking** about a career in Web design."

Some retirees **are using** their free time to volunteer. "I retired as an accountant six months ago, and now I **volunteer** as a math tutor in a public library near my house. I **go** to the library twice a week to help students who **are having** trouble with math," says Ron Meyers of Miami. "I **work** in a food pantry and **feed** the homeless three times a week," says Linda Carlson of Washington, DC. "It **gives** me a lot of satisfaction."

Today healthy retirees **are exploring** many options, from relaxing to starting a new business or making a hobby into a new career. How **do** you **see** yourself as a retiree?

2.2 | Using the Present Continuous for Longer Actions

Examples	Explanation
Judy **is meeting** new people. She **is getting** her pension and **earning** money from her new job. She **is enjoying** her new career. My grandfather **is planning** to retire soon.	We use the present continuous tense to show a long-term action that is in progress. It may not be happening at this exact moment.
More and more retired Americans **are looking** for a second career. Some older people **are working** because of economic necessity. Americans **are living** longer. Many older women **are returning** to work after their children are grown.	We use the present continuous tense to describe a *trend*. A trend is a behavior that many people in society are doing at this time. It describes a change in behavior from an earlier time.

EXERCISE 3 Fill in the blanks with an appropriate verb. Answers may vary.

EXAMPLE More and more retired people ____are working____ these days.

1. Many people _____ at a younger age.
2. They _____ their time at the beach or
    (not)
babysitting for their grandchildren.

The Present Continuous Tense; Action and Nonaction Verbs; the Future Tense   49

3. They _____ new careers.

4. People _____ longer and healthier lives.

5. Some people _____ new talents and abilities.

6. Some older women _____ to work after raising a family.

EXERCISE 4 ABOUT YOU Write three sentences about being a student. Tell what is happening in your life as a student. (You may share your sentences with the class.)

EXAMPLES *I'm taking five courses this semester.*

I'm staying with my sister this semester.

I'm majoring in math.

You may use these verbs: *learn, study, take courses, stay, live, major,* and *plan*.

1. _____
2. _____
3. _____

EXERCISE 5 ABOUT YOU Write three sentences to tell which things in your life are changing. Then find a partner and ask your partner if he or she is experiencing the same changes.

EXAMPLES *I'm gaining weight. Are you gaining weight?*

I'm planning to buy a house. Are you planning to buy a house?

My English pronunciation is improving. Is your pronunciation improving?

You may use the following verbs: *plan, get (become), learn, grow, gain, lose, improve, think about, change,* and *start*.

1. _____
2. _____
3. _____

EXERCISE 6 Tell if these things are happening at this point in time in the U.S., in the world, or in another country you know about. Discuss your answers.

1. Older people are getting more respect than before.
2. People are living healthier lives.
3. People are living longer.
4. The world is becoming a more dangerous place.

5. The economy is getting better.
6. Medical science is advancing quickly.
7. A lot of people are losing their jobs.
8. People are working harder than before.
9. People are doing more and enjoying less.
10. The cost of a college education is going down.
11. The cost of computers is going down.
12. More and more people are using cell phones.
13. Cars are getting bigger.
14. Kids are growing up faster than before.

2.3 | Questions with the Present Continuous Tense

Affirmative Statements and Questions

Wh- Word	Be	Subject	Be	Verb + -ing	Complement	Short Answer
		Jerry	is	designing	something.	
	Is	he		designing	a house?	No, he isn't.
What	is	he		designing?		A Web site.
		They	are	taking	courses at college.	
	Are	they		taking	biology?	No, they aren't.
What courses	are	they		taking?		Computer courses.
		He	is	thinking	about a new career.	
	Is	he		thinking	about a career in computers?	No, he isn't.

Language Notes:
1. We can leave a preposition at the end of a question.
   What kind of career is he thinking about?
2. When the question is "What . . . doing?" we usually answer with a different verb.
   What are they **doing**? They're **taking** an aerobics class.
   What are those people **doing**? They're **playing** chess.

Negative Statements and Questions

Wh- Word	Be + n't	Subject	Be + n't	Verb + -ing	Complement
		Mary	isn't	dancing.	
Why	isn't	she		dancing?	
		You	aren't	using	the computer.
Why	aren't	you		using	the computer?

EXERCISE 7 Fill in the blanks to make *yes / no* questions about the readings in this lesson.

EXAMPLE _Are those men playing_ checkers? No, they aren't. Those men are playing chess.

1. _____ this retirement home? Yes, I am. I'm considering it now that my wife is gone.

2. _____ a Web site. Yes, she is. Marge is designing a Web site with pictures of her vacations.

3. _____ pictures now? No, he isn't taking pictures. He's putting his pictures on his Web site.

4. _____ something? No, not everyone is doing something. Some people are just relaxing.

5. _____ art classes? Yes, they are. Judy and Charles love art so they're taking a lot of classes.

6. _____ too many questions? No, you're not. You can ask as many questions as you want.

EXERCISE 8 Read each statement. Then write a question using the word in parentheses ( ). An answer is not necessary.

EXAMPLE Some retirees are discovering new interests. (how)
How are they discovering new interests?

1. Judy is having more fun now. (why)
   _____

2. Judy is traveling to many new places. (where)
   _____

3. I am starting a new career. (what kind of career)
   _____

4. Some students are having trouble with math. (why)
   _____

5. My father is thinking about retirement. (why)
   _____

6. My mother is looking for a new career. (what kind)
   _____

7. We're not planning to retire. (why)
   _____

8. People are living longer nowadays. (why)
   _____

9. I'm doing things that interest me. (what kinds of things)
   _____

EXERCISE 9 Fill in the blanks to form *yes / no* questions about the reading on pages 44-45. Use the present continuous tense.

Jack (J) is talking to his neighbor Alan (A).

A: What ____*are you doing*____, Jack?
   (example: you/do)

J: I _____ at some brochures.
   (1 look)

A: What kind of brochures _____?
   (2 you/look at)

J: They're from a retirement village.

A: So _____ about moving?
   (3 you/think)

J: Yes, I'm thinking about moving into a retirement village.

A: Why?

J: Now that Rose is gone, I feel lonely.

A: But you have a lot of good neighbors here.

J: Most of the people here are young. My neighbors to the north are never home. Right now they _____. And my
   (4 work)
   neighbors across the street are never home.

A: They're older people. _____ too?
   (5 work)

J: No. They _____ now. Right now
   (6 travel)
   they _____ a cruise[7] to Alaska.
   (7 take)

---

[7] A *cruise* is a pleasure trip on a large passenger boat.

A: But I'm here. I _____ (8 water) my lawn, as usual. And my wife is inside. She _____ (9 talk) on the phone, as usual.

J: I'm sorry I'm complaining so much.

A: You _____ (10 not/complain). You _____ (11 just/look) for something to do.

J: There's a lot to do. I just don't want to do things alone.

A: But your daughter lives with you.

J: She's in her 20s. She doesn't want to do things with her dad. Right now she _____ (12 watch) a movie with her friends.

A: What movie _____ (13 they/watch)?

J: Who knows? Something for young people. Her movies don't interest me.

A: What retirement village _____ (14 you/plan) to go to?

J: Sun Valley Senior Village seems nice.

A: What about your daughter?

J: She _____ (15 plan) to move in with a friend of hers.

EXERCISE 10 Fill in the blanks to complete the questions. Answers may vary.

EXAMPLE
A: Why _____is your sister wearing_____ sunglasses? It's not sunny.
B: My sister's wearing sunglasses because she wants to look like a movie star.

1. **A:** What _____?
   B: I'm reading an article about older Americans.
   A: _____ the article?
   B: Oh, yes. I'm enjoying it very much.

2. **A:** Where _____ now?
   B: She's going to the park. Grandma always goes to the park on Sundays to jog.
   A: (not) _____ now?
   B: Yes, it's raining. But that doesn't matter. The park has an indoor track.

3. **A:** Martha is on her cell phone. Who _____?

   B: She's talking to her best friend.

   A: Why _____ on her cell phone?

   Why _____ her home phone?

   B: Because her sister is using the home phone.

4. **Student:** _____?

   Teacher: Yes. You're accent is improving a lot.

   Student: How _____ with my grammar?

   Teacher: You're doing very well.

5. **Wife:** Something smells good. What _____?

   Husband: I'm cooking your favorite dinner—steak and potatoes.

   (*A few minutes later . . .*)

   Wife: _____ something _____?

   Husband: Uh, oh. The steaks are burning.

6. **A:** The kids are watching TV. What _____?

   B: They're watching cartoons.

   A: Why _____ their homework?

   B: They're not doing their homework because they don't have homework today.

7. **A:** I'm leaving.

   B: Where _____?

   A: I'm going to the library.

   B: Why _____?

   A: Because you're making too much noise. I have to study.

8. **Dad:** I'm planning to retire next year.

   Son: You're so young. Why _____?

   Dad: First of all, I'm not so young. I'm almost 60. I'm planning to travel.

   Son: _____ alone?

   Dad: No, of course not. I _____ with Mom.

   Son: But she's still _____.

   Dad: She is now. But she's thinking about retiring too. She loves her work, but enough's enough. It's time to have fun.

The Present Continuous Tense; Action and Nonaction Verbs; the Future Tense

2.4 Contrasting the Simple Present and the Present Continuous

Form

Simple Present Tense	Present Continuous Tense
He sometimes **travels** in the summer. He **doesn't travel** in the winter. **Does** he **travel** with his daughter? No, he **doesn't**. How often **does** he **travel**? Why **doesn't** he **travel** with his daughter?	He **is planning** his vacation. He **isn't planning** his retirement. **Is** he **planning** a trip to Hawaii? No, he **isn't**. Where **is** he **planning** to go? Why **isn't** he **planning** to retire?

Use

Examples	Explanation
a. Many people **retire** at age 65. a. Retirees **get** Social Security. a. People **like** to feel useful. b. Jack *sometimes* **feels** lonely. b. He *rarely* **watches** movies with his daughter. b. Ron **volunteers** in a library *twice a week*. b. Judy *often* **travels**. c. Grown children **live** separately from their parents. c. Parents **call** their grown children before they visit them. c. Some singles **belong** to a singles group.	Use the **simple present tense** to talk about: a. a general truth b. a habitual activity c. a custom
a. Jack **is visiting** a retirement village now. a. We **are studying** this grammar chart now. b. Judy **is meeting** a lot of new people at this time. b. She**'s earning** money at her hobby. c. People **are living** longer these days. c. People **are retiring** earlier these days.	Use the **present continuous tense** for: a. an action that is in progress now b. a longer action that is in progress at this general time c. recent trends in society
Compare: a. My parents **live** in a retirement village. b. My sister **is living** in a dorm this semester.	a. *Live* in the simple present shows a person's home. b. *Live* in the present continuous shows a temporary, short-term residence.

Compare:
a. **What does she do (for a living)?**
    She's a nurse.
b. **What is she doing?**
    She's waiting for the bus.
	Sentence (a) asks about a job or profession. It uses the simple present tense.
	Sentence (b) asks about an activity now. It uses the present continuous tense.

EXERCISE 11 Fill in the blanks with the simple present or the present continuous tense of the verb in parentheses ( ).

1. **A:** What _____are you eating_____? Is it a hamburger?
   (example: you/eat)

   B: No, it isn't. It's a veggie burger. I never _____
   (1 eat)

   meat. Where's your lunch?

   A: I don't want to eat lunch. I _____ too much weight.
   (2 gain)

   I _____ to lose weight. I _____
   (3 try)   (4 eat)

   only twice a day—breakfast and dinner.

   B: But you _____ a soda now.
   (5 drink)

   A: It's a diet cola.

2. **A:** What _____?
   (6 you/do)

   B: I _____ in the answers.
   (7 fill)

   A: Why _____ a pen? A pencil is better. What if
   (8 you/use)

   you make a mistake?

   B: I never _____ mistakes. My grammar is perfect!
   (9 make)

   A: That's not true. We all _____ mistakes. That's
   (10 make)

   why we're in this class.

The Present Continuous Tense; Action and Nonaction Verbs; the Future Tense

B: I'm just kidding. Of course I _____ (11 make) mistakes all the time.

3. **A:** What _____ (12 your father/do) for a living?

   B: He's a commercial artist. He _____ (13 work) for a big company downtown. But this week he's on vacation.

   A: What _____ (14 he/do) this week?

   B: He _____ (15 play) golf with his friends.

   A: Is your mom on vacation too?

   B: No. She _____ (16 take) a vacation every December.

4. **A:** Where _____ (17 the teacher/go)?

   B: She _____ (18 go) to her office.

   A: She _____ (19 carry) heavy books. Let's help her.

   B: I'm late for my next class. My math teacher always _____ (20 start) on time. He _____ (21 get) angry if someone is late.

5. **A:** You _____ (22 sleep), Daniel. Wake up.

   B: I'm so tired. I never _____ (23 get) enough sleep.

   A: How many hours _____ (24 you/sleep) a night?

   B: Only about four or five.

   A: That's not enough. You always _____ (25 fall) asleep in class.

   B: I know. But I _____ (26 take) 18 credit hours this semester.

   A: That's too much. I never _____ (27 take) more than 12.

Lesson 2

2.5 Action and Nonaction Verbs

Some verbs are action verbs. These verbs show physical or mental activity (*run, play, study, drive, eat,* etc.). Some verbs are nonaction verbs. These verbs describe a state, condition, or feeling, not an action.

Examples	Explanation
Miriam says, "My kids **don't need** me now. I **have** free time now." Judy says, "I **love** my second career now." My grandmother is old. She **needs** a lot of care now.	With nonaction verbs, we use the simple present tense, even when we talk about now. We do not usually use a continuous form with these verbs.
a. Jack **is watching** the dancers. b. He **sees** more women than men.	*Watch* is an action verb. *See* is a nonaction verb.
a. Some people **are listening** to music. b. Jack **hears** the music.	*Listen* is an action verb. *Hear* is a nonaction verb.
a. Judy **is meeting** new people. b. She **knows** a lot of people.	*Meet* is an action verb. *Know* is a nonaction verb.
a. Miriam is **thinking** *about* a career in Web design. b. She **thinks** *that* Web design is interesting.	a. When you think *about* or *of* something, *think* is an action verb. b. *Think that* shows an opinion about something. It is a nonaction verb.
a. Judy **is having** a lot of fun now. a. I **am having** a burger for lunch. b. Miriam **has** free time now. b. I **have** three brothers. b. Ron **has** a fever now.	a. When *have* means to experience something or to eat or drink something, it is an action verb. b. When *have* shows possession, relationship, or illness, it is a nonaction verb.
a. Jack **is looking** at the people in the swimming pool. a. Mary **is smelling** the flowers. b. The aerobics class **looks** interesting. b. The flowers **smell** nice.	a. When the sense-perception verbs describe an action, they are action verbs. b. When the sense-perception verbs describe a state, they are nonaction verbs.

Nonaction Verbs:

like	know	see	cost
love	believe	smell	own
hate	think (that)	hear	have (for possession)
want	care (about)	taste	matter
need	understand	feel	mean
prefer	remember	seem	

The Present Continuous Tense; Action and Nonaction Verbs; the Future Tense

EXERCISE 12

Fill in the blanks with the simple present or the present continuous tense of the verb in parentheses ( ).

1. **A:** Grandpa volunteers his time. Twice a week he __reads__ (example: read) for blind people.

   B: My grandmother _____ (1 work) part-time in a bookstore. She _____ (2 love) books. She usually _____ (3 ride) her bike to work. She _____ (4 like) the exercise.

   A: Where is she now? _____ (5 she/work) now?

   B: Now she's on vacation. She _____ (6 sail) in Florida.

2. **A:** Can I borrow your dictionary?

   B: I'm sorry. I _____ (7 use) it now. Where's your dictionary?

   A: I never _____ (8 bring) it to class. It's too heavy.

   B: _____ (9 expect) to use my dictionary all the time? You _____ (10 need) an electronic dictionary. It's very light.

3. **A:** What _____ (11 the teacher/say) ?

   She _____ (12 talk) too fast, so I _____ (13 not/understand) her now.

   B: I don't know. I _____ (14 not/listen). I _____ (15 think) about my girlfriend.

   A: I _____ (16 think) you are a very romantic guy.

   B: Yes. I _____ (17 think) about asking her to marry me.

4. **A:** What _____ (18 you/write)?

   B: I _____ (19 write) a composition about my grandparents. I _____ (20 love) them very much.

   A: _____ (21 they/live) with you?

   B: No, they don't. They live in Pakistan. They _____ (22 visit) us once a year.

   A: _____ (23 you/ever/send) them e-mail?

   B: Sometimes I do. But right now their computer _____ (24 not/work). Anyway, they _____ (25 prefer) handwritten letters.

   A: I do too.

5. **A:** Look at that girl. Who is she?

   B: She's in my math class. I _____ (26 know) her pretty well.

   A: What _____ (27 she/wear)?

   B: She _____ (28 wear) a dress and army boots.

   A: She _____ (29 look) strange. _____ (30 she/always/wear) a dress and army boots?

   B: No, not always. Sometimes she _____ (31 wear) sandals. And sometimes she _____ (32 not/wear) any shoes at all.

6. **A:** _____ (33 you/see) that guy over there? Who is he?

   B: That's my English teacher.

   A: He _____ (34 wear) jeans and gym shoes. And he _____ (35 have) an earring in his ear. He _____ (36 look) like a student.

   B: I _____ (37 know). Everyone _____ (38 think)

The Present Continuous Tense; Action and Nonaction Verbs; the Future Tense   **61** he's a student. But he's a very professional teacher.

A: What level _____ ?
(39 he/teach)

B: He teaches level four. But now he _____ for
(40 look)

another job because he _____ a full-time job
(41 not/have)

here. He _____ to work full-time.
(42 want)

7. A: What _____ this semester?
(43 you/study)

B: English, math, and biology.

A: _____ well in all your courses?
(44 you/do)

B: I _____ well in English and math. But biology
(45 do)

is hard for me. I _____ to drop it.
(46 need)

I _____ the teacher very well.
(47 not/understand)

He _____ too fast for me.
(48 talk)

8. A: What _____ for a living?
(49 your mother/do)

B: She's retired now.

A: _____ old?
(50 be)

B: No, she's only 58.

A: What _____ with her free time?
(51 she/do)

B: She does a lot of things. In fact, she _____ any
(52 not/have)

free time at all. She _____ two art courses at the
(53 take)

art center this semester. Right now she _____ a
(54 paint)

beautiful picture of me. She also _____ at a
(55 volunteer)

hospital twice a week.

A: That's wonderful. A lot of retired people _____
(56 volunteer)

these days.

62   Lesson 2

EXERCISE 13 This is a phone conversation between two friends, Patty (P) and Linda (L). Fill in the blanks with the missing words. Use the simple present or the present continuous tense.

P: Hello?

L: Hi, Patty. This is Linda.

P: Hi, Linda. What _____*are you doing*_____ now?
(example: you/do)

L: Not much. _____ to meet for coffee?
(1 you/want)

P: I can't. I _____ . I _____
(2 cook)   (3 have)

dinner in the oven now, and I _____ for it to be
(4 wait)

finished. What _____?
(5 you/do)

L: I _____ for a test. But I _____
(6 study)   (7 want)

to take a break now. Besides, I _____ to talk to
(8 need)

someone. I usually _____ to my roommate when
(9 talk)

I _____ a problem, but
(10 have)

she _____ some friends in New York now.
(11 visit)

P: We can talk while I _____ dinner.
(12 prepare)

It _____ serious.
(13 sound)

L: My parents _____ to put Grandma in a nursing
(14 plan)

home.

P: But why?

L: My mom _____ she'll receive better care there.
(15 think)

P: I _____ that's such a good idea. In my family,
(16 not/think)

we _____ our parents and grandparents in a
(17 never/put)

nursing home. We _____ of them at home.
(18 always/take care)

L: My mom _____ what else to do. Grandma
(19 not/know)

_____ all the time.
(20 fall)

P: Maybe she _____ a cane or a walker.
(21 need)

L: Her memory is terrible too. She _____
(22 never/remember)

where she puts things.

P: I _____ my husband coming in the door, and
(23 hear)

dinner is almost ready. I'll call you later when we can talk more about it.

L: Thanks for listening. Talk to you later.

THE GRAYING OF AMERICA

Before You Read

1. In your native culture, who takes care of people when they get old?
2. Do old people in your native culture get a lot of respect?

Read the following article. Pay special attention to future tense verbs.

The overall population of the U.S. is growing slowly. In the year 2004, the American population was 293 million. By the middle of this century, it **is going to be** 404 million. Even though this is not a big growth, one group is growing very fast—the elderly (65 years old and over). By 2030, twenty percent of the American population **will be** 65 or over. Today there are three million people 85 or older. In 2050, 28 million **will be** 85 or older.

There are two reasons for this sudden rise in the number of older Americans. First, life expectancy is increasing. In 1900, when the life expectancy was 47, 1 in 25 Americans was elderly. In 2000, with a life expectancy of 79.5 years for women and 74 for men, 1 in 8 was elderly. By 2050, 1 in 5 **will be** elderly.

The second reason for this growth is the aging of the "baby boomers." In the eighteen years after World War II, from 1946 to 1964, a large number of babies were born—75 million. The people born during this period, known as the baby boomers, are now middle-aged and **will** soon **be** elderly. The average age of the population is increasing as the baby boomers get older and live longer. The median age of Americans in 1970 was 28; in 2000 it was 35.3. By 2050, it **will be** 40.3.

What does this mean for America? First, there **will be** a labor shortage as the baby boomers retire. There are fewer younger people to take their place at work. For taxpayers, the aging of Americans means that they **are going to pay** more taxes as one-fifth of the population uses one-half of the resources. Also, the country **will see** an increase in the number of nursing homes and the need for people to work in them.

The housing market **will have** to respond to the needs of the baby boomers too. As their children grow up and move out, many baby boomers **will sell** their bigger houses and **move** to smaller ones. Others **will convert** extra bedrooms to offices and home gyms. Also, we **will see** more and more retirement villages for active seniors. Some seniors will move from the suburbs to the city. "We live in a suburb of Chicago now," says Paula Hoffman, 52, "because the schools for our teenage children are good. But when they go away to college, we **are going to move** back into the city. There's much more activity for us there."

Susan Brecht, a housing consultant in Philadelphia, Pennsylvania, says, "Baby boomers do not view retirement the way their parents and grandparents did. For starters, they're much more active. My 55 is not my mother's 55," Brecht stated. "I think there is a change in how different generations respond to the aging process. And, that's what we're seeing now and **will see** in a dramatic way for the next 10 to 20 years."

It **will be** interesting to see how the baby boomers **are going to continue** to influence the future of America.

The Present Continuous Tense; Action and Nonaction Verbs; the Future Tense

2.6 The Future Tense with *Will*

Examples	Explanation
We **will move** back to the city. You **will see** a big change in the next 10 to 20 years.	We use *will* + the base form for the future tense.
I *will* **always** help my parents. My parents *will* **never** go to a nursing home.	We can put a frequency word between *will* and the main verb.
I'll be 72 in 2050. **You'll** take care of your elderly parents.	We can contract *will* with the subject pronouns: *I'll, you'll, he'll, she'll, it'll, we'll,* and *they'll*.
The population **will not** go down. I **won't** live with my children.	To form the negative, put *not* after *will*. The contraction for *will not* is *won't*.

Compare affirmative statements and questions with *will*.

Wh- Word	Will	Subject	Will	Verb (Base Form)	Complement	Short Answer
		She	will	live	with her daughter.	
	Will	she		live	with her son?	No, she won't.
When	will	she		live	with her daughter?	Soon.

Compare negative statements and questions with *will*.

Wh- Word	Won't	Subject	Won't	Verb (Base Form)	Complement
		They	won't	need	a large house.
Why	won't	they		need	a large house?

EXERCISE 14 Fill in the blanks with an appropriate verb in the future tense. Use *will*. Answers may vary.

EXAMPLE In the future, people _____*will live*_____ longer.

1. The population of old people _____.

2. There _____ more older people by 2050.

3. Where _____ you _____ when you are old?

4. _____ your children _____ care of you?

5. How old _____ you _____ in 2050?

6. The baby boomers are middle-aged now. They _____ soon _____ elderly.

EXERCISE 15 A 30-year-old woman is saying good-bye to her 60-year-old parents. They are leaving on a trip in their recreational vehicle (RV). Fill in the blanks to complete this conversation. Use the future with *will*. Answers may vary.

A: I'm worried about you. You ___will be___ gone for a long time.
(example)

B: Don't worry. We _____(1)_____ only _____(2)_____ gone for the summer months.

A: You _____(3)_____ alone on the road.

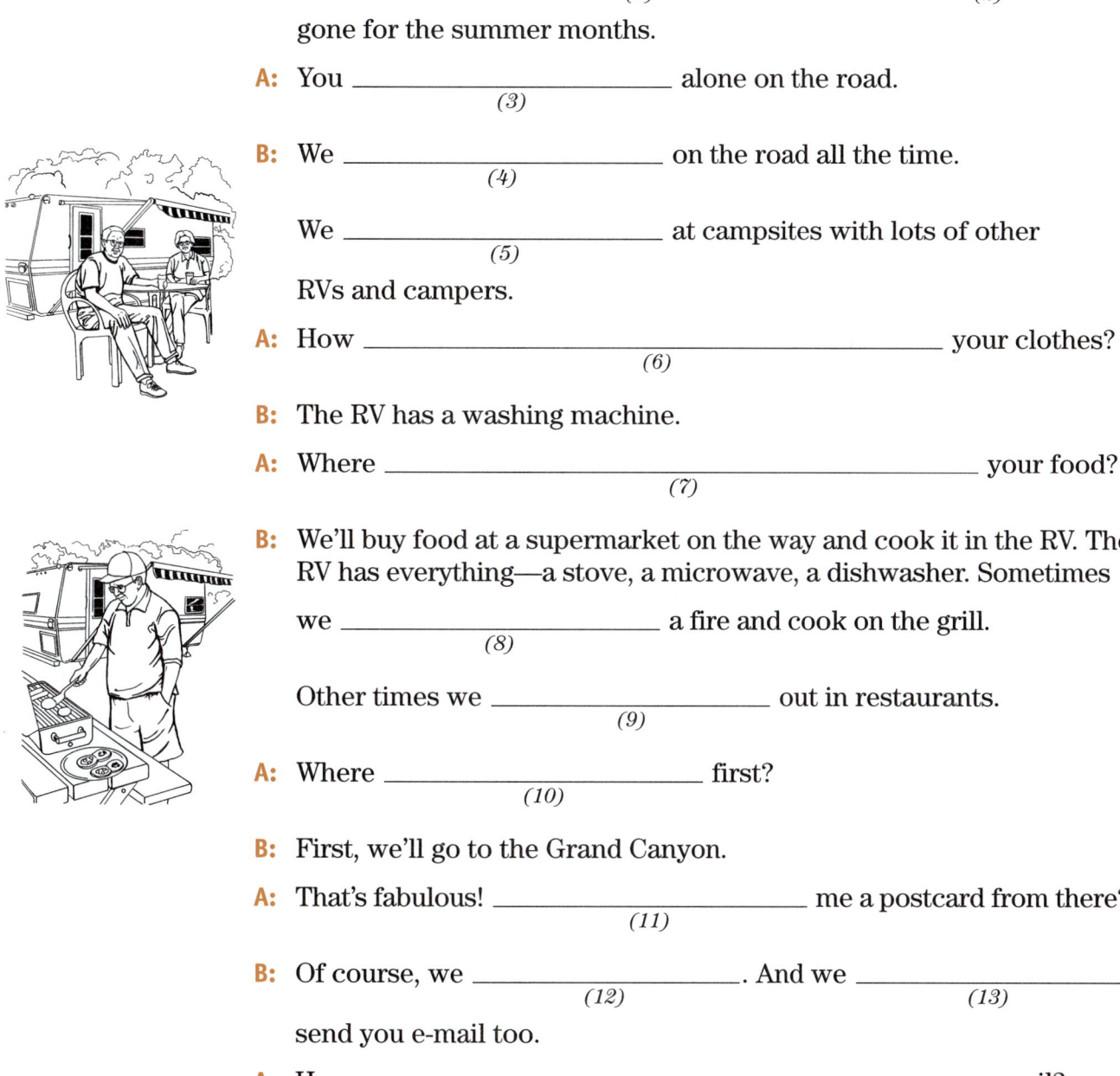

B: We _____(4)_____ on the road all the time.

We _____(5)_____ at campsites with lots of other RVs and campers.

A: How _____(6)_____ your clothes?

B: The RV has a washing machine.

A: Where _____(7)_____ your food?

B: We'll buy food at a supermarket on the way and cook it in the RV. The RV has everything—a stove, a microwave, a dishwasher. Sometimes we _____(8)_____ a fire and cook on the grill.

Other times we _____(9)_____ out in restaurants.

A: Where _____(10)_____ first?

B: First, we'll go to the Grand Canyon.

A: That's fabulous! _____(11)_____ me a postcard from there?

B: Of course, we _____(12)_____. And we _____(13)_____ send you e-mail too.

A: How _____(14)_____ e-mail?

B: From our computer, of course. We _____(15)_____ it with us.

A: Where _____(16)_____ electricity for all these things?

The Present Continuous Tense; Action and Nonaction Verbs; the Future Tense   **67**

B: At the campsites. There are electrical hookups.

A: You _____(17)_____ all the comforts of home. Why, then, are you leaving?

B: We can't see the Grand Canyon from our home.

A: _____(18)_____ pictures?

B: Yes, we'll take a lot of pictures. We'll have our digital camera with us. There _____(19)_____ a lot of beautiful things to take pictures of. We _____(20)_____ them to you by e-mail.

A: Have a good time. I _____(21)_____ you.

B: We'll miss you too.

2.7 The Future Tense with *Be Going To*

Examples	Explanation
People **are going to live** longer. They **are going to need** help from their children. There **are going to be** more elderly people in 50 years.	We use a form of *be* + *going to* + the base form to form the future tense.
I'**m not** going to live with my children. He **isn't** going to retire.	To form the negative, put *not* after *am*, *is,* or *are*.
We're **going to go** on a long trip in the RV. We're **going** on a long trip in the RV.	We often shorten *going to go* to *going*.
We're going to return **in** two months. I'm going to retire **in** ten years.	We use the preposition *in* with the future tense to mean *after*.

Pronunciation Notes:

1. In informal speech, *going to* before another verb often sounds like "gonna." In formal English, we don't write "gonna." Listen to your teacher's pronunciation of *going to* in the following sentences.
    Where's he going to live?   (Where's he "gonna" live?)
    He's going to live in a dorm.   (He's "gonna" live in a dorm.)
2. Only *going to* before another verb sounds like "gonna." We don't pronounce "gonna" at the end of a sentence or before a noun.
    Where is he going?
    He's going to the bookstore.

Compare affirmative statements and questions with *be going to*.

Wh- Word	Be	Subject	Be	Going to + Verb (Base Form)	Complement	Short Answer
		They	are	going to sell	their house.	
	Are	they		going to sell	it soon?	Yes, they are.
Why	are	they		going to sell	it?	Because they don't need a big house.

Compare negative statements and questions with *be going to*.

Wh- Word	Be + n't	Subject	Be + n't	Going to + Verb (Base Form)	Complement
		She	isn't	going to retire	from her job.
Why	isn't	she		going to retire?	

EXERCISE 16 Fill in the blanks with an appropriate verb in the future tense. Use *be going to*. Answers may vary.

EXAMPLE ____*Are*____ your children ____*going to take care of*____ you?

1. The cost of health care _____.
2. People _____ higher taxes.
3. How old _____ your daughter _____ in 2050?
4. _____ you _____ care of your elderly parents?
5. A lot of people _____ over 100 years old in 2050.

EXERCISE 17 Two co-workers are talking. Fill in the blanks with the future using *be going to*.

A: I'm so excited. I __*'m going to retire*__ at the end of this year.
   (example: retire)

B: That's wonderful news. What _____ next?
   (1 you/do)

A: I don't really know yet. I _____ new things.
   (2 explore)

B: For example, what _____?
   (3 you/explore)

A: I think I have a talent for art. I _____ (4 take) art classes.

B: _____ (5 you/work) part-time?

A: No way! I _____ (6 do) exactly what I want to do, when I want to do it.

B: Is your wife happy about your retirement?

A: Yes. She _____ (7 retire) too.

B: But you're not that old.

A: I'm 58 and she's 56. Our children aren't going to need us much anymore.

B: Why _____ (8 not/need) you?

A: Our youngest son _____ (9 leave) for college in September. And the other two are already on their own. The oldest _____ (10 get) married next year, and the middle one has her own apartment and a job.

B: I _____ (11 miss) you at work.

A: I _____ (12 miss) you too. But I _____ (13 not/miss) the boss and the long hours.

EXERCISE 18 Do you have questions for the teacher about this semester, next semester, or his or her life in general? Write three questions to ask the teacher about the near or distant future.

EXAMPLES *What time are you going to leave today?*

When are you going to give us a test?

Are you going to retire soon?

1. _____
2. _____
3. _____

2.8 Will vs. Be Going To

In some cases, *will* is the better choice for the future tense. In some cases, *be going to* is the better choice. In some cases, both forms of the future work.

Uses	Will	Be Going To
Prediction	My father always exercises and eats well. I think he **will live** a long time.	I think my father **is going to live** a long time.
Fact	The sun **will set** at 6:43 tonight. The population of older people **will increase**.	The sun **is going to set** at 6:43 tonight. The population of older people **is going to increase**.
Scheduled event	The movie **will begin** at 8 o'clock.	The movie **is going to begin** at 8 o'clock.
Plan		My grandfather **is going to move** to Florida next year. I **am going to return** to my native country in three years.
Promise	I **will** always **take** care of you, Mom.	
Offer to help	A: This box is heavy. B: I'**ll carry** it for you.	

Language Note:
We sometimes use the present continuous tense with a future meaning. We can do this with planned events in the near future. We do this especially with verbs of motion.
   My grandmother **is moving** into a retirement home on Friday.
   I'**m helping** her move on Friday.

EXERCISE 19 Choose *will* or *be going to* to fill in the blanks. In some cases, both are possible.

1. **A:** Where are you going?

   B: I'm going to the park this afternoon. I ___*am going to meet*___
   (example: meet)

   my friend and play tennis with her. I have to return some videos to the video store, but I don't have time.

   A: Give them to me. I _____ that way.
   (1 pass)

   I _____ them for you.
   (2 return)

2. **A:** I have to go to the airport. My sister's plane _____ at four o'clock this afternoon.
   (3 arrive)

   B: I _____ with you. I _____ in the car while you go into the airport. That way, you _____ pay for parking.
   (4 go) *(5 stay)* *(6 not/have to)*

3. **A:** My sister's birthday is next week.

   B: _____ her a birthday present?
   (7 you/give)

   A: Of course, I _____.
   (8)

   B: What _____ her?
   (9 you/give)

   A: She loves the theater. I _____ her tickets to a play.
   (10 buy)

   B: How old _____?
   (11 be)

   A: She _____ 21 years old.
   (12 be)

4. **Teacher:** Next week we _____ our midterm test.
   (13 have)

   Student: _____ hard?
   (14 it/be)

   Teacher: Yes, but I _____ you prepare for it.
   (15 help)

5. **Wife:** I won't have time to pick up the children this afternoon. I have to work late.

   Husband: Don't worry. I _____ them up.
   (16 pick)

   Wife: I won't have time to cook either.

   Husband: Just relax. I _____ dinner tonight.
   (17 prepare)

The Present Continuous Tense; Action and Nonaction Verbs; the Future Tense

6. **Man:** I want to marry you.

   Woman: But we're only 19. We're too young.

   Man: I _____ 20 in April.
   (18 be)

   Woman: But you don't even have a job.

   Man: I _____ a job.
   (19 find)

   Woman: Let's wait a few years.

   Man: I _____ for you forever. I _____ you.
   (20 wait) (21 always/love)

7. **A:** Do you want to watch the football game with me on Saturday?

   B: I can't. My brother _____.
   (22 move)

   I _____ him.
   (23 help)

   A: Do you need any help?

   B: We need boxes. Do you have any?

   A: No, but I _____ for boxes. I _____
   (24 look) (25 go)
   to the supermarket this afternoon. I _____
   (26 get)
   boxes there. I _____ them to your house.
   (27 bring)

   B: Thanks.

8. **A:** I'm so excited! I _____ a puppy.
   (28 get)

   B: That's a big responsibility. You're never home. How
   _____ care of it?
   (29 take)

   A: My cousin lives with me now. She doesn't have a job.
   She _____ me take care of the dog.
   (30 help)

   B: What about your landlord? Is it OK with him?

   A: I _____ him.
   (31 not/tell)

   B: You have to tell him. He _____ if you have a
   (32 know)
   dog. You _____ take the dog out
   (33 have to)
   three times a day. And the dog _____.
   (34 bark)

Lesson 2

2.9 Future Tense + Time/If Clause[8]

Some future sentences have two clauses: a main clause and a time or *if* clause.

Time or *if* Clause (Simple Present Tense)	Main Clause (Future Tense)	Explanation
When the children **grow** up,	we **will move** back to the city.	We use the *future* only in the main clause; we use the *simple present tense* in the time/*if* clause.
If I **am** healthy,	I **will continue** to work for the rest of my life.	
Main Clause (Future Tense)	**Time or *If* Clause (Simple Present Tense)**	We can put the time/*if* clause before the main clause. Or we can put the main clause before the time/*if* clause.
He **will move** to a warm climate	as soon as he **retires**.	
My parents **are going to travel**	if they **take** an early retirement.	

Punctuation Note:
If the time/*if* clause comes before the main clause, we use a comma to separate the two parts of the sentence. If the main clause comes first, we don't use a comma.

EXERCISE 20 Connect the sentences using the word in parentheses ( ).

EXAMPLE I will retire. I will play golf. (when)
  When I retire, I will play golf. OR *I will play golf when I retire.*

1. I will retire. I'm not going to live with my children. (when)
   _____

2. I will be old. I will take care of myself. (when)
   _____

3. My parents will need help. I'll take care of them. (if)
   _____

4. I won't be healthy. I'll live with my children. (if)
   _____

5. I won't have money. I will get help from the government. (if)
   _____

6. My parents will die. I'll move to another city. (after)
   _____

[8] A *clause* is a group of words that has a subject and a verb. Some sentences have more than one clause.

7. I will get a pension. I won't need to depend on my children. (if)

_____

8. I'll retire. I'm going to save my money. (before)

_____

EXERCISE 21 ABOUT YOU Think about a specific time in your future (when you graduate, when you get married, when you have children, when you find a job, when you return to your native country, when you are old, etc.). Write three sentences to tell what will happen at that time. Find a partner who is close to your age. Compare your answers to your partner's answers.

EXAMPLES When I have children, I won't have as much free time as I do now.

When I have children, I'm going to have a lot more responsibilities.

When I have children, my parents will be very happy.

1. _____
2. _____
3. _____

EXERCISE 22 A foreign student (F) is talking to an American (A) about getting old. Fill in the blanks with the correct form of the verb to complete this conversation. In many cases, you can use either *be going to* or *will*.

F: How's your grandfather?

A: He's OK. I __'m going to visit__ him this afternoon.
(example: visit)

F: How's he doing?

A: He's in great health. Next week he _____
(1 go)

to Hawaii to play golf.

F: How old is he?

A: He _____ 78 next month. Did I tell you?
(2 be)

In June, he _____ married to a widow
(3 get)

he met in the retirement home.

F: That seems so strange to me. Why _____ that?
(4 he/do)

A: Why not? They like each other, and they want to be together.

F: What _____ when he's no longer
(5 you/do)

able to take care of himself?

76 Lesson 2

A: We never think about it. He's in such great shape that we think he _____ healthy forever. I think
(6 be)
he _____ us all.
(7 outlive)

F: But he _____ help as he gets older.
(8 probably/need)

A: We _____ that bridge when we come
(9 cross)
to it. Do you have plans for your parents as they get older?

F: They're in their 50s now. But when they _____
(10 be)
older, they _____ with me and my wife.
(11 live)
In our country, it's an honor to take care of our parents.

A: That sounds like a great custom. But I think older people should be independent. I'm glad that Grandpa doesn't depend on us. And when
I _____ old, I _____
(12 be)   (13 take)
care of myself. I don't want to depend on anyone.

F: You _____ your mind when
(14 change)
you _____ old.
(15 be)

A: Maybe. I have to catch my bus now. Grandpa is waiting for me.
I _____ you later.
(16 see)

F: Wait. I have my car. I _____
(17 drive)
you to your grandfather's place.

A: Thanks.

EXERCISE 23 This is a conversation between two co-workers. They are talking about retirement. Fill in the blanks with the correct form and tense of the verb in parentheses ( ).

A: I hear you're going to retire this year.

B: Yes. Isn't it wonderful? I ___*will be*___ 65 in September.
(example: be)

A: What _____ after you
(1 you/do)

_____?
(2 retire)

The Present Continuous Tense; Action and Nonaction Verbs; the Future Tense

B: I'm trying to sell my house now. When I _____ (3 sell)

it, I _____ (4 move) to Florida and buy a condo.

A: What _____ (5 you/do) in Florida?

B: I _____ (6 buy) a sailboat and spend most of my time on the water.

A: But a sailboat is expensive.

B: When I _____ (7 be) 65, I _____ (8 start) to use my savings

Also, I _____ (9 get) a lot of money when I _____ (10 sell) my house.

What _____ (11 you/do) when you _____ (12 retire)?

A: I'm only 45 years old. I have another 20 years until I _____ (13 retire).

B: Now is the time to start thinking about retirement. If you _____ (14 save) your money for the next 20 years,

you _____ (15 have) a comfortable retirement.

But if you _____ (16 not/think) about it until the time

_____ (17 come), you _____ (18 not/have)

enough money to live on.

A: I _____ (19 worry) about it when the time _____ (20 come).

I'm too young to worry about it now.

B: If you _____ (21 wait) until you _____ (22 be)

65 to think about it, you _____ (23 be) a poor, old man.

On Monday morning when we _____ (24 be) at work,

78 Lesson 2

I _____ you to a woman who can explain the
(25 introduce)

company's savings plan to you. After you _____
(26 talk)

to her, I'm sure you _____ your mind about
(27 change)

when to worry about retirement.

SUMMARY OF LESSON 2

Uses of Tenses	
Simple Present Tense	
General truths, facts	Many people **retire** in their sixties. Retirees **get** Social Security.
Regular activities, habits, customs	Jack **plays** golf twice a week. I **always** visit my grandparents on the weekend.
Place of origin	My grandfather **comes** from Mexico. My grandmother **comes** from Peru.
In a time clause or in an *if* clause of a future statement	When she **retires,** she will enjoy life. If Grandma **needs** help, she will live with her daughter.
With nonaction verbs	I **care** about my grandparents. Your grandfather **needs** help now. My grandfather **prefers** to live alone now.
Present Continuous (with action verbs only)	
Now	We**'re comparing** verb tenses now. I**'m looking** at page 79 now.
A long-term action in progress at this general time	Judy **is earning** money by making dolls. Jack is retired now. He **is starting** a new career.
A trend in society	The population of the U.S. **is getting** older. Americans **are living** longer.
A plan in the near future	She **is retiring** next month. She **is going** on a long trip soon.
A descriptive state	Mary **is standing** over there. She **is wearing** blue jeans and a T-shirt.

The Present Continuous Tense; Action and Nonaction Verbs; the Future Tense

Future		
	will	*be going to*
A plan		He **is going to retire** in two years.
A fact	The number of old people **will increase**.	The number of old people **is going to increase**.
A prediction	I think you **will enjoy** retirement.	I think you **are going to enjoy** retirement.
A promise	I **will** take care of you when you're old.	
An offer to help	Grandma, I**'ll carry** your grocery bags for you.	
A scheduled event	Dance instruction **will begin** at 8 p.m. on Saturday.	Dance instruction **is going to begin** at 8 p.m. on Saturday.

EDITING ADVICE

1. Always include *be* in a present continuous tense verb.

   She ^is working now.

2. Don't use the present continuous tense with a nonaction verb.

   I ~~am liking~~ your new car. (like)

3. Don't use *be* with another verb for the future.

   I will ~~be~~ go back to my native country in five years.

4. Include *be* in a future sentence that has no other verb.

   He will ^be angry.

   There will ^be a party soon.

5. Don't combine *will* and *be going to*.

   He will ~~going to~~ leave. OR *He's going to leave.*

6. Use the future tense with an offer to help.

   The phone's ringing. I ^'ll get it.

Lesson 2

7. Don't use the future tense after a time word or *if*.

   When they ~~will~~ go home, they are going to watch TV.

   If I ~~will be~~ *am* late, I'll call you.

8. Use a form of *be* with *going to*.

   He ^*is* going to help me.

9. Use correct word order in questions.

   When ~~you will~~ *will you* go back to your native country?

   Why ~~she isn't~~ *isn't she* going to buy a new car?

LESSON 2 TEST/REVIEW

PART 1 Find the mistakes with the underlined words, and correct them. Not every sentence has a mistake. If the sentence is correct, write *C*.

EXAMPLES You can't move this sofa alone. <u>I'll help</u> you.   **C**

Where <u>will you be</u> live when you are old?

1. He <u>sitting</u> near the door.
2. What <u>will you do</u> after you graduate?
3. <u>I'm going to buy</u> a new car soon.
4. He's listening to the radio. <u>He's hearing</u> the news.
5. <u>She going to leave</u> on Friday.
6. <u>I'll going to watch</u> TV tonight.
7. <u>I going to do</u> my homework when I get home.
8. What <u>you going to do</u> tonight?
9. <u>I'm leaving</u> for New York on Friday.
10. There <u>will a</u> test on Friday.
11. <u>I will be know</u> English well in a few years.
12. If you don't eat dinner, you <u>will hungry</u> later.
13. She <u>won't leave</u> her family.
14. If you need something, let me know. <u>I get</u> it for you.

15. Why <u>won't you</u> tell me about your problem?
16. She's looking at the report. She <u>sees</u> the problem now.
17. Why <u>she isn't</u> going to visit her grandmother?
18. I'll cross that bridge when I <u>come</u> to it.

PART 2 Mary (M) is talking to her friend Sue (S) on the phone. Fill in the blanks with the correct tense and form of the words in parentheses ( ). Use the simple present, present continuous, or future tenses. In some cases, more than one answer is possible.

S: Hi, Mary.

M: Hi, Sue. How are you?

S: Fine. What are you doing?

M: I _____*am packing*_____ now. We _____
    (example: pack)   (1 move)
next Saturday.

S: Oh, really? Why? You _____ such a lovely
                              (2 have)
apartment now.

M: Yes, I know we do. But my father _____
                                            (3 come)
soon, so we _____ a bigger apartment.
                (4 need)

S: When _____?
            (5 come)

M: He _____ as soon as he _____
        (6 come)   (7 get)
his visa. That'll probably be in about four months.

S: But your present apartment _____ an extra bedroom.
                                        (8 have)

M: Yes. But my husband _____ to have an extra room
                                (9 always/like)
for an office. He usually _____ a lot of work home.
                                (10 bring)
He _____ a place where he can work without noise.
    (11 need)

S: _____ his own apartment after he
        (12 your father/get)
_____ a job?
    (13 find)

M: He's retired now. He _____ with us.
                                (14 live)
He _____ to live alone.
    (15 not/like)

S: Do you need help with your packing?

M: Not really. Bill and I _____ home this week to
(16 stay)

finish the packing. And my sister _____ me now too.
(17 help)

S: I _____ over next Saturday to help you move.
(18 come)

M: We _____ professional movers on
(19 use)

Saturday. We don't want to bother our friends.

S: It's no bother. I _____ to help.
(20 want)

M: Thanks. There probably _____ a few things you
(21 be)

can help me with on Saturday. I have to go now. I

_____ Bill. He _____ me. He
(22 hear)   (23 call)

_____ me to help him in the basement.
(24 want)

I _____ you back later.
(25 call)

S: You don't have to call me back. I _____ you on
(26 see)

Saturday. Bye.

PART 3 Fill in the blanks with the negative form of the underlined verb.

EXAMPLE Mary is busy. Sue ___isn't___ busy.

1. Sue is talking to Mary. She _____ to her husband.
2. Mary is going to move to a bigger apartment. She _____
   _____ to a house.
3. Mary's husband needs an extra room. He _____ a big room.
4. Sue will go to Mary's house on Saturday. She _____
   _____ tomorrow.
5. Mary will move the small things. She _____ the furniture.
6. Her new apartment has an extra room. Her old apartment
   _____ an extra room.
7. Her father likes to live with family. He _____ to live alone.

PART 4 Write a *yes / no* question about the words in parentheses ( ). Then write a short answer based on the conversation in Part 2 on pages 82–83.

EXAMPLE Mary is busy. (her husband)
Is her husband busy? Yes, he is.

1. Mary's husband is helping her pack. (her sister)
___

2. Her husband works in an office. (at home)
___

3. Her present apartment has an extra room for an office. (for her father)
___

4. Professional movers will move the furniture. (her friends)
___

5. Mary is staying home this week. (her husband)
___

6. Mary's going to move. (Sue)
___

PART 5 Write a *wh-* question about the words in parentheses ( ). An answer is not necessary.

EXAMPLE Mary's packing now. (why)
Why is Mary packing?

1. They're going to move to a bigger apartment. (why)
___

2. Her husband needs an extra bedroom. (why)
___

3. She doesn't want her friends to help her move. (why)
___

4. Her father is going to come soon. (when)
___

5. Bill is calling Mary now. (why)
___

6. They'll use professional movers. (when)
___

Lesson **2**

EXPANSION ACTIVITIES

Classroom Activities

1. Check (✓) your predictions about the future. Form a small group and discuss your predictions with your group. Give reasons for your beliefs.

   a. ____ People are going to have fewer children than they do today.
   b. ____ People will live longer.
   c. ____ People will have a healthier life.
   d. ____ People are going to be happier.
   e. ____ People will be lonelier.
   f. ____ People will be more educated.
   g. ____ Everyone is going to have a computer.
   h. ____ There will be a cure for cancer and other serious illnesses.
   i. ____ There will be a cure for the common cold.

2. Check (✓) the activities that you plan to do soon. Form a group of between five and seven students. Ask questions about the items another student checked.

   EXAMPLE   ✓ move
   When are you going to move?
   Why are you moving?
   Are your friends going to help you?
   Are you going to rent a truck?
   Where are you going to move to?

   a. ____ send an e-mail
   b. ____ visit a friend
   c. ____ invite guests to my house
   d. ____ buy something new
   e. ____ take a vacation
   f. ____ celebrate a birthday or holiday
   g. ____ go to a concert or sporting event
   h. ____ transfer to another school
   i. ____ move
   j. ____ take the citizenship test
   k. ____ start a new job
   l. ____ have an out-of-town visitor
   m. ____ get married

Write About it

1. Write a short composition telling how you think your life will be when you are ten years older than you are now. *Sample beginning*: I'm 25 years old now. When I'm 35 years old, I think I will . . .

2. Write a short composition describing the life of an old person you know—a family member, a friend, a neighbor, etc.

3. Write a short composition telling what you want your life to be like when you retire.

Outside Activities

1. Give the list from Classroom Activity 1 to an American. Find out his or her predictions. Report to the class something interesting that the American told you.

2. Keep a small notebook and a pen with you at all times for a week. Write down all the behaviors of older people that seem strange to you. Observe food, clothes, shopping, recreation, relationships between parents and children, behaviors on public transportation, etc. Write what people are doing as you are observing.

    EXAMPLE An old woman is standing on the bus. No one is giving her a seat.
    An old man is jogging in the park.

Internet Activities

1. Find a Web site for the elderly. Find out what kinds of products and services are available for senior citizens. Search under *senior citizens* or try the *National Council of Senior Citizens* (NCSC) or *American Association of Retired Persons* (AARP).

2. Look for a life expectancy calculator on the Internet. Calculate how long you will probably live.

3. At a search engine, type in *baby boomers*. Find an article about the baby boomers and bring it to class.

4. Find information about a retirement community in the area where you live. Get information about the cost, types of activities, and types of housing.

Additional Activities at http://elt.heinle.com/gic

LESSON 3

GRAMMAR
Habitual Past with *Used To*
The Simple Past Tense

CONTEXT: Working Towards a Better Life
Equal Rights for All
George Dawson—Life Is So Good

Martin Luther King Jr., 1929–1968

Rosa Parks, 1913–2005

EQUAL RIGHTS FOR ALL

Before You Read

1. In your native country, does the government give equality to everyone?
2. Is there one group of people that has a harder life than other groups? Which group? What kind of problems do these people have?

 Read the following article. Pay special attention to simple past tense verbs and *used to* + base form.

Did You Know?
Martin Luther King Jr., was interested in the ideas of Mahatma Gandhi of India. He studied and used Gandhi's technique of nonviolent protest.

Today all people in the United States have equal rights under the law. But this **was** not always the case, especially for African-Americans[1]. Even though slavery in the U.S. **ended** in 1865, blacks **continued** to suffer discrimination[2] and segregation[3], especially in the South. Many hotels, schools, and restaurants **were** for whites only. Many businesses there **used to have** signs in their windows that **said**: "Blacks Not Allowed." Black children **used to go** to separate, and often inferior, schools. Many professions **were** for whites only. Even in sports, blacks could not join the major leagues; there **used to be** separate leagues for blacks.

In many places in the South, buses **used to reserve** the front seats for white people. One evening in December of 1955, a 42-year-old woman, Rosa Parks, **got** on a bus in Montgomery, Alabama, to go home from work. She **was** tired when she **sat** down. When some white people **got** on the crowded bus, the bus driver **ordered** Ms. Parks to stand up. Ms. Parks **refused** to leave her seat. The bus driver **called** the police, and they **came** and **arrested** Ms. Parks.

Martin Luther King Jr.[4], a black minister living in Montgomery, Alabama, **wanted** to put an end to discrimination. When King **heard** about Ms. Park's arrest, he **told** African-Americans in Montgomery to boycott the bus company. People who **used to** ride the bus to work **decided** to walk instead. As a result of the boycott, the Supreme Court **outlawed**[5] discrimination on public transportation.

[1] *African-Americans*, whose ancestors came from Africa as slaves, are sometimes called "blacks." They used to be called "negroes" or "colored."
[2] *Discrimination* means giving some people unfair treatment, especially because of race, age, religion, etc.
[3] *Segregation* means separation of the races.
[4] When a father and son have the same name, the father uses *senior* (Sr.) after his name; the son puts *junior* (Jr.) after his name.
[5] *To outlaw* means to make an action illegal or against the law.

In 1964, about 100 years after the end of slavery, Congress **passed** a new law that officially **gave** equality to all Americans. This law **made** discrimination in employment and education illegal. King **won** the Nobel Peace Prize[6] for his work in creating a better world.

In 1968, a great tragedy **occurred**. Someone **shot** and **killed** King when he was only 39 years old.

In 1983, Martin Luther King's birthday (January 15) **became** a national holiday.

African-American Firsts

1947   Jackie Robinson was the first African-American to play on a major league baseball team.

1983   Guion Bluford was the first African-American to go into space.

1989   Oprah Winfrey became the first African-American to own her own television and film production company.

1997   Tiger Woods, whose father is African-American and whose mother is Thai, became both the first African-American and the first Asian-American to win the Masters golf tournament.

2001   Halle Berry was the first African-American woman to win an Oscar for best actress.

2001   General Colin Powell became the first African-American secretary of state.

2005   Condoleezza Rice became the first female African-American secretary of state.

Tiger Woods

Halle Berry

---

[6] The *Nobel Peace Prize* is one of six international prizes given once a year for great work in literature, science, economics, and world peace.

3.1 Habitual Past with *Used To*

Examples	Explanation
Black children **used to** have separate schools. Many professions **used to** be for white people only. There **used to** be special baseball teams for black people.	*Used to* + a base form shows a habit or custom over a past period of time. This custom no longer exists.
Some restaurants **didn't use to** serve African-Americans.	For negatives, omit the *d* in *used to*.

Language Note:
Used to is for past habits or customs. It is not for an action that happened once or a few times.
   Many restaurants **used to** serve white people only. (This happened over a period of time.)
   Rosa Parks **used to** ride the bus to work. (This happened over a period of time.)
   In 1955, Rosa Parks **got** on the bus and **refused** to stand. (This happened one time.)
   The bus driver **called** the police. (This happened one time.)

EXERCISE 1 ABOUT YOU Tell which of the following you used to do when you were a child.

EXAMPLE cry a lot
I used to cry a lot.
   OR
I didn't use to cry a lot.

1. enjoy school
2. obey my parents
3. attend religious school
4. play with dolls
5. play soccer
6. fight with other children
7. draw pictures
8. have a pet
9. tell lies
10. read mystery stories
11. live on a farm
12. eat a lot of candy
13. live with my grandparents
14. believe in Santa Claus
15. watch a lot of TV
16. read comic books

EXERCISE 2 ABOUT YOU Name something. Practice *used to*.

EXAMPLE Name something you used to know when you were in elementary school.

I used to know the names of all the presidents (but I don't know them anymore).

1. Name something you used to do when you were a child.
2. Tell what kind of stories you used to enjoy when you were a child.
3. Name something you used to believe when you were a child.
4. Name something you used to like to eat when you were a child.
5. Tell about some things your parents, grandparents, or teachers used to tell you when you were a child.
6. Tell about some things you used to do when you were younger.

EXERCISE 3 ABOUT YOU Write sentences comparing the way you used to live with the way you live now. Share your sentences with a partner or with the entire class.

EXAMPLES *I used to live with my whole family. Now I live alone.*

I used to work in a restaurant. Now I'm a full-time student.

I didn't use to speak English at all. Now I speak English pretty well.

Ideas for sentences:
school   job   hobbies   apartment / house   family life   friends

1. _____
2. _____
3. _____
4. _____
5. _____

Habitual Past with *Used To*; The Simple Past Tense

EXERCISE 4 A young man is comparing how his life used to be five years ago and how his life is now. Complete his statements. Answers may vary.

EXAMPLE I used to _____be lazy_____. Now I'm hardworking.

1. I used to _____. Now I save my money.
2. I used to _____. Now I'm a serious student.
3. I used to _____. Now I live alone.
4. I used to _____. Now I almost never watch TV.
5. I used to _____. Now I come home after work and study.
6. I used to _____. Now I have short hair.
7. I used to _____. Now I have a car and drive everywhere.
8. I used to _____. Now I'm on a diet and I'm losing weight.
9. I used to _____. Now I make my own decisions.
10. I used to _____. Now I use my credit card for most of my purchases.

GEORGE DAWSON—LIFE IS SO GOOD

Before You Read

1. Is it necessary to know how to read in order to have a good life?
2. Is it hard for old people to learn new things?

Read the following article. Pay special attention to the simple past tense.

> George Dawson **lived** in three centuries—the end of the nineteenth, all through the twentieth, and the start of the twenty-first. He **was** born in 1898 in Texas, the grandson of slaves. He **was** the oldest of five children. His family **was** very poor, so George **had** to go to work to help his family. He **started** working full-time for his father when he was four years old. As a result, he **didn't attend** school. He **worked at** many jobs during his lifetime: he **chopped** wood, **swept** floors, **helped** build the railroad, and **cleaned** houses. For most of his adult life, he **ran** farm machinery at a dairy farm[7].

[7] On a *dairy farm*, cows are used to produce milk and milk products.

In his lifetime, great technological changes **occurred:** cars, television, airplanes, spaceships, and computers **came** into being. He **saw** several wars and political changes in the U.S. He **outlived**[8] four wives and two of his seven children.

He **lived** at a time when African-Americans **had** fewer opportunities than they do today. And he **lived** in the South, where there **was** a lot of discrimination against African-Americans; African-Americans **were** segregated from others, and job possibilities **were** limited. By the end of his life, he **saw** others have the opportunities that he didn't have when he **was** young. He **witnessed** the success of many African-Americans.

George Dawson (1898–2001)

Because he **didn't know** how to read or write, he **signed** his name with an X. Then, when he **was** 98 years old, Dawson **started** attending school. He **went** to adult literacy classes in Dallas County. The teacher **asked** him, "Do you know the alphabet?" He **answered,** "No." Over the next few years, his teacher, Carl Henry, **taught** Dawson to read and write. Dawson **said,** "Every morning I get up and I wonder what I might learn that day."

In 1998, an elementary school teacher, Richard Glaubman, **read** an article about Dawson in the newspaper. He **wanted** to meet Dawson. Together Glaubman and Dawson **wrote** a book about Dawson's life, called *Life Is So Good*. In this book, Dawson tells about what makes a person happy. Dawson **had** a close family and never **felt** lonely. He **learned** from his father to see the good things in life. His father **told** him, "We **were** born to die. You **didn't come** here to stay, and life is something to enjoy." He **taught** his children to see the richness in life. Dawson says in the book, "We make our own way. Trouble is out there, but a person can leave it alone and just do the right thing. Then, if trouble still finds you, you've done the best you can. . . . People worry too much. Life is good, just the way it is."

> **Excerpt from Dawson's book:**
> "My first day of school was January 4, 1996. I was ninety-eight years old and I'm still going. . . . I'm up by five-thirty to make my lunch, pack my books, and go over my schoolwork. Books was[9] something missing from my life for so long. . . . I learned to read my ABC's in two days—I was in a hurry. . . . Now I am a man that can read."

---

[8] *To outlive* means to live longer than others.
[9] These are Dawson's exact words. However, this sentence is not grammatically correct. The correct way is: Books *were* . . . .

3.2 Past Tense of *Be*

The past tense of *be* has two forms: *was* and *were*.

Examples	Explanation
Life **was** hard for George Dawson. He **was** poor. His grandparents **were** slaves.	The past of the verb *be* has two forms: *was* and *were*. I, he, she, it → was we, you, they → were
There **was** discrimination in the South. There **were** many changes in the twentieth century.	After *there*, use *was* or *were* depending on the noun that follows. Use *was* with a singular noun. Use *were* with a plural noun.
Dawson's life **wasn't** easy. Education and books **weren't** available to Dawson as a child.	To make a negative statement, put *not* after *was* or *were*. The contraction for *was not* is *wasn't*. The contraction for *were not* is *weren't*.
Dawson **was born** in 1898.	Always use a form of *be* with *born*.
Dawson **was** married four times. He **was** interested in reading at the age of 98.	Use *be* with adjectives that end in *-ed*: *crowded, tired, bored, interested, worried, married, divorced, allowed,* and *permitted*.

Compare statements and questions

Affirmative Statements and Questions

Wh- Word	Was/Were Wasn't/Weren't	Subject	Was/Were Wasn't/Weren't	Complement	Short Answer
		Dawson	was	poor.	
		He	wasn't	in school.	
	Was	he		a slave?	No, he **wasn't**.
Where	was	he		from?	
Why	wasn't	he		in school?	

Negative Statements and Questions

Wh- Word	Wasn't/Weren't	Subject	Wasn't/Weren't	Complement
		Dawson	wasn't	in school.
Why	wasn't	he		in school?
		There	weren't	many opportunities.
Why	weren't	there		many opportunities?

EXERCISE 5 Fill in the blanks with an appropriate word. Answers may vary.

EXAMPLE George Dawson _____was_____ poor.

1. Dawson was _____ in 1898.
2. At that time, there _____ a lot of discrimination.
3. His parents _____ poor.
4. Life for most African-Americans in the South was _____.
5. Job possibilities for African-Americans _____ limited.
6. When he was _____, he learned how to read.
7. Dawson's father used to tell him, "We _____ born to die."
8. He was poor, but he wasn't _____.

EXERCISE 6 Fill in the blanks with the correct word(s).

EXAMPLE Martin Luther King Jr., ___was___ a great American.

1. Martin Luther King Jr., _____ born in Georgia.
2. He (not) _____ born in Alabama.
3. He and his father _____ ministers.
4. He _____ tired of discrimination toward African-Americans.
5. African-Americans (not) _____ allowed to enter some restaurants in the South.
6. There _____ discrimination on public transportation.
7. _____ discrimination in employment? Yes, there _____.
8. Rosa Parks was a citizen of Montgomery, Alabama. _____ an African-American? Yes, she was.
9. She was tired and took a seat on the bus. Why _____ tired?
10. African-Americans weren't allowed to sit down on a crowded bus in Montgomery. Why _____ allowed to sit down?
11. How old _____ when he was killed? He was 39.

3.3 The Simple Past Tense of Regular Verbs

To form the simple past tense of regular verbs, add -ed to the base form.[10]

Examples	Explanation
Dawson **signed** his name with an X. Dawson **learned** a lot from his father. African-Americans **suffered** discrimination. Dawson **lived** to be 103 years old.	Base Form / Past Form sign / signed learn / learned suffer / suffered live / lived If the verb ends in an -e, add only -d.[10] The past forms are the same for all persons.
Dawson **learned** to read and write. A teacher **wanted** to meet Dawson.	The verb after *to* does **not** use the past form.

EXERCISE 7 Fill in the blanks with the past tense of the verb in parentheses ( ).

EXAMPLE Dawson __learned__ to read when he was 98.
(learn)

1. He _____ many, many years.
   (live)

2. He _____ his name with an X.
   (sign)

3. He _____ all his wives.
   (outlive)

4. Many changes _____ during his long life.
   (occur)

5. He _____ school when he was 98.
   (attend)

6. His teacher _____, "Do you know the alphabet?"
   (ask)

7. Dawson _____ from his father to enjoy life.
   (learn)

8. Richard Glaubman _____ to meet Dawson.
   (want)

EXERCISE 8 Fill in the blanks with the simple past tense of the verb in parentheses ( ).

EXAMPLE King __lived__ in the South.
(live)

1. Slavery _____ in 1865, but discrimination
   (end)
   _____.
   (continue)

[10] For a review of the spelling and pronunciation of the -ed past form, see Appendix A.

2. King _____(want)_____ equality for all people.

3. King _____(work)_____ as a minister.

4. In many places, the law _____(separate)_____ whites from blacks.

5. In 1968, a great tragedy _____(occur)_____. Someone _____(kill)_____ King.

6. The bus driver _____(order)_____ Rosa Parks to stand up, but she _____(refuse)_____.

7. The bus driver _____(call)_____ the police.

8. The police _____(arrest)_____ Ms. Parks.

9. King _____(organize)_____ a peaceful protest.

10. In 1964, Congress _____(change)_____ the law.

11. Black children _____(attend)_____ separate schools.

Habitual Past with *Used To;* The Simple Past Tense

3.4 The Simple Past of Irregular Verbs[11]

Many past tense verbs are irregular. They do not have an -ed ending.

Verbs with no change

beat	fit	put	spit
bet	hit	quit	split
cost	hurt	set	spread
cut	let	shut	

Final d changes to t

bend—bent	send—sent
build—built	spend—spent
lend—lent	

Verbs with Vowel Changes

feel—felt	mean—meant[12]	dig—dug	sting—stung
keep—kept	sleep—slept	hang—hung	strike—struck
leave—left	sweep—swept	spin—spun	swing—swung
lose—lost	weep—wept	stick—stuck	win—won
awake—awoke	speak—spoke	begin—began	sing—sang
break—broke	steal—stole	drink—drank	sink—sank
choose—chose	wake—woke	forbid—forbade	spring—sprang
freeze—froze		ring—rang	swim—swam
		shrink—shrank	
bring—brought	fight—fought	blow—blew	grow—grew
buy—bought	teach—taught	draw—drew	know—knew
catch—caught	think—thought	fly—flew	throw—threw
arise—arose	rise—rose	bleed—bled	meet—met
drive—drove	shine—shone	feed—fed	read—read[13]
ride—rode	write—wrote	flee—fled	speed—sped
		lead—led	
sell—sold	tell—told	find—found	wind—wound
mistake—mistook	take—took	lay—laid	say—said[14]
shake—shook		pay—paid	
swear—swore	wear—wore	bite—bit	light—lit
tear—tore		hide—hid	slide—slid
become—became		fall—fell	hold—held
come—came			
eat—ate			
forgive—forgave		run—ran	
give—gave		sit—sat	
lie—lay		see—saw	
forget—forgot	shoot—shot	stand—stood	
get—got		understand—understood	

Miscellaneous Changes

be—was/were	go—went	hear—heard
do—did	have—had	make—made

[11] For an alphabetical list of irregular verbs, see Appendix M.

Language Note:
[12] There is a change in the vowel sound. *Meant* rhymes with *sent*.
[13] The past form of *read* is pronounced like the color *red*.
[14] *Said* rhymes with *bed*.

EXERCISE 9 Fill in the blanks with the past tense of the verb in parentheses ( ).

EXAMPLE Dawson ____had____ a hard life.
(have)

1. His father was poor, so he _____ to work.
(have)

2. He _____ to work for his father when he was four years old.
(begin)

3. He _____ many changes in his lifetime.
(see)

4. He _____ interested in reading when he was 98.
(become)

5. He _____ to the adult literacy program in Dallas County.
(go)

6. His teacher _____ him the alphabet.
(teach)

7. Dawson _____, "I wonder what I might learn today."
(say)   (write)

EXERCISE 10 Fill in the blanks with the past tense of the verb in parentheses ( ).

EXAMPLE King ____fought____ for the rights of all people.
(fight)

1. King _____ born in 1929.
(be)

2. King _____ a minister.
(become)

3. He _____ married in 1953.
(get)

4. He _____ a job in a church in Montgomery, Alabama.
(find)

Habitual Past with *Used To*; The Simple Past Tense   **99**

5. Rosa Parks was tired and _____ (sit) down on the bus.

6. Some white people _____ (get) on the bus.

7. The bus driver _____ (tell) Parks to stand up.

8. Police _____ (come) and arrested Parks.

9. King _____ (hear) about her arrest.

10. In 1963, he _____ (give) a beautiful speech in Washington, D.C.

11. Many people _____ (go) to see King in Washington in 1963.

12. King _____ (win) an important prize for his work.

13. A man _____ (shoot) King in 1968.

EXERCISE 11 Fill in the blanks with the correct past tense form of the verb in parentheses ( ) in this short biography of Oprah Winfrey.

Oprah Winfrey, talk show host, publisher, and actress, is one of the richest women in the U.S. today. But she ___*came*___ (example: come) from a poor family. In fact, she _____ (1 be) born to unmarried teenage parents and _____ (2 have) a very difficult childhood. She _____ (3 live) first with her grandmother, later with her mother, and when she was a teenager, she _____ (4 go) to live with her father. Her father _____ (5 encourage) her to read a lot. She _____ (6 enter) Tennessee State University in 1971 and _____ (7 begin) working as a reporter for a radio station at age 19. In 1976, Winfrey _____ (8 move) to

Oprah Winfrey

100 Lesson 3

Baltimore and _____ (9 get) her own talk show on TV. It

_____ (10 become) very popular.

In 1986, Oprah's show went national. In its first year,

the show _____ (11 bring) in $125 million and Oprah

_____ (12 earn) $30 million. Around this time, Oprah

_____ (13 begin) an acting career. In 2000, she _____ (14 start)

publishing a magazine, *O: The Oprah Magazine*. Oprah

_____ (15 go) from being a poor black farm girl from

Mississippi to a national celebrity.

3.5 | Negative Statements

Compare affirmative (A) and negative (N) statements with past tense verbs.

Examples	Explanation

A. Dawson **learned** to read when he was old.
N. He **didn't learn** to read when he was a child.
 	
A. Dawson **lived** in the South.
N. He **didn't live** alone.
 	
A. He **knew** many things.
N. He **didn't know** the alphabet.
 	
A. He **went** to school when he was old.
N. He **didn't go** to school when he was young.
	For the negative past tense, we use *didn't* + base form for ALL verbs (except *be*), regular and irregular.
	Compare:
	    learned—didn't learn
	    lived—didn't live
	    knew—didn't know
	    went—didn't go

Language Note:
Remember: Some past tense verbs are the same as the base form.
  A. He **put** an X on the line.
  N. He **didn't put** his name on the line.	

EXERCISE 12 Fill in the blanks with the negative form of the underlined word.

EXAMPLE Dawson came from a poor family. He _didn't come_ from a middle-class family.

1. He felt happy because he had a good family. He _____ lonely.

2. Children from families with money attended school. Dawson _____ school.

3. He went to school when he was old. He _____ to school when he was young.

4. He learned to read when he was old. He _____ to read when he was a child.

5. He knew many things. He _____ how to write or read.

6. Carl Henry taught Dawson. Richard Glaubman _____ Dawson.

EXERCISE 13 Write the negative form of the underlined words.

EXAMPLE Slavery ended in 1865. Discrimination _didn't end_.

1. King lived in the South. He _____ in the North.

2. King wanted equality for everyone. He _____ separate schools for blacks and whites.

3. He thought about the future of his children. He _____ about his own safety.

4. He believed in peace. He _____ in violence.

5. He became a minister. He _____ a politician.

6. He was in jail for his protests. He _____ in jail for a crime.

7. African-Americans had to stand on a crowded bus. White people _____ to stand.

8. African-Americans rode the buses in Montgomery every day. They _____ the buses after the arrest of Rosa Parks.

9. King went to Memphis in 1968. His wife _____ there.

10. He died violently. He _____ peacefully.

3.6 Questions with the Simple Past Tense

Compare affirmative statements and questions

Wh- Word	Did	Subject	Verb	Complement	Short Answer
		Dawson	**learned**	to read.	
	Did	he	**learn**	to read when he was young?	No, he didn't.
When	**did**	he	**learn**	to read?	When he was 98.
		Dawson	**wrote**	a book.	
	Did	he	**write**	it alone?	No, he didn't.
Why	**did**	he	**write**	a book?	Because he wanted to tell his life story.

Language Note:
The base form is used in questions after *did*.

Compare negative statements and questions

Wh- Word	Didn't	Subject	Verb	Complement
		Dawson	**didn't learn** to read	when he was young.
Why	**didn't**	he	**learn** to read	when he was young?
		Dawson	**didn't go**	to school.
Why	**didn't**	he	**go**	to school?

EXERCISE 14 A student is interviewing her teacher about Martin Luther King Jr. Fill in the blanks with the correct form of the verb.

S: Do you remember Martin Luther King Jr.?

T: Of course I do. I ____*saw*____ him on TV many times when I
             (example: see)

   _____ young.
   (1 be)

S: _____ him on TV when he was in Washington, D.C.?
   (2 see)

T: Yes, I _____. I remember his famous speech in
          (3)
   Washington in 1963.

S: What _____ about?
          (4 speak)

T: He _____ about equality for everyone.
       (5 speak)

S: _____ (6 a lot of people/go) to Washington?

T: Oh, yes. 250,000 people _____ (7 go) to Washington.

S: Do you remember when he died?

T: I was in high school when he _____ (8 die). The principal _____ (9 come) to our class and _____ (10 tell) us the news.

S: What _____ (11 do) when you heard the news?

T: At first we _____ (12 not/believe) it. Then we all started to _____ (13 cry). We _____ (14 go) home from school and _____ (15 watch) the news on TV.

S: Where _____ (16 be) he when he died?

T: He _____ (17 be) on the balcony of a hotel in Memphis when a man _____ (18 come) and _____ (19 shoot) him. It was terrible. But we should remember King for his life, not his death. We celebrate Martin Luther King Jr.'s birthday.

S: Really? I _____ (20 not/know) that. When is it?

T: He _____ (21 be) born on January 15. We don't have school on that date.

S: _____ (22 this date/become) a holiday right after he died?

T: No. It _____ (23 become) a holiday in 1983.

S: How do you remember so much about King?

T: I _____ (24 write) a paper on him when I was in college.

EXERCISE 15 ABOUT YOU Check (✓) the things you did this past week. Exchange books with another student. Ask the other student about the items he or she checked.

EXAMPLE ✓ I made a long-distance phone call.

A: I made a long-distance phone call.
B: Who(m) did you call?
A: I called my father in Mexico.
B: How long did you talk?
A: We talked for about 15 minutes.

1. ____ I made a long-distance phone call.
2. ____ I shopped for groceries.
3. ____ I met someone new.
4. ____ I got together with a friend.
5. ____ I wrote a letter.
6. ____ I bought some new clothes.
7. ____ I went to the bank.
8. ____ I read something interesting (a book, an article).
9. ____ I went to the post office.
10. ____ I did exercises.
11. ____ I received a letter.
12. ____ I went to an interesting place.

EXERCISE 16 Decide which is better: the simple past tense or *used to* + base form. Fill in the blanks.

EXAMPLES Martin Luther King Jr. ____went____ to Alabama in 1955.
(go)

Oprah Winfrey ____used to be____ poor.
(be)

1. There _____ a lot more discrimination in the past
(be)
than there is today.

2. President Lincoln _____ slavery in 1865.
(end)

3. African-Americans _____ a hard time getting into
(have)
certain professions.

4. Black children _____ to separate schools in the
(go)
South.

5. In 1964, Congress _____ a law that gave equality to all.
(pass)

6. Colin Powell _____ secretary of state in 2001.
(become)

Habitual Past with *Used To*; The Simple Past Tense 105

SUMMARY OF LESSON 3

1. Simple Past Tense

   Be

   Dawson **was** happy.
   He **wasn't** rich.
   Was he from a large family? Yes, he **was**.
   Where **was** he born?
   Why **wasn't** he in school?

   Regular Verb

   Dawson **lived** for 103 years.
   He **didn't live** in the time of slavery.
   Did he **live** in the North? No, he **didn't**.
   Where **did** he **live**?
   Why **didn't** he **live** in the North?

   Irregular Verb

   Dawson **felt** happy.
   He **didn't feel** lonely.
   Did he **feel** good when he learned to read? Yes, he **did**.
   How **did** he **feel** about his life?
   Why **didn't** he **feel** lonely?

2. Habitual Past with *Used To*

   Oprah **used to** be poor. Now she's rich.
   Black children and white children **used to** go to separate schools. Now schools are for all children.

EDITING ADVICE

1. Use *was / were* with *born*.

   He ^*was*^ born in Germany.

2. Don't use *was / were* with *die*.

   He ~~was~~ died two years ago.

3. Don't use a past form after *to*.

   I decided to ~~left~~ *leave* early.

   I wanted to go home and ~~watched~~ TV.

106 Lesson 3

4. Don't use *was* or *were* to form a simple past tense.

   He ~~was go~~ *went* home yesterday.

5. Use *there* when a new subject is introduced.

   There w~~W~~as a big earthquake in 1906.

6. Use a form of *be* before an adjective. Remember, some *-ed* words are adjectives.

   They *were* excited about their trip to America.

7. Don't use *did* with an adjective. Use *was / were*.

   Why ~~did~~ *were* you afraid?

8. Use the correct word order in a question.

   Why ~~you didn't~~ *didn't you* return?

9. Use *did* + the base form in a question.

   What kind of car *did* you ~~bought~~ *buy*?

10. Use the base form after *didn't*.

    He didn't worke~~d~~ yesterday.

11. Don't forget the *d* in *used to*.

    She use*d* to live in Miami.

12. Don't add the verb *be* before *used to* for habitual past.

    ~~I'm~~ I used to play soccer in my country.

Habitual Past with *Used To*; The Simple Past Tense

LESSON 3 TEST/REVIEW

PART 1 Write the past form of the following verbs.

EXAMPLE draw ____*drew*____

1. eat _____
2. put _____
3. give _____
4. write _____
5. send _____
6. listen _____
7. read _____
8. take _____
9. bring _____
10. talk _____
11. know _____
12. find _____
13. stand _____
14. leave _____
15. sit _____
16. go _____
17. make _____
18. hear _____
19. feel _____
20. fall _____
21. get _____

PART 2 Find the mistakes with the underlined words, and correct them. Not every sentence has a mistake. If the sentence is correct, write *C*.

EXAMPLES She <u>losed</u> her umbrella.   *lost*

Did she <u>lose</u> her glove?   *C*

1. My mother <u>borned</u> in Italy.
2. Why <u>you didn't eat</u> breakfast?
3. <u>Did you studied</u> English in your country?
4. When <u>arrived your uncle</u>?
5. Last night <u>were</u> a lot of people at the airport.
6. Why <u>was you</u> late?
7. <u>Did you afraid</u> of the robber?
8. I <u>enjoyed</u> the concert.
9. Last night I <u>read</u> an interesting article.
10. My grandmother <u>was died</u> ten years ago.
11. They <u>decided to drove</u> to New York.
12. I <u>excited</u> about my trip to London last year.
13. What <u>did she do</u> about her problem?
14. Why <u>he wasn't</u> happy?
15. Where <u>you bought</u> your coat?
16. She <u>use to</u> live in Miami.

PART 3 Write the negative form of the underlined word.

EXAMPLE Rosa Parks lived in Alabama. She ___didn't live___ in Washington.

1. She was tired when she got out of work. She _____ sick.

2. She went to work by bus. She _____ to work by car.

3. The bus driver told African-Americans to stand. He _____ white Americans to stand.

4. Some African-Americans stood up. Rosa Parks _____ up.

5. The police came to the bus. They _____ to her house.

6. They took her to jail. They _____ her to her house.

7. Martin Luther King, Jr., organized a protest. Rosa Parks _____ a protest.

8. Slavery ended in 1865. Discrimination _____ in 1865.

9. King believed in peaceful protest. He _____ in violence.

10. King spoke about brotherhood. He _____ about violence.

11. Many people had the opportunity for education. George Dawson _____ the opportunity for education.

12. George Dawson wrote a book. He _____ it alone.

Habitual Past with *Used To*; The Simple Past Tense

PART 4 Write a question beginning with the word given. An answer is not necessary.

EXAMPLE Martin Luther King Jr., lived in the South.
Where _____*did he live?*_____

1. King became a minister.
Why _____

2. King was born in Georgia.
When _____

3. King didn't like segregation.
Why _____

4. Black children went to separate schools.
Why _____

5. Some restaurants didn't permit black people to eat there.
Why _____

6. King was in jail many times because of his protests.
How many times _____

7. King won the Nobel Peace Prize.
When _____

8. Rosa Parks worked in Montgomery.
Where _____

9. She was tired.
Why _____

10. She went home by bus.
How many times _____

11. She lived in the South.
Where _____

12. She didn't want to obey the law.
Why _____

13. The police took her to jail.
Why _____

14. George Dawson believed in the goodness of life.
Why _____

15. Dawson taught his children to see the richness in life.

    How _____

16. Dawson didn't feel lonely.

    Why _____

PART 5 Write two sentences with *used to* comparing your life ten years ago with your life today.

1. _____

2. _____

EXPANSION ACTIVITIES

Classroom Activities

1. Check (✓) the sentences that are true for you. Find a partner and exchange books. Give each other more information about the things you checked. Ask each other questions about these activities.

    (a) ____ I bought a CD in the past week.

    (b) ____ I worked last Saturday.

    (c) ____ I rode a bike this past week.

    (d) ____ I went to a party last weekend.

    (e) ____ I got a driver's license in the past year.

    (f) ____ I took a trip in the past year.

    (g) ____ I got married in the last two years.

    (h) ____ I found a job this month.

    (i) ____ I spent more than $50 today.

    (j) ____ I received some money this week.

    (k) ____ I ate pizza in the past month.

    (l) ____ I bought a car in the past year.

    (m) ____ I came to the U.S. alone.

2. Who did it?

    Teacher: Pass out an index card to each student.

    Students: Write something you did last weekend. It can be something unusual or something ordinary. (Examples: I went fishing. I baked a pie. I did my laundry.)

    Teacher: Collect the cards. Pull out one card at a time and read the sentence to the class. The students have to guess who wrote the card.

3. Who used to do it?

   Teacher: Pass out an index card to each student.

   Students: Think of some things you used to be, wear, do, etc. when you were younger. Think of things that other students would not guess about you. Write two or three of these things on the card.

   Teacher: Collect the cards. Pull out one card at a time and read the sentences to the class. The students have to guess who wrote the card.

   EXAMPLES I used to hate studying a foreign language.
   I used to have very long hair.
   I used to be a terrible student.

4. Bring in a picture of yourself when you were younger. Describe how you were at that time and compare yourself to how you are now.

   EXAMPLE I used to play soccer all day with my friends. Now I don't have time for it.

5. Fill in the blank. Discuss your answers in a small group or with the entire class.

   Before I came to the U.S., I used to believe that _____, but now I know it's not true.

6. With a partner, write a few questions to ask George Dawson.

   EXAMPLES Why didn't you go to school?
   What kind of jobs did you have?
   What was the first book you read?

Talk About it

In a small group or with the entire class, discuss the following:

1. Changes in daily life: Compare how life used to be when you were younger with how it is now.

2. Fashions: Talk about different styles or fashions in the past.

   EXAMPLE In the 1960s, men used to wear their hair long.

Write About it

Choose one of the following topics to write a short composition.

1. Write a paragraph or paragraphs telling about your childhood.

2. Write a paragraph or paragraphs telling about changes in your native country. Compare how life used to be with how it is now.

3. If you are married, write a paragraph or paragraphs comparing your life as a married person with your life as a single person.

Outside Activity

Interview an American-born person. Ask this person to tell you about changes he or she sees in American society. Ask this person to compare how he or she used to live with how he or she lives now. Report some interesting information to the class.

Internet Activities

1. Find information about one of the people below. Tell the class why this person was (or is) famous.

Jesse Jackson	James Earl Ray
Malcolm X	Jesse Owens
John Wilkes Booth	Nat Turner
Mahatma Gandhi	

2. At a search engine, type in *I Have a Dream* to find Martin Luther King Jr.'s most famous speech. Summarize his dream.

3. Find a description of George Dawson's book *Life Is So Good*. (Try using amazon.com or barnesandnoble.com.) Print it and bring it to class.

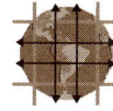

Additional Activities at http://elt.heinle.com/gic

LESSON 4

GRAMMAR

Possessive Forms
Object Pronouns
Reflexive Pronouns
Questions

CONTEXT: Weddings

A Traditional American Wedding
New Wedding Trends
Economizing on a Wedding
Questions and Answers About an American Wedding

115

A TRADITIONAL AMERICAN WEDDING

Before You Read

1. What kind of clothes do a bride and groom wear in your native culture?
2. At what age do people usually get married in your native culture?

 Read the following article. Pay special attention to object pronouns and possessive forms.

Did You Know?

- Most American weddings (85%) take place in a church or synagogue.
- The average number of guests is 190.
- Hawaii is the favorite honeymoon destination.
- August is the most popular month for weddings.
- Money is the most desired wedding gift.
- About 50 percent of marriages end in divorce.

Many young couples consider **their** wedding to be one of the most important days of **their** life. They save for **it** and often spend a year planning for **it**: finding a place, selecting a menu and cake, buying a wedding dress, ordering invitations and sending **them** to friends and relatives, selecting musicians, and much more. The bride chooses **her** maid of honor and bridesmaids, and the groom chooses **his** best man[1] and groomsmen. The bride and groom want to make this day special for themselves and for their guests.

When the day arrives, the groom doesn't usually see the bride before the wedding. It is considered bad luck for **him** to see **her** ahead of time. The guests wait with excitement to see **her** too. When the wedding begins, the groom and groomsmen enter first. Then the bridesmaids enter. When the bride finally enters in **her** white dress, everyone turns around to look at **her**. Sometimes guests stand up when the bride enters. Often the **bride's** father or both of **her** parents walk **her** down the aisle to the groom's side.

During the ceremony, the bride and groom take vows[2]. They promise to love and respect each other for the rest of their lives. The groom's best man holds the rings for **them** until they are ready to place **them** on each **other's** fingers. At the end of the ceremony, the groom lifts the **bride's** veil and kisses **her.**

[1] The *best man* is the man who stands beside the groom and helps him.
[2] A *vow* is a promise.

116   Lesson 4

There is a party after the ceremony. People make toasts[3], eat dinner, and dance. The bride and groom usually dance the first dance alone. Then guests join **them.**

Before the bride and groom leave the party, the bride throws **her** bouquet over **her** head, and the single women try to catch **it**. It is believed that the woman who catches **it** will be the next one to get married.

The newlyweds[4] usually take a trip, called a honeymoon, immediately after the wedding.

4.1 Possessive Forms of Nouns

We use possessive forms to show ownership or relationship.

Noun	Ending	Examples
Singular noun: 　bride 　groom	Add apostrophe + s	The **bride's** dress is white. The **groom's** tuxedo is black.
Plural noun ending in **-s**: 　parents 　guests	Add apostrophe only	She got married in her **parents'** house. The **guests'** coats are in the coat room.
Irregular plural noun: 　men 　women	Add apostrophe + s	The **men's** suits are black. The **women's** dresses are beautiful.
Names that end in **-s**: 　Charles	Add apostrophe only OR Add apostrophe + s	Do you know **Charles'** wife? OR Do you know **Charles's** wife?
Inanimate objects: 　the church 　the dress	Use "the _____ of _____." Do not use apostrophe + s.	St. Peter's is **the name of the church.** **The front of the dress** has pearls.

[3] A *toast* is a wish for good luck, usually while holding a glass.
[4] For a short time after they are married, the bride and groom are called *newlyweds*.

EXERCISE 1 Fill in the blanks to make the possessive form of the noun.

EXAMPLE The bride '*s* grandfather looks very handsome.

1. The groom _____ mother is very nice.
2. The bride _____ flowers are beautiful.
3. The bridesmaids _____ dresses are blue.
4. They invited many guests to the wedding. They didn't invite the guests _____ children.
5. The women _____ dresses are very elegant.
6. Charles _____ sister is a bridesmaid.
7. The newlyweds _____ picture is in the newspaper.
8. Do you know the children _____ names?

EXERCISE 2 Fill in the blanks with the two nouns in parentheses ( ). Put them in the correct order. Use the possessive form of one of the nouns, except with nonliving things.

EXAMPLES The ___*bride's name*___ is Lisa.
(name/the bride)

I don't like the ___*color of your outfit*___ .
(your outfit/color)

1. The _____ came to the wedding from London.
(bride/grandmother)
2. The _____ has a red carpet.
(church/floor)
3. The _____ are very beautiful.
(windows/church)
4. The _____ is crying.
(bride/mother)
5. The _____ is Saint Paul's.
(church/name)
6. The _____ are black.
(men/tuxedos)
7. The _____ is white.
(limousine/color)
8. The _____ are pretty.
(dresses/girls)
9. Who chose the _____ ?
(flowers/color)
10. Some people get married in their _____ .
(house/parents)

118   Lesson 4

4.2 | Possessive Adjectives

Possessive adjectives show ownership or relationship.

Examples	Explanation
My brother is getting married. **Your** gift is wonderful. The groom chooses **his** best man. The bride chooses **her** bridesmaids. The restaurant has **its** own reception hall. **Our** cousins came from out of town. The wedding is the most important day of **their** life.	**Subject Pronouns** / **Possessive Adjectives** I / my you / your he / his she / her it / its we / our they / their

My sister loves **her** husband.
My uncle lives with **his** daughter.
	Be careful not to confuse *his* and *her*.
	  Wrong: My sister loves *his* husband.
	  Wrong: My uncle lives with *her* daughter.

The **bride's mother's** dress is blue.	We can use two possessive nouns together.
My brother's wife did not attend the wedding.	We can use a possessive adjective (*my*) before a possessive noun (*brother's*).

EXERCISE 3 Fill in the blanks with a possessive adjective.

EXAMPLE I love _____my_____ parents.

1. I have one sister. _____ sister got married five years ago.
2. She loves _____ husband very much.
3. He's an accountant. He has _____ own business.
4. They have one child. _____ son's name is Jason.
5. They bought a house last year. _____ house isn't far from my house.
6. My sister and I visit _____ parents once a month. They live two hours away from us.
7. My sister said, "My car isn't working this week. Let's visit them in _____ car."

EXERCISE 4 Fill in the blanks with a possessive adjective.

A: What are you going to wear to _____your_____ sister's
(example)
wedding?

B: I'm going to wear _____(1)_____ new blue dress.

A: Did your sister buy a new dress for her wedding?

B: No. She's going to borrow _____(2)_____ best friend's dress.

A: Will the wedding be at your home?

B: Oh, no. We live in an apartment. _____(3)_____ apartment is too small. We're going to invite over 200 guests. The wedding is going to be at a church. Afterwards, we're going to have a dinner in a restaurant. The restaurant has _____(4)_____ own reception hall.

A: Are the newlyweds going on a honeymoon after the wedding?

B: Yes. They have friends who have a cottage. They're going to stay at _____(5)_____ friends' cottage in the country for a week.

A: Is the groom's mother a nice woman?

B: I don't know _____(6)_____ mother. I'll meet her at the wedding for the first time.

4.3 Possessive Pronouns

We can use possessive pronouns (*mine, yours, his, hers, ours, theirs*) to show ownership or relationship.

Possessive Adjective	Possessive Pronoun	Explanation
Her dress is white. **Their wedding** was big. We had **our wedding** in a church.	**Mine** is blue. **Ours** was small. They had **theirs** in a garden.	When we use a possessive pronoun, we omit the noun. *mine* = my dress *ours* = our wedding *theirs* = their wedding
The groom's parents look happy.	**The bride's** do too.	After the possessive form of a noun, we can omit the noun. *The bride's* = the bride's parents

Compare the three forms below.		
Subject Pronoun	**Possessive Adjective**	**Possessive Pronoun**
I	my	mine
you	your	yours
he	his	his
she	her	hers
it	its	—
we	our	ours
they	their	theirs

EXERCISE 5   Fill in the blanks with an appropriate possessive pronoun.

A: I heard your brother got married last month. How was the wedding? Was it anything like your wedding? I remember _____yours_____ (example) very well.

B: It was very different from _____ . _____ was a
(1)   (2)
very formal wedding in a church last month. _____ was
(3)
very informal, in a garden.

A: I prefer informal weddings. I don't like to get dressed up in a suit and tie. At _____ , I just wore comfortable clothes.
(4)

B: Our honeymoon was a two-day trip. _____ was a two-week
(5)
stay in a luxury hotel in Hawaii. Their honeymoon was expensive.
_____ was very economical. We drove to Chicago and
(6)
stayed in a motel there.

A: I remember your wife made her own dress. You saved a lot of money.

B: My sister-in-law, Gina, spent a lot of money on her dress.
_____ cost over $1,000. My wife's was only about $100.
(7)

A: The cost of a wedding isn't the most important thing. The most important thing is the happiness that follows. My uncle's wedding cost over $30,000. _____ was the most beautiful
(8)
wedding you can imagine. But his marriage lasted only eight months.

Possessive Forms; Object Pronouns; Reflexive Pronouns; Questions   **121**

EXERCISE 6 Fill in the blanks with *I, I'm, me, my,* or *mine.*

1. _____ a student.
2. _____ live in an apartment near school.
3. _____ apartment is on the first floor.
4. _____ parents often visit _____.
5. They don't have a computer. They use _____.

EXERCISE 7 Fill in the blanks with *we, we're, us, our,* or *ours.*

1. _____ classroom is large.
2. _____ study English here.
3. _____ foreign students.
4. The teacher helps _____ learn English.
5. The teacher brings her book, and we bring _____.

EXERCISE 8 Fill in the blanks with *you, you're, your,* or *yours.* Pretend you are talking directly to the teacher.

1. _____ the teacher.
2. _____ come from the U.S.
3. My first language is Polish. _____ is English.
4. _____ pronunciation is very good.
5. We see _____ every day.

EXERCISE 9 Fill in the blanks with *he, he's, his,* or *him.*

1. I have a brother. _____ name is Paul.
2. _____ married.
3. _____ has four children.
4. My apartment is small. _____ is big.
5. I see _____ on the weekends.

EXERCISE 10 Fill in the blanks with *she, she's, her,* or *hers.*

1. I have a sister. _____ name is Marilyn.
2. I visit _____ twice a week.
3. _____ lives in a suburb.
4. _____ a teacher. _____ husband is a doctor.
5. My children go to private school. _____ go to public school.

EXERCISE 11 Fill in the blanks with *it*, *it's*, or *its*.

1. The school has a big library. _____ comfortable and clean.
2. _____ has many books and magazines.
3. _____ hours are from 8 a.m. to 8 p.m.
4. I use _____ every day.
5. _____ on the first floor.

EXERCISE 12 Fill in the blanks with *they*, *they're*, *them*, *their*, or *theirs*.

1. My parents rent _____ apartment.
2. My apartment is small, but _____ is big.
3. _____ very old now.
4. _____ live in a suburb.
5. I visit _____ on the weekends.

4.4 | Questions with *Whose*

Whose + a noun asks a question about ownership.

Whose + Noun	Auxiliary Verb	Subject	Verb	Answer
Whose dress	did	the bride	borrow?	She borrowed her sister's dress.
Whose last name	will	the bride	use?	She'll use her husband's last name.
Whose flowers	are	those?		They're the bride's flowers.

Language Note:
You can drop the noun after *whose* if the meaning is clear.
   Whose flowers are these? **Whose** are those?

EXERCISE 13 Write a question with *whose*. The answer is given.

EXAMPLE   *Whose flowers are these* ? They're the bride's flowers.

1. _____? That's my father's car.
2. _____? Those are the newlyweds' gifts.
3. _____? She's wearing her sister's necklace.
4. _____? I'm wearing my friend's suit.
5. _____? I follow my parents' advice.
6. _____? The bride borrowed her sister's dress.

4.5 Object Pronouns

We can use an object pronoun (*me, you, him, her, it, us,* or *them*) after the verb.

Object Noun	Object Pronoun	Explanation
Daniel loves **Sofia**. Sofia loves **Daniel**. You know **my parents**.	He loves **her** very much. She loves **him** very much. You met **them**.	We can use an object pronoun to substitute for an object noun.
Do you know **the guests**? The bride and groom sent **invitations**.	Yes, we know **them**. They sent **them** last month.	We use *them* for plural people and things.
I see **the bride**. The bride is with her **father**.	Everyone is looking *at* **her**. She will dance *with* **him**.	An object pronoun can follow a preposition (*at, with, of, about, to, from, in,* etc.).

Compare Subject and Object Pronouns

Subject	Object	Examples		
		Subject	**Verb**	**Object**
I	me	You	love	me.
you	you	I	love	you.
he	him	She	loves	him.
she	her	He	loves	her.
it	it	We	love	it.
we	us	They	love	us.
they	them	We	love	them.

EXERCISE 14 Fill in the blanks with an object pronoun in place of the underlined word.

EXAMPLE The groom doesn't walk down the aisle with <u>the bride</u>. Her father walks with ____her____.

1. <u>The bride</u> doesn't enter with <u>the groom</u>. He waits for _____, and she goes to _____.

2. The groom takes <u>the ring</u>. He puts _____ on the bride's hand.

3. <u>The bride</u> wears <u>a veil</u>. The groom lifts _____ to kiss _____.

4. The bride doesn't throw <u>the bouquet</u> to all the women. She throws _____ to the single women only.

5. People make toasts to <u>the bride and groom</u>. They wish _____ health and happiness.

6. <u>The groom</u> promises to love the bride, and the bride promises to love _____.

EXERCISE 15 Fill in the blanks with the correct subject pronoun, object pronoun, or possessive adjective. Answers may vary.

A: How was your cousin Lisa's wedding last Saturday?

B: _____It_____ was great.
       (example)

A: How many guests were there?

B: Maybe about 200. I couldn't count _____(1)_____.

A: Wow! That's a lot. It sounds like an expensive wedding. How did they pay for _____(2)_____?

B: Lisa and Ron worked when _____(3)_____ graduated from college and saved money for _____(4)_____ wedding. _____(5)_____ parents helped _____(6)_____ a little, but they couldn't depend on _____(7)_____ too much. _____(8)_____ parents aren't wealthy.

A: Did Lisa wear a traditional white dress?

B: Yes. In fact, _____(9)_____ wore _____(10)_____ mother's wedding dress. She looked beautiful in _____(11)_____.

A: Where did _____(12)_____ go on their honeymoon?

B: They went to Hawaii. I was surprised—they sent _____(13)_____ a postcard. They had a great time.

A: I hope _____(14)_____ will be happy. The wedding and honeymoon are important, but the marriage that follows is what really counts.

B: I agree with _____(15)_____. But I'm sure they'll be happy. _____(16)_____ loves _____(17)_____ and _____(18)_____ loves _____(19)_____ very much.

A: Did you take pictures?

B: Yes. Do you want to see _____(20)_____? I took _____(21)_____ with my new digital camera.

A: I don't have time now. Can you show _____(22)_____ the pictures tomorrow?

B: Yes. I'll bring _____(23)_____ tomorrow to show _____(24)_____.

Possessive Forms; Object Pronouns; Reflexive Pronouns; Questions   **125**

NEW WEDDING TRENDS[5]

Before You Read

1. American wedding customs are changing. Are wedding customs changing in your native culture?

2. In your native culture, what kind of vows do the bride and groom make to each other?

 Read the following article. Pay special attention to direct and indirect objects after verbs.

Wedding traditions are changing. More and more young couples are choosing to create a unique wedding experience for themselves and for their guests. In traditional weddings, a clergy **reads the bride and groom their vows.** "Do you, Mary Jones, take Roger Smith to be your husband, for better or for worse, for richer, for poorer, in sickness and in health, to love and to cherish, until death parts you?" The bride and groom simply **say, "I do"** in response to this question. But more and more couples today **are writing their own vows** and **saying them** in their own words. They **face the guests** while they **say** or **read their vows to each other.**

Churches and synagogues are still the most popular places for a wedding. But some couples are choosing to have a destination wedding. They get married on the beach, on a mountain top, or other unusual place. These weddings **have fewer guests** because of the expense of traveling. Often the bride and groom pay for the hotel rooms of their guests. They **tell their guests the date** at least three to four months in advance. Often they **send them "save-the-date" cards** so that their guests can make plans to attend the wedding.

Another new trend in weddings is to create a wedding based on the couple's ethnic background. For example, in an African-American wedding,

---
[5]A *trend* is a current style.

some couples want to **show respect to their ancestors**[6] by jumping over a broom, a tradition coming from the time of slavery. The jumping of the broom **symbolizes a new beginning** by sweeping away of the old and welcoming the new. Some African-Americans **use colorful clothing** inspired by African costumes, rather than a white dress for the bride and a suit or tuxedo for the groom.

One thing stays the same. The newlyweds **send the guests thank-you cards** by mail to **thank them** for attending the wedding and for the gifts they gave.

4.6 | Direct and Indirect Objects

Some verbs are followed by both a direct and an indirect object. The order of the objects depends on the verb.[7]

Examples				Explanation
Pattern A:				With the following verbs, we follow Pattern A or Pattern B.
Subj.	**Verb**	**Indirect Obj.**	**Direct Obj.**	bring read show
We	gave	the couple	a wedding gift.	give sell tell
They	sent	us	a thank-you card.	offer send write
She	read	the groom	her vows.	pay
They	showed	me	their pictures.	
Pattern B:				
Subj.	**Verb**	**Direct Obj.**	***To* Indirect Obj.**	
We	gave	a wedding gift	to the couple.	
She	read	her vows	to the groom.	
He gave her a ring. He gave **it to her** on her birthday. Do you have the pictures? Can you show **them to me**?				When the direct object is a pronoun, we follow Pattern B.
		Direct Obj.	***To* Indirect Obj.**	With the following verbs, we follow Pattern B.
Please explain		wedding customs	to me.	announce mention say
Please describe		the wedding	to us.	describe prove suggest
				explain report

[6] *Ancestors* are your grandparents, great-grandparents, great-great grandparents, etc.
[7] For a more detailed list of verbs and the order of direct and indirect objects, see Appendix I.

EXERCISE 16 Fill in the blanks with the words in parentheses ( ). Put them in the correct order. Add *to* if necessary. In some cases, more than one answer is possible.

A: How was your cousin's wedding? Can you describe __it to me__? (example: it/me)

B: It was beautiful. The bride read _____, and (1 a lovely poem/the groom)

then the groom read _____ too. (2 a poem/her)

A: Did they get married in a church?

B: No. They got married in a beautiful garden. Why didn't you go? I thought they sent _____? (3 an invitation/you)

A: They did. But I couldn't go. I wrote _____ and (4 a letter/them)

I explained _____. I had to take an important (5 them/my problem)

exam for college that day. But I sent _____. (6 a lovely present/them)

B: I'm sure they'll appreciate it. It's too bad you couldn't go.

A: I'm sure I mentioned _____ a few weeks ago. (7 you/it)

B: You probably did, but I forgot.

A: Do you have pictures from the wedding?

B: I have some at home. I'll bring them tomorrow and show _____. (8 you/them)

A: Thanks.

4.7 | Say and Tell

Say and tell have the same meaning but we use them differently.

Examples	Explanation
Compare: a. She **said** her name. b. She **told** me her name. c. She **said** her name to me. d. They **told** the musicians to start the music.	a. We *say* something. b. We *tell* someone something. c. We *say* something to someone. d. We *tell* someone to do something.
The bride and groom **say** "I do." They **say** "thank you" to the guests.	*Say* is followed by a direct object.
They **told** the guests the wedding date. **Tell** me the bride's name.	*Tell* is followed by an indirect object and a direct object.
Tell the truth, do you love me?	We can use *tell the truth* or *tell a lie* without an indirect object.

EXERCISE 17 Fill in the blanks with the correct form of *say* or *tell*.

EXAMPLES The bride ____said____, "I love you."

They ____told____ me the date of the wedding.

1. You _____ me the groom's name, but I forgot it.
2. Can you _____ me where the wedding is?
3. _____ the truth, do you love him?
4. The bride hates to _____ good-bye to her family.
5. During the ceremony, the bride and groom _____, "I do."
6. We _____ the band to play romantic music.
7. My neighbor wants to come to the wedding. I wasn't planning on inviting her, but I can't _____ no.
8. We _____ our daughter to economize on her wedding, but she _____ she wanted a fancy wedding.

ECONOMIZING ON A WEDDING

Before You Read
1. Why are weddings so expensive?
2. How can people economize on their weddings?

Read the following article. Pay special attention to the reflexive pronouns.

The average cost of a wedding in the U.S. today is $20,000 to $25,000 for about 200 guests. In days past, the bride's parents usually paid for the wedding. But as today's brides and grooms are older when they get married, they often pay for things **themselves.** There are many couples who put **themselves** in debt[8] to create a dream wedding.

(*continued*)

[8] When you are *in debt*, you owe money and have to pay it back.

Some recently married people give advice on how to economize on a wedding and still have a lovely, memorable event. Here are their tips:

- "I always pictured **myself** in a beautiful white dress. But when I went shopping and saw that most dresses are at least $1,000, I decided to look for a secondhand dress. I found something for $200, and it was lovely. When my sister got married, she made her dress **herself** and spent only $100 on fabric and lace. It isn't necessary to spend so much money on a dress. A bride is always beautiful."

- "We were going to use a professional printer for the invitations, but we decided to make the invitations **ourselves**. We designed them on the computer and added ribbons. The guests told us that they were beautiful and original."

- "I always wanted live music at my wedding. But when I saw the cost of musicians, I was shocked. My cousin plays piano well, so I asked her to play the piano for the wedding. And we used a DJ[9] for the dancing afterwards. We had to remind **ourselves** that the music wasn't the focus for the day, our marriage was."

- "Most couples want to get married in the summer. Ask **yourself** how important a summer wedding really is. You can cut costs by having a wedding at a less popular time. For example, a wedding in January is cheaper than a wedding in August."

According to some couples, it is not good to economize on some things.

- "Don't try to save money by sending invitations or thank-you cards through e-mail. Guests are offended. You should use postal mail."

- "We asked a friend to take pictures at our wedding but were very disappointed with the results. Our advice: Hire a professional photographer. You want to look at **yourselves** and guests for years to come."

The best way to economize is to cut the guest list and invite only your closest relatives and friends.

While most young couples want a perfect wedding, the most important thing is to have a good marriage.

Did You Know?

The average age of marriage is 27 for men and 25 for women.

---

[9]A *DJ* is a disk jockey, a person who plays recorded music from CDs.

4.8 | Reflexive Pronouns

We use reflexive pronouns for the object when the subject and object are the same.
Compare:
The groom loves **her.** (object pronoun)
The bride loves **herself.** (reflexive pronoun)

Examples	Explanation
a. I pictured **myself** in a beautiful white dress. (D.O.) b. We tell **ourselves** that money makes us happy, but it's not true. (I.O.) c. They like to look at **themselves** in their wedding photos. (O.P.)	A reflexive pronoun can be a. a direct object (D.O.) b. an indirect object (I.O.) c. the object of a preposition (O.P.)
She made the dress **all by herself.** The bride and groom made the invitations **themselves.**	We often use a reflexive pronoun to mean alone, without help. We often add (*all*) *by* before the reflexive pronoun.
We enjoyed **ourselves** at the wedding. Help **yourself** to more cake. Make **yourself** at home.	We use reflexive pronouns in a few idiomatic expressions.

Forms

Subject	Verb	Reflexive Pronoun
I	see	myself.
You	see	yourself.
He	sees	himself.
She	sees	herself.
It	sees	itself.
We	see	ourselves.
You	see	yourselves.
They	see	themselves.

EXERCISE 18 Frank and Sylvia are like many American couples. They have problems balancing their relationship, children, careers, families, and other responsibilities. Read each one's story and fill in the blanks with a reflexive pronoun.

Sylvia's Story:

Now that I'm married, I don't have time for ___*myself*___ anymore.
(example)

We used to spend time with each other. Now that we have kids, we

never have time for _____. We both work, but Frank doesn't
(1)

help me with housework or with the kids. I have to do everything all by

_____. My husband only thinks of _____. When he
(2) (3)

wants something, like a new digital camera or new software, he buys it.

He never buys me flowers or presents anymore. I tell _____ that
(4)
he still loves me, but sometimes I'm not so sure. Sometimes I think the problem is his fault, but sometimes I blame _____.
(5)

Frank's Story:

Sylvia never has time for me anymore. We used to do things together. Now I have to do everything by _____. If I want to
(6)
go to a movie, she says that she's too busy or too tired or that the kids are sick. I rarely go to the movies, and if I do, I go by _____.
(7)
It seems that all I do is work and pay bills. Other married people seem to enjoy _____ more than we do. She says she wants me to
(8)
help her with the housework, but she really prefers to do everything _____ because she doesn't like the way I do things. She
(9)
wants us to see a marriage counselor, but I don't like to tell other people about my problems. I like to solve my problems _____.
(10)

What do you think Frank and Sylvia should do?

EXERCISE 19 ABOUT YOU Write two sentences telling about things you like to do by yourself. Write two sentences telling about things you don't like to do by yourself.

EXAMPLES *I like to shop by myself.*

I don't like to eat by myself.

_____

_____

_____

_____

EXERCISE 20 *Combination Exercise.* Fill in the blanks with the correct pronoun or possessive form.

Frank and Sylvia used to do a lot of things together. __They__ (example) went to movies, went out to restaurants, and took vacations together.

But now _____(1)_____ are always too busy for each other. _____(2)_____ have two children and spend most of _____(3)_____ time taking care of _____(4)_____.

Frank and Sylvia bought a house recently and spend _____(5)_____ free time taking care of _____(6)_____. It's an old house and needs a lot of work.

When Frank and Sylvia have problems, _____(7)_____ try to solve _____(8)_____ by _____(9)_____. But sometimes Sylvia goes to _____(10)_____ mother for advice. Frank never goes to _____(11)_____ mother. He doesn't want to bother _____(12)_____ with _____(13)_____ problems. Frank often complains that Sylvia cares more about the kids and the house than about _____(14)_____.

Sylvia wants to go to a marriage counselor, but Frank doesn't want to go with _____(15)_____. He always says to Sylvia, "We don't need a marriage counselor. We can solve _____(16)_____ problems by _____(17)_____. You just need to pay more attention to _____(18)_____. If you want to see a counselor, you can go by _____(19)_____. I'm not going." Sylvia feels very frustrated. She thinks that the marriage isn't going to get better by _____(20)_____.

QUESTIONS AND ANSWERS ABOUT AN AMERICAN WEDDING

Before You Read

1. Do you have any questions about American weddings?
2. How is a traditional American wedding different from a wedding in your native culture?

Read the following questions and answers about American weddings. Pay special attention to questions.

Q: Who pays for the wedding?
A: In the past, the bride's parents paid for most of the wedding. Today only about 20 percent of weddings are the responsibility of the bride's parents. As men and women are getting married after starting careers and earning money, more and more weddings are becoming the responsibility of the bride and groom.

Q: What is a shower?
A: A shower is a party for the bride (and sometimes the groom) before the wedding. The purpose of the party is to give the couple gifts that will help them start their new home. Typical gifts are towels, cookware, linens[10], and small kitchen and household appliances.

Q: Who hosts the shower?
A: Usually the maid of honor hosts the shower. She invites friends and relatives of the bride and groom.

Q: When do they have the shower?
A: Usually the shower is two to six weeks before the wedding.

Q: How long does it take to plan a wedding?
A: Most couples plan their wedding for seven to twelve months.

Q: When do the couples send invitations?
A: They usually send the invitations about eight weeks before the wedding.

Q: When guests come in from out of town, who pays for their hotel and transportation?
A: The out-of-town guests pay for their own hotel. However, the groom pays for the hotel for his groomsmen and the bride pays for her bridesmaids. The guests usually pay for their own transportation.

Q: Whom does the groom choose as his best man?
A: Often the groom chooses his brother or best friend. However, he chooses the man he feels closest to. The groom chooses other close friends or male relatives as the groomsmen.

Q: When do the bride and groom open their gifts?
A: They open their gifts at home, not at the wedding.

Q: How do the guests know what the bride and groom want as gifts?
A: The bride and groom usually register for gifts at stores. They list the gift items they want and need for their new home, such as dishes, cookware, small appliances, and towels. When the guests go to buy a gift, they check the registry in the store. Of course, money is always a popular gift.

Q: How do I know how much money to give?
A: Most guests spend about $100 on a gift. People who are closer to the bride or groom often spend more. Casual friends usually spend less.

---

[10] *Linens* are sheets, pillowcases, and tablecloths.

4.9 Questions About the Subject or Complement

Questions about the complement include *do, does,* or *did*. Questions about the subject do not include *do, does,* or *did*.

Examples	Explanation
Who wears a white dress? The bride **does**. **Who paid** for the wedding? The parents **did**. **How many people came** to the wedding? About 150 people **did**.	We usually answer a subject question with a subject and an auxiliary verb.
What happened after the wedding? The bride and groom **went** on a honeymoon.	*What happened* is a subject question. We usually answer with a different verb.
Who **has** the prettiest dress? Which woman **has** the prettiest dress? Which women **have** the prettiest dresses? How many people **want** to dance?	• After *who*, use the **s** form for the simple present tense. • After *which* + noun, use either the base form or the **s** form. • After *how many*, use the base form.

Compare these statements and related questions.

Wh- Word	Do/Does/Did	Subject	Verb	Complement
What	did	The groom the bride Someone Who	paid for pay for? paid for paid for	the rings. the wedding. the wedding?
Whom	does	The groom he The bride Who	chooses choose? chooses chooses	a best man. her dress. the rings?
Why	do	Out-of-town guests they Who	stay stay stays	at a hotel. at a hotel? at a hotel?
		Something What	happened happened	next. next?

Language Note:

In a question about the object, *whom* is very formal. Informally, many Americans say *who*.
    Formal: *Whom* did your brother marry?
    Informal: *Who* did your brother marry?

EXERCISE 21 Read each statement. Then write a question about the words in parentheses ( ). No answer is necessary.

EXAMPLE Someone takes the bride to the groom. (who)

Who takes the bride to the groom?

1. Someone dances the first dance. (who)
   _____

2. Someone holds the rings. (who)
   _____

3. Two people say, "I do." (how many people / "congratulations")
   _____

4. The bridesmaids sometimes wear matching dresses.[11] (which woman / a white dress)
   _____

5. The bride pays for her white dress. (who / the bridesmaids' dresses)
   _____

EXERCISE 22 ABOUT YOU Use the simple present tense of the verb in parentheses ( ) to ask a question about this class. Any student may volunteer an answer.

EXAMPLES Who (ride) a bike to school?
 A: Who rides a bike to school?
 B: I do.

How many students (have) the textbook?
 A: How many students have the textbook?
 B: We all do.

1. Who (explain) the grammar?
2. How many students (speak) Spanish?
3. What usually (happen) after class?
4. Who (need) help with this lesson?
5. Who (have) a computer?
6. Who (have) a digital camera?
7. Who (live) alone?

[11] *Matching dresses* are all the same color.

EXERCISE 23 ABOUT YOU Use the simple past tense of the verb in parentheses ( ) to ask a question. Any student may volunteer an answer.

EXAMPLE Who (buy) a used textbook?
A: Who bought a used textbook?
B: I did.

1. Who (move) last year?
2. Who (understand) the explanation?
3. Who (take) a trip recently?
4. Who (bring) a dictionary to class today?
5. Who (pass) the last test?
6. Which students (come) late today?
7. Which student (arrive) first today?
8. How many students (do) today's homework?
9. How many students (study) English in elementary school?
10. How many students (bring) a cell phone to class?

EXERCISE 24 Read each statement. Then write a question about the words in parentheses ( ). Some of the questions are about the subject. Some are not. No answer is necessary.

EXAMPLES The bride wears a white dress. (what / the groom)
What does the groom wear?

The bride enters last. (who / first)
Who enters first?

1. The bride throws the bouquet. (when)
   _____

2. Some women try to catch the bouquet. (which women)
   _____

3. The groom puts the ring on the bride's finger. (on which hand) OR (which hand . . . on)
   _____

4. The band plays music. (what kind of music)
   _____

5. Someone dances with the bride. (who)
   _____

Possessive Forms; Object Pronouns; Reflexive Pronouns; Questions

6. Guests give presents. (what kind of presents)
   _____

7. Some people cry at the wedding. (who)
   _____

8. There's a dinner after the ceremony. (what / happen / after the dinner)
   _____

EXERCISE 25 In the conversation below, two women are talking about their families. Fill in the blanks to complete the questions. Some of the questions are about the subject. Some are about the object. Answers may vary.

A: How do you have time to work, go to school, and take care of a family?

B: I don't have to do everything myself.

A: Who _____*helps you*_____?
         (example)

B: My husband helps me.

A: I usually cook in my house. Who _____(1)_____?

B: Sometimes my husband cooks; sometimes I cook. We take turns.

A: I usually clean. Who _____(2)_____?

B: I usually clean the house.

A: How many ___(3)___?

B: I have five children.

A: How many ___(4)___?

B: Three children go to school. The younger ones stay home.

A: Do you send them to public school or private school?

B: One of my sons goes to private school.

A: Which _____(5)_____?

B: The oldest does. He's in high school now.

A: It's hard to take care of so many children. How do you find the time to go to class?

B: As I said, my husband helps me a lot. And sometimes I use a babysitter.

A: I'm looking for a sitter. Who(m) _____(6)_____?

B: I recommend our neighbor, Susan. She's 16 years old, and she's very good with our children.

A: Maybe she's too busy to help me. How many families _____
_____(7)_____?

B: I think she works for only one other family. I'll give you her phone number. If she's not busy, maybe she can work for you too.

A: Thanks. I can use some help.

EXERCISE 26 Fill in the blanks with *who, whom, who's,* or *whose.*

1. _____ your English teacher? Cindy Kane is my teacher.

2. _____ do you live with? I live with my sister.

3. _____ has the right answer? I have the right answer.

4. There's no name on this book. _____ is it?

5. _____ parents speak English? My parents do.

SUMMARY OF LESSON 4

1. Pronouns and Possessive Forms

Subject Pronoun	Object Pronoun	Possessive Adjective	Possessive Pronoun	Reflexive Pronoun
I	me	my	mine	myself
you	you	your	yours	yourself
he	him	his	his	himself
she	her	her	hers	herself
it	it	its	—	itself
we	us	our	ours	ourselves
you	you	your	yours	yourselves
they	them	their	theirs	themselves
who	whom	whose	whose	—

EXAMPLES

Robert and Lisa are **my** friends.
They come from Canada.
I like **them**.
Their wedding was beautiful.
My wedding was small.
　Theirs was big.
They paid for the wedding **themselves**.

Who has a new car?
With **whom** do you live?
　(FORMAL)
Who do you live with?
　(INFORMAL)
Whose book is that?
This is **my** dictionary.
　Whose is that?

2. Possessive Form of Nouns

　Singular Nouns
　　the **bride's** dress
　　my **father's** house
　　the **child's** toy
　　the **man's** hat
　　Charles' wife / **Charles's** wife

　Plural Nouns
　　the **bridesmaids'** dresses
　　my **parents'** house
　　the **children's** toys
　　the **men's** hats

3. *Say* and *Tell*

　He **said** his name.
　He **told** me his name.

　He **said** good-bye to his friends.
　He **told** them to write often.

4. Questions About the Subject

　Simple Present:
　　Who has the rings?
　　How many bridesmaids have a pink dress?
　　Which bridesmaid has a red dress?
　　Which bridesmaids have pink flowers?

　Simple Past:
　　Who kissed the bride?
　　Which man kissed the bride?
　　What happened next?

EDITING ADVICE

1. Don't confuse *you're* (you are) and *your* (possessive form).

   You're
   ~~Your~~ late.

   Your
   ~~You're~~ class started ten minutes ago.

2. Don't confuse *he's* (he is) and *his* (possessive form).

   He's
   ~~His~~ married.

   His
   ~~He's~~ wife is a friend of mine.

3. Don't confuse *it's* (it is) and *its* (possessive form).

   It's
   This college is big. ~~Its~~ a state university.

   Its
   ~~It's~~ library has many books.

4. Don't confuse *his* (masculine possessor) and *her* (feminine possessor).

   her
   My sister loves ~~his~~ son.

   his
   My brother loves ~~her~~ daughter.

5. Don't confuse *my* and *mine*.

   my
   I don't have ~~mine~~ book today.

6. Don't confuse *they're* and *their*.

   Their
   ~~They're~~ last name is Williams.

7. Use the correct pronoun (subject or object).

   her
   I have a daughter. I love ~~she~~ very much.

8. For a compound subject, use "another person and I." Don't use *me* in the subject position.

   I
   My father and ~~me~~ like to go fishing.

   My father and I
   ~~Me and my father~~ like to go fishing.

Possessive Forms; Object Pronouns; Reflexive Pronouns; Questions

9. For a compound object, use "another person and me." Don't use *I* in the object position.

   My parents gave my brother and ~~I~~ *me* a present.

10. Don't use *the* with a possessive form.

    ~~The~~ *M*my wife's mother is very nice.

11. Don't use an apostrophe to make a plural form.

    They invited many ~~guest's~~ *guests* to the wedding.

12. Don't use an auxiliary verb in a question about the subject.

    Who ~~does~~ speak*s* Spanish?

13. Don't separate *whose* from the noun.

    Whose is this (book)?

14. Don't confuse *whose* and *who's*.

    ~~Who's~~ *Whose* coat is that?

15. Use the correct word order for possession.

    ~~Mother my wife~~ *My wife's mother* helps us a lot.

16. Put the apostrophe after the *s* of a plural noun that ends in *s*.

    My ~~parent's~~ *parents'* house is small.

17. The *s* in a possessive pronoun is not for a plural.

    Theirs~~ parents live in Canada.

18. Don't use a form of *be* with *what happened*.

    What ~~was~~ happened to your new car?

19. Use correct word order with direct and indirect objects.

    She explained ~~me the grammar~~ *the grammar to me*.

    I gave ~~him it~~ *it to him*.

LESSON 4 TEST/REVIEW

PART 1 Find the mistakes with the underlined words, and correct them. Not every sentence has a mistake. If the sentence is correct, write *C*.

EXAMPLES The bride's ~~the~~ parents are very proud.

They are going to get married in their parents' house. **C**

1. Do you like the bridesmaid's dresses?
2. The groom puts the ring on the brides' left hand.
3. The bride throws his bouquet to the single women.
4. The groom dances with her new wife.
5. When will they open their friends gifts?
6. They're car has a sign that says "Just Married."
7. The groom's friend's often have a party for him before the wedding.
8. Your wedding was very beautiful.
9. She married his best friend's brother.
10. Her husband's mother's friend is wearing a beautiful dress.
11. The womens' dresses are very elegant.
12. My sister's the wedding will be in March.
13. Your name is different from your husband's name.
14. She visits hers parents once a week.
15. The groom graduated from college. His an accountant now.
16. Our friends invited my wife and me to their wedding.
17. My wife and me went to a beautiful wedding.
18. Who did get married in a church?
19. Whose mother is that? I think it's mother the bride.
20. How many people brought gifts to the wedding?
21. Please describe me the painting.
22. Who throw the bouquet at an American wedding? The bride does.
23. Theirs dresses are green. Mine is black.
24. The your wedding was lovely.
25. What was happened after the wedding?
26. Show me the wedding pictures.

Possessive Forms; Object Pronouns; Reflexive Pronouns; Questions   143

PART 2 Choose the correct word to complete each sentence.

EXAMPLE   Do you like ____c____ neighbors?

      a. you   **b.** you're   **c.** your   **d.** yours

1. Where do your parents live? _____ live in Colombia.
   - **a.** My
   - **b.** Mine
   - **c.** Mine's
   - **d.** Mines

2. _____ coat is that?
   - **a.** Whose
   - **b.** Who's
   - **c.** Who
   - **d.** Whom

3. _____ is usually white.
   - **a.** The bride's dress
   - **b.** The brides' dress
   - **c.** Dress the bride
   - **d.** The dress of bride

4. My sister's daughter is 18. _____ son is 16.
   - **a.** His
   - **b.** Her
   - **c.** Hers
   - **d.** Her's

5. What's _____?
   - **a.** the name your son
   - **b.** the name your son's
   - **c.** your son's name
   - **d.** your the son's name

6. Look at those dogs. Do you see _____?
   - **a.** they
   - **b.** its
   - **c.** them
   - **d.** it's

7. We have your phone number. Do you have _____?
   - **a.** us
   - **b.** our
   - **c.** ours
   - **d.** our's

8. What is _____?
   - **a.** that building name
   - **b.** the name of that building
   - **c.** the name that building
   - **d.** the name's that building

9. _____
   - **a.** Whose is this sweater?
   - **b.** Who's is this sweater?
   - **c.** Whose sweater is this?
   - **d.** Who's sweater is this?

10. _____ the correct answer?
    - **a.** Who knew
    - **b.** Whom knows
    - **c.** Who does know
    - **d.** Who knows

11. They have my address, but I don't have _____.
    - **a.** their
    - **b.** them
    - **c.** they're
    - **d.** theirs

12. We did it by _____.
    - **a.** self
    - **b.** oneself
    - **c.** ourself
    - **d.** ourselves

13. They can help _____.
    a. theirself   b. theirselves   c. themself   d. themselves
14. I know _____ very well.
    a. myself   b. mineself   c. meself   d. self
15. My teacher speaks Spanish. My _____ teacher doesn't.
    a. husbands   b. husbands'   c. husband's   d. the husband's

PART 3 Fill in the blanks with *said* or *told*.

1. She _____, "Excuse me."
2. She _____ them to study.
3. She _____ him the truth.
4. She _____ "hello" to her neighbor.
5. She _____ them the answers.
6. She _____ us about her trip.
7. She _____ an interesting story.
8. She _____ them her name.

PART 4 Complete the question. Some of these questions ask about the subject. Some do not. The answer is underlined.

EXAMPLES What *does the bride wear* _____?

The bride wears a white dress and a veil.

Who *usually cries at the wedding* _____?

The bride's mother usually cries at the wedding.

1. When _____?

   She throws the bouquet at the end of the wedding party.

2. Which women _____?

   The single women try to catch the bouquet.

3. On which hand _____?

   The groom puts the ring on the bride's left hand.

4. Whom _____?

   The groom kisses the bride.

5. Whose _____?
   The bride's ring has a diamond.

6. Whose _____?
   The bride uses her husband's last name.

7. Who _____?
   A professional photographer took pictures at my wedding.

8. Whose _____?
   I borrowed my sister's dress.

9. Whose _____, yours or your sisters?
   My sister's wedding was bigger.

10. How many people _____?
    Over 250 people came to the wedding.

11. Who _____?
    The bride and groom cut the cake.

PART 5 Fill in the blanks with a reflexive pronoun.

EXAMPLE She likes to talk about ____herself____.

1. I made the cake all by _____.
2. The bride made her dress _____.
3. They prepared _____ financially before getting married.
4. We helped _____ to another piece of cake.
5. The groom bought _____ a new pair of shoes.
6. All of you should help _____ to more cake and coffee.
7. Did you go to the wedding by _____ or did your wife go with you?

EXPANSION ACTIVITIES

Classroom Activities

1. Form a small group. The group should have people from different cultures and countries, if possible. Talk about weddings and marriages in your native cultures and countries.

    a. Who chooses a husband for a woman?

    b. Who pays for the wedding?

    c. What happens at the wedding?

    d. What happens after the wedding?

    e. Do the guests bring gifts to the wedding? What kind of gifts do they give? Where do the bride and groom open the gifts?

    f. How many people attend a wedding?

    g. Where do people get married?

    h. Do people dance at a wedding?

    i. Who takes pictures?

    j. What color dress does the bride wear?

    k. At what age do people usually get married?

2. In a small group, interview one person who is married. Ask this person questions about his or her wedding.

    EXAMPLES Where did you get married?
    How many people did you invite?
    How many people came?
    Where did you go on your honeymoon?

3. According to an American tradition, the bride should wear:
    Something old,
    Something new,
    Something borrowed,
    Something blue.

    Do you have any traditions regarding weddings in your native culture?

4. Do you have a video of a wedding in your family? If so, can you bring it to class and tell the class about it? The teacher may have a video of an American wedding to show the class.

Possessive Forms; Object Pronouns; Reflexive Pronouns; Questions

5. Write some advice for newlyweds in each of the following categories. Discuss your sentences in a small group.

home	problem solving
children	mother-in-law
housework	money
careers	time together / time apart
family obligations	

Write About it

1. Write about a typical wedding in your native culture, or describe your own wedding.

2. Write about a problem you once had or have now. Tell what you did (or are doing) to help yourself solve this problem or how others helped you (or are helping you).

Talk About it

1. What kind of problems do most married people have today? Do you think American married couples have the same problems as couples in other countries?

2. Do you think married couples can solve their problems by themselves? At what point should they go to a marriage counselor?

3. Do you think married people should spend most of their time together, or should they spend time by themselves?

4. Do you think young people are realistic about marriage? How can they prepare themselves for the reality of marriage?

5. Some people go on TV in the U.S. and talk about themselves and their personal problems. What do you think about this?

Internet Activities

1. Do a search on *bridal registry* on the Internet. Make a list of the types of wedding gifts couples ask for.

2. Do a search on *weddings* on the Internet. Find out how Americans plan for a wedding.

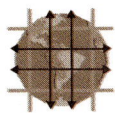

Additional Activities at http://elt.heinle.com/gic

LESSON 5

GRAMMAR

Singular and Plural
Count and Noncount Nouns
There + Be
Quantity Words

CONTEXT: Thanksgiving, Pilgrims, and American Indians

A Typical Thanksgiving
The Origin of Thanksgiving
Recipe for Turkey Stuffing
Taking the Land from the Native Americans
Navajo Code Talkers

A TYPICAL THANKSGIVING

Before You Read

1. When you celebrate a holiday, what kind of food do you prepare?
2. Do you think a holiday meal is a healthy meal?

Thanksgiving Day Parade

Read the following article. Pay special attention to singular and plural nouns.

Thanksgiving is a very special American **holiday.** We celebrate it on the fourth Thursday of November. **People** get together with **family** and **friends. Airports** are especially crowded as people travel to be with their **families** on this day. In fact, there are more **travelers** on the Sunday after Thanksgiving than any other day in the year.

On Thanksgiving, people eat a very big meal. While waiting for the **guests** to arrive, the host family usually puts out **snacks,** such as potato **chips** and **nuts.** The main part of the meal is **turkey.** Most people stuff the turkey with a mixture of **bread, onions, celery, nuts,** and **spices.** Some people add **fruit,** such as **apples** or **apricots** to the stuffing. Other parts of the **meal** include **sweet potatoes, mashed potatoes, gravy**[1]**, corn bread,** and **cranberry sauce.** Then there is **dessert. Pumpkin pie** with whipped **cream** is a favorite dessert.

[1] *Gravy* is made from meat drippings, flour, water, and sometimes bacon fat.

The typical Thanksgiving meal contains more than 3,000 **calories** and is 45 percent **fat**. Many people talk about going on **a diet** the day after Thanksgiving.

In addition to eating a big meal, many **people** relax and watch TV. It is a typical **tradition** to watch professional football on Thanksgiving day. The **men** are especially interested in football. Many **cities** also have a **parade** on Thanksgiving morning. New York City has a very big parade. **Millions** of people go to see the parade.

Thanksgiving is a relaxing and fun day for **families** and **friends**.

5.1 Noun Plurals

We use the plural to talk about more than one. Regular noun plurals add -s or -es. Some noun plurals are irregular.

Regular Noun Plurals

Word Ending	Example Noun	Plural Addition	Plural Form	Pronunciation
Vowel	bee banana	+ s	bees bananas	/z/
s, ss, sh, ch, x, z	church dish box watch class	+ es	churches dishes boxes watches classes	/əz/
Voiceless consonants	cat lip month	+ s	cats lips months	/s/
Voiced consonants	card pin	+ s	cards pins	/z/
Vowel + y	boy day	+ s	boys days	/z/
Consonant + y	lady story	~~y~~ + ies	ladies stories	/z/
Vowel + o	video radio	+ s	videos radios	/z/
Consonant + o	potato hero	+ es	potatoes heroes	/z/
Exceptions: photos, pianos, solos, altos, sopranos, autos, and avocados				
f or fe	leaf knife	~~f~~ + ves	leaves knives	/z/
Exceptions: beliefs, chiefs, roofs, cliffs, chefs, and sheriffs				

(continued)

Irregular Noun Plurals			
Singular	Plural	Examples	Explanation
man woman mouse tooth foot goose	men women mice teeth feet geese	The **men** watched the football game. The **women** washed the dishes.	Vowel change
sheep fish deer	sheep fish deer	There are three **fish** in the bowl.	No change
child person	children people (or persons) **Note:** *People* is more commonly used than *persons*.	The **children** set the table. We invited a lot of **people** to dinner.	Different word form

EXERCISE 1 Write the plural form of each noun. Pronounce each plural form.

EXAMPLE hour ___*hours*___

1. holiday _____
2. turkey _____
3. cranberry _____
4. potato _____
5. child _____
6. family _____
7. spice _____
8. nut _____
9. guest _____
10. man _____
11. woman _____
12. snack _____
13. apple _____
14. peach _____
15. tomato _____
16. pie _____
17. knife _____
18. deer _____
19. watch _____
20. tax _____
21. month _____
22. goose _____
23. dish _____
24. path _____

EXERCISE 2 Fill in the blanks with the plural form of the words in parentheses ( ).

A: Who prepares the Thanksgiving meal in your family?

B: The _____women_____ in my family do most of the cooking.
(example: woman)

But the _____ help a little too. My husband usually
(1 man)

makes the _____ and gravy. I always prepare the
(2 potato)

turkey. Even the _____ help. Last year, my two
(3 child)

_____ made the cranberry sauce.
(4 daughter)

A: Do you use fresh _____?
(5 cranberry)

B: Yes, we do. We boil them with sugar and add _____
(6 apple)

or orange _____ and some _____.
(7 slice)   (8 nut)

A: How do you make the stuffing?

B: I use bread, garlic _____, _____,
(9 clove)   (10 onion)

butter, and _____. I add _____.
(11 mushroom)   (12 spice)

A: What do you make for dessert?

B: My neighbor always comes and brings several _____.
(13 pie)

A: Does she make them herself?

B: No, she doesn't make them. She buys them.

A: Thanksgiving is such a lovely holiday, isn't it?

B: I love it. The only thing I don't like is washing the

_____ afterwards.
(14 dish)

A: Why don't the _____ wash the _____?
(15 man)   (16 dish)

B: They're too busy watching the football game. They always say that

they'll wash them later, but the _____ are in a hurry
(17 woman)

to clean up. So we do it ourselves.

Singular and Plural; Count and Noncount Nouns; *There + Be*; Quantity Words   153

5.2 Using the Singular and Plural for Generalizations

We can use the singular or plural to make a generalization. A generalization says something is true of all members of a group.

Examples	Explanation
a. **A football game** lasts about three hours. b. **Football games** last about three hours. a. **A sweet potato** is nutritious. b. **Sweet potatoes** are nutritious.	To make a generalization about the subject, use the indefinite article (*a* or *an*) with a singular subject (examples **a**) or no article with a plural subject (examples **b**).

EXERCISE 3 Make a generalization about the following nouns. Use the plural form. You may work with a partner.

EXAMPLE American teachers *are very informal.*

1. American children _____
2. American colleges _____
3. Buses in this city _____
4. Elderly Americans _____
5. American cities _____
6. American doctors _____
7. American women _____
8. American men _____
9. American holidays _____
10. Football games _____

EXERCISE 4 Make a generalization about these professions. Use the singular form. You may work with a partner.

EXAMPLE A taxi driver *has a dangerous job.*

1. A teacher _____
2. A doctor _____
3. A nurse _____
4. A garbage collector _____
5. A lawyer _____

6. A musician _____
7. A librarian _____
8. A movie star _____
9. An accountant _____
10. A newspaper reporter _____

5.3 Special Cases of Singular and Plural

Examples	Explanation
a. The U.S. has over 290 **million** people. b. **Millions** of people go shopping the day after Thanksgiving.	a. Exact numbers use the singular form. b. Inexact numbers use the plural form.
One of my **neighbors** brought a pie to the Thanksgiving dinner. One of the **men** helped with the dishes.	We use the plural form in the following expressions: *one of* (*the, my, his, her,* etc.).
Every **guest** brought something. We washed all the **dishes.**	We use a singular noun and verb after *every*. We use a plural noun after *all*.
After dinner, the girl put on her **pajamas** and went to bed. We're wearing our best **clothes** today.	Some words have no singular form: *pajamas, clothes, pants, slacks, (eye)glasses, scissors.*
Let's watch the **news.** It's on after dinner. Let's not discuss **politics** during dinner. It's not a good subject	Even though *news* and *politics* end in *-s*, they are singular.

Language Note:
Do not make adjectives plural.
  He made three **wonderful** pies.

EXERCISE 5 Find the mistakes with the underlined words, and correct them. Not every sentence has a mistake. If the sentence is correct, write *C*.

EXAMPLES Five <u>man</u> watched the football game. *men*

Ten <u>guests</u> came to dinner.   **C**

1. The <u>childrens</u> helped serve the dinner.
2. One of her <u>daughter</u> came from New York on Thanksgiving.
3. Ten <u>millions</u> people passed through the airports that day.
4. <u>Millions</u> of people travel for Thanksgiving.

5. After the news is over, we can watch the football game.
6. His pants is new.
7. Five women prepared the dinner.
8. Every guests stayed to watch the game.
9. Thanksgiving is one of my favorite holiday.
10. Hundreds of people saw the parade.
11. My grandmother came for Thanksgiving. She's in her eighties.
12. Politics is not a good subject to discuss at the dinner table.
13. The child should go to bed. His pajamas are on the bed.
14. Do you like sweets potatoes?

THE ORIGIN OF THANKSGIVING

Before You Read
1. What do you know about the origin of American Thanksgiving?
2. Do you have a day of thanks in your native culture?

Read the following article. Pay special attention to count and noncount nouns.

On Thanksgiving, **Americans** come together to give thanks for all the good **things** in their **lives**. Thanksgiving officially began in 1863 when President Lincoln declared that Americans would have a **day** of thanks. What is the origin of this great day?

In 1620, a **group** of 120 **men, women,** and **children** left England for America on a **ship** called the Mayflower. They came to America in search of religious **freedom**. They started their new **life** in a deserted[2] Indian **village** in what is now the **state** of Massachusetts. But half of the **Pilgrims** did not survive their first cold, hard **winter**. In the **spring**, two American **Indians**[3] found the **people** from England in very bad **condition**. They didn't have enough **food**, and they were in bad **health**. Squanto, an English-speaking American Indian, stayed with them for several **months** and taught them how to

[2] *Deserted* means empty of people.
[3] The natives of America are called *American Indians, Indians,* or *Native Americans.*

survive in this new **land.** He brought them deer **meat** and animal **skins;** he showed them how to grow **corn** and other **vegetables;** he showed them how to use **plants** as **medicine;** he explained how to use **fish** for **fertilizer**[4]—he taught them many **skills** for survival in their new land.

By the time their second **fall** arrived, the Pilgrims had enough **food** to get through their second winter. They were in better **health.** They decided to have a Thanksgiving **feast**[5] to celebrate their good **fortune.**

They invited Squanto and neighboring Indian **families** of the Wampanoag **tribe** to come to their **dinner.** The Pilgrims were surprised when 90 Indians showed up. The Pilgrims did not have enough **food** for so many people. Fortunately, the Indian **chief** sent some of his people to bring food to the **celebration.** They brought five **deer, fish, beans, squash,** corn **bread, berries,** and many wild **turkeys.** The feast lasted for three **days.** There was a short **time** of **peace** and **friendship** between the Indians and the Pilgrims.

Now on Thanksgiving, we eat some of the traditional **foods** from this period in American **history.**

[4] *Fertilizer* is made of natural things. We put fertilizer in the earth to help plants grow.
[5] A *feast* is a large dinner.

5.4 Noncount Nouns

We classify nouns into two groups: **count nouns** and **noncount nouns.** A count noun is something we can count. It has a singular and plural form.
> one potato — two potatoes
> one day — three days

A noncount noun is something we don't count. It has no plural form (*corn, bread, health, medicine, freedom,* etc.).
There are several types of noncount nouns.

Group A: Nouns that have no distinct, separate parts. We look at the whole.

milk	wine	bread	electricity
oil	yogurt	meat	lightning
water	pork	butter	thunder
coffee	poultry[6]	paper	cholesterol
tea	soup	air	blood

Group B: Nouns that have parts that are too small or insignificant to count

rice	hair	sand
sugar	popcorn	corn
salt	snow	grass

Group C: Nouns that are classes or categories of things. The members of the category are not the same.

money or cash (nickels, dimes, dollars)	fruit (cherries, apples, grapes)
food (vegetables, meat, spaghetti)	makeup (lipstick, rouge, eye shadow)
furniture (chairs, tables, beds)	homework (compositions, exercises, reading)
clothing (sweaters, pants, dresses)	jewelry (necklaces, bracelets, rings)
mail (letters, packages, postcards, fliers)	

Group D: Nouns that are abstractions

love	happiness	nutrition	music	information
life	education	intelligence	art	nature
time	experience	unemployment	work	help
truth	crime	pollution	health	noise
beauty	advice	patience	trouble	energy
luck/fortune	knowledge	poverty	fun	friendship

Group E: Subjects of study

history	grammar	biology
chemistry	geometry	math (mathematics*)

*__Note:__ Even though *mathematics* ends with *s,* it is not plural.

---

[6] *Poultry* includes domestic birds that we eat, such as chickens and turkeys.

EXERCISE 6 Fill in the blanks with a noncount noun from the box below.

| advice | turkey | freedom ✓ | friendship |
| health | food | corn | snow |

EXAMPLE The Pilgrims wanted to find ____freedom____ in America.

1. They had poor _____.
2. The Indians gave the Pilgrims a lot of _____ about how to grow food.
3. Squanto taught them to plant _____.
4. The first winter was hard. It was cold and there was a lot of _____.
5. During the second winter, the Pilgrims had enough _____.
6. In the beginning, there was _____ between the Pilgrims and the Indians.
7. Today people eat _____ on Thanksgiving.

5.5 | Count and Noncount Nouns[7]

Examples	Explanation
I eat a lot of **rice** and **beans**. rice = noncount noun beans = count noun	*Count* and *noncount* are grammatical terms, but they are not always logical. *Rice* is very small and is a noncount noun. *Beans* and *peas* are also very small, but they are count nouns.
a. We put some **fruit** in the cranberry sauce. b. Oranges and lemons are **fruits** that contain Vitamin C. a. We prepared a lot of **food** for Thanksgiving. b. Cranberries and sweet potatoes are typical **foods** for Thanksgiving.	a. Use *fruit* and *food* as noncount nouns when you mean fruit and food in general. b. Use *fruits* and *foods* as count nouns when you mean kinds of fruit or categories of food.
a. The Indians brought many **turkeys** to the feast. b. We eat **turkey** on Thanksgiving. a. He brought 3 **pies** to the Thanksgiving dinner. b. I ate some **pie** after dinner.	a. When referring to the whole thing (*turkey, pie*), these words are count nouns. b. When referring to a part, these words are noncount nouns.
a. Children like to eat **candy**. b. There are 3 **candies** on the table.	a. When you talk about candy in general, *candy* is noncount. b. When you look at individual pieces of candy, you can use the plural form.
We have a lot of **information** about American history. The Indians gave the English people **advice** about how to plant food.	Some nouns that have a plural form in other languages are noncount in English. *Advice, information, knowledge, equipment, furniture,* and *homework* are always noncount nouns in English.

[7] For a list of nouns that can be both count or noncount, see Appendix G.

EXERCISE 7 Decide if the noun in parentheses ( ) is count or noncount. If it is a count noun, change it to the plural form. If it is a noncount noun, do not use the plural form.

EXAMPLE The ___*Pilgrims*___ wanted ___*freedom*___.
(Pilgrim)   (freedom)

1. American Indians have a lot of respect for _____.
(nature)

   They love _____, _____,
   (flower)   (tree)

   _____, and _____.
   (bird)   (fish)

2. Thanksgiving is a celebration of _____ and
   (peace)

   _____.
   (friendship)

3. On Thanksgiving, Americans eat a lot of _____
   (food)

   and sometimes gain weight.

4. Squanto gave the Pilgrims a lot of _____ about
   (advice)

   planting _____ and other _____.
   (corn)   (vegetable)

   He had a lot of _____ about the land.
   (knowledge)

5. The Pilgrims didn't have any _____ with American food.
   (experience)

6. On the first Thanksgiving, Indians brought _____,
   (meat)

   _____, _____, and _____.
   (bean)   (bread)   (berry)

7. The Pilgrims celebrated because they had a lot of good

   _____.
   (fortune)

8. American Indians use _____ for _____.
   (plant)   (medicine)

9. My friends went to the Southwest last summer. They bought

   American Indian _____, such as _____
   (jewelry)   (ring)

   and _____.
   (necklace)

10. Do you have a lot of _____ about American
    (information)

    _____?
    (holiday)

RECIPE FOR TURKEY STUFFING

Before You Read

1. Do you like to cook?
2. What is a favorite recipe of yours?

Read the following recipe. Pay special attention to quantities.

Turkey Stuffing

1/4 cup of butter or olive oil
2 cloves of garlic, minced[8]
1 cup of mushrooms
1 onion, chopped
3 stalks of celery, chopped
1/4 cup pieces of bacon
4 cups of dry bread, cut into cubes
1/4 teaspoon of salt
1/4 teaspoon of pepper
1/4 teaspoon of oregano
2 teaspoons of dry parsley
1 1/4 cup of hot chicken broth

Brown garlic in butter (or olive oil). Add mushrooms and sauté. Add the rest of the vegetables and cook until they begin to soften. Stir bacon bits into mixture, then lower heat to medium and add bread cubes and seasonings.

Continue cooking for approximately 5 more minutes, stirring continuously.

Add hot chicken broth and mix well. Cover and cook over low heat for at least 30 minutes, stirring frequently.

Use as turkey stuffing and bake with turkey OR place in a covered casserole dish and bake for 30 minutes in 350–375 degree oven.

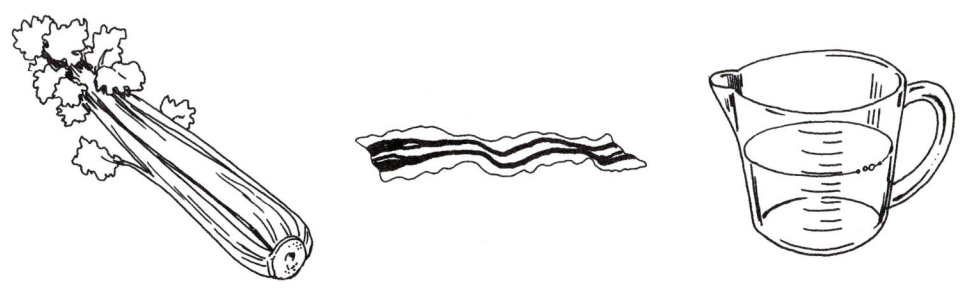

[8] *Minced* means cut into very small pieces.

Singular and Plural; Count and Noncount Nouns; *There + Be*; Quantity Words

5.6 Quantities with Count and Noncount Nouns

We can put a number before a count noun. We cannot put a number before a noncount noun. We use a unit of measure, which we can count—two **cloves** of garlic.

By container	By portion	By measurement[9]	By shape or whole piece	Other
a bottle of water a carton of milk a jar of pickles a bag of flour a can of soda (pop) a cup of coffee a glass of water a bowl of soup	a slice (piece) of bread a piece of meat a piece of cake a strip of bacon a piece (sheet) of paper a slice of pizza a scoop of ice cream	an ounce of sugar a quart of oil a pound of meat a gallon of milk a pint of cream	a loaf of bread an ear of corn a piece of fruit a head of lettuce a candy bar a roll of film a tube of toothpaste a bar of soap a clove of garlic a stalk of celery	a piece of mail a piece of furniture a piece of advice a piece of information a work of art a homework assignment

EXERCISE 8 Fill in the blanks with a specific quantity or unit of measure. Answers may vary.

EXAMPLE I drink three ___glasses of___ water a day.

1. You should take a few _____ film on your vacation.
2. I'm going to buy two _____ meat to make dinner for the family.
3. _____ milk is heavy to carry.
4. She drinks two _____ coffee every morning.
5. Buy _____ bread for dinner.
6. He eats _____ fruit a day.
7. Some Americans carry _____ water with them.
8. I ate two _____ cake.
9. Let me give you _____ advice before you apply to colleges.
10. How many _____ gas did you buy at the gas station?
11. How many _____ garlic are you going to use in the recipe?
12. The recipe calls for ¼ _____ butter or oil.
13. The recipe calls for ¼ _____ pepper.

[9] For a list of conversions from the American system of measurement to the metric system, see Appendix D.

TAKING THE LAND FROM THE NATIVE AMERICANS

Before You Read

1. Who were the original inhabitants of your native country?
2. Are there any ethnic minorities in your native country? Do they have the respect of the majority population?

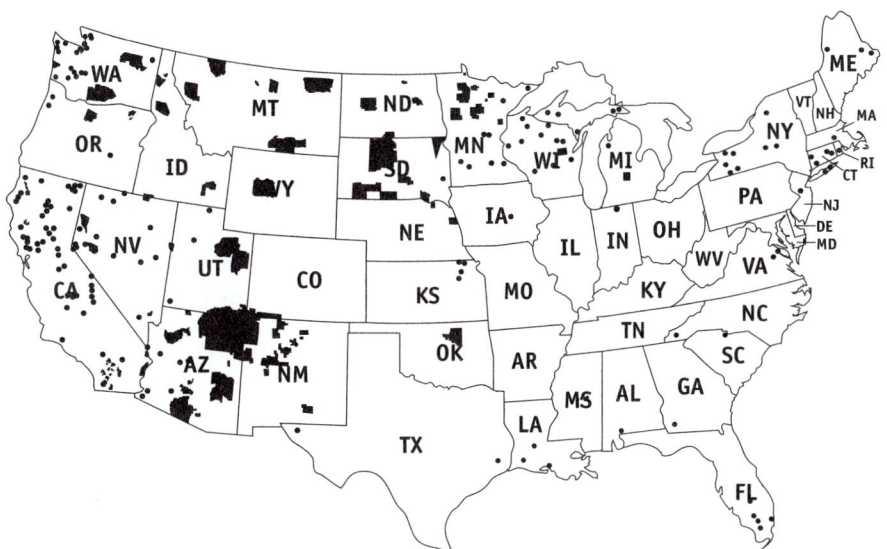

American Indian Reservations in the U.S.

 Read the following article. Pay special attention to *there* + a form of *be*.

Did You Know?

Many place names in the U.S. are American Indian names. Chicago, for example, comes from an Indian word meaning smelly onion.

Before the arrival of Europeans, **there were** between 10 and 16 million Native Americans in America. Today **there are** fewer than two million. What happened to these natives of America?

The friendship between the Indians and Europeans did not last for long. As more English people came to America, they did not need the help of the Indians, as the first group of Pilgrims did. The white people started to take the land away from the Indians. As Indians fought to keep their land, many of them were killed. Also, **there were** many deaths from diseases that Europeans brought to America. In 1830, President Andrew Jackson took the Indians' lands and sent them to live on reservations. Indian children had to learn English. Often they were punished for speaking their own language. As a result, **there are** very few Indians today who speak the language of their ancestors.[10]

Today **there are** about 500 tribes in the U.S., each with its own traditions. **There are** about 300 reservations, but only 22 percent of American Indians live on this land. **There is** a lot of unemployment and poverty on many reservations. As a result, many Indians move to big cities to find work. Many return to their reservations only for special celebrations such as Pow-Wows, when Indians wear their traditional clothing and dance to traditional music.

It is becoming harder and harder for Indians to keep their traditions and languages alive.

[10] *Ancestors* are grandparents, great-grandparents, etc.

Singular and Plural; Count and Noncount Nouns; *There* + *Be*; Quantity Words

5.7 | *There* + a Form of *Be*

We use *there* + a form of *be* to introduce a subject, either count or noncount, into the conversation. After the noun, we often give a time or place.

There	Be	A / An / One	Singular Subject	Complement
There	is	a	reservation	in Wyoming.
There	is	an	onion	in the recipe.
There	will be	a	football game	on TV tonight.
There	was	one	guest	for dinner.

There	Be	(Quantity Word)	Noncount Subject	Complement
There	is	a lot of	unemployment	on some reservations.
There	is	some	garlic	in the recipe for stuffing.
There	was		peace	between the Indians and the Pilgrims.

There	Be	(Quantity Word)	Plural Subject	Complement
There	are	500	Indian tribes	in the U.S.
There	were	many	deaths	from diseases after the Europeans arrived.
There	are	a lot of	calories	in a typical Thanksgiving meal.
There	are		reservations	in California.

Negative Forms

There	Be + Not + A / An	Singular Subject	Complement
There	wasn't a	problem	between the Pilgrims and Indians in 1620.

There	Be + No	Singular Subject	Complement
There	was no	problem	between the Pilgrims and Indians in 1620.

There	Be + Not + (Any)	Noncount Subject	Complement
There	isn't any	milk	in the recipe.

There	Be + No	Noncount Subject	Complement
There	is no	milk	in the recipe.

There	Be + Not + (Any)	Plural Subject	Complement
There	aren't any	reservations	in Illinois.

There	Be + No	Plural Subject	Complement
There	are no	reservations	in Illinois.

5.8 | Using *There*

We use *there* + a form of *be* to introduce a subject, either count or noncount, into the conversation.

Examples	Explanation
There's a reservation in Wyoming.	The contraction for *there is* = *there's*. We don't write a contraction for *there are*.
There is one onion and three celery stalks in the recipe. **There are** three celery stalks and one onion in the recipe. **There is** dessert and coffee after the dinner.	If two nouns follow *there*, use a singular verb (*is*) if the first noun is singular. Use a plural verb (*are*) if the first noun is plural.
Informal: There's a lot of reservations in California. **Formal: There are** a lot of reservations in California.	In conversation, you will sometimes hear *there's* with plural nouns.
There are over 500 tribes of Native Americans in the U.S. **They** each have their own traditions. There's a Navajo reservation in Arizona. **It's** very big. There's a Navajo woman in my chemistry class. **She** comes from Arizona.	After we introduce a noun with *there*, we can continue to speak of this noun with a pronoun (*they, it, she,* etc.)

Is there unemployment on some reservations?
   Yes, there is.
Are there any reservations in California?
   Yes, there are.
How many Navajo Indians **are there** in Arizona?
	Observe the word order in questions with *there*.

Wrong: **There's** the Grand Canyon in Arizona. *Right:* The Grand Canyon is in Arizona.	*There* never introduces a specific or unique noun. Don't use a noun with the definite article (*the*) after *there*.

EXERCISE 9 Fill in the blanks with the correct form and tense.

EXAMPLE There _____*are*_____ a lot of Indians in Oklahoma.

1. There _____ a lot of reservations in California.
2. There _____ more American Indians 200 years ago than there _____ today.
3. In the beginning, there _____ peace between the Indians and the Pilgrims.

Singular and Plural; Count and Noncount Nouns; *There* + *Be*; Quantity Words   **165**

4. Later, there _____ wars between the Indians and the white people who took their land.

5. _____ _____ enough food to eat at the first Thanksgiving? Yes, there was.

6. How many people _____ _____ at the first Thanksgiving celebration?

7. Next week there _____ _____ a test on noncount nouns.

8. How many questions _____ _____ _____ on the test?

EXERCISE 10 Fill in the blanks with a time or place.

EXAMPLE There was a war *in my country from 1972 to 1975.*

1. There will be a test _____
2. There's a lot of snow _____
3. There are a lot of people _____
4. There are a lot of reservations _____
5. There was a presidential election _____

NAVAJO CODE TALKERS

Before You Read
1. Are some languages more complicated than others?
2. Why is a code important during wartime?

166   Lesson 5

Read the following article. Pay special attention to quantity words.

American Indian languages are very complicated. There are **many** different languages and each one has **several** dialects. **Some** languages, like Navajo, have **no** alphabet or symbols.

Philip Johnston was not an Indian but he grew up on the Navajo reservation and learned **a lot of** their language. Later, when Johnston served in World War I, he understood the importance of developing a code that the enemy could not understand. In World War II, the U.S. was at war with Japan. The Japanese were very skillful at breaking codes. In 1942, Johnston met with an American military general and explained his idea of using the Navajo language in code to send messages. Indians living on Navajo land in the Southwest U.S. could speak and understand the language. **Very few** non-Navajos could speak or understand it.

The general agreed to try this idea. The U.S. Marines recruited **200** native speakers of Navajo to create a code based on their language. There were **many** military words that did not exist in the Navajo language, so the Navajo recruits had to develop words for these things. For example, the commanding general was a "war chief"; a battleship was a "whale"; a submarine was an "iron fish."

In the first **two** days of code talking, more than **800** messages were sent without **any** errors.

During and after the war, the Navajo code talkers got **little** recognition for their great help in World War II. It wasn't until 1992 that the U.S. government honored the Navajo code talkers for their help in winning major battles of the war.

5.9 Quantity Expressions—An Overview

We can use quantity expressions to talk about the quantity of count and noncount nouns.

There are about **two million** American Indians today.
There were about **400** code talkers during World War II.
Very few non-Navajos could speak the Navajo language.
Navajo code talkers got **little** recognition for their work.
The Pilgrims had **very little** food during the first winter.
The American Indians had **a lot of** knowledge about the land.
The Pilgrims didn't have **much** knowledge about the land.
Many Indians died from disease after the Europeans came.
Some Indians today live on reservations.
The Navajo language has **no** alphabet.
The Navajo language has **several** dialects.

Singular and Plural; Count and Noncount Nouns; *There + Be*; Quantity Words

EXERCISE 11 Fill in the blanks to complete these statements. Answers may vary.

EXAMPLE There are 500 ___tribes___ of American Indians in the United States.

1. Two hundred native speakers of _____ served as code talkers.

2. There is no word for _____ in Navajo.

3. The Navajo language has no _____.

4. Before the arrival of the white people from Europe, there were at least _____ American Indians.

5. After the first cold winter in America, the Pilgrims didn't have much _____.

6. Many Pilgrims _____ during the first winter.

7. Some _____ helped the Pilgrims.

8. The Indians taught them many _____ to help them survive.

9. The second year in America was much better. They had a lot of _____.

10. As more white people came to America, many _____ lost their land.

11. Many Indians can't find work on their reservations. There is a lot of _____ on a reservation.

Native American at a Pow-Wow

168 Lesson 5

5.10 Some, Any, A, No

	Examples	Explanation
Affirmative	There is **a** big reservation in the Southwest. There is **an** onion in the recipe.	Use *a* or *an* with singular count nouns.
Affirmative	I used **some** raisins in the recipe. I used **some** bread in the recipe.	Use *some* with both plural count nouns and noncount nouns.
Negative	I didn't eat **any** potatoes. I didn't eat **any** gravy.	Use *any* for negatives with both plural count nouns and noncount nouns.
Question	Did the code talkers make **any** mistakes? Did the enemy get **any** information?	Use *any* for questions with both plural count nouns and noncount nouns.
No* vs. *any	There isn't **any** sugar in the stuffing. There is **no** sugar in the stuffing. There aren't **any** potatoes in the soup. There are **no** potatoes in the soup.	Use *any* after a negative verb. Use *no* after an affirmative verb. *Wrong:* There *aren't no* potatoes in the soup.

Language Notes:

1. Don't use the indefinite article after *no*.
   Wrong: I have no *an* answer to your question.
   Right: I have no answer to your question.
2. You will sometimes see *any* with a singular count noun.
   Which pen should I use for the test? You can use *any* pen.
   Any, in this case, means whichever you want. It doesn't matter which pen.

EXERCISE 12 ABOUT YOU Use *there* + *be* + the words given to tell about your hometown. If you use *no*, delete the article. You can add a statement to give more information.

EXAMPLES a mayor
There's a mayor in my hometown. He's a young man.

a subway
There's no subway in my hometown.

1. a university
2. a subway
3. an English language newspaper
4. an airport
5. a soccer team
6. a river
7. a jail
8. an art museum
9. an English language institute
10. a cemetery

EXERCISE 13 Fill in the blanks with *some, any, a, an,* or *no.*

EXAMPLES

I have ___some___ money in my pocket.

Do you have ___any___ time to help me?

Do you have ___a___ new car?

I have ___no___ experience as a babysitter.

1. Do you have _____ questions about this exercise?
2. Do you have _____ dictionary with you?
3. Did you have _____ trouble with the homework?
4. If we have _____ extra time, we'll go over the homework.
5. The teacher can't help you now because he has _____ time.
6. The teacher can't help you now because he doesn't have _____ time.
7. I'm confused. I need _____ answer to my question.
8. I have _____ questions about the last lesson. Can you answer them for me?
9. I understand this lesson completely. I have _____ questions.
10. I understand this lesson completely. I don't have _____ questions.
11. I work hard all day and have _____ energy late at night.
12. I don't have _____ computer.

5.11 A Lot Of, Much, Many

	Examples	Explanation
Affirmative	**A lot of** Indians served in the military. It takes **a lot of** time to develop a code.	Use *a lot of* with count and noncount nouns.
Affirmative	On Thanksgiving, we give thanks for the **many** good things in our lives. We eat **a lot of** food on Thanksgiving.	Use *many* with count nouns. Use *a lot of* with noncount nouns in affirmative statements. *Much* is rare in affirmative statements.
Negative	Today the Indians don't have **much** land. The Pilgrims didn't have **many** skills.	Use *much* with noncount nouns. Use *many* with count nouns.
Negative	Today the Indians don't have **a lot of** land. The Pilgrims didn't have **a lot of** skills.	Use *a lot of* with both count and noncount nouns.
Question	Did you eat **much** turkey? Did you eat **many** cookies?	Use *much* with noncount nouns. Use *many* with count nouns.
Question	Did you eat **a lot of** turkey? Did you eat **a lot of** cookies?	Use *a lot of* with both count and noncount nouns.
Question	**How much** experience did the code talkers have? **How many** code talkers were in the military?	Use *how much* with noncount nouns. Use *how many* with count nouns.

Language Note:
When the noun is omitted (in this case, **water**), use *a lot,* not *a lot of.*

Compare:
I usually drink **a lot of** water, but I didn't drink **a lot** today.

EXERCISE 14 Fill in the blanks with *much, many,* or *a lot (of).* Avoid *much* in affirmative statements. In some cases, more than one answer is possible.

A: Did you prepare ___*a lot of*___ food for Thanksgiving?
    (example)

B: No, I didn't prepare _____.
                                (1)

A: You didn't? Why not?

B: This year I didn't invite _____ people. I just invited my
                                    (2)
immediate family.

A: How _____ people are there in your immediate family?
              (3)

Singular and Plural; Count and Noncount Nouns; *There + Be*; Quantity Words **171**

B: Just seven. I bought a twelve-pound turkey. It was more than enough.

A: I don't know how to prepare a turkey. Is it _____(4)_____ work to prepare a turkey?

B: Not really. But you have to cook it for _____(5)_____ hours.

A: Did you make _____(6)_____ other dishes, like sweet potatoes and cranberry sauce?

B: No. Each person in my family made something. That way I didn't have _____(7)_____ work. But we had _____(8)_____ work cleaning up. There were _____(9)_____ dirty dishes. I hate washing dishes after a big dinner, so I'm planning to buy a dishwasher soon.

A: Does a dishwasher cost _____(10)_____ money?

B: Yes, but I'd like to have one for that one day a year.

A: Maybe you should just use paper plates.

B: I know _____(11)_____ people do that, but I want my dinner to look elegant. For me, paper plates are for picnics.

5.12 | *A Lot Of* vs. *Too Much / Too Many*

Examples	Explanation
a. **A lot of** Navajo Indians live in the Southwest. b. My friend left the reservation because there was **too much** unemployment and she couldn't find a job. a. **A lot of** people came to dinner. We all had a great time. b. **Too many** people came to dinner. There wasn't enough food for everyone.	Sentences (a) show a large quantity. No problem is presented. *A lot of* has a neutral tone. Sentences (b) show an excessive quantity. A problem is presented or implied. A sentence with *too much/too many* can have a complaining tone.
I feel sick. I ate **too much**.	We can put *too much* at the end of a verb phrase.

Language Note:
Sometimes you can use *a lot of* in place of *too much/too many*.
  Too many people came to dinner. There wasn't enough food for everyone.
  A lot of people came to dinner. There wasn't enough food for everyone.

172 Lesson 5

EXERCISE 15 Fill in the blanks with *a lot of*, *too much*, or *too many*. In some cases, more than one answer is possible.

EXAMPLE I love garlic. This recipe calls for ____a lot of____ garlic, so it's going to be delicious.

1. I can't eat this soup. It has _____ salt.
2. A Thanksgiving dinner has about 3,000 calories. Most people eat _____ and gain a few pounds.
3. The Navajo code talkers gave _____ help during World War II.
4. The code talkers sent _____ messages successfully.
5. Before the Europeans arrived, there were _____ Indians in America.
6. There are _____ American Indian languages.
7. You put _____ pepper in the potatoes, and they taste terrible.
8. She's going to bake a cherry pie. She needs _____ cherries.
9. I think I ate _____ pieces of pumpkin pie. Now I feel sick.

EXERCISE 16 Use *a lot of*, *too much*, or *too many* to fill in the blanks in the story below. In some cases, more than one answer is possible.

My name is Coleen Finn. I'm a Ho-chunk Indian. My tribal land is in Wisconsin. But I live in Chicago because there is ____too much____ *(example)* unemployment on my tribal land, and I can't find a good job there. There are _____ *(1)* opportunities in Chicago, and I found a job as a secretary in the English Department at Truman College. I like my job very much. I have _____ *(2)* responsibilities and I love the challenge.

I like Chicago, but I miss my land, where I still have _____ *(3)* relatives and friends. I often go back to visit them whenever I get tired of life in Chicago. My friends and I have _____ *(4)* fun together, talking, cooking our native food,

Coleen Finn

Singular and Plural; Count and Noncount Nouns; *There + Be*; Quantity Words   **173**

walking in nature, and attending Indian ceremonies, such as Pow-Wows.

I need to get away from Chicago once in a while to feel closer to nature.

Even though there are _____(5)_____ nice things about Chicago, there are _____(6)_____ cars and trucks in the big city and there is _____(7)_____ pollution. A weekend with my tribe gives me time to relax and smell fresh air.

EXERCISE 17 ABOUT YOU Fill in the blanks after *too* with *much* or *many*. Then complete the statement.

EXAMPLE If I drink too __much__ coffee, *I won't be able to sleep tonight.*

1. If I try to memorize too _____ words, _____

2. If I make too _____ mistakes on my homework, _____

3. If I spend too _____ money on clothes, _____

4. If I drink too _____ coffee, _____

5. If I spend too _____ time with my friends, _____

6. If I stay up _____ late, _____

5.13 | *A Few, Several, A Little*

	Examples	Explanation
Count	The Navajo language has **several** dialects. She speaks **a few** languages. Put **a few** teaspoons of salt in the potato recipe.	Use *a few* or *several* with count nouns or with quantities that describe noncount nouns (*teaspoon, cup, bowl, piece*, etc.).
Noncount	He put **a little** salt in the potatoes. Please add **a little** milk to the coffee.	Use *a little* with noncount nouns.

Lesson 5

EXERCISE 18 Fill in the blanks with *a few*, *several*, or *a little*. In some cases, more than one answer is possible.

EXAMPLE We have ____*a little*____ information about American Indians.

1. _____ Indians came to help the Pilgrims.
2. They taught the Pilgrims _____ skills for planting.
3. They gave them _____ help.
4. _____ Navajo Indians developed a code.
5. It took _____ time to develop the code.
6. The Navajos had to create _____ new words.
7. There were _____ Japanese experts at code breaking.
8. You need _____ butter for the recipe.
9. You need _____ bread for the recipe.
10. You need _____ cloves of garlic for the recipe.

5.14 | *A Few* vs. *Few*; *A Little* vs. *Little*

A few and *a little* have a positive emphasis. *Few* and *little* (without *a*) have a negative emphasis.

Examples	Explanation
a. **A few** Indians helped the Pilgrims. b. **Few** non-Navajos could speak the Navajo language. c. **Very few** young American Indians speak the language of their ancestors.	a. *A few* means some or enough. b. and c. *Few* and *very few* mean not enough; almost none. We use *very* to emphasize the negative quantity.
a. There's **a little** food in the refrigerator. Let's make a sandwich. b. The Navajo code talkers got **little** recognition for their help in World War II. c. The Pilgrims had **very little** food the first winter.	a. *A little* means some or enough. b. and c. *Little* and *very little* mean not enough; almost none. We use *very* to emphasize the negative quantity.

Language Note:
Whether something is enough or not enough does not depend on the quantity. It depends on the perspective of the person. Is the glass half empty or half full?
- ☺ One person may say the glass is half full. He sees something positive about the quantity of water in the glass: The glass has *a little* water.
- ☹ Another person may say the glass is half empty. He sees something negative about the quantity of water in the glass. The glass has *(very) little* water.

EXERCISE 19 Fill in the blanks with *a little*, *very little*, *a few*, or *very few*. In some cases, more than one answer is possible.

EXAMPLES He has ____*a little*____ extra money. He's going to buy a sandwich.

He has ____*very little*____ extra money. He can't buy anything.

1. I have _____ food in my refrigerator. Let's make dinner at my house.

2. In some countries, people have _____ food, and many people are starving.[11]

3. That worker has _____ experience. He probably can't do that job.

4. That worker has _____ experience. He can probably do that job.

5. I eat _____ meat every day because I want protein in my diet.

6. I want to bake cookies, but I can't because I have _____ sugar in the house.

7. When there is _____ rain, plants can't grow.

8. Tomorrow there may be _____ rain, so you should take an umbrella.

9. Twenty-five years ago, home computers were very rare. _____ people had a home computer.

10. Before I bought my computer, I talked to _____ people about which computer to buy.

11. There are _____ monkeys in the zoo. Let's go to see them.

12. There are _____ gray whales in the world. These animals are an endangered species.[12]

13. If you want to study medicine, I can give you a list of _____ good medical schools in the United States.

14. _____ high schools teach Latin. It is not a very popular language to study anymore.

15. I want to say _____ words about my country. Please listen.

16. My father is a man of _____ words. He rarely talks.

17. English is the main language of _____ countries.

18. Women are still rare as political leaders. _____ countries have a woman president.

---

[11] *To starve* means to suffer or die from not having enough food.
[12] An *endangered species* is a type of living thing that is becoming more and more rare. The species is in danger of disappearing completely if it is not protected.

EXERCISE 20 ABOUT YOU Ask a question with "*Are there . . . ?*" and the words given about another student's hometown. The other student will answer with an expression of quantity. Practice count nouns.

EXAMPLE museums

A: Are there any museums in your hometown?
B: Yes. There are a lot of (a few, three) museums in my hometown.
OR
No. There aren't any museums in my hometown.

1. department stores
2. churches
3. synagogues
4. skyscrapers
5. supermarkets
6. open markets
7. hospitals
8. universities
9. mosques
10. bridges

EXERCISE 21 ABOUT YOU Ask a question with "*Are there any . . . ?*" or "*Are there many . . . ?*" and the words given about another student's native country. The other student will answer with an expression of quantity. Practice count nouns.

EXAMPLE single mothers

A: Are there many single mothers in your country?
B: There are very few.

1. homeless people
2. working women
3. fast-food restaurants
4. factories
5. American businesses
6. nursing homes
7. rich people
8. good universities

EXERCISE 22 ABOUT YOU Ask a question with "*Is there . . . ?*" and the words given about another student's native country or hometown. The other student will answer with an expression of quantity. Practice noncount nouns.

EXAMPLE petroleum / in your native country

A: Is there much petroleum in your native country?
B: Yes. There's lot of petroleum in my native country.
OR
No. There isn't much petroleum in my native country.

In Your Native Country

1. petroleum
2. industry
3. agriculture
4. tourism

In Your Hometown

5. traffic
6. rain
7. pollution
8. noise

Singular and Plural; Count and Noncount Nouns; *There + Be*; Quantity Words

EXERCISE 23 ABOUT YOU Ask a student a question with "*Do you have . . . ?*" and the words given. The other student will answer. Practice both count and noncount nouns.

EXAMPLES American friends

A: Do you have any American friends?
B: Yes. I have many (OR a lot of) American friends.
   OR
   No. I don't have many American friends.

free time

A: Do you have a lot of free time?
B: Yes. I have some free time.
   OR
   No. I have very little free time.

1. problems in the U.S.
2. American friends
3. relatives in New York
4. time to relax
5. brothers and sisters (siblings)
6. experience with small children
7. questions about American customs
8. trouble with English pronunciation
9. information about points of interest in this city
10. knowledge about computer programming

EXERCISE 24 Cross out the phrase that doesn't fit and fill in the blanks with an expression of quantity to make a **true** statement about another country you know about. Discuss your answers.

EXAMPLE There's / There isn't ____*much*____ unemployment in ____*Korea*____.

1. There's / There isn't _____ opportunity to make money in _____.

2. There are / There aren't _____ divorced people in _____.

3. There are / There aren't _____ foreigners in _____.

4. There's / There isn't _____ freedom in _____.

5. There are / There aren't _____ American cars in _____.

6. There are / There aren't _____ political problems in _____.

7. There is / There isn't _____ unemployment in _____.

8. There is / There isn't _____ crime in _____.

SUMMARY OF LESSON 5

1. Study the words that are used before count and noncount nouns.

Singular Count	Plural Count	Noncount
a tomato	some tomatoes	some coffee
no tomato	no tomatoes	no coffee
	any tomatoes (with questions and negatives)	any coffee
	a lot of tomatoes	a lot of coffee
	many tomatoes	much coffee (with questions and negatives)
	a few tomatoes	a little coffee
	several tomatoes	
	How many tomatoes?	How much coffee?

2. Sentences with *There*
   Count
   > **There's** an onion in the recipe.
   > **There are** two carrots in the recipe.

   Noncount
   > **There's** some butter in the recipe.
   > How much salt **is there** in the recipe?

3. *Too Much / Too Many / A Lot Of*
   - *A lot of* + count or noncount noun (no problem is presented)
      She's a healthy woman. She gets **a lot of** exercise.
      She walks **a lot of** miles.
   - *Too much* + noncount noun (a problem is presented)
      She doesn't qualify for financial aid because her parents make **too much** money.
   - *Too many* + count noun (a problem is presented)
      There are **too many** students in the class. The teacher doesn't have time to help everyone.

EDITING ADVICE

1. Some plural forms are irregular and don't take -s.

    She has two ~~childrens~~.

2. Use a singular noun and verb after *every*.

    Every ~~children~~ need love. (child, needs)

3. Use the plural form of the noun after *one of*.

    One of my sister*s* is a lawyer.

4. Don't use *a* or *an* before a plural noun.

    She bought ~~a~~ (some) new socks.

5. Don't put *a* or *an* before a noncount noun.

    I want to give you ~~an~~ advice. (some OR a piece of)

6. A noncount noun is always singular.

    I have ~~many~~ (a lot of) homeworks to do.

    She bought three (pieces of) furnitures.

7. Use *there* to introduce a noun.

    ~~Are~~ (There are a) lot of people in China.

8. Be careful with *there* and *they're*. They sound the same.

    ~~They're~~ (There) are many problems in the world.

9. Don't use a specific noun after *there*.

    ~~There's~~ (T)he Golden Gate bridge (is) in San Francisco.

10. Include *of* with a unit of measure.

    He bought three rolls (of) film.

11. Omit *of* after *a lot* when the noun is omitted.

    I have a lot of time, but my brother doesn't have a lot ~~of~~.

180   Lesson 5

12. Use *a little / a few* for a positive meaning. Use *little / few* for a negative meaning.

            (very)
  He can't help you because he has a little time.

13. Don't use *too much* or *too many* if the quantity doesn't present a problem.

         a lot of
  He's a lucky man. He has ~~too many~~ friends.

14. Don't use a double negative.

       any
  He doesn't have ~~no~~ money. OR
    He has no money.

LESSON 5 TEST/REVIEW

PART 1 Find the mistakes with the underlined words, and correct them. Not every sentence has a mistake. If the sentence is correct, write *C*.

      much
EXAMPLES How ~~many~~ milks did you drink?

  How <u>much</u> time do you have? **C**

1. He doesn't have <u>no</u> job.
2. One of my <u>friend</u> moved to Montana.
3. I can't go out tonight because I have <u>too much</u> work.
4. Three <u>womens</u> came into the room.
5. I had a lot of friends in my country, but in the U.S. I don't have <u>a lot of</u>.
6. <u>A lot of American</u> own a computer.
7. A person can be happy if he has <u>a few</u> good friends.
8. I have <u>much</u> information about my country.
9. Every <u>workers</u> in the U.S. pays taxes.
10. Are there <u>any</u> mistakes in this sentence?
11. My mother gave me a lot of <u>advices</u>.
12. You need <u>a luck</u> to win the lottery.
13. There's <u>the White House</u> in Washington, D.C.
14. I can help you on Saturday because I'll have <u>too much</u> time.
15. <u>Are</u> a lot of students in the cafeteria, and I can't find a seat.

Singular and Plural; Count and Noncount Nouns; *There + Be*; Quantity Words **181**

16. A few of my <u>teacher</u> speak English very fast.
17. Did you buy <u>a new furniture</u> for your apartment?
18. Some <u>man</u> are very polite.
19. I have <u>many</u> problems with my landlord.
20. Did you have <u>much fun</u> at the party?
21. I have <u>a</u> new dishes in my kitchen.
22. Several <u>students</u> in this class speak French.
23. I have a dog. I don't have <u>any</u> cat.
24. <u>Many</u> people like to travel.
25. He doesn't need <u>any</u> help from you.
26. I have a <u>little</u> time. I can help you.
27. I have a <u>little</u> time. I can't help you.
28. He bought three <u>pounds meat.</u>
29. How <u>much</u> apples did you eat?
30. How many <u>cup of coffees</u> did you drink?
31. <u>They're are</u> four Mexican students in the class.
32. I want to give you <u>an</u> advice about your education.

PART 2 Fill in the blanks with the singular or plural form of the word in parentheses ( ).

EXAMPLE The Pilgrims didn't have a lot of _____*experience*_____ with
(experience)

American land.

1. The Indians had many _____ with white
(war)

_____ over their lands.
(person)

2. Some _____ have a big problem with
(reservation)

_____ and _____. There aren't
(unemployment)   (poverty)

enough _____ for everyone.
(job)

3. My father gave me a lot of _____. He told me that
(advice)

there are more _____ in big _____
(job)   (city)

than on reservations.

182 Lesson 5

4. We like to visit the art museum. We like to see the _____ (sculpture)

   and _____ (painting) by famous _____ (artist).

   We like all kinds of _____ (art).

5. My brother likes all kinds of _____ (music). He has a large

   collection of _____ (CD) and _____ (tape).

PART 3 Fill in the blanks with an appropriate measurement of quantity. In some cases, several answers are possible.

EXAMPLE I bought a ___*loaf*___ of bread.

1. I drank a _____ of tea.
2. She drank a _____ of milk.
3. I usually put a _____ of sugar in my coffee.
4. There's a _____ of milk in the refrigerator.
5. I'm going to buy a _____ of furniture for my living room.
6. The teacher gave a long homework _____.
7. My father gave me an important _____ of advice.
8. I took three _____ of film on my vacation.
9. I need a _____ of paper to write my composition.
10. We need to buy a _____ of soap.

PART 4 Read this composition by an American Indian. Circle the correct words to complete the composition.

My name is Joseph Falling Snow. I'm (*an*, *a*, *any*) Native American from a Sioux[13] reservation in South Dakota. I don't live in South Dakota anymore because I couldn't find (*a*, *any*, *no*) job. There's (*a little*, *a few*, *very little*, *very few*) work on my reservation. There's (*much*, *a lot of*, *many*) poverty. My uncle gave me (*a*, *an*, *some*, *any*) good advice. He told me to go to Minneapolis to find (*a*, *an*, *some*) job. Minneapolis is a big city, so there are (*much*, *many*, *any*) job opportunities there. It was easy for me to find a job as a carpenter. I had (*no*, *not*, *any*) trouble finding a job because I have (*a lot of*, *many*, *much*) experience.

My native language is Lakota, but I know (*any*, *a few*, *very few*) words in my language. Most of the people on my reservation speak English. (*A few*, *Any*, *A little*) older people still speak Lakota, but the language is dying out as the older people die.

(*A few*, *A little*, *Few*, *Little*) times a year, I go back to the reservation for a Pow-Wow. We wear our native costumes and dance our native dances. It gets very crowded at these times because (*much*, *any*, *a lot of*) people from our reservation and nearby reservations attend this celebration. We have (*much*, *many*, *a lot of*) fun.

[13] *Sioux* is pronounced /su/.

EXPANSION ACTIVITIES

Classroom Activities

1. Work with a partner. Imagine that you have to spend a few weeks alone on a deserted island. You can take 15 things with you. What will you need to survive? Give reasons for each item.

    EXAMPLE I'll take a lot of water because I can't drink ocean water. It has salt in it.

2. Game: Where am I? Teacher: Write these words on separate index cards: *at the airport, downtown, at the library, at a supermarket, at a department store, on the highway, at the zoo, at church, at the beach, at home, on an elevator, on a bus, on an airplane, at the post office,* and *in the school cafeteria*. Students: One student picks an index card with a place name and says, "Where am I?" Other students have to guess where he / she is by asking questions.

    EXAMPLES Are you indoors or outdoors?
    Are there a lot of cars in this place?
    Is it noisy in this place?
    Are there a lot of people in this place?

3. Find a partner. Take something from your purse, pocket, book bag, or backpack. Say, "I have _____ with me." Then ask your partner if he or she has this. If you're not sure if the item is a count or noncount noun, ask the teacher.

    EXAMPLES I have a comb in my pocket. Do you have a comb in your pocket?
    I have some makeup in my purse. Do you have any makeup in your purse?
    I have some money from my country in my pocket. Do you have any money from your country?

Talk About it

Read the following quotes and discuss what they mean to you.

1. "Once I was in a big city and I saw a very large house. They told me it was a bank and that the white men place their money there to be taken care of, and that by and by they got it back with interest. We are Indians and we have no such bank. When we have plenty of money or blankets, we give them away to other chiefs and people, and by and by they return them with interest, and our hearts feel good. Our way of giving is our bank."

    —Chief Maquinna, Nootka tribe

2. "Treat the Earth well. It was not given to you by your parents; it was loaned to you by your children."

3. "Today is a time of celebrating for you—a time of looking back to the first days of white people in America. But it is not a time of celebrating for me. It is with a heavy heart that I look back upon what happened to my people. When the Pilgrims arrived, we, the Wampanoags, welcomed them with open arms, little knowing that it was the beginning of the end. . . . Let us always remember, the Indian is and was just as human as the white people."
From a speech by a Wampanoag Indian given on Thanksgiving in 1970 in Massachusetts, at the 350th anniversary of the Pilgrim's arrival in America.

Write About it

1. Write about an ethnic minority in your native country or another country you know about. Where and how do they live? Use expressions of quantity.

2. Write a paragraph telling about the advantages or disadvantages of living in this city. You may write about pollution, job opportunities, weather, traffic, transportation, and crime. Use expressions of quantity.

Outside Activity

Rent one of the following movies and write a summary of the movie: *Smoke Signals*, *Windtalkers*, or *Dances with Wolves*.

Internet Activities

1. Search for American Indian Web sites. Find the names and locations of three tribes.

2. Search for more information about the Pilgrims. Why did they leave England? Where did they go before coming to America?

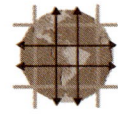

Additional Activities at http://elt.heinle.com/gic

LESSON 6

GRAMMAR
Adjectives
Noun Modifiers
Adverbs
Too / Enough / Very / A Lot Of

CONTEXT: Health
Obesity: A National Problem
Obesity: The Solution
Sleep

OBESITY: A NATIONAL PROBLEM

Before You Read

1. Do you ever eat at fast-food restaurants?
2. What kind of food commercials do you see on TV?

Read the following article.
Pay special attention to adjectives and noun modifiers.

Everyone knows that it's important to eat well and get **enough** exercise. We see **beautiful, thin** fashion models and want to look like them. We see commercials for **exercise** machines on TV showing **fit, thin, smiling** people exercising. **Health** clubs are full of people trying to get in shape. Sales of **diet** colas and low-calorie and low-carbohydrate foods indicate that Americans want to be **thin.** However, two-thirds of **American** adults are **overweight,** and one in six American children is overweight. This is a **large** increase in the **last** 20 years, when 50 percent of adults and only five percent of children were **overweight.**

Fifty-eight percent of Americans are **concerned** about their weight. They spend billions of dollars on **weight-loss** products and **health** clubs. But weight is also becoming a **national** problem as **health** costs go up in response to diseases related to obesity: **heart** disease, **high blood** pressure, diabetes, arthritis, and stroke.

What is the reason for this **growing** problem? First, **today's** lifestyle does not include enough **physical** activity. When the U.S. was an **agricultural** society, farmers ate a **big, heavy** meal, but they burned off the calories by doing **hard physical** labor. **Modern** technology has removed **physical** activity from our **daily** lives. Seventy-five percent of all trips are less than a mile from home, but Americans drive. Only 17 percent of **school** children walk to school even though most of them live within one mile of school. And the **average American** child spends 24 hours a week watching TV. In most **physical education** classes, kids are **active** for just three minutes.

Another reason for the **weight** problem is the **American** diet. The **average** child sees more than 10,000 **food** commercials a year. Most of these are for high-calorie foods, such as **sweetened** cereals, **sugary** soft drinks, **salty**

EXERCISE 1 Fill in the blanks with an appropriate word. Answers may vary.

EXAMPLE Burgers and fries are _____high_____ in calories.

1. Fries are cooked in oil. They are very _____.
2. I ate a terrible meal and I got _____.
3. Do you want a large cola or a small _____?
4. She's very _____ about her children's health because they prefer candy to fruit.
5. I didn't sleep at all last night. I'm very _____ today.
6. Have a piece of fresh apple pie. I just had a piece. It _____ good.
7. Potato chips are very _____.
8. Ice cream is _____ in calories.
9. Most Americans have _____ lives and don't make the time to eat well.
10. Obesity in the U.S. is a _____ problem. It is a much bigger problem today than it was 20 years ago.

EXERCISE 2 Circle the correct words in *italics* to complete this conversation.

A husband (H) and wife (W) are discussing weight.

H: We're gaining weight. We used to be *(thin)/ thins*, but when we got
(example)
marry / married, we started to gain weight.
(1)

W: Let's go jogging after work. There's a *beautiful park / park beautiful*
(2)
where we can go. It's *locate / located* just a few blocks away from our
(3)
apartment.

H: But after work I'm always too *tire / tired*. I just want to eat dinner
(4)
and watch TV.

W: It's not good to eat a big meal so late at night. I know that's what most Americans do, but in other countries people eat a big meal

during the day and *a small one / a small* at night.
(5)

H: What difference does it make?

W: If we eat a big meal in the middle of the day, we have the rest of the day to burn off the calories.

H: I'm sure that's *an idea very good / a very good idea* but I don't have
(6)
time to eat a big meal in the middle of the day. My lunch break is
kind / kind of short.
(7)

W: We should cook more at home. We're always eating out in
expensive / expensives restaurants that have *fatty / fattied* foods.
(8) (9)

H: Maybe doctors will find a pill that will make us thin with no effort.

W: You know what they say, "No pain, no gain." It takes a lot of effort to lose weight.

6.2 | Noun Modifiers

Examples	Explanation
Do you have an **exercise machine**? A **farm worker** gets a lot of exercise. Some people eat at a **fast-food restaurant**. I joined a **health club**.	A noun can modify (describe) another noun. The second noun is more general than the first. An *exercise machine* is a machine. A *leg exercise* is an exercise.
I bought new **running** shoes. Do you ever use the **swimming** pool?	Sometimes a gerund describes a noun. It shows the purpose of the noun.
My **five-year-old** son prefers candy to fruit. **Potato** chips have a lot of grease. I can't read the small print on this box. I need my **eye**glasses.	The first noun is always singular. A five-**year**-old son is a son who is five **years** old. **Potato** chips are chips made from **potatoes**. **Eye**glasses are glasses for **eyes**.
Do you have your **driver's** license? I can't understand the **owner's** manual for my new DVD player. **Today's** lifestyle doesn't include much physical activity.	Sometimes a possessive form describes a noun.

Pronunciation Note:
When a noun describes a noun, the first noun usually receives the greater emphasis in speaking.
    I wear my **running** shoes when I go to the **health** club and use the **exercise** machines.

EXERCISE 3 Find the noun modifiers in the article on pages 188–189. Underline them.

EXERCISE 4 A mother (M) and son (S) are shopping at a big supermarket. Fill in the blanks by putting the nouns in parentheses ( ) in the correct order. Remember to use the singular form for the first noun.

S: What are we going to buy today? Just a few things?

M: No. We need a lot. Let's take a ___*shopping cart*___.
(example: cart/shopping)

S: Can I sit in the _____?
(1 child/seat)

M: You're much too big. You're a six- _____ -old boy.
(2 year/years)

S: Mom, buy me that cereal. It looks good. I saw it on a _____.
(3 commercial/TV)

M: Let's read the ingredients on the _____ first. I want to see the _____ before we buy it. Let me put on my _____. Oh, dear. This cereal has 20 grams of sugar.
(4 cereal/box)
(5 content/sugar)
(6 glasses/eyes)

S: But I like sugar, Mom.

M: You know it causes _____. Remember what the dentist told you?
(7 teeth/decay)

S: But I brush my teeth once a day.

M: I want you to use your _____ after every meal, not just once a day.
(8 teeth/brush)

S: Mom, can we buy those _____?
(9 chips/potatoes)

M: They have too much fat.

S: How about some soda?

M: You should drink more juice. How about some _____?
(10 juice/oranges)

S: I don't like juice.

M: It seems you don't like anything that's good for you. Maybe we should shop at the _____ store next time.
(11 food/health)

S: Oh, Mom, you're no fun.

M: Let's get in the _____ and pay now.
(12 line/check-out)

Adjectives; Noun Modifiers; Adverbs; *Too/Enough/Very/A Lot Of* **193**

OBESITY: THE SOLUTION

Before You Read

1. Where and when do you eat your big meal of the day?
2. When you see commercials for food on TV, do you want to buy that food?

 Read the following article. Pay special attention to adverbs.

Millions of Americans are overweight. Health experts agree that the problem comes from a combination of things: the kind of food we eat, our lifestyle, and even technology. Experts have the following recommendations for living a healthier lifestyle.

1. Get active. Ride a bike or walk places instead of driving. Cars and other machines **greatly** reduce the need for physical activity. We can move from place to place **easily** and **quickly** and work **efficiently** without using much physical energy.
2. Eat a **well**-balanced meal, consisting of protein, grains, vegetables, and fruit. Unfortunately, many people often eat alone and **quickly.** Some even just eat snacks all day. Nutritionists recommend that families eat together like they used to. As they eat their big meal together **slowly,** they can discuss the events of their day and enjoy each other's company.
3. Take the soft drink and snack machines out of the schools and educate children **early** about nutrition and exercise. The typical teenager gets about 10 to 15 percent of his or her calories from soft drinks, which have no nutrition at all. Replace the food in the machines with water, juices, and healthy snacks such as raisins.

4. Be careful of the food messages you hear from advertisers that say, "Eat this. Buy that." Technology allows advertisers to send us messages **constantly** through commercials. Many of these foods are high in fat and calories. Choose natural foods, such as fruits and nuts, instead of manufactured foods.

In addition to what individuals can do, communities need to build their housing more **carefully.** In many communities in the U.S., it is hard to walk from place to place **easily** because there are no sidewalks. If we want people to get exercise in their communities, they need sidewalks and bike paths with stores and activities within walking distance.

Can you think of any other ways to solve the problem of obesity?

6.3 Adverbs of Manner

An adverb of manner tells *how* or *in what way* a person does something.

Examples	Explanation
Subject / **Verb Phrase** / **Adverb** He / does his job / **efficiently.** They / ate lunch / **quickly.** We / walk together / **slowly.**	We form most adverbs of manner by putting -*ly*[1] at the end of an adjective. An adverb usually follows the verb phrase.
Cars **greatly** reduce the need for physical activity. We **constantly** see ads on TV for food.	The -*ly* adverb of manner can come before the verb. This position is more formal.
Do you eat **well**?	The adverb for *good* is *well*.
You should eat a **well**-balanced meal. We live in a **carefully** planned community.	An adverb can come before an adjective.
ADJ: He is a **hard** worker. ADV: He works **hard.** ADJ: He wants a **fast** meal. ADV: Don't eat so **fast.** ADJ: He has an **early** class. ADV: We need to educate our children **early.** ADJ: I have a **late** class. ADV: I get home **late.**	Some adjectives and adverbs have the same form: *hard, fast, early,* and *late*.
She worked **hard** to prepare a good meal, but her son **hardly** ate anything.	*Hard* and *hardly* are both adverbs, but they have completely different meanings. *She worked **hard*** means she put a lot of effort into the work. *He **hardly** ate anything* means he ate almost nothing.
He came home **late** and missed dinner. **Lately,** he doesn't have time to eat a good meal.	*Late* and *lately* are both adverbs, but they have completely different meanings. *Late* means not on time. *Lately* means recently.
Compare: She is a **friendly** person. She behaves **in a friendly manner.** He is a **lively** person. He dances **in a lively way.**	Some adjectives end in -*ly*: *lovely, lonely, early, friendly, lively, ugly*. They have no adverb form. We use an adverbial phrase (*in a ___-ly way*) to describe the action.
He loses weight **very** easily. She cooks **extremely** well. He eats **so** fast. She exercises **real** hard. You eat **quite** slowly.	*Very, extremely, so, real,* and *quite* can come before an adverb.

[1] For the spelling of -*ly* adverbs, see Appendix C.

EXERCISE 5 Fill in the blanks with an adverb from the box below (or choose your own adverb). Several answers may be possible.

| cheaply | differently | constantly | poorly |
| briskly ✓ | regularly | quickly | well |

EXAMPLE If you walk ___briskly___ every day, you can lose weight.

1. TV gives us messages _____, telling us to buy, buy, buy more food.

2. Do you eat _____ or slowly?

3. You should exercise _____ if you want to lose weight.

4. If you eat _____, you will not be healthy and strong.

5. If you eat _____, you will have no need to snack between meals.

6. In a fast-food restaurant, a family can eat _____. In another kind of restaurant, they have to spend a lot of money.

7. Some immigrants eat _____ when they come to the U.S. because they can't find food from their native countries.

EXERCISE 6 ABOUT YOU Write the adverb form of the word in parentheses ( ). Then check (✓) the activities that you do in this way. Make statements telling how you do these activities.

EXAMPLES ✓ shop ___carefully___
(careful)

I shop carefully. I always try to buy healthy food for my family.

___ dance ___well___
(good)

I don't dance well. I never learned.

1. ___ answer every question _____
(honest)

2. ___ drive _____
(fast)

3. ___ cook _____
(good)

4. ___ talk _____
(constant)

5. ___ work _____
(hard)

Adjectives; Noun Modifiers; Adverbs; *Too/Enough/Very/A Lot Of*

6. ___ study _____
   (hard)

7. ___ speak Spanish _____
   (fluent)

8. ___ type _____
   (fast)

9. ___ type _____
   (accurate)

10. ___ choose my food _____
    (careful)

6.4 | Adjective vs. Adverb

\	\
An adjective describes a noun. An adverb describes a verb (phrase).	
Examples	**Explanation**
Jim is **serious** about good health. He takes his doctor's advice **seriously**.	*Serious* is an adjective. It describes Jim. *Seriously* is an adverb. It tells how he takes his doctor's advice.
a. Your composition looks **good**. b. The teacher is looking at it **carefully**. a. The soup tastes **delicious**. b. I tasted the soup **slowly** because it was hot.	a. Use an adjective, not an adverb, after the following verbs if you are describing the subject: *smell, sound, taste, look, seem, appear,* and *feel*. b. Use an adverb if you are telling *how* the action (the verb phrase) is done.
a. The children got **hungry**. b. They ate lunch **hungrily**.	Use an adjective, not an adverb, in expressions with *get*: get hungry, get tired, get sick, get rich, etc. a. *Hungry* describes the children. b. *Hungrily* describes how they ate lunch.

Her health is **absolutely** perfect.
The refrigerator is **completely** empty.
You should eat a **well**-balanced diet.
	An adverb can come before an adjective in phrases such as these:
	  completely right extremely important
	  pleasantly surprised well-known
	  perfectly clear absolutely wrong

He's sick. He doesn't feel **well** today.	For health, use *well*. In conversational English, people often use *good* for health. He's sick. He doesn't feel **good** today.
Compare: **As usual,** she cooked the dinner. Her husband **usually** cooks on Saturday.	Use the adjective, not the adverb, in the expression *as usual*.

198   Lesson 6

EXERCISE 7 Fill in the blanks with the correct form of the adjective or adverb in parentheses ( ).

Last week I was invited to a "potluck" dinner at my math teacher's house. This is my first month in the U.S., so I didn't know what that was. A ___good___ friend of mine told me that this is a dinner
(example: good)
where each person brings some food. I wanted to make a _____
(1 good)
impression, so I prepared my _____ dish from Mexico. I
(2 favorite)
worked _____ hard to make it look and taste _____.
(3 extreme)   (4 good)
Most of the people at the dinner looked at my dish _____.
(5 strange)
They didn't know what it was. They thought _____ that
(6 foolish)
Mexicans just eat tacos. They tasted my food _____, thinking
(7 careful)
that Mexicans make everything very hot and spicy. But I didn't. I know that some people don't like _____ food, so I put the hot sauce
(8 spicy)
on the side.

A student from India brought Indian food. I was _____ to
(9 surprised)
find out how hot Indian food is. The taste was very _____ to
(10 strange)
me, but I ate it anyway.

The party was great. I went home very _____. I had to get
(11 late)
up early the next morning, so I _____ slept at all that night.
(12 hard)

SLEEP

Before You Read

1. How many hours do you sleep a night?
2. How many hours would you like to sleep a night?

 Read the following article. Pay special attention to *too, enough, a lot of,* and *very*.

Did You Know?

Albert Einstein said he needed 10 hours of sleep a night to function well.

Most people need eight hours of sleep but don't get **enough.** Most Americans get less than seven hours a night. Only 35 percent get **enough sleep.** When people aren't rested **enough,** there are bad results. For example, if people drive when they're **too tired,** they can cause serious accidents on the road. According to the National Transportation Administration, sleepy drivers cause 100,000 accidents each year. There are many work-related accidents too. But that's not all. If you stay awake **too long,** your mind and nervous system begin to malfunction[2]. In the long term, if you don't get **enough sleep,** you will have less resistance to infection and disease.

Are we **too busy** to get enough sleep? Not always. Besides job and family responsibilities, Americans have **a lot of** other things that keep them out of bed. Twenty-four-hour-a-day Internet and TV keep us awake. Supermarkets, shopping malls, and laundromats are open late.

A lot of Americans report having trouble sleeping a few nights per week. About two-thirds complain to doctors about not getting **enough sleep.** Maybe they have **too much** stress in their lives or don't have good sleep habits. Sleep experts have some recommendations:

- Don't nap during the day.
- Don't get **too stimulated** before going to bed. Avoid activities such as watching TV or eating before bed.
- Go to bed at the same time every night.
- Avoid caffeine after lunchtime. If you drink **too much** coffee during the day, don't expect to get a good night's sleep.
- Exercise. Physical activity is **very** good for sleep. But if you exercise **too late** in the day, it will interfere with your sleep.

A good night's sleep is **very** important, so turn off the TV, shut down the computer, and sleep well.

[2] *To malfunction* means to function, or work, poorly.

6.5 | Too and Enough

Too indicates a problem. The problem is stated or implied. *Enough* means sufficient.

Examples	Explanation
adjective I'm **too tired** to drive. **adverb** She drove **too fast** and got a ticket.	Put *too* **before** adjectives and adverbs.
noncount noun a. Children eat **too much food** that is high in calories. **count noun** b. You spend **too many hours** watching TV. c. He doesn't sleep well because he worries **too much**.	a. Use *too much* before a noncount noun. b. Use *too many* before a count noun. c. *Too much* can come at the end of the verb phrase.
adjective Five hours of sleep is not **good enough**. **adverb** I walked **quickly enough** to raise my heart rate.	Put *enough* **after** adjectives and adverbs.
noun Some children don't get **enough exercise**. **noun** I don't have **enough time** to exercise.	Put *enough* **before** nouns.

Language Notes:
1. An infinitive phrase can follow a phrase with *too* and *enough*.
   He's **too young to understand** that candy isn't good for you.
   I don't have **enough money to join** a health club.
2. *Too good to be true* shows a positive, surprised reaction.
   I just won a million dollars. It's **too good to be true.**

EXERCISE 8 Fill in the blanks to complete these statements. Answers may vary.

EXAMPLES Are Americans too ___*busy*___ to get a good night's sleep?

Some people don't get enough ___*exercise*___, so they're overweight.

1. It's hard to sleep if you exercise too _____ in the afternoon.
2. If you're too _____ when you drive, you can fall asleep at the wheel.

Adjectives; Noun Modifiers; Adverbs; *Too/Enough/Very/A Lot Of*

3. Some people spend too much _____ on the Internet. They should shut down the computer and go to bed.

4. If you drink too much _____, it can affect your sleep.

5. People drive everywhere. They don't _____ enough.

6. When children eat too _____, they get fat.

7. Children shouldn't drink so much soda because it contains too many _____.

8. Most Americans don't get enough _____.

9. Many people say, "I don't have enough _____ to do all the things I need to do."

10. It's never too _____ to change your bad habits.

11. His clothes don't fit him anymore because he got too _____.

EXERCISE 9 ABOUT YOU Complete each statement with an infinitive.

EXAMPLES I'm too young *to retire.*

I'm not strong enough *to move a piano.*

1. I'm not too old _____
2. I'm too young _____
3. I don't have enough money _____
4. I don't have enough time _____
5. I don't speak English well enough _____

EXERCISE 10 A person is complaining about the school cafeteria. Fill in the blanks with *too, too much,* or *too many.*

EXAMPLE It's _____*too*_____ noisy, so I can't talk with my friends.

1. They serve _____ junk food there.
2. The fries have _____ grease.
3. The hamburgers have _____ calories.
4. The food is _____ expensive.
5. The tables are _____ dirty.
6. There are _____ people there, and sometimes there's no place to sit.

6.6 Too and Very and A Lot Of

Examples	Explanation
a. I'm **too** tired to drive. Would you drive for a while? b. I was **very** tired, but I stayed up late and studied for my test. a. The speed limit on the highway is 55, and you're driving 40. You're driving **too** slowly. b. The speed limit on this road is 15 miles per hour. You need to drive **very** slowly. a. My brother is 14 years old. He's **too** old to get into the movie theater at half price. b. My grandmother is 85. She's **very** old, but she's in great health.	Don't confuse *very* and *too*. *Too* always indicates a problem in a specific situation. The problem can be stated or implied. *Very* is a neutral word. In examples (a), *too* shows a problem in a specific situation. In examples (b), *very* does not show any problem.
a. You put **too much** salt in the soup, and I can't eat it. b. She puts **a lot of** sugar in her coffee. She likes it that way. a. I ate **too many** cookies, and now I feel sick. b. She baked **a lot of cookies** for the party. Everyone enjoyed them.	Don't confuse *a lot of* and *too much/too many*. a. *Too* always indicates a problem in a specific situation. b. *A lot of* is a neutral expression.

EXERCISE 11 Fill in the blanks with *too, too much, too many, a lot of,* or *very*.

A: Your dinner was ____*very*____ delicious tonight.
   (example)

B: I'm _____ glad you liked it.
   (1)

A: Everything was great. But the soup had _____ salt.
   (2)

B: Oh. I thought you liked everything.

A: I did. Other than the salt, it was good. And I especially liked the potatoes.

B: I'm glad.

A: But you put a little _____ butter in the potatoes.
   (3)

   They were _____ greasy.
   (4)

B: Oh.

A: But don't worry. I ate them anyway.

Adjectives; Noun Modifiers; Adverbs; *Too/Enough/Very/A Lot Of*

B: I'm afraid the steak was burned. I left it in the oven _____(5)_____ long.

A: Well, no one's perfect. I ate it anyway.

B: What about the cake I made? Did you like that?

A: Yes. It was _____(6)_____ good. The only problem was it was _____(7)_____ small. I was hoping to have another piece, but there was nothing left.

B: I thought you wanted to lose weight. You always say you're _____(8)_____ fat and need to go on a diet.

A: Fat? I'm not fat.

B: But you can't wear your old pants anymore.

A: I'm not _____(9)_____ fat. My clothes are _____(10)_____ small. When I washed them, the water I used was _____(11)_____ hot and they shrank.

B: They didn't shrink. You gained weight.

SUMMARY OF LESSON 6

1. Adjectives and Adverbs

ADJECTIVES	ADVERBS
We had a **quick** lunch.	We ate **quickly**.
We had a **late** dinner.	We ate **late**.
She is a **good** cook.	She cooks **well**.
She looks **serious**.	She is looking at the label **seriously**.
As usual, he drank a cup of coffee.	He **usually** drinks coffee in the morning.

2. Adjective Modifiers and Noun Modifiers

ADJECTIVE MODIFIER	NOUN MODIFIER
a **new** machine	an **exercise** machine
old shoes	**running** shoes
a **short** vacation	a **two-week** vacation
a **valid** license	a **driver's** license

3. **Very / Too / Enough / Too Much / Too Many**
   He's **very** healthy.
   He's **too** young to retire.
   I'm relaxed **enough** to drive.
   I had **enough** sleep last night.
   She doesn't eat ice cream because it has **too much** fat.
   She doesn't eat ice cream because it has **too many** calories.
   He loves coffee, but when he drinks **too much,** he can't sleep.

EDITING ADVICE

1. Adjectives are always singular.

   I had two important~~s~~ meetings last week.

2. Certain adjectives end with *-ed*.

   He was tire*d* after his trip.

3. Put an adjective before the noun.

   She is a ~~girl very intelligent~~ *very intelligent girl*.

4. Use *one(s)* after an adjective to take the place of a noun.

   He has an old dictionary. She has a new *one*.

5. Put a specific noun before a general noun.

   She made a ~~call phone~~ *phone call*.

6. A noun modifier is always singular.

   She took a three-week~~s~~ vacation.

7. An adverb describes a verb. An adjective describes a noun.

   The teacher speaks English fluent*ly*.

   The teacher looks serious~~ly~~.

8. Don't put the *-ly* adverb between the verb and the object.

   He opened (carefully) the envelope.

9. Adverbs of manner that don't end in *-ly* follow the verb phrase.

    He ~~late~~ came home. *(late circled with arrow to after "home")*

10. *Too* indicates a problem. If there is no problem, use *very*.

                    very
    Your father is ~~too~~ intelligent.

11. *Too much / too many* is followed by a noun. *Too* is followed by an adjective or adverb.

    She's too ~~much~~ old to take care of herself.

12. Put *enough* after the adjective.

            old enough
    He's ~~enough old~~ to get married.

13. Don't use *very* before a verb.

                very much
    He ~~very~~ likes his job.

14. Don't confuse *hard* and *hardly*.

    I'm tired. I worked hard~~ly~~ all day.

15. Don't use *too much / too many* when there is no problem.

                                  a lot of
    I love juice. Every day I drink ~~too much~~ juice.

LESSON 6 TEST/REVIEW

PART 1 Find the mistakes with the underlined words, and correct them. Not every sentence has a mistake. If the sentence is correct, write *C*.

                                                  license
EXAMPLES When did you get your ~~license~~ driver's?

He <u>gets up early</u> and walks the dog. **C**

1. Do you know where I can find the <u>shoes</u> department in this store?
2. She doesn't feel <u>well</u> today.
3. The <u>language English</u> is very different from my language.
4. I'm very <u>tire</u> because I worked <u>hard</u> all week.
5. Your answer seems <u>wrongly</u>.
6. My grandfather is <u>too much</u> old to work.
7. I don't like red apples. I like <u>yellows</u> ones.

8. The singer's voice sounds sweet.
9. I wrote carefully my name.
10. She bought a car very expensive.
11. I'm too happy to meet you.
12. He stayed in the library late to finish his class project.
13. She looked beautiful when she got marry.
14. You speak English very fluently.
15. He's not old enough to work.
16. I like your new shoes very much.
17. I made too much food for the party, and everyone had enough to eat.
18. He hardly speaks a word of English. He just came to the U.S.
19. She's going to take her driving test. She looks nervously.
20. I'm completely surprised by the news of your marriage.
21. I very like your new apartment.
22. If you spend too much time in front of the TV, you'll get fat.
23. You have too many friends. You're a lucky person.

PART 2 Fill in the blanks with the correct form, adjective or adverb, of the word in parentheses ( ).

EXAMPLES She has ___*clear*___ pronunciation.
(clear)

She pronounces very ___*clearly*___.
(clear)

1. You need to find time to eat _____. Don't eat food that
(good)

   is _____ for you.
   (bad)

2. Don't drive _____. It's important to arrive _____.
(fast) (safe)

3. I can't understand you. Could you speak more _____,
(slow)

   please?

4. Some people learn languages _____.
(easy)

5. Some people think that math is _____, but it's
(hard)

   _____ for me.
   (easy)

Adjectives; Noun Modifiers; Adverbs; *Too/Enough/Very/A Lot Of*

6. As _____ (usual), we will have a test at the end of the lesson.

7. She spoke _____ (soft), and I couldn't hear her _____ (good).

8. I need to learn English _____ (quick).

9. Do you exercise _____ (regular), or are you _____ (lazy)?

10. You seem _____ (tired) today.

11. I'm very _____ (busy).

12. She works very _____ (hard), but she's _____ (happy) with her job.

13. She is a _____ (lovely) woman. She's very _____ (friendly).

14. John sounds _____ (angry), but he's not angry. He just talks _____ (loud).

15. You speak English _____ (extreme) well. You have _____ (perfect) pronunciation. Everything you say is _____ (absolute) _____ (clear).

EXPANSION ACTIVITIES

Classroom Activities

1. Make a list of things that you ate when you were younger that you don't eat now. Make a list of things that you eat now that you didn't eat when you were younger. Form a small group and compare your lists.

Things I ate before that I don't eat now:	Things I eat now that I didn't eat before:

Lesson 6

2. Make a list of your lifestyle changes in the past few years. Find a partner. Compare your list with your partner's list. Which of these activities affect your health?

Things I do (or don't do) now:	Things I did (or didn't do) before:
I watch TV more often.	I hardly ever watched TV before.
I shop once a week.	I shopped almost every day when I lived in my country.

3. Bad habits. Make a list of bad habits that you or someone in your family has.

   EXAMPLES   I don't get enough exercise.
   My daughter talks on the phone too much.

4. Take something from your purse, pocket, or bag, but don't show it to anyone. Describe it. Another student will try to guess what it is.

5. Game: "In the manner of"

   Teacher: Write these adverbs on separate pieces of paper or on index cards:

accurately	excitedly	gladly	quietly	smoothly
carefully	fearfully	indecisively	repeatedly	steadily
carelessly	fearlessly	neatly	simply	suddenly
comfortably	foolishly	promptly	slowly	surprisingly
efficiently				

   Make sure the students know the meaning of each of these adverbs. Ask one student to leave the room. The other students pick one adverb. When the student returns to the room, he/she asks individuals to do something by giving imperatives. The others do this task in the manner of the adverb that was chosen. The student tries to guess the adverb.

   EXAMPLES   Edgar, write your name on the blackboard.
   Sofia, take off one shoe.
   Maria, open the door.
   Elsa, walk around the room.
   Nora, give me your book.

6. In some schools, students evaluate teachers. Work with a partner and write an evaluation form for teachers at this school or for another profession you are familiar with.

EXAMPLES

	Strongly Agree	Agree	Disagree	Strongly Disagree
1. Begins class promptly. 2. Treats students with respect. 3. Explains assignments clearly.				

Talk About it

1. In a small group or with the entire class, discuss what kind of food you usually eat. Do you think people eat healthful food in your native culture?

2. Americans often say, "You are what you eat." What do you think this means?

3. Do you get enough sleep? How much is enough for you? Do you remember your dreams?

Write About it

1. Think of a place in this city (a museum, a government office, a park, a shopping center, the airport, etc.). Write a brief description of this place.

2. Write a paragraph about your hometown (or a specific place in your hometown). Use descriptions.

3. Write a short composition comparing food in your native culture to food in the U.S.

Internet Activities

1. Go to the Web site for the U.S. Department of Agriculture (USDA). Find an article about food and nutrition and bring it to class. How does your diet compare to the USDA's recommendations?

2. At a search engine, type in *height weight*. Find a copy of a height/weight chart. Print it. See if you are the right weight for your height.

3. Find a conversion chart from the metric system to the English system. See how much you weigh in pounds.

Additional Activities at http://elt.heinle.com/gic

LESSON 7

GRAMMAR
Time Words and Time Clauses
The Past Continuous Tense[1]

CONTEXT: Immigrants
Ellis Island
Albert Einstein—Immigrant from Germany
Gloria Estefan—Cuban Immigrant

Ellis Island, New York, 1907

[1] The *past continuous tense* is also called the *past progressive tense*.

ELLIS ISLAND

Before You Read

1. Who was the first member of your family to come to the U.S.?
2. How did you or your family come to the U.S.?
3. Was the process of entering the U.S. difficult for your family? How was it difficult?

Read the following article. Pay special attention to time words.

Ellis Island today with Wall of Honor

Did You Know?

The largest number of immigrants in the U.S. between 1820 and 1996 came from Germany. The largest number of immigrants today come from Mexico, India, the Philippines, and China.

For many years, Ellis Island, an island in New York harbor, was the main door through which millions of immigrants entered the United States. **From** the time it opened **in** 1892 **until** the time it closed **in** 1924, the U.S. Bureau of Immigration used Ellis Island to receive and process new arrivals. **During** this time, 12 million foreigners passed through this door with the hope of becoming Americans. They came from Italy, Poland, Russia, Germany, China, and many other countries. Sometimes more than 10,000 people passed through the registry room in one 24-hour period. New arrivals often waited **for** many hours **while** inspectors checked to see if they met legal and medical standards. Most did not speak English, and they were tired, hungry, and confused. Two percent (250,000 people) did not meet the requirements to enter the U.S. and had to return to their countries.

After Congress passed an immigration law that limited the number and nationality of new immigrants, immigration slowed down and Ellis Island was closed as an immigration processing center. It remained abandoned **until** 1965, **when** President Lyndon Johnson decided to restore it as a monument. Restoration of Ellis Island was finished **by** 1990. Now visitors to this monument can see the building as it looked **from** 1918 **to** 1920. In addition, they can see the Wall of Honor with the names of many of those who passed through on their way to becoming American citizens.

7.1 When, Until, While

Examples	Explanation
When immigration slowed down, Ellis Island was closed. **When** it reopened, visitors could see the history of immigration.	*When* means *at that time* or *starting at that time*.
Ellis Island was closed **until** 1990. Immigrants could not enter the U.S. **until** they passed an inspection.	*Until* means *before that time*.
While they waited, they were often tired, confused, and hungry. New arrivals waited **while** inspectors checked their documents. **While** they were crossing the ocean, they thought about their uncertain future.	*While* means *during that time*. We can sometimes use *when* in place of *while*: **When** they were crossing the ocean, they thought about their uncertain future.

EXERCISE 1 Fill in the blanks with *when, while,* or *until*. In some cases, more than one answer is possible.

EXAMPLE My grandfather came to the U.S. ____when____ he was 25 years old.

1. _____ he lived in Poland, he had a hard life.

2. _____ he left Poland, he didn't speak English at all.

3. _____ he was at Ellis Island, he had to wait for hours. He was nervous _____ he waited.

4. He was nervous _____ he got permission to enter the country. Then he felt more relaxed.

5. _____ he passed the inspection, he entered the country.

6. In Poland, he didn't study English. He didn't speak a word of English _____ he started to work in the U.S. Then he learned a little.

7. _____ he worked, he saved money to bring his wife and children to America.

8. My grandmother couldn't come to the U.S. _____ my grandfather had enough money to send for her and their children.

9. My grandfather lived in the U.S. _____ he died in 1968.

EXERCISE 2 ABOUT YOU Add a main clause to complete each statement.

EXAMPLE Before I got to class today, *I finished all my homework.*

1. While I was in high school, _____
2. When I finished high school, _____
3. Until I came to this city / school, _____
4. When I arrived in the U.S., _____
5. Until I started this course, _____

EXERCISE 3 ABOUT YOU Finish the time expression to complete each statement.

EXAMPLE I stayed in my country until *a civil war broke out.*

1. I found my apartment / house while _____
2. I enrolled in this English class when _____
3. I didn't understand English until _____
4. I got married / found a job / bought a car / came to this country (*choose one*) when _____

EXERCISE 4 ABOUT YOU If you are from another country, name something *you never . . . until you came to the U.S.*

EXAMPLE Name something you never had.
I never had a car until I came to the U.S.

1. Name something you never did.
2. Name something or someone you never heard of.
3. Name something you never saw.
4. Name something you never thought about.
5. Name something you never had.
6. Name something you never ate.
7. Name something you never knew.

7.2 When and Whenever

Examples	Explanation
When I went to New York last year, I visited Ellis Island.	*When* means *at that time* or *after that time*.
Whenever I go to New York, I go to the theaters there.	*Whenever* means *any time* or *every time*. With the general present, *when* and *whenever* have almost the same meaning.

EXERCISE 5 ABOUT YOU Add a main clause to complete each statement. Use the general present.

EXAMPLE Whenever I take a test, *I feel nervous.*

1. Whenever I feel sad or lonely, _____
2. Whenever I get angry, _____
3. Whenever I need advice, _____
4. Whenever I receive a present, _____
5. Whenever I get a letter from my family, _____
6. Whenever I'm sick, _____
7. Whenever the weather is bad, _____
8. Whenever the teacher explains the grammar, _____

EXERCISE 6 ABOUT YOU Finish each sentence with a time clause.

EXAMPLES I feel nervous *before I take a test.*
I feel nervous *whenever I have to speak in class.*

1. I feel relaxed _____
2. I get angry _____
3. I get bored _____
4. I can't concentrate _____
5. I'm happy _____
6. I'm in a bad mood _____
7. I sometimes daydream[2] _____
8. Time passes quickly for me _____

[2] *To daydream* means to dream while you are awake. Your mind does not stay in the present moment.

7.3 | Time Words

Time Word	Examples	Explanation
on	We came to the U.S. **on** April 16, 2003. We came to the U.S. **on** Monday.	Use *on* with a specific date or day.
in	Ellis Island closed **in** 1924. My cousins came to the U.S. **in** August.	Use *in* with a specific year or month.
in vs. after	a. My brother will come to the U.S. **in** two months. b. My brother will come to the U.S. **after** he gets his visa.	a. Use *in* to mean after a period of time. b. Use *after* with an activity. *Wrong:* My brother will come to the U.S. *after* two months.
during	a. Many immigrants came to America **during** the war. b. Ellis Island was open from 1892 to 1924. **During** that time, 12 million immigrants came through there.	a. Use *during* with an event (*the war, the trip, the movie,* etc.). b. Use *during* with a period of time (*during that time, during the month of May, during the first week in August,* etc.).
for	**For** many years, Ellis Island was the main entrance for immigrants to America. My grandfather waited at Ellis Island **for** ten hours.	Use *for* with the quantity of years, months, weeks, days, etc. *Wrong:* They waited at Ellis Island *during* ten hours.
before vs. by	a. **Before 1990,** Ellis Island was closed. b. **By 1990,** restoration of Ellis Island was complete.	a. In the example to the left, if you use *before,* 1990 is not included. b. If you use *by,* 1990 is included.
before vs. ago	a. She got married **before** she came to the U.S. b. She got married three years **ago.**	Do not confuse *before* and *ago.* *Wrong:* She got married three years *before.*
from . . . to till until	Ellis Island was open **from** 1892 **to** 1924. You can visit Ellis Island **from** 9:30 *till* 5:00.	Use *from* with the starting time. Use *to, till,* or *until* with the ending time.

EXERCISE 7 Circle the correct time word to fill in the blanks.

EXAMPLE He lived with his parents (*during* /(*until*)/ *by*) he was 19 years old.

1. (*When* / *During* / *Whenever*) he was a child, he lived with his grandparents.
2. (*During* / *For* / *While*) several years, he lived with his grandparents.
3. (*For* / *While* / *During*) his childhood, he lived with his grandparents.

4. (*While / Until / When*) he got married, he lived with his grandparents. Then he found an apartment with his wife.
5. (*While / During / Whenever*) he was in elementary school, he lived with his grandparents.
6. (*Whenever / While / When*) he was ten years old, his grandparents gave him a bike.
7. She worked for her father (*during / while / whenever*) she was in college.
8. She worked for her father (*for / during / while*) her free time.
9. She worked for her father (*during / whenever / when*) she was single.
10. She worked for her father (*for / during / while*) three years.
11. She worked for her father full-time (*while / when / during*) her summer vacation.
12. She worked for her father (*when / until / while*) she got married. Then she quit her job to take care of her husband and children.
13. She worked for her father 12 years (*before / ago / after*).
14. (*Until / Whenever / During*) her husband needs help in his business, she helps him out.
15. She can't help you now. She's busy. She'll help you (*by / after / in*) an hour.
16. Please finish this exercise (*by / in / until*) 8:30.
17. Please finish this exercise (*by / before / until*) you go home. The teacher wants it today.
18. Please finish this exercise (*in / after / by*) ten minutes.
19. He'll retire (*after / in / by*) two years.
20. He'll retire (*when / while / until*) he's sixty-five years old.
21. He'll work (*when / while / until*) he's sixty-five years old. Then he'll retire.
22. I'm not going to eat dinner (*when / while / until*) my wife gets home. Then we'll eat together.
23. The Ellis Island Museum is open every day (*for / from / by*) 9:30 a.m. (*at / by / till*) 5:00 p.m.
24. The Ellis Island Museum is not open (*in / at / on*) December 25.

7.4 | The Past Continuous Tense—An Overview

We use the past continuous tense to show that something was in progress at a particular moment in time.

Examples	Explanation
In 1998, I **was living** in the U.S. In 1998, my parents **were living** in Ecuador.	To form the past continuous tense, we use *was* or *were* + verb-*ing*. 　I, he, she, it → *was* 　you, we, they → *were*
In 1998, I **wasn't living** in Ecuador. My parents **weren't living** with me.	To form the negative, put *not* after *was* or *were*. The contraction for *was not* is *wasn't*. The contraction for *were not* is *weren't*.

ALBERT EINSTEIN—IMMIGRANT FROM GERMANY

Before You Read

1. Can you name any famous immigrants to the U.S.?
2. Did anyone from your native culture become famous in the U.S.?

 Pay special attention to the relationship of the past and the past continuous tenses.

Albert Einstein, 1879–1955

Did You Know?

After Einstein died, Princeton University kept his brain in a jar to study how the brain of a genius is different from an ordinary brain.

Of the many immigrants who came to the U.S., one will always be remembered throughout the world: Albert Einstein. Einstein changed our understanding of the universe. When people think of the word "genius," Einstein's name often comes to mind. However, in Einstein's early years, he was not successful in school or at finding a job.

Einstein was born in Germany in 1879 to Jewish parents. He loved math and physics, but he disliked the discipline of formal German schooling. Because of his poor memory for words, his teachers believed that he was a slow learner. Einstein left school before receiving his diploma and tried to pass the exam to enter the Swiss Polytechnic Institute, but he failed on his first attempt. On his second attempt, he passed. He graduated in 1900. He **was planning** to become a teacher of physics and math, but he could not find a job in those fields. Instead, he went to work in a patent[3] office as a third-class technical expert from 1902 to 1909. While he **was working** at this job, he **studied** and **wrote** in his spare time. In 1905, when he was only 26 years old, he published three papers that explained the basic structure of the universe. His theory of relativity explained the relationship of space and time. Einstein was finally respected for his brilliant discovery. He returned to Germany to accept a research position at the University of Berlin. However, in 1920, while he **was lecturing** at the university, anti-Jewish groups often **interrupted** his lectures, saying they were "un-German."

In 1920, Einstein visited the United States for the first time. During his visits, he talked not only about his scientific theories, but also about world peace. While he **was visiting** the U.S. again in 1933, the Nazis **came** to power in Germany. They took his property, burned his books, and removed him from his university job. The U.S. offered Einstein a home. In 1935, he became a permanent resident of the U.S., and in 1940, he became a citizen. He received many job offers from all over the world, but he decided to accept a position at Princeton University in New Jersey. He lived and worked there until he died in 1955.

	Einstein's Life
1879	Born in Germany
1902–1909	Worked in a Swiss patent office
1905	Published his theory of relativity
1919	Scientists recognized his theory to be correct
1933	Visited the U.S.
1940	Became a U.S. citizen
1955	Died

[3] A *patent* is a document that identifies the owner of a new invention. Only the person or company who has the patent can sell the invention.

7.5 The Past Continuous Tense—Forms

Compare affirmative statements, questions, and short answers using the past continuous tense.

Wh- Word	Was/Were	Subject	Was/Were	-ing[4] Form	Complement	Short Answer
		Einstein	was	living	in the U.S.	
	Was	he		living	in New Jersey?	Yes, he **was.**
Where	was	he		living?		
		Who	was	living	in Germany?	

Compare negative statements and questions using the past continuous tense.

Wh- Word	Wasn't/Weren't	Subject	Wasn't/Weren't	-ing Form	Complement
		He	wasn't	living	in Germany.
Why	wasn't	he		living	in Germany?

EXERCISE 8 Fill in the blanks with the correct forms.

EXAMPLE In 1889, Einstein ___was studying___ in the Swiss Polytechnic Institute.
(study)

1. He _____ to become a teacher.
   (plan)

2. He _____ to become a doctor.
   (not/plan)

3. In 1907, he _____ in a patent office.
   (work)

4. In 1933, he _____ the U.S.
   (visit)

5. What _____ in the U.S.?
   (he/do)

6. _____ to go back to Germany? Yes,
   (he/plan)
   he _____.

7. Why _____ in Germany?
   (he/not/work)

[4] For the spelling of the *-ing* form, see Appendix A.

7.6 | The Past Continuous Tense—Uses

We use the past continuous to show the relationship of an action of some duration to a specific point in time or to a shorter past action.

Example	Explanation
Einstein **was working** in a patent office in 1905. I **was sleeping** at 3:00 in the morning.	We use the past continuous tense to show what was in progress at a specific moment in the past.
Einstein **was living** in Switzerland when he **developed** his theory of relativity. While Einstein **was visiting** the U.S., the Nazis **took** his property. Einstein **was living** in New Jersey when he **died**.	We use the past continuous tense with the simple past to show the relationship of a longer past action to a shorter past action.
Compare: a. Einstein was living in Switzerland **when** he **discovered** his theory of relativity. b. Einstein discovered his theory of relativity **while** he **was living** in Switzerland.	a. Use *when* + the simple past with the shorter action. b. Use *while* + the past continuous with the longer action.
Where **was** Einstein **living** when the Nazis **took** his home?	In a question with two clauses, only the verb in the main clause is in a question form.
While Einstein **was** in Switzerland, he developed his theory.	We don't use the continuous form with the verb *be*.

Punctuation Note:
If the main clause precedes the time clause, do not separate the two clauses with a comma. If the time clause precedes the main clause, separate the two clauses with a comma.
    He was living in New Jersey when he died. (No Comma)
    While he was living in New Jersey**,** he died. (Comma)	

EXERCISE 9   **ABOUT YOU** Tell if the following things were happening in January 2004.

EXAMPLE   go to school
I was (not) going to school in January 2004.

1. work
2. go to school
3. study English
4. live in the U.S.
5. live with my parents
6. take a vacation

EXERCISE 10   **ABOUT YOU** Ask a question with *"What were you doing . . . ?"* at these specific times. Another student will answer.

EXAMPLE   at 6 o'clock this morning

A: What were you doing at 6 o'clock this morning?
B: I was sleeping.

1. at 10 o'clock last night
2. at 4 o'clock this morning
3. at 5 o'clock yesterday afternoon
4. at this time yesterday
5. at this time last year[5]

EXERCISE 11   Decide which of these two verbs has longer action. Fill in the correct tense (simple past or past continuous) of the verb in parentheses ( ) and *when* or *while*.

EXAMPLES   She __was taking__ a shower __when__ the telephone __rang__.
                          (take)   *(ring)*

It __started__ to rain __while__ I __was walking__ to school.
        (start)   *(walk)*

1. _____ the teacher _____ on the blackboard,
                                   (write)
she _____ the chalk.
       (drop)

2. He _____ and _____ his arm _____
        (fall)   *(break)*
he _____ a tree.
       (climb)

3. Mary _____ in a department store _____ she
           (shop)
_____ her purse.
   (lose)

4. I _____ my homework _____ my friend
       (do)
_____ over.
   (come)

5. She _____ her husband _____ she _____ college.
        (meet)   *(attend)*

[5] *At this time last year* is very general; it does not refer to a specific hour.

6. _____ I _____ to work, I
   　　　　　　　(drive)
   _____ out of gas.[6]
   　(run)

7. _____ he _____ at the airport,
   　　　　　　　(arrive)
   his friends _____ for him.
   　　　　　　　(wait)

8. They _____ dinner _____
   　　　　(eat)
   someone _____ on the door.
   　　　　　　(knock)

9. _____ I _____ a test,
   　　　　　　　(take)
   my pencil point _____.
   　　　　　　　　(break)

10. The baby _____ me _____
    　　　　　　(interrupt)
    I _____ to a friend.
    　　(talk)

11. I _____ my tooth _____ I _____ a nut.
    　　(break)　　　　　　　　　　　　(eat)

12. I _____ an old friend _____
    　　　(meet)
    I _____ in the park.
    　　(walk)

13. She _____ dinner _____
    　　　(cook)
    the smoke alarm _____ off.[7]
    　　　　　　　　　(go)

14. He _____ snow _____ he
    　　　(shovel)
    _____ his glove.
    　(lose)

15. I _____ a fuse _____
    　　(blow)
    I _____.
    　(iron)

16. She _____ _____ the baby
    　　　(sleep)
    _____ to cry.
    　(start)

17. She _____ her favorite plate _____
    　　　(break)
    she _____ the dishes.
    　　(wash)

---

[6] To *run out of* means to use up everything.
[7] When an alarm *goes off*, it starts to sound.

Time Words and Time Clauses; The Past Continuous Tense

EXERCISE 12 Fill in the blanks with the simple past or the past continuous form of the verb in parentheses ( ) in the following conversations.

Conversation 1, between a wife (W) and husband (H)

W: Look what I found today! Your favorite watch!

H: Where ___did you find___ it?
    (example: find)

W: In your top drawer. I _____ away your
    (1 put)
    socks when I _____ it.
    (2 find)

H: I wonder how it got there.

W: Probably while you _____ something
    (3 put)
    in that drawer, it _____ off your wrist.
    (4 fall)

Conversation 2, between two students

A: When did you come to the U.S.?

B: Two months ago.

A: Really? But you speak English so well.

B: While I _____ in a refugee camp in
    (1 live)
    Kenya, I studied English.

A: _____ to come to the U.S.?
    (2 you/plan)

B: Not really. I had no plans at all. I _____
    (3 just/wait)
    in the refugee camp.

A: Are you from Kenya?

B: No. I'm from Sudan. But while I _____
    (4 live)
    in Sudan, a war _____ there and
    (5 start)
    I had to leave my country.

A: Are you here with your family?

B: No. I'm alone. When the war _____, I
    (6 start)
    _____ far away from my family. I
    (7 live)
    escaped to Kenya, but I don't know where my family is today.

224   Lesson 7

Conversation 3, between a son (S) and mother (M)

S: I _____(1 look)_____ through some old boxes when I _____(2 find)_____ this picture of you and Dad when you were young. By the way, how _____ you _____(3 meet)_____ Dad?

M: One day I _____(4 walk)_____ in the park in my hometown when he _____(5 stop)_____ me to ask what time it was. We _____(6 start)_____ to talk, and then he _____(7 ask)_____ me to go out with him.

S: Did you date for a long time?

M: We _____(8 date)_____ for ten months. During that time, his family _____(9 apply)_____ for the green card lottery in the U.S. While we _____(10 date)_____, they _____(11 receive)_____ a letter that gave them permission to immigrate to the U.S.

S: What _____(12 happen)_____?

M: At first, I was worried that I'd never see your dad again. But he _____(13 write)_____ to me often and _____(14 call)_____ me whenever he could. About a year later, he _____(15 go)_____ back to our country to visit me. While we _____(16 eat)_____ in a beautiful restaurant, he _____(17 ask)_____ me to marry him.

S: _____(18 you/marry)_____ him right away?

M: Yes, we got married a few weeks later and then he _____(19 return)_____ to the U.S. But I couldn't go to the U.S. with him. I _____(20 have)_____ to wait for permission. Finally, I _____(21 get)_____ permission to come.

7.7 Was / Were Going To

We use *was/were going to* + the base form to describe a plan that we didn't carry out. It means the same thing as *was/were planning to*.

Examples	Explanation
a. Einstein **was going to** return to Germany, but the Nazis came to power.	a. Einstein was planning to return, but didn't.
b. I **was going to** call you, but I lost your phone number.	b. I was planning to call, but didn't.

EXERCISE 13 Fill in the blanks with *was going to* + one of the verbs from the box below.

use	write ✓	go
say	call	

A: What did you write for your composition today?

B: I ___was going to write___ about Einstein, but I couldn't find any information.
(example)

A: What? There's tons of[8] information. Did you go to the library?

B: I _____ to the library, but the library near my
(1)

house is closed for construction.

A: How about the college library?

B: I didn't think of it.

A: Why didn't you use the Internet? You can find plenty of information there.

B: I _____ the Internet, but my computer
(2)

crashed.

A: Why didn't you call me? I have Internet access at home. You're welcome to use my computer.

B: I _____ you, but I lost your phone number.
(3)

A: I'm beginning to think you didn't really want to do your homework.

B: Maybe you're right. I'm kind of lazy.

A: I _____ that, but I didn't want to hurt your
(4)

feelings.

[8] *Tons of* means *a lot of*.

EXERCISE 14 Fill in the blanks to tell what prevented a plan from happening.

EXAMPLE He was going to return to his country, but _he couldn't get permission._

1. My cousin was going to come to the U.S., but _____
_____

2. He was going to work in the U.S. for only three months, but _____
_____

3. We were going to return to our country, but _____
_____

4. I was going to call my grandparents last night, but _____
_____

5. We were going to rent an apartment in this city, but _____
_____

GLORIA ESTEFAN—CUBAN IMMIGRANT

Before You Read

1. Is there anyone from your native culture who is famous in the U.S.?
2. Do you like Latin music?

Read the following article. Pay special attention to the verb tenses with *when* and *while*.

Gloria Estefan

Immigrants who come to the U.S. bring their skills and talents. The U.S. benefits from these diverse abilities. One especially talented immigrant came from Cuba.

On September 1, 1957, Gloria Maria Fajardo was born in Havana, Cuba. **When** Fidel Castro **took** over in Cuba, Gloria was only two years old. Her father was taken as a political prisoner. Gloria and her mother moved to Miami to escape the Communist government.

Life as a child was not easy for Gloria. **When** Gloria's father **joined** the family in Miami a few years later, he **became** very sick. Gloria **took** care of him **while** her mother **worked**. She **practiced** singing and playing the guitar **while taking** care of her father.

In 1985, Gloria's mother asked her to sing some songs at a wedding. The bandleader at the wedding, Emilio Estefan, was very impressed by Gloria's singing and asked her to join his band, The Miami Sound Machine. (Emilio Estefan later became Gloria's husband.) The band played a combination of Cuban and American pop music. In 1989, Gloria started to perform solo and had several hit songs.

(continued)

Awards, fame, and fortune followed—until one day in 1990 **when** a tragedy **happened.** Gloria, her husband, and son **were riding** in her music tour bus **when** a truck **hit** the bus. Gloria's back was broken. She had to undergo painful surgery. Her career was on hold for a year. **When** she **recovered**, she **started** singing again.

Today, Gloria Estefan has a successful career and millions of fans among Americans and Latinos. Gloria's story is one of talent, a little luck, and a lot of hard work.

7.8 | Simple Past vs. Past Continuous with *When*

Both the simple past and the past continuous can be used in a sentence that has a *when* clause. However, the time sequence is completely different.

Examples	Explanation
a. **When** the truck hit the tour bus, Gloria **was** hurt. b. **When** the truck hit the tour bus, Gloria and her band **were riding** to a concert.	In sentences (a), the simple past in the main clause shows what happened **after** an action.
a. Einstein came to live in the U.S. **when** he lost his German citizenship. b. Einstein **was living** in the U.S. **when** he died.	In sentences (b), the past continuous in the main clause shows what was happening **at the same time** a shorter action occurred.

EXERCISE 15 Fill in the blanks with the simple past or the past continuous of the verb in parentheses ( ).

EXAMPLES When the movie was over, we ___*left*___ the theater.
(leave)

We ___*were leaving*___ the theater when we met an old friend.
(leave)

A

1. Gloria Estefan _____ in a bus when the
   (ride)
   accident happened.

2. Gloria Estefan _____ to the hospital when the
   (go)
   accident happened.

3. Einstein _____ in the U.S. when he died.
   (live)

4. A scientist _____ Einstein's brain in a jar
   (put)
   when he died.

5. When I got home, I _____ dinner with my family. (picture A)
   (eat)

6. When I got home, my family _____ dinner. (picture B)
   (eat)

B

7. When I got to class, the teacher _____ (give) a test. Luckily I got there just in time.

8. When I got to class, the teacher _____ (give) a test. I missed the first ten minutes of it.

9. When the phone rang, I _____ (take) a shower.

10. When the phone rang, my roommate _____ (answer) it.

11. When she heard the news about the disaster, she _____ (start) to cry.

12. When she heard the news about the disaster, she _____ (watch) TV.

13. When the accident happened, I _____ (call) the police.

14. When the accident happened, I _____ (drive) to work. I called my boss to tell him I would be late.

7.9 | Simple Past vs. Past Continuous

Examples	Explanation
Gloria took care of her father **while** her mother **worked**. **While** Einstein **worked** at a patent office, he **studied** and **wrote**.	We can connect two past actions that happened in the same time period with *while* and the simple past tense in both clauses.
While I **was reading** the story about Gloria Estefan, I **was underlining** the verbs. **While** we **were doing** the last exercise, the teacher **was helping** us.	We can connect two past actions that happened in the **exact** same time period with *while* and the past continuous tense in both clauses.
When the accident **happened,** Gloria had to stop performing.	Use *when* to mean *at a specific time*. Use the simple past tense.

EXERCISE 16 Fill in the blanks with *when* for an action at a specific time or *while* for an action that continues over time.

EXAMPLE She learned to play guitar ___*while*___ she took care of her father.

1. _____ her mother worked, Gloria stayed home with her sick father.

2. _____ Emilio Estefan met Gloria, he liked her very much.

3. Gloria was hurt very badly _____ a truck hit her bus.
4. _____ Gloria had an accident, she had to stop singing.
5. _____ she was recovering, she received a lot of mail from fans.
6. _____ she recovered, she went back to her singing career.

7.10 Using the -ing Form After Time Words

When the main clause and the time clause have the same subject, we can delete the subject of the time clause and use a present participle (verb + -ing) after the time word.

Examples

Einstein left high school **before he finished** his studies.
∨
Einstein left high school **before finishing** his studies.

After Einstein left high school, he studied mathematics and physics.
∨
After leaving high school, Einstein studied mathematics and physics.

Gloria Estefan practiced the guitar **while she took** care of her father.
∨
Gloria Estefan practiced the guitar **while taking** care of her father.

EXERCISE 17 Change these sentences. Use a present participle after the time word. Make any necessary changes.

entering   *Einstein*
EXAMPLE After ~~Einstein entered~~ the university, ~~he~~ developed his theory.

1. Einstein passed an exam before he entered the university.
2. He left high school before he received his diploma.
3. After Einstein developed his theory of relativity, he became famous.
4. He became interested in physics after he received books on science.
5. After Einstein came to the U.S., he got a job at Princeton.
6. Before she came to the U.S., Gloria lived in Cuba.
7. While Gloria was taking care of her father, she practiced the guitar.
8. Gloria was injured while she was riding in a music tour bus.
9. After she recovered from her injuries, Gloria went back to making music.

SUMMARY OF LESSON 7

1. Time Words

Time Word	Examples
When	**When** immigrants came to America, they passed through Ellis Island.
While	They waited **while** inspectors checked their health.
Until	Ellis Island remained closed **until** 1990.
Before	**Before** 1920, many immigrants came to America.
After	**After** 1920, Congress limited the number of immigrants.
From . . . to / until / till	**From** 1892 **to** 1924, Ellis Island was an immigrant processing center. The Ellis Island Museum is open **from** 9:30 **till** 5:00.
During	**During** this time, 12 million immigrants passed through Ellis Island.
For	New arrivals had to wait **for** hours.
In	**In** 1905, Einstein wrote about relativity. We will finish the test **in** an hour.
By	Restoration of Ellis Island was finished **by** 1990.
Ago	One hundred years **ago,** new arrivals passed through Ellis Island.
On	We came to the U.S. **on** Wednesday.

2. Uses of the past continuous tense:
   A. To describe a past action that was in progress at a specific moment:
   He **was sleeping** at 6 o'clock this morning.
   Where **were** you **living** in December 2001?

   B. With the past tense, to show the relationship of a longer past action to a shorter past action:
   Gloria **was riding** in a bus when the accident **happened.**
   Einstein **was living** in New Jersey when he **died.**
   While Gloria **was taking** care of her father, she **practiced** the guitar.

   C. To show past intentions:
   I **was going to call** you, but I lost your phone number.
   She **was going to cook** dinner, but she didn't have time.

EDITING ADVICE

1. Put the subject before the verb in all clauses.

   When ~~entered the teacher~~ *the teacher entered*, the students stood up.

2. Use *when*, not *while*, if the action has no duration.

   ~~While~~ *When* she spilled the milk, she started to cry.

3. Don't confuse *during* and *for*.

   He watched TV ~~during~~ *for* three hours.

4. Don't confuse *until* and *when*.

   She will eat dinner ~~until~~ *when* her husband comes home.

5. Don't confuse *before* and *ago*.

   They came to the U.S. three years ~~before~~ *ago*.

6. After a time word, use an *-ing* form, not a base form.

   After ~~find~~ *finding* a job, he bought a car.

LESSON 7 TEST/REVIEW

PART 1 Find the mistakes with the underlined words, and correct them. Not every sentence has a mistake. If the sentence is correct, write *C*.

EXAMPLES She came to the U.S. two weeks ~~before~~ *ago*.

While I was walking in the park, I saw my friend.   **C**

1. When he arrived, he ate dinner with his family.
2. After leaving my country, I went to Thailand.
3. When arrived the teacher, the students had a test.
4. I graduated until I finished all my courses.
5. While she was washing the dishes, she dropped the glass.
6. While she dropped the glass, it broke.
7. He studied English until he became fluent.
8. She served dinner when her guests arrived.

9. Einstein lived in the U.S. <u>until</u> he died.
10. They went home <u>until</u> the movie was over.
11. I'll be back <u>in</u> ten minutes.
12. <u>During</u> three weeks, he was on vacation.
13. Please return your library books <u>by</u> Friday.
14. She found a job three weeks <u>before</u>.
15. He was sick <u>for</u> a week.
16. I ate dinner an hour <u>ago</u>.
17. Einstein was in the U.S. <u>during</u> the Second World War.
18. I <u>was going</u> to call you, but I lost your phone number.

PART 2 Fill in the blanks with the simple past or the past continuous form of the verb in parentheses ( ).

EXAMPLE   He __was walking__ (walk) to his car when he __lost__ (lose) his glove.

1. What _____ (you/do) at 4 p.m. yesterday afternoon? I tried to call you, but you weren't home.

2. She _____ (live) in Paris when the war _____ (start).

3. I _____ (find) your necklace while I _____ (look) for my watch.

4. She _____ (buy) a house three years ago.

5. He _____ (meet) his wife while he _____ (work) in a restaurant.

6. When my grandfather _____ (come) to America, he _____ (find) a job in a factory.

7. When he _____ (arrive) at Ellis Island, his uncle _____ (wait) for him.

8. While she _____ (use) the computer, it _____ (crash).

9. He _____ (cook) dinner when the fire _____ (start).

10. I _____ (drive) my car and _____ (listen) to the radio when I _____ (hear) about the plane crash.

PART 3 Fill in the blanks with an appropriate time word. Choose *when, whenever, while, until, before, after, by, ago, in, for, on, from, till, to,* or *during*. In some cases, more than one answer is possible.

EXAMPLE I will continue to work ____*until*____ I am 65 years old. Then I will retire.

1. _____ it snows, there are a lot of traffic accidents.
2. I was walking to my friend's house _____ it started to rain. I was glad I had my umbrella with me.
3. _____ I was driving to school, I was listening to the radio.
4. _____ I finished my homework last night, I watched the news on TV.
5. I got my visa _____ coming to the U.S.
6. He must stay in his country _____ he gets permission to come to the U.S.
7. _____ he dropped his glasses, they broke.
8. We have to finish this lesson _____ 10 o'clock.
9. He found a job two months _____.
10. He found a job three weeks _____ coming to the U.S.
11. He found a job _____ April.
12. It's 7:50. The movie will begin _____ ten minutes, at 8:00.
13. _____ the movie began, everyone became quiet.
14. _____ she was watching the sad movie, she started to cry.

Lesson 7

15. Einstein was 61 years old _____ he became a U.S. citizen.
16. Einstein lived in the U.S. _____ 22 years.
17. I had a doctor's appointment _____ Monday.
18. I work everyday _____ 9 a.m. _____ 5 p.m.

EXPANSION ACTIVITIES

Classroom Activities

1. Pick an important event in your life (*immigrating to a new country, moving to a new town, going to a new school, getting married*, etc.) and make a list of things you did before, during, and after the event. Discuss your answers with a small group.

   Event:_____

Before	During	After

2. Form a small group. Turn to the person next to you and say a year or a specific time of the year. The person next to you tells what was happening in his or her life at that time.

   EXAMPLES   1996
   I was living with my parents.

   January 2004
   I was studying to be a nurse.

Talk About it

1. Read these quotes by Einstein. Discuss their meaning.
   - "Imagination is more important than knowledge."
   - "The only real valuable thing is intuition."
   - "A person starts to live when he can live outside himself."
   - "I never think of the future. It comes soon enough."
   - "Anyone who has never made a mistake has never tried anything new."

Time Words and Time Clauses; The Past Continuous Tense

- "Science is a wonderful thing if one does not have to earn one's living at it."
- "Peace cannot be kept by force. It can only be achieved by understanding."
- "Education is what remains after one has forgotten everything he learned in school."
- "Not everything that counts can be counted, and not everything that can be counted counts." (Sign hanging in Einstein's office at Princeton)

2. Einstein is often called a genius. Can you think of any other famous people who are geniuses?

3. In a small group or with the entire class, discuss your experience of immigration. Was the process difficult? How did you feel during the process?

Write About it

1. Write a paragraph about the changes that took place after a major historical event in your country or elsewhere in the world.

   EXAMPLES After the communists took over in Cuba . . .
   After the Khmer Rouge took power in Cambodia . . .
   After the coup failed in the former Soviet Union . . .
   After the president of my country was assassinated . . .
   After the fall of the Berlin Wall . . .

2. Write about the life of a famous person who interests you.

3. Write about how you met your spouse or how your father and mother met.

Outside Activities

1. Most people remember what they were doing when they heard shocking news. Do you remember what you were doing when you heard about the terrorist attacks in the U.S. on September 11, 2001? Ask another classmate or a friend or neighbor, "What were you doing when you heard about the attack on September 11?" Report this information to the class.

2. Is there another famous event that most people remember well? What was it? Ask people what they were doing when this event happened. Report your findings to the class.

Internet Activities

1. Look for the Ellis Island Web site. Find out what time the museum is open. See what names are on the wall of the museum. Is your family's name on the wall?

2. At a search engine, type in *famous immigrants*. Find information about an immigrant that you find interesting. Report this information to the class.

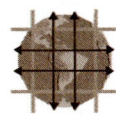

Additional Activities at http://elt.heinle.com/gic

LESSON 8

GRAMMAR

Modals
Related Expressions

CONTEXT: Renting an Apartment

An Apartment Lease
Tenants' Rights
The New Neighbors
At a Garage Sale

8.1 Modals and Related Expressions—An Overview

A modal adds meaning to the verb that follows it.

List of Modals	Modals are different from other verbs in several ways.

can
could
should
will
would
may
might
must
	1. The base form of a verb follows a modal.[1]
	    You **must pay** your rent. (*Not:* You must <u>to</u> pay your rent.)
	    He **should clean** his apartment now. (*Not:* He should clean<u>ing</u> his apartment now.)
	2. Modals never have an *-s, -ed,* or *-ing* ending.
	    He **can** rent an apartment. (*Not:* He can<u>s</u> rent an apartment.)

Related Expressions	Some verbs are like modals in meaning.
have to be able to be supposed to be permitted to be allowed to	He **must** sign the lease. = He **has to** sign the lease. He **can** pay the rent. = He **is able to** pay the rent. I **must** pay my rent by the first of the month. = I**'m supposed to** pay my rent by the first of the month. You **can't** change the locks in your apartment. = You **are not permitted to** change the locks in your apartment. = You **are not allowed to** change the locks in your apartment.

AN APARTMENT LEASE

Before You Read

1. Do you live in an apartment? Do you have a lease? Did you understand the lease when you signed it?
2. What kinds of things are not allowed in your apartment?

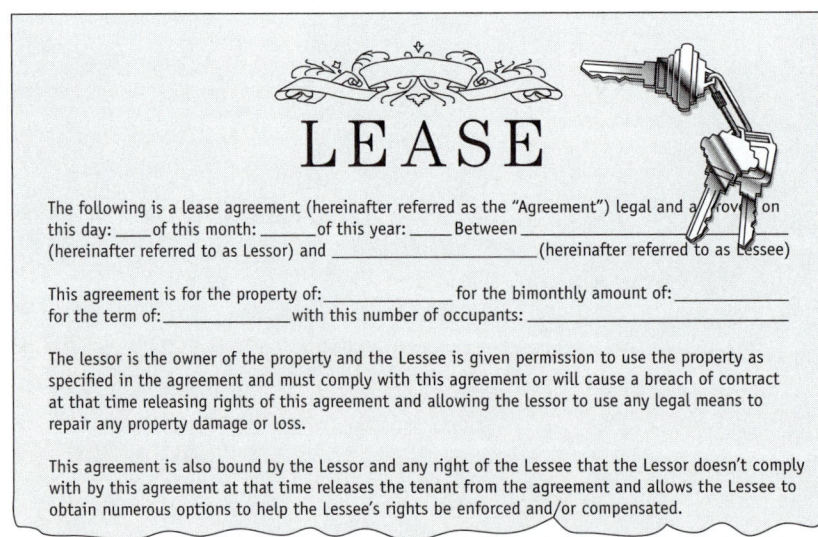

---

[1] Do not follow a modal with an infinitive. There is one exception: *ought to. Ought to* means *should.*

Read the following article. Pay special attention to modals and related expressions.

When people rent an apartment, they often **have to** sign a lease. A lease is an agreement between the owner (landlord[2]) and the renter (tenant). A lease states the period of time for the rental, the amount of the rent, and the rules the renter **must** follow. Some leases contain the following rules:

- Renters **must not** have a water bed.
- Renters **must not** have a pet.
- Renters **must not** change the locks without the owner's permission.
- Renters **must** pay a security deposit.

Many owners ask the renters to pay a security deposit in case there are damages. When the renters move out, the owners **are supposed to** return the deposit plus interest if the apartment is in good condition. If there is damage, the owners **can** use part or all of the money to repair the damage. However, they **may not** keep the renters' money for normal wear and tear (the normal use of the apartment).

Renters **do not have to** agree to all the terms of the lease. They **can** ask for changes before they sign. A pet owner, for example, **can** ask for permission to have a pet by offering to pay a higher security deposit.

There are laws that protect renters. For example, owners **must** provide heat during the winter months. In most cities, they **must** put a smoke detector in each apartment and in the halls. In addition, owners **can't** refuse to rent to a person because of sex, race, religion, nationality, or disability.

When the lease is up for renewal, owners **can** offer the renters a new lease or they **can** ask the renters to leave. The owners **are supposed to** notify the renters (usually at least 30 days in advance) if they want the renters to leave.

smoke detector

[2] A *landlord* is a man. A *landlady* is a woman.

Modals; Related Expressions

8.2 Negatives with Modals

Negatives and negative contractions	You form the negative of a modal by putting *not* after the modal. You can make a negative contraction with some, but not all, modals.

cannot → can't
could not → couldn't
should not → shouldn't
will not → won't
would not → wouldn't
may not → (no contraction)
might not → (no contraction)
must not → mustn't
	• The negative of *can* is *cannot* (one word) or *can't*.
	    We **cannot** pay the rent.
	    You **can't** have a dog in your apartment.
	• The negative contraction of *will not* is *won't*.
	    We **will not** renew our lease.
	    We **won't** stay here.
	• Don't make a contraction for *may not* or *might not*.
	    You **may not** know legal terms.
	    You **might not** understand the lease.

EXERCISE 1 Write the negative form of the underlined words. Use a contraction whenever possible.

EXAMPLE You <u>must</u> pay a security deposit. You ___must not___ have a water bed.

1. I <u>can</u> have a cat in my apartment. I _____ have a dog.

2. You <u>should</u> read the lease carefully. You _____ sign it without reading it.

3. The landlord <u>must</u> install a smoke detector. You _____ remove it.

4. You <u>may</u> have visitors in your apartment. You _____ make a lot of noise and disturb your neighbors.

5. If you damage something, the landlord <u>can</u> keep part of your deposit. He _____ keep all of your deposit.

6. You <u>might</u> get back all of your security deposit. If you leave your apartment in bad condition, you _____ get all of it back.

8.3 Statements and Questions with Modals

Compare **affirmative** statements and questions with a modal.

Wh-Word	Modal	Subject	Modal	Verb (base form)	Complement	Short Answer
		He	can	have	a cat in his apartment.	
	Can	he		have	a water bed?	No, he **can't**.
What	can	he		have	in his apartment?	
		Who	can	have	a dog?	

Compare **negative** statements and questions with a modal.

Wh-Word	Modal	Subject	Modal	Verb (base form)	Complement
		He	shouldn't	pay	his rent late.
Why	shouldn't	he		pay	his rent late?

EXERCISE 2 Read each statement. Fill in the blanks to complete the question.

EXAMPLE You should read the lease before you sign it. Why _____*should I*_____ read the lease before I sign it?

1. You can't have a water bed. Why _____ a water bed?

2. We must pay a security deposit. How much _____?

3. Someone must install a smoke detector. Who _____ a smoke detector?

4. The landlord can't refuse to rent to a person because of race, religion, or nationality. Why _____ to rent to a person for these reasons?

5. Tenants shouldn't make a lot of noise in their apartments. Why _____ a lot of noise?

6. I may have a cat in my apartment. _____ have a dog in my apartment?

7. The landlord can have a key to my apartment. _____ _____ enter my apartment when I'm not home?

Modals; Related Expressions

8.4 Must, Have To, Have Got To

Must has a very official tone. For nonofficial situations, we usually use *have to* or *have got to*.

Examples	Explanation
The landlord **must** give you a smoke detector. The tenant **must** pay the rent on the first of each month.	For formal obligations, use *must*. *Must* is often used in legal contracts, such as apartment leases.
The landlord **has to** give you a smoke detector. The landlord **has got to** give you a smoke detector.	In conversation or informal writing, we usually use *have to* or *have got to*, not *must*.

You **must** leave the building immediately. It's on fire!
You **have to** leave the building immediately. It's on fire!
You**'ve got to** leave the building immediately. It's on fire!
	Must, *have to*, and *have got to* express a sense of urgency. All three sentences to the left have the same meaning.
	
	Have got to is usually contracted:
	   I have got to = I've got to
	   He has got to = He's got to

Our apartment is too small. We **have to** move. Our apartment is too small. We**'ve got to** move. The landlord **has to** give you a smoke detector.	Avoid using *must* for personal obligations. It sounds very official or urgent and is too strong for most situations. Use *have to* or *have got to*. (You can use *have to* in formal situations. But don't use *must* in informal situations.)
At the end of my lease last May, I **had to** move. I **had to** find a bigger apartment.	*Must* has no past form. The past of both *must* and *have to* is *had to*. *Have got to* has no past form.

Language Notes:
1. In fast, informal speech, *have to* is often pronounced "hafta." *Has to* is often pronounced "hasta." *Got to* is often pronounced "gotta." Listen to your teacher pronounce the sentences in the above box.
2. We don't usually use *have got to* for questions and negatives.

EXERCISE 3 Fill in the blanks with an appropriate verb. Answers may vary.

EXAMPLE The landlord must _____give_____ you heat in cold weather.

1. You must _____ the lease with a pen. A pencil is not acceptable.

2. The landlord must _____ your security deposit if you leave your apartment in good condition.

3. The landlord must _____ you if he wants you to leave at the end of your lease.

4. You must _____ quiet in your apartment at night. Neighbors want to sleep.

5. To get a driver's license, you must _____ a driving test.

6. When you are driving, you must _____ your seat belt.

7. When you see a red light, you must _____.

EXERCISE 4 ABOUT YOU Make a list of personal necessities you have.

EXAMPLE *I have to change the oil in my car every three months.*

1. _____
2. _____
3. _____

EXERCISE 5 ABOUT YOU Make a list of things you had to do last weekend.

EXAMPLE *I had to do my laundry.*

1. _____
2. _____
3. _____

EXERCISE 6 Finish these statements. Practice *have got to*. Answers will vary.

EXAMPLE When you live in the U.S., you've got to *learn English.*

1. When I don't know the meaning of a word, I've got to _____
   _____

2. English is so important in the U.S. We've got to _____
   _____

3. For this class, you've got to _____
   _____

4. If you rent an apartment, you've got to _____
   _____

5. If you want to drive a car, you've got to _____
   _____

8.5 Obligation with *Must* or *Be Supposed To*

Examples	Explanation
Landlord to tenant: "You **must** pay your rent on the first of each month." Judge to landlord: "You have no proof of damage. You **must** return the security deposit to your tenant."	*Must* has an official, formal tone. A person in a position of authority (like a landlord or judge) can use *must*. Legal documents use *must*.
You're **supposed to** put your name on your mailbox. The landlord **is supposed to** give you a copy of the lease.	Avoid using *must* if you are not in a position of authority. Use *be supposed to*.
We're **not supposed to** have cats in my building, but my neighbor has one. The landlord **was supposed to** return my security deposit, but he didn't. I'm **supposed to** pay my rent on the first of the month, but sometimes I forget.	*Be supposed to*, not *must*, is used when reporting on a law or rule that was broken or a task that wasn't completed.

Pronunciation Note:
The *d* in *supposed to* is not pronounced.

EXERCISE 7 Make these sentences less formal by changing from *must* to *be supposed to*.

EXAMPLE You must wear your seat belt.
You're supposed to wear your seat belt.

1. You must carry your driver's license with you when you drive.
2. You must stop at a red light.
3. We must put money in the parking meter during business hours.
4. Your landlord must notify you if he wants you to leave.
5. The landlord must give me a smoke detector.
6. The teacher must give a final grade at the end of the semester.
7. We must write five compositions in this course.
8. We must bring our books to class.

EXERCISE 8 Finish these statements. Use *be supposed to* plus a verb. Answers may vary.

EXAMPLE I <u>'m supposed to pay my rent</u> on the first of the month.

1. Pets are not permitted in my apartment. I (not) _____ _____ a pet.
2. The landlord _____ us heat in the winter months.
3. The tenants _____ before they move out.
4. The landlord _____ a smoke detector in each apartment.
5. I _____ my rent last week, but I forgot.
6. My stove isn't working. My landlord _____ it.
7. We're going to move out next week. Our apartment is clean and in good condition. The landlord _____ our security deposit.

EXERCISE 9 ABOUT YOU Write three sentences to tell what you are supposed to do for this course. You may work with a partner.

EXAMPLE <u>We're supposed to write three compositions this semester.</u>

1. _____
2. _____
3. _____

Modals; Related Expressions

8.6 Can, May, Could, and Alternate Expressions

Example with a Modal	Alternate Expression	Explanation
I **can** clean the apartment by Friday.	It **is possible** (for me) **to** clean the apartment by Friday.	Possibility
I **can't** understand the lease.	I **am not able to** understand the lease.	Ability
I **can't** have a pet in my apartment.	I **am not permitted to** have a pet. I **am not allowed to** have a pet.	Permission
The landlord **may not** keep my deposit if my apartment is clean and in good condition.	The landlord **is not permitted to** keep my deposit. The landlord **is not allowed to** keep my deposit.	Permission
I **couldn't** speak English five years ago, but I can now.	I **wasn't able to** speak English five years ago, but I can now.	Past Ability
I **could** have a dog in my last apartment, but I can't have one in my present apartment.	I **was permitted to** have a dog in my last apartment, but I can't have one in my present apartment.	Past Permission

Language Notes:
1. *Can* is not usually stressed in affirmative statements. Sometimes it is hard to hear the final *t*, so we must pay attention to the vowel sound to hear the difference between *can* and *can't*. Listen to your teacher pronounce these sentences:

    I can gó. /kIn/

    I cán't go. /kænt/

    In a short answer, we pronounce *can* as /kæn/.

    Can you help me later?

    Yes, I can. /kæn/
2. We use *can* in the following common expression:

    I *can't afford* a bigger apartment. I don't have enough money.

EXERCISE 10 Fill in the blanks with an appropriate permission word to talk about what is or isn't permitted at this school. Answers may vary.

EXAMPLES We __aren't allowed to__ bring food into the classroom.

We __can__ leave the room without asking the teacher for permission.

1. We _____ eat in the classroom.
2. Students _____ talk during a test.
3. Students _____ use their dictionaries when they write compositions.
4. Students _____ write a test with a pencil.
5. Students _____ sit in any seat they want.
6. Students _____ use their textbooks during a test.

EXERCISE 11 Complete each statement. Answers may vary.

EXAMPLE The landlord may not __refuse to rent__ to a person because of his or her nationality.

1. The tenants may not _____ the locks without the landlord's permission.
2. Each tenant in my building has a parking space. I may not _____ in another tenant's space.
3. Students may not _____ during a test.
4. Teacher to students: "You don't need my permission to leave the room. You may _____ the room if you need to."
5. Some teachers do not allow cell phones in class. In Mr. Klein's class, you may not _____ during class.
6. My teacher says that after we finish a test, we may _____. We don't have to stay in class.

EXERCISE 12 ABOUT YOU Write statements to tell what is or is not permitted in this class, in the library, at this school, or during a test. If you have any questions about what is permitted, write a question for the teacher. You may work with a partner.

EXAMPLES *We aren't allowed to talk in the library.*

May we use our textbooks during a test?

EXERCISE 13 ABOUT YOU Write three sentences telling about what you couldn't do in another class or school that you attended.

EXAMPLE *In my high school, I couldn't call a teacher by his first name, but I can do it here.*

1.
2.
3.

EXERCISE 14 ABOUT YOU If you come from another country, write three sentences telling about something that was prohibited there that you can do in the U.S.

EXAMPLE *I couldn't criticize the political leaders in my country, but I can do it now.*

1.
2.
3.

TENANTS' RIGHTS

Before You Read

1. What are some complaints you have about your apartment? Do you ever tell the landlord about your complaints?
2. Is your apartment warm enough in the winter and cool enough in the summer?

 Read the following conversation. Pay special attention to *should* and *had better*.

brochure

A: My apartment is always too cold in the winter. I've got to move.
B: You don't have to move. The landlord is supposed to give enough heat.
A: But he doesn't.
B: You **should** talk to him about this problem.
A: I did already. The first time I talked to him, he just told me I **should** put on a sweater. The second time I said, "You**'d better** give me heat, or I'm going to move."
B: You **shouldn't** get so angry. That's not the way to solve the problem. You know, there are laws about heat. You **should** get information from the city so you can know your rights.
A: How can I get information?
B: Tomorrow morning, you **should** call the mayor's office and ask for a brochure about tenants' rights. When you know what the law is exactly, you **should** show the brochure to your landlord.
A: And what if he doesn't want to do anything about it?
B: Then you **should** report the problem to the mayor's office.
A: I'm afraid to do that.
B: Don't be afraid. You have rights. Maybe you **should** talk to other tenants and see if you can do this together.

Modals; Related Expressions

8.7 Should; Had Better

Examples	Explanation

You **should** talk to the landlord about the problem.
You **should** get information about tenants' rights.
You **shouldn't** get so angry.
	For advice, use *should*.
	    Should = It's a good idea.
	    Shouldn't = It's a bad idea.

Compare: Your landlord **must** give you a smoke detector. You **should** check the battery in the smoke detector occasionally.	Remember, *must* is very strong and is not for advice. It is for rules and laws. For advice, use *should*.
You **had better** give me heat, or I'm going to move. We**'d better not** make so much noise, or our neighbors will complain.	For a warning, use *had better (not)*. Something bad can happen if you don't follow this advice. The contraction for *had* (in *had better*) is *'d*. I'd you'd he'd she'd we'd they'd

Pronunciation Note:
Native speakers often don't pronounce the *had* or *'d* in *had better*. You will hear people say, "**You better** be careful; **You better** not make so much noise."

EXERCISE 15 Give advice using *should*. Answers may vary.

EXAMPLE I'm going to move next week, and I hope to get my security deposit back.

    Advice: *You should clean the apartment completely.*

1. I just rented an apartment, but the rent is too high for me alone.

   Advice: _____

2. My upstairs neighbors make a lot of noise.

   Advice: _____

3. The battery in the smoke detector is old.

   Advice: _____

4. I want to paint the walls.

   Advice: _____

5. The rent was due last week, but I forgot to pay it.

   Advice: _____

6. My landlady doesn't give us enough heat in the winter.

   Advice: _____

7. I can't understand my lease.

    Advice: _____

8. I broke a window in my apartment.

    Advice: _____

9. My landlord doesn't want to return my security deposit.

    Advice: _____

10. The landlord is going to raise the rent by 40 percent.

    Advice: _____

EXERCISE 16 Fill in the blanks with an appropriate verb (phrase) to complete this conversation. Answers may vary.

A: My mother is such a worrier.

B: What does she worry about?

A: Everything. Especially me.

B: For example?

A: Even if it's warm outside, she always says, "you'd better ___take a sweater___ (example) because it might get cold later," or "You'd better _____ (1) because it might rain." When I drive, she always tells me, "You'd better _____ (2), or you might get a ticket." If I stay out late with my friends, she tells me, "You'd better _____ (3), or you won't get enough sleep." If I read a lot, she says, "You'd better not _____ (4), or you'll ruin your eyesight."

B: Well, she's your mother. So naturally she worries about you.

A: But she worries about other things too.

B: Like what?

A: You'd better _____(5)_____ your shoes when you enter the apartment, or the neighbors downstairs will hear us walking around.

We'd better _____(6)_____, or the neighbors will complain about the noise in our apartment.

B: It sounds like she's a good neighbor.

A: That's not all. She unplugs the TV every night. She says, "I'd better _____(7)_____, or the apartment will fill up with radiation."

And she doesn't want to use a cell phone. She says it has too much radiation. I think that's so silly.

B: I don't think that's silly. You'd better _____(8)_____ some articles about cell phones because they do produce radiation.

A: I don't even use my cell phone very much. But my mother always tells me, "You'd better _____(9)_____ in case I need to call you."

B: Do you live with your mother?

A: Yes, I do. I think I'd better _____(10)_____ to my own apartment, or she'll drive me crazy.

252   Lesson 8

8.8 Negatives of Modals

In negative statements, *must not, don't have to,* and *shouldn't* have very different meanings. *Must not, may not,* and *can't* have similar meanings.

Examples	Explanation
You **must not** change the locks without the landlord's permission. You **must not** take the landlord's smoke detector with you when you move.	Use *must not* for prohibition. These things are against the law or rules. *Must not* has an official tone.
I **can't** have a dog in my apartment. I **may not** have a water bed in my apartment.	Use *cannot* or *may not* to show no permission. The meaning is about the same as *must not*. (*May not* is more formal than *cannot*).
The landlord **is not supposed to** keep your security deposit. You **are not supposed to** paint the walls without the landlord's permission. You **are not supposed to** park in another tenant's parking space.	*Be not supposed to* indicates that something is against the law or breaks the rules. *Be not supposed to* is more common than *must not*. Remember, *must not* has an official tone.
My landlord offered me a new lease. I **don't have to** move when my lease is up. The janitor takes out the garbage. I **don't have to** take it out.	*Not have to* indicates that something is not necessary, not required. A person can do something if he wants, but he has no obligation to do it.
If you turn on the air-conditioning, you **shouldn't** leave the windows open. You **shouldn't** make noise late at night.	*Shouldn't* is for advice, not for rules.
You**'d better not** play your music so loud, or your neighbors will complain to the landlord.	*Had better not* is used for a warning.
Compare: a. I **don't have to pay** my rent with cash. I can use a check. b. I **must not pay** my rent late. c. I **don't have to use** the elevator. I can use the stairs. d. There's a fire in the building. You **must not use** the elevator.	In affirmative statements, *must* and *have to* have very similar meanings. However, in negative statements, the meaning is very different. In the examples on the left: a. It is not necessary to use cash. b. It is against the rules to pay late. c. You have options: stairs or elevator. d. It is prohibited or dangerous to use the elevator.
Compare: a. You **must not change** the locks without permission from the landlord. b. You**'re not supposed to change** the locks without permission from the landlord. c. You **shouldn't leave** your door unlocked. A robber can enter your apartment.	a. *Must not* is for prohibition. b. *Be not supposed to* is also for prohibition, but it sounds less official or formal. c. *Should not* expresses that something is a bad idea. It does not express prohibition.

EXERCISE 17 Practice using *must not* for prohibition. Use *you* in the impersonal sense.

EXAMPLE Name something you must not do.
You must not steal.

1. Name something you must not do on the bus.
2. Name something you mustn't do during a test.
3. Name something you mustn't do in the library.
4. Name something you must not do in the classroom.
5. Name something you mustn't do on an airplane.

EXERCISE 18 ABOUT YOU Tell if you *have to* or *don't have to* do the following. For affirmative statements, you can also use *have got to*.

EXAMPLES work on Saturdays
I have to work on Saturdays.   OR   I've got to work on Saturdays.

wear a suit to work
I don't have to wear a suit to work.

1. speak English every day
2. use a dictionary to read the newspaper
3. pay rent on the first of the month
4. type my homework
5. work on Saturdays
6. come to school every day
7. pay my rent in cash
8. use public transportation
9. talk to the teacher after class
10. cook every day

EXERCISE 19 Ask a student who comes from another country these questions.

1. In your native country, does a citizen have to vote?
2. Do men have to serve in the military?
3. Do schoolchildren have to wear uniforms?
4. Do divorced fathers have to support their children?
5. Do people have to get permission to travel?
6. Do students have to pass an exam to get their high school or university diploma?
7. Do students have to pay for their own books?
8. Do citizens have to pay taxes?
9. Do people have to make an appointment to see a doctor?

EXERCISE 20 Fill in the blanks with *be not supposed to* (when there is a rule) or *don't have to* (when something is not necessary).

A: Would you like to see my new apartment?

B: Yes.

A: I'll take you there after class today. The teacher says we ____*don't have to*____ go to the lab this afternoon. We can take the day off today.
(example)

(*at the apartment*)

B: Why do you carry your bicycle up to the third floor? Wouldn't it be better to leave it near the front door?

A: The landlord says we _____(1)_____ leave anything near the door.
The rule is to leave the front lobby empty. Besides, I can take it up in the elevator. I _____(2)_____ use the stairs, but I don't mind carrying it. My bicycle is light.

B: This is a great apartment. But it's so big. Isn't it expensive?

A: Yes, but I _____(3)_____ pay the rent alone. I have a roommate.

B: I see you have lots of nice pictures on the walls. In my apartment, we _____(4)_____ make holes in the walls.

Modals; Related Expressions   255

A: You can't even put up pictures? If you use picture hooks, you _____(5)_____ make big holes. Why don't you ask your landlord if you can do it? If you can, I can give you some picture hooks.

B: Thanks. In my apartment, the landlord has so many rules. For example, we _____(6)_____ hang our laundry out the window. We have to use the washing machine in the basement. And we _____(7)_____ use electric heaters.

A: An electric heater can sometimes cause a fire. I'm sure the apartment has heaters for each room. And in the U.S. people don't usually hang clothes to dry out the window. People use driers.

B: There are so many different rules and customs here.

A: Don't worry. If you do something wrong, someone will tell you.

EXERCISE 21 Students (S) are asking the teacher (T) questions about the final exam. Fill in the blanks with the negative form of *have to, should, must, had better, can, may, be supposed to*. In some cases, more than one answer is possible.

S: Do I have to sit in a specific seat for the test?

T: No, you __*don't have to*__ *(example)*. You can choose any seat you want.

S: Is it OK if I talk to another student during a test?

T: No. Absolutely not. You _____(1)_____ talk to another student during a test.

S: Is it OK if I use my book?

T: Sorry. You _____(2)_____ use your book.

S: What if I don't understand something on the test? Can I ask another student?

T: You _____(3)_____ talk to another student, or I'll think you're getting an answer. Ask me if you have a question.

S: What happens if I am late for the test? Will you let me in?

T: Of course I'll let you in. But you _____(4)_____ come late. You'll need a lot of time for the test.

S: Do I have to bring my own paper for the final test?

T: If you want to, you can. But you _____(5)_____ bring paper. I'll give you paper if you need it.

S: Must I use a pen?

T: You can use whatever you want. You _____(6)_____ use a pen.

S: Do you have any advice on test-taking?

T: Yes. If you see an item that is difficult for you, go on to the next item. You _____(7)_____ spend too much time on a difficult item, or you won't finish the test.

S: Can I bring coffee into the classroom?

T: The school has a rule about eating or drinking in the classroom. You _____(8)_____ bring food into the classroom.

S: If I finish the test early, must I stay in the room?

T: No, you _____(9)_____ stay. You can leave.

THE NEW NEIGHBORS

Before You Read

1. Are people friendly with their neighbors in your community?
2. Do you know any of your neighbors now?

 Read the following conversation. Pay special attention to *must*.

crib

Lisa (L) knocks on the door of her new upstairs neighbor, Paula (P).

L: Hi. You **must be** the new neighbor. I saw the moving truck out front this morning. Let me introduce myself. My name is Lisa. I live downstairs from you.

P: Nice to meet you, Lisa. My name is Paula. We just moved in.

L: I saw the movers carrying a crib upstairs. You **must have** a baby.

P: We do. We have a ten-month-old son. He's sleeping now. Do you have any kids?

L: Yes. I have a 16-year-old-daughter and an 18-year-old son.

P: It **must be** hard to raise teenagers.

L: Believe me, it is! I **must spend** half my time worrying about where they are and what they're doing. My daughter talks on the phone all day. She **must spend** half of her waking hours on the phone with her friends. They're always whispering to each other. They **must have** some big secrets.

P: I know what you mean. My brother has a teenage daughter.

L: Listen, I don't want to take up any more of your time. You **must be** very busy. I just wanted to bring you these cookies.

P: Thanks. That's very nice of you. They're still warm. They **must be** right out of the oven.

L: They are. Maybe we can talk some other time when you're all unpacked.

8.9 | *Must* for Conclusions

In Section 8.4, we studied *must* to express necessity. *Must* has another use: we use it to show a logical conclusion or deduction based on information we have or observations we make. *Must*, in this case, is for the present only, not the future.

Examples	Explanation
a. The new neighbors have a crib. They **must have** a baby. b. Paula just moved in. She **must be** very busy. c. The teenage girls whisper all the time. They **must have** secrets.	a. You see the crib, so you conclude that they have a baby. b. You know how hard it is to move, so you conclude that she is busy. c. You see them whispering, so you conclude that they are telling secrets.
I didn't see Paula's husband. He **must not be** home.	For a negative deduction, use *must not*. Do not use a contraction.

EXERCISE 22 A week later, Paula goes to Lisa's apartment and notices certain things. Use *must* + base form to show Paula's conclusions about Lisa's life. Answers may vary.

EXAMPLE There is a bowl of food on the kitchen floor.
Lisa must have a pet.

1. There are pictures of Lisa and her two children all over the house. There is no picture of a man.
   _____

2. There is a nursing certificate on the wall with Lisa's name on it.
   _____

3. There are many different kinds of coffee on a kitchen shelf.
   _____

4. There are a lot of classical music CDs.
   _____

5. In Lisa's bedroom, there's a sewing machine.
   _____

6. In the kitchen, there are a lot of cookbooks.
   _____

Modals; Related Expressions

7. There's a piano in the living room.
   _____

8. On the bookshelf, there are a lot of books about modern art.
   _____

9. On the kitchen calendar, there's an activity filled in for almost every day of the week.
   _____

10. There are pictures of cats everywhere.
    _____

EXERCISE 23 Two neighbors, Alma (A) and Eva (E), meet in the hallway of their building. Fill in the blanks with an appropriate verb to show deduction.

A: Hi. My name's Alma. I live on the third floor. You must ____be____ new in this building.
   (example)

E: I am. We just moved in last week. My name's Eva.

A: I noticed your last name on the mailbox. It'sKović. That sounds like a Bosnian name. You must _____ from Bosnia.
   (1)

E: I am. How did you know?

A: I'm from Bosnia too. Did you come directly to the U.S. from Bosnia?

E: No. I stayed in Germany for three years.

A: Then you must _____ German.
   (2)

E: I can speak it pretty well, but I can't write it well.

A: Are you going to school now?

E: Yes, I'm taking English classes at Washington College.

A: What level are you in?

E: I'm in Level 5.

A: Then you must _____ my husband. He takes classes
   (3)

   there too. He's in Level 5 too.

260 Lesson 8

E: There's only one guy with a Bosnian last name. That must _____(4)_____ your husband.

A: His name is Hasan.

B: Oh, yes, I know him. I didn't know he lived in the same building. I never see him here. He must not _____(5)_____ home very much.

A: He isn't. He has two jobs.

E: Do you take English classes?

A: Not anymore. I came here 15 years ago.

E: Then your English must _____(6)_____ perfect.

A: I don't know if it's perfect, but it's good enough.

8.10 | *Will* and *May / Might*

Examples	Explanation
My lease **will** expire on April 30. We **won't** sign another lease.	For certainty about the future, use *will*. The negative contraction for *will not* is *won't*.
a. My landlord **might** raise my rent at that time. a. I **may** move. b. I don't know what "tenant" means. Let's ask the teacher. She **might** know. b. The teacher **may** have information about tenants' rights.	*May* and *might* both have about the same meaning: possibility or uncertainty. a. about the future b. about the present
He **may not** renew our lease. He **might not** renew our lease.	We don't use a contraction for *may not* and *might not*.
Compare: a. **Maybe** I will move. b. I **might** move. a. **Maybe** he doesn't understand the lease. b. He **might** not understand the lease. a. **Maybe** the apartment is cold in winter. (*maybe* = adverb) b. The apartment **may** be cold in winter. (*may* + *be* = modal + verb)	*Maybe* is an adverb. It is one word. It usually comes at the beginning of the sentence and means *possibly* or *perhaps*. *May* and *might* are modals. They follow the subject and precede the verb. Sentences (a) and (b) have the same meaning. *Wrong:* I *maybe* will move. *Wrong:* He *maybe* doesn't understand. *Wrong:* The apartment *maybe* is cold.

EXERCISE 24 The following sentences contain *maybe*. Take away *maybe* and use *may* or *might* + base form.

EXAMPLE   Maybe your neighbors will complain if your music is loud.
Your neighbors might complain if your music is loud.

1. Maybe my sister will come to live with me.
2. Maybe she will find a job in this city.
3. Maybe my landlord will raise my rent.
4. Maybe I will get a dog.
5. Maybe my landlord won't allow me to have a dog.
6. Maybe I will move next year.
7. Maybe I will buy a house soon.
8. Maybe I won't stay in this city.
9. Maybe I won't come to class tomorrow.
10. Maybe the teacher will review modals if we need more help.

EXERCISE 25   ABOUT YOU Fill in the blanks with a possibility.

EXAMPLES   If I don't pay my rent on time, _I might have to pay a late fee._

If I make a lot of noise in my apartment, _the neighbors may complain._

1. When my lease is up, _____
2. If I don't clean my apartment before I move out, _____
_____
3. If I don't study for the next test, _____
4. If we don't register for classes early, _____
_____
5. If I don't pass this course, _____

EXERCISE 26   Fill in the blanks with possibilities. Answers may vary.

EXAMPLE   **A:** I'm going to move on Saturday. I might ____need____ help. Can you help me?

B: I'm not sure. I may ____go____ to the country with my family if the weather is nice. If I stay here, I'll help you.

1. **A:** My next door neighbor's name is Terry Karson. I see her name on the doorbell but I never see her.

   B: Why do you say "her"? Your neighbor may _____.
   Terry is sometimes a man's name.

262   Lesson 8

2. **A:** I need coins for the laundry room. Do you have any?

   B: Let me look. I might _____ some. No, I don't have any. Look in the laundry room. There might _____ a dollar-bill changer there.

3. **A:** Do you know the landlord's address?

   B: No, I don't. Ask the manager. She might _____.

   A: Where's the manager now?

   B: I'm not sure. She might _____ in a tenant's apartment.

4. **A:** Do they allow cats in this building?

   B: I'm not sure. I know they don't allow dogs, but they might _____ cats.

5. **A:** We'd better close the windows before going out.

   B: Why? It's a hot day today.

   A: Look how gray the sky is. It might _____.

6. **A:** Are you going to stay in this apartment for another year?

   B: I'm not sure. I may _____.

   A: Why?

   B: The landlord might _____ the rent. If the rent goes up more than 25 percent, I'll move.

7. **A:** I have so much stuff in my closet. There's not enough room for my clothes.

   B: There might _____ lockers in the basement where you can store your things.

   A: Really? I didn't know that.

   B: Let's look. I may _____ a key to the basement with me.

   A: That would be great.

   B: Hmm. I don't have one on me. Let's go to my apartment. My basement keys might _____ there.

AT A GARAGE SALE

Before You Read

1. People often have a garage sale or yard sale or an apartment sale before they move. At this kind of sale, people sell things that they don't want or need anymore. Did you ever buy anything at this kind of sale?

2. At a garage or yard sale, it is usually not necessary to pay the asking price. You may be able to bargain[3] with the seller. Can you bargain the price in other places?

This is a conversation at a garage sale between a seller (S) and a buyer (B). Read the conversation. Pay special attention to modals and related expressions.

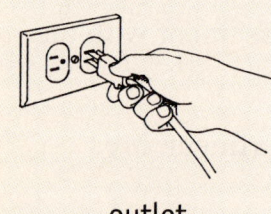

outlet

S: I see you're looking at my microwave oven. **May** I answer any questions?
B: Yes. I'm interested in buying one. Does it work well?
S: It's only two years old, and it's in perfect working condition. **Would** you **like** to try it out?
B: Sure. **Could** you plug it in somewhere?
S: I have an outlet right here. **Why don't we** boil a cup of water so you can see how well it works.

A few minutes later . . .

B: It seems to work well. **Would** you tell me why you're selling it, then?
S: We're moving next week. Our new apartment already has one.
B: How much do you want for it?[4]
S: $40.

---

[3] When a buyer *bargains* with the seller, the buyer makes an offer lower than the asking price and hopes that he or she and the seller will agree on a lower price.

[4] We ask "How much is it?" when the price is fixed. We ask "How much do you want for it?" when the price is negotiable—you can bargain for it.

B: **Will** you take $30?
S: **Can** you wait a minute? I'll ask my wife.

A few minutes later . . .

S: My wife says she'll let you have it for $35.
B: OK. **May** I write you a check?
S: I'm sorry. **I'd rather** have cash.
B: **Would** you hold it for me for an hour? I can go to the ATM and get cash.
S: **Could** you leave me a small deposit? Ten dollars, maybe?
B: Yes, I can.
S: Fine. I'll hold it for you.

8.11 | Using Modals and Questions for Politeness

Modals and questions are often used to make direct statements more polite.
Compare:
  Plug it in. (very direct)
  Would you plug it in? (more polite)

	Examples	Explanation
To ask permission	**May** / **Can** / **Could** I write you a check?	*May* and *could* are considered more polite than *can* by some speakers of English.
To request that someone do something	**Can** / **Could** / **Will** / **Would** you plug it in?	For a request, *could* and *would* are softer than *can* and *will*.
To express want or desire	**Would** you **like** to try out the microwave oven? Yes, I **would like** to see if it works. I**'d like** a cup of coffee.	*Would like* has the same meaning as *want*. *Would like* is softer than *want*. The contraction for *would* after a pronoun is **'d.**
To express preference	**Would** you **rather** pay with cash or by credit card? I**'d rather** pay by credit card (than with cash).	Use *or* in questions with *would rather*. Use *than* in statements.
To offer a suggestion	**Why don't you** go to the ATM to get cash? **Why don't we** boil a cup of water? **Compare:** Go to the ATM. Boil a cup of water.	We can make a suggestion more polite by using a negative question.

EXERCISE 27 Change each request to make it more polite. Practice *may, can,* and *could + I?*

EXAMPLES I want to use your phone.
May I use your phone?

I want to borrow a quarter.
Could I borrow a quarter?

1. I want to help you.
2. I want to close the door.
3. I want to leave the room.
4. I want to write you a check.

EXERCISE 28 Change these commands to make them more polite. Practice *can you, could you, will you,* and *would you?*

EXAMPLES Call the doctor for me.
Would you call the doctor for me?

Give me a cup of coffee.
Could you give me a cup of coffee, please?

1. Repeat the sentence.
2. Give me your paper.
3. Spell your name.
4. Tell me your phone number.

EXERCISE 29 Make these sentences more polite by using *would like.*

EXAMPLE Do you want some help?
Would you like some help?

1. I want to ask you a question.
2. The teacher wants to speak with you.
3. Do you want to try out the oven?
4. Yes. I want to see if it works.

EXERCISE 30 Make each suggestion more polite by putting it in the form of a negative question.

EXAMPLES Plug it in.
Why don't you plug it in?

Let's eat now.
Why don't we eat now?

1. Take a sweater.
2. Let's turn off the light.
3. Turn left here.
4. Let's leave early.

EXERCISE 31 ABOUT YOU Make a statement of preference using *would rather*.

EXAMPLE own a house / a condominium
I'd rather own a condominium (than a house).

1. live in the U.S. / in another country
2. own a condominium / rent an apartment
3. have young neighbors / old neighbors
4. have wood floors / carpeted floors
5. live in the center of the city / in a suburb
6. drive to work / take public transportation
7. pay my rent by check / cash
8. have nosy neighbors / noisy neighbors

EXERCISE 32 ABOUT YOU Ask a question of preference with the words given. Another student will answer.

EXAMPLE eat Chinese food / Italian food
A: Would you rather eat Chinese food or Italian food?
B: I'd rather eat Italian food.

1. read fact / fiction
2. watch funny movies / serious movies
3. listen to classical music / popular music
4. visit Europe / Africa
5. own a large luxury car / a small sports car
6. watch a soccer game / take part in a soccer game
7. write a letter / receive a letter
8. cook / eat in a restaurant

EXERCISE 33 This is a conversation between a seller (S) and a buyer (B) at a garage sale. Make this conversation more polite by using modals and other polite expressions in place of the underlined words. Answers may vary.

S: ~~What do you want?~~ *May I help you?*
(example)

B: I'm interested in that lamp. <u>Show it to me</u>. Does it work?
(1)

S: I'll go and get a light bulb. <u>Wait a minute</u>.
(2)

A few minutes later . . .

B: <u>Plug it in</u>.
(3)

S: You see? It works fine.

B: How much do you want for it?

S: This is one of a pair. I have another one just like it. They're $10 each. I <u>prefer to sell</u> them together.
(4)

B: <u>Give them both to me for $15</u>.
(5)

S: I'll have to ask my husband.

(*A few seconds later*)

My husband says he'll sell them to you for $17.

B: Fine. I'll take them. Will you take a check?

S: I <u>prefer to</u> have cash.
(6)

B: I only have five dollars on me.

S: OK. I'll take a check. <u>Show me some identification</u>.
(7)

B: Here's my driver's license.

S: That's fine. Just write the check to James Kucinski.

B: <u>Spell your name for me</u>.
(8)

S: K-U-C-I-N-S-K-I.

SUMMARY OF LESSON 8

Modals		
Modal	**Example**	**Explanation**
can	I **can** stay in this apartment until March. I **can** carry my bicycle up to my apartment. You **can't** paint the walls without the landlord's permission. **Can** I borrow your pen? **Can** you turn off the light, please?	Permission Ability/Possibility Prohibition Asking permission Request
should	You **should** be friendly with your neighbors. You **shouldn't** leave the air-conditioner on. It wastes electricity.	A good idea A bad idea
may	**May** I borrow your pen? You **may** leave the room. You **may not** talk during a test. I **may** move next month. The landlord **may** have an extra key.	Asking permission Giving permission Prohibition Future possibility Present possibility
might	I **might** move next month. The landlord **might** have an extra key.	Future possibility Present possibility
must	The landlord **must** install smoke detectors. You **must not** change the locks. Mary has a cat box. She **must** have a cat.	Rule or law: Official tone Prohibition: Official tone Conclusion/Deduction
would	**Would** you help me move?	Request
would like	I **would like** to use your phone.	Want
would rather	I **would rather** live in Florida than in Maine.	Preference
could	In my country, I **couldn't** choose my own apartment. The government gave me one. In my country, I **could** attend college for free. **Could** you help me move? **Could** I borrow your car?	Past permission Past ability Request Asking permission

Related Expressions

Expression	Example	Explanation
have to	She **has to** leave. He **had to** leave work early today.	Necessity Past necessity
have got to	She **has got to** see a doctor. I**'ve got to** move.	Necessity
not have to	You **don't have to** pay your rent with cash. You can pay by check.	No necessity
had better	You **had better** pay your rent on time, or the landlord will ask you to leave. You**'d better** get permission before changing the locks.	Warning
be supposed to	I **am supposed to** pay my rent by the fifth of the month. We**'re not supposed to** have a dog here.	Reporting a rule
be able to	The teacher **is able to** use modals correctly.	Ability
be permitted to be allowed to	We**'re not permitted to** park here overnight. We**'re not allowed to** park here overnight.	Permission

EDITING ADVICE

1. After a modal, we use the base form.

    I must ~~to~~ study.

    I can help~~ing~~ you now.

2. A modal has no ending.

    He can~~s~~ cook.

3. We don't put two modals together. We change the second modal to another form.

            have to
    She will ~~must~~ take the test.

4. Don't forget *to* after *be permitted, be allowed, be supposed,* and *be able.*

                     to
    We're not permitted ∧ talk during a test.

5. Don't forget *be* before *permitted to, allowed to, supposed to,* and *able to.*

    am
    I ^ not supposed to pay my rent late.

6. Use the correct word order in a question.

    should I
    What ~~I should~~ do about my problem?

7. Don't use *can* for past. Use *could* + a base form.

    couldn't go
    I ~~can't went~~ to the party last week.

8. Don't forget *would* before *rather.*

    'd
    I ^ rather live in Canada than in the U.S.

9. Don't forget *had* before *better.*

    'd
    You ^ better take a sweater. It's going to get cold.

10. Don't forget *have* before *got to.*

    've
    It's late. I ^ got to go.

11. Don't use *maybe* before a verb.

    may
    It ~~maybe will~~ rain later.

Modals; Related Expressions **271**

LESSON 8 TEST/REVIEW

PART 1 Find the grammar mistakes with the underlined words, and correct them. Not every sentence has a mistake. If the sentence is correct, write *C*.

EXAMPLES You <u>must to stop</u> at a red light.

You <u>have to stop</u> at a red light.   **C**

1. We're <u>not permitted use</u> our books during the test.
2. When I was a child, I <u>couldn't rode</u> a bike.
3. When <u>she can</u> leave?
4. What <u>must I</u> write on this application?
5. She <u>has to taking</u> her daughter to the doctor now.
6. What <u>we should</u> do for homework?
7. You <u>not supposed</u> to talk during the test.
8. We're <u>not allowed to</u> take food into the computer lab.
9. He <u>can't have</u> a dog in his apartment.
10. <u>Could I</u> use your pen, please?
11. <u>I rather</u> walk than drive.
12. <u>You'd better</u> hurry. It's late.
13. I <u>got to</u> talk to my boss about a raise.
14. We <u>maybe will buy</u> a house.
15. She <u>might buy</u> a new car next year.
16. I <u>may have to</u> go home early tonight.
17. He <u>can speak</u> English now, but he <u>can't spoke</u> it five years ago.

PART 2 This is a conversation between two friends. Circle the correct expression in parentheses ( ) to complete the conversation.

A: I'm moving on Saturday. (**Could** / *May*) you help me?
    (example)

B: I (*should / would*) like to help you, but I have a bad back. I went to
    (1)

   my doctor last week, and she told me that I (*shouldn't / don't have to*)
    (2)

272   Lesson 8

lift anything heavy for a while. (*Can / Would*) I help you any other
                                        (3)

way besides moving?

A: Yes. I don't have enough boxes. (*Should / Would*) you help me find
                                              (4)

some?

B: Sure. I (*have to / must*) go shopping this afternoon. I'll pick up some
              (5)

boxes while I'm at the supermarket.

A: Boxes can be heavy. You (*would / had*) better not lift them yourself.
                              (6)

B: Don't worry. I'll have someone put them in my car for me.

A: Thanks. I don't have a free minute. I (*couldn't go / can't went*) to
                                            (7)

class all last week. There's so much to do.

B: I know what you mean. You (*might / must*) be tired.
                                (8)

A: I am. I have another favor to ask. (*Can / Would*) I borrow your van
                                         (9)

on Saturday?

B: I (*should / have to*) work on Saturday. How about Sunday? I
        (10)

(*must not / don't have to*) work on Sunday.
      (11)

A: That's impossible. I (*'ve got to / should*) move out on Saturday. The
                          (12)

new tenants are moving in Sunday morning.

B: Let me ask my brother. He has a van too. He (*must / might*) be able
                                                  (13)

to let you use his van. He (*has to / should*) work Saturday too, but
                          (14)

only for half a day.

A: Thanks. I'd appreciate it if you could ask him.

B: Why are you moving? You have a great apartment.

A: We decided to move to the suburbs. It's quieter there. And I want to
have a dog. I (*shouldn't / 'm not supposed to*) have a dog in my
              (15)

present apartment. But my new landlord says I (*might / may*) have
                                              (16)

a dog.

B: I (*had / would*) rather have a cat. They're easier to take care of.
        (17)

EXPANSION ACTIVITIES

1. A student will read one of the following problems out loud to the class, pretending that this is his or her problem. Other students will ask for more information and give advice about this problem.

   EXAMPLE   My mother-in-law comes to visit all the time. When she's here, she always criticizes everything we do. I told my wife that I don't want her here, but she says, "It's my mother, and I want her here." What should I do?

   A: How long does she usually stay?
   B: She might stay for about two weeks or longer.
   C: How does she criticize you? What does she say?
   B: She says I should help my wife more.
   D: Well, I agree with her. You should help with housework.
   B: My children aren't allowed to watch TV after 8 o'clock. But my mother-in-law lets them watch TV as long as they want.
   E: You'd better have a talk with her and tell her your rules.

   Problem 1. My mother is 80 years old, and she lives with us. It's very hard on my family to take care of her. We'd like to put her in a nursing home, where she can get better care. Mother refuses to go. What can we do?

   Problem 2. I have a nice one-bedroom apartment with a beautiful view of a park and a lake. I live with my wife and one child. My friends from out of town often come to visit and want to stay at my apartment. In the last year, ten people came to visit us. I like to have visitors, but sometimes they stay for weeks. It's hard on my family with such a small apartment. What should I tell my friends when they want to visit?

   Problem 3. My upstairs neighbors make noise all the time. I can't sleep at night. I asked them three times to be quieter, and each time they said they would. But the noise still continues. What should I do?

   Write your own problem to present to the class. It can be real or imaginary. (Suggestions: a problem with a neighbor, your landlord, a teacher or class, a service you are dissatisfied with)

   _____
   _____
   _____

2. Circle a game you like from the following list. Find a partner who also likes this game. Write a list of some of the rules of this game. Tell what you *can, cannot, should, have to,* and *must not* do.

   chess   tennis   football   poker   other _____
   checkers   baseball   soccer   volleyball

   EXAMPLE checkers
   You have to move the pieces on a diagonal. You can only move in one direction until you get a king. Then you can move in two directions.

   _____
   _____
   _____

3. Many people get vanity license plates that tell something about their professions, hobbies, or families. Often words are abbreviated: M = am, U = you, 4 = for, 8 = the "ate" sound. Words are often missing vowels. If you see the following license plates, what conclusion can you make about the owner? You may work with a partner and get help from the teacher.

   EXAMPLE EYE DOC *The owner must be an eye doctor.*

   1. I TCH ENGLSH _____
   2. I LV CARS _____
   3. I M GRANDMA _____
   4. MUSC LVR _____
   5. I LV DGS _____
   6. TENNIS GR8 _____
   7. I SK8 _____
   8. CRPNTR _____
   9. BSY MOM _____
   10. SHY GUY _____
   11. DAD OF TWO _____
   12. RMNTIC GAL _____
   13. NO TIME 4 U _____
   14. CITY GAL _____
   15. LDY DOC _____
   16. LUV GLF _____
   17. MXCAN GUY _____
   18. I M GD COOK _____

19. ALWAYS L8 _____

20. WE DANCE _____

4. Work with a partner from your own country, if possible. Talk about some laws in your country that are different from laws in the United States. Present this information to the class.

   EXAMPLE Citizens must vote in my country. In the U.S., they don't have to vote.

   People are supposed to carry identification papers at all times. In the U.S., people don't have to carry identification papers.

   In my country, citizens must not own a gun.

Talk About it

1. Compare getting a driver's license here with getting a driver's license in another country or state. Are the requirements the same?

2. How did you find your apartment?

Write About it

1. Write a short composition comparing rules in an apartment in this city with rules in an apartment in your hometown or native country.

2. Write about the differences between rules at this school and rules at another school you attended. Are students allowed to do things here that they can't do in another school?

3. Find out what a student has to do to register for the first time at this school. You may want to visit the registrar's office to interview a worker there. Write a short composition explaining to a new student the steps for admission and registration.

Outside Activities

1. Look at the Sunday newspaper for notices about garage sales or apartment sales. What kind of items are going to be sold? If you have time, go to a sale. Report about your experience to the class.

2. Get a newspaper. Look for the advice column. Read the problems and the advice. Circle the modals. Do you agree with the advice?

3. Look at your lease. Can you understand what the rules are in your apartment?

Internet Activities

1. Try to find information online about tenants' rights in the city where you live. Circle the modals.

2. Find a phone directory online. Look up the names and addresses of moving companies in your city. Call a company to find out the price of a move.

3. Find apartments for rent online. Print a page. Discuss with your classmates the price of apartments and what is included.

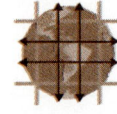

Additional Activities at http://elt.heinle.com/gic

LESSON 9

GRAMMAR
The Present Perfect
The Present Perfect Continuous[1]

CONTEXT: Searching the Web
Google
Genealogy

[1] The *present perfect continuous* is sometimes called the *present perfect progressive*.

9.1 The Present Perfect Tense—An Overview

We form the present perfect with *have* or *has* + the past participle.

Subject	*have*	Past Participle	Complement	Explanation
I	have	been	in the U.S. for three years.	Use *have* with *I, you, we, they,* and plural nouns.
You	have	used	your computer a lot.	
We	have	written	a job résumé.	
They	have	bought	a new computer.	
Computers	have	changed	the world.	

Subject	*has*	Past Participle	Complement	Explanation
My sister	has	gotten	her degree.	Use *has* with *he, she, it,* and singular nouns.
She	has	found	a job as a programmer.	
My father	has	helped	me.	
It	has	rained	a lot this month.	

There	*has/have*	been	Complement	Explanation
There	has	been	a problem with my computer.	After *there*, we use *has* or *have*, depending on the noun that follows. Use *has* with a singular noun. Use *have* with a plural noun.
There	have	been	many changes in the world.	

GOOGLE

Before You Read

1. Do you surf the Internet a lot? Why?
2. What search engine do you usually use?

Larry Page and Sergey Brin

Read the following article. Pay special attention to the present perfect tense.

Did You Know?

The word "Google" started as a noun, the company's name. Today people use it as a verb: "I'm going to *google* the Civil War to get more information about it."

Since its start in 1998, Google **has become** one of the most popular search engines. It **has grown** from a research project in the dormitory room of two college students to a business that now employs approximately 1,000 people.

Google's founders, Larry Page and Sergey Brin, met in 1995 when they were in their 20s and graduate students in computer science at Stanford University in California. They realized that Internet search was a very important field and began working together to make searching easier. Both Page and Brin left their studies at Stanford to work on their project. Interestingly, they **have** never **returned** to finish their degrees.

Brin was born in Russia, but he **has lived** in the U.S. since he was five years old. His father was a mathematician in Russia. Page, whose parents were computer experts, **has been** interested in computers since he was six years old.

When Google started in 1998, it did 10,000 searches a day. Today it does 200 million searches a day in 90 languages. It indexes[2] three billion Web pages.

How is Google different from other search engines? **Have** you ever **noticed** how many ads and banners there are on other search engines? News, sports scores, stock prices, links for shopping, mortgage rates, and more fill other search engines. Brin and Page wanted a clean home page. They believed that people come to the Internet to search for specific information, not to be hit with a lot of unwanted data. The success of Google over its rivals[3] **has proved** that this is true.

Over the past few years, Google **has added** new features to its Web site: Google Images, where you can type in a word and get thousands of pictures; Google News, which takes you to today's news; Froogle, which takes you to a shopping site; and more. But one thing **hasn't changed:** the clean opening page that Google offers its users.

In 2003, *Fortune* magazine ranked Page and Brin among the top ten richest people under 30. So far these two men **haven't changed** their lifestyles very much. They continue to live modestly.

[2] *To index* means to sort, organize, and categorize information.
[3] *Rivals* are competitors.

EXERCISE 1 Underline the present perfect tense in each sentence. Then tell if the sentence is true or false.

EXAMPLE Google <u>has become</u> the number one search engine.   T

1. Google has grown over the years.
2. Sergey Brin has lived in the U.S. all his life.
3. Larry Page and Sergey Brin have known each other since they were children.
4. Larry Page has been interested in computers since he was a child.
5. Brin and Page have returned to college to finish their degrees.
6. Since they became rich, Brin and Page have changed their lifestyles.
7. The word "Google" has become a verb.

9.2 The Past Participle

Forms			Explanation
Regular Verbs			The past participle of regular verbs ends in *-ed*. The past form and the past participle for regular verbs are the same.
Base Form	Past Form	Past Participle	
work	worked	**worked**	
improve	improved	**improved**	
Irregular Verbs			The past participle of irregular verbs is sometimes the same as the past form and sometimes different from it. For an alphabetical list of irregular past tenses and past participles, see Appendix M.
Base Form	Past Form	Past Participle	
have	had	**had** *(same as past)*	
write	wrote	**written** *(different from past)*	

9.3 Irregular Past Participle Forms of Verbs[4]

Base Form	Past Form	Past Participle
become	became	become
come	came	come
run	ran	run
blow	blew	blown
draw	drew	drawn
fly	flew	flown
grow	grew	grown
know	knew	known
throw	threw	thrown
swear	swore	sworn
tear	tore	torn
wear	wore	worn
break	broke	broken
choose	chose	chosen
freeze	froze	frozen
speak	spoke	spoken
steal	stole	stolen
begin	began	begun
drink	drank	drunk
ring	rang	rung
sing	sang	sung
sink	sank	sunk
swim	swam	swum
arise	arose	arisen
bite	bit	bitten
drive	drove	driven
ride	rode	ridden
rise	rose	risen
write	wrote	written
be	was/were	been
eat	ate	eaten
fall	fell	fallen
forgive	forgave	forgiven
give	gave	given
mistake	mistook	mistaken
see	saw	seen
shake	shook	shaken
take	took	taken
do	did	done
forget	forgot	forgotten
get	got	gotten
go	went	gone
lie	lay	lain
prove	proved	proven (or proved)
show	showed	shown (or showed)

[4] For an alphabetical listing of irregular past tenses and past participles, see Appendix M.

EXERCISE 2 Write the past participle of these verbs.

EXAMPLE   eat _____*eaten*_____

1. go _____
2. see _____
3. look _____
4. study _____
5. bring _____
6. take _____
7. say _____
8. be _____
9. find _____
10. leave _____
11. live _____
12. know _____
13. like _____
14. fall _____
15. feel _____
16. come _____
17. break _____
18. wear _____
19. choose _____
20. drive _____
21. write _____
22. put _____
23. begin _____
24. want _____
25. get _____
26. fly _____
27. sit _____
28. drink _____
29. grow _____
30. give _____

9.4 | The Present Perfect—Contractions, Negatives

For an affirmative statement, we can make a contraction with the subject pronoun. For a negative statement, we can make a contraction using *have/has* + *n't*.

Examples	Explanation
I've had a lot of experience with computers. **We've** read the story about Google. **He's** been interested in computers since he was a child. **There's** been an increase in searching over the years.	We can make a contraction with subject pronouns and *have* or *has*. I have = I've He has = He's You have = You've She has = She's We have = We've It has = It's They have = They've There has = There's
Larry's lived in the U.S. all his life. **Sergey's** been in the U.S. since he was five years old.	Most singular nouns can contract with *has*.
I **haven't** studied programming. Brin **hasn't** finished his degree.	Negative contractions: have not = haven't has not = hasn't

Language Note:
The *'s* in *he's, she's, it's,* and *there's* can mean *has* or *is*. The word following the contraction will tell you what the contraction means.
   He**'s** working. = He **is** working.
   He**'s** worked. = He **has** worked.

EXERCISE 3 Fill in the blanks to form the present perfect. Make a contraction, if possible.

EXAMPLE You _'ve_____ bought a new computer.

1. I _____ learned a lot about computers.
2. We _____ read the story about Google.
3. Larry _____ known Sergey since they were at Stanford University.
4. They (not) _____ known each other since they were children.
5. It _____ been easy for me to learn about computers.
6. You _____ used the Internet many times.
7. Larry and Sergey (not) _____ finished their degrees.

9.5 | Adding an Adverb

Subject	has/have	Adverb	Past Participle	Complement	Explanation
Page and Brin	have	never	finished	their degrees.	You can put an adverb between the auxiliary verb (have/has) and the past participle.
They	have	already*	made	a lot of money.	
They	have	even	become	billionaires in their 30s.	
Larry Page	has	always	been	interested in computers.	
You	have	probably	used	a search engine.	

Language Note:
Already frequently comes at the end of the verb phrase.
They have made a lot of money **already.**

EXERCISE 4 Add the word in parentheses ( ) to the sentence.

EXAMPLE You have gotten an e-mail account. (probably)
You have probably gotten an e-mail account.

1. The teacher has given a test on this lesson. (not)
   _____

2. We have heard of Page and Brin. (never)
   _____

The Present Perfect; The Present Perfect Continuous

3. They have been interested in search technology. (always)

_____

4. You have used Google. (probably)

_____

5. Brin hasn't finished his degree. (even)

_____

9.6 | The Present Perfect—Statements and Questions

Compare affirmative statements and questions

Wh-Word	have/has	Subject	have/has	Past Participle	Complement	Short Answer
		Larry	has	lived	in the U.S. all his life.	
	Has	Sergey		lived	in the U.S. all his life?	No, he hasn't.
How long	has	Sergey		lived	in the U.S.?	Since 1979.

Language Note:
For a short *yes* answer, we cannot make a contraction.
  Has Larry lived in the U.S. all his life? Yes, he has. (Not: *he's*)

Compare negative statements and questions

Wh-Word	haven't/hasn't	Subject	haven't/hasn't	Past Participle	Complement
		They	haven't	finished	their degrees.
Why	haven't	they		finished	their degrees?

EXERCISE 5   Change the statement to a question.

EXAMPLE   Google has changed the way people search. (how)
How has Google changed the way people search?

1. I have used several search engines. (which ones)

_____

2. Larry and Sergey haven't finished their degrees. (why)

_____

3. They haven't changed their lifestyles. (why)

_____

4. Sergey has been in the U.S. for many years. (how long)

_____

5. Larry and Sergey have hired approximately 1,000 people to work for Google. (how many)

   _____

6. We have used the computer lab several times this semester. (how many times)

   _____

7. The memory and speed of computers have increased. (why)

   _____

8. Computers have become part of our daily lives. (how)

   _____

9.7 Continuation from Past to Present

We use the present perfect tense to show that an action or state started in the past and continues to the present.

Past ←——— I **have had** my computer for two months. ———Now——————————→ Future

Examples	Explanation
Larry Page **has been** interested in computers **for many years.** My sister **has been** a programmer **for three years.**	Use *for* + an amount of time: *for two months, for three years, for one hour, for a long time,* etc.
Brin's family **has been** in the U.S. **since 1979.** I **have had** my computer **since March.** Personal computers **have been** popular **since the 1980s.**	Use *since* with the date, month, year, etc. that the action began.
Brin *has been* interested in computers *since he* **was** *a child.* I *have had* an e-mail account *since I* **bought** *my computer.*	Use *since* with the beginning of the continuous action or state. The verb in the *since* clause is simple past.
How long *has* Brin's family *been* in the U.S.? **How long** *have* you *had* your computer?	Use *how long* to ask about the amount of time from the past to the present.
Larry Page *has* **always** *lived* in the U.S. He *has* **always** *been* interested in computers.	We use the present perfect with *always* to show that an action began in the past and continues to the present.
My grandmother *has* **never** *used* a computer. Google *has* **never** *put* advertising on its opening page.	We use the present perfect with *never* to show that something has not occurred from the past to the present.

EXERCISE 6 Fill in the blanks with the missing words.

EXAMPLE I've known my best friend ____since____ we were in high school.

1. My brother has been in the U.S. _____ 1998.
2. My mother _____ never been in the U.S.
3. How _____ have you been in the U.S.?
4. I've known the teacher since I _____ to study at this college.
5. She's _____ married for two years.
6. She's had the same job _____ ten years.
7. My wife and I _____ known each other since we _____ in elementary school.
8. She' _____ been a student at this college _____ September.
9. I've had my car for three years. _____ long have you _____ your car?
10. I'm interested in art. I' _____ _____ interested in art since I was in high school.
11. _____ always wanted to have my own business.

EXERCISE 7 ABOUT YOU Write **true** statements using the present perfect with the words given and *for, since, always,* or *never*. Share your sentences with the class.

EXAMPLES
know *My parents have known each other for over 40 years.*
have *I've had my car since 2002.*
want *I've always wanted to learn English.*

1. have _____
2. be _____
3. want _____
4. know _____

EXERCISE 8 ABOUT YOU Make statements with *always*.

EXAMPLE Name something you've always thought about.
I've always thought about my future.

1. Name something you've always enjoyed.
2. Name a person you've always liked.

3. Name something you've always wanted to do.
4. Name something you've always wanted to have.
5. Name something you've always been interested in.

EXERCISE 9 ABOUT YOU Make statements with *never*.

EXAMPLE Name a machine you've never used.
I've never used a fax machine.

1. Name a movie you've never seen.
2. Name a food you've never liked.
3. Name a subject you've never studied.
4. Name a city you've never visited.
5. Name a sport you've never played.
6. Name a food you've never tasted.

EXERCISE 10 ABOUT YOU Write four sentences telling about things you've always done (or been). Share your sentences with the class.

EXAMPLES *I've always cooked the meals in my family.*
I've always been lazy.

1. _____
2. _____
3. _____
4. _____

EXERCISE 11 ABOUT YOU Write four sentences telling about things you've never done (or been) but would like to. Share your sentences with the class.

EXAMPLES *I've never studied photography, but I'd like to.*
I've never acted in a play, but I'd like to.

1. _____
2. _____
3. _____
4. _____

The Present Perfect; The Present Perfect Continuous

9.8 The Simple Present vs. the Present Perfect

Examples	Explanation
a. Larry Page **is** in California. b. Larry Page **has been** in California since he was in his 20s.	Sentences (a) refer only to the present.
a. He **loves** computers. b. He **has** always **loved** computers.	Sentences (b) connect the past to the present.
a. Google **doesn't have** advertising on its homepage. b. Google **has** never **had** advertising on its homepage.	
a. **Do** you **work** at a computer company? Yes, I **do**. b. **Have** you always **worked** at a computer company? Yes, I **have**.	

EXERCISE 12 Read each statement about your teacher. Then ask the teacher a question beginning with the words given. Include *always* in your question. Your teacher will answer.

EXAMPLE You're a teacher. Have you _____*always been a teacher*_____?

No. I was an accountant before I became a teacher. I've only been a teacher for five years.

1. You teach English. Have you _____?

2. You work at this college / school. Have you _____?

3. You think about grammar. Have you _____?

4. English is easy for you. Has English _____?

5. Your last name is _____. Has your last name _____?

6. You're interested in languages. Have you _____?

7. You live in this city. Have you _____?

288 Lesson 9

EXERCISE 13 Fill in the blanks with the missing words.

Two students meet by chance in the computer lab.

A: ___Have___ you ___been___ in the U.S. for long?
(examples)

B: No, I _____.
(1)

A: How _____ _____ you been in the U.S.?
(2) (3)

B: I _____ _____ here for about a year.
(4) (5)

A: Where did you come from?

B: Burundi.

A: Burundi? I _____
(6)

never _____ of it.
(7)

Where is it?

B: It's a small country in Central Africa.

A: Do you have a map? Can you show me where it is?

B: Let's go on the Internet. We can do a search.

A: Did you learn to use a computer in your country?

B: No. When I came here, a volunteer at my church gave me her old computer. Before I didn't know anything about computers. I've

_____ a lot about computers since I came here.
(8)

A: Oh, now I see Burundi. It's very small. It's near Congo.

B: Yes, it is.

A: Why did you come to the U.S.?

B: My country _____ political problems for many years.
(9)

It wasn't safe to live there. My family left in 1995.

A: So you _____ _____ here since 1995?
(10) (11)

B: No. First we lived in a refugee camp in Zambia.

A: I' _____ never _____ of Zambia either.
(12) (13)

Can we search for it on the Internet?

B: Here it is.

A: You speak English very well. Is English the language of Burundi?

B: No. Kirundi is the official language. Also French. I _____
(14)
_____ French since I was a small child. Where
(15)
are you from?

A: I'm from North Dakota.

B: I _____ never _____ of North Dakota.
(16)   (17)
Is it in the U.S.?

A: Of course. Let's search for an American map on the Internet. Here it is. Winter in North Dakota is very cold. It's cold here too.

B: I don't know how people live in a cold climate. I _____
(18)
never _____ in a cold climate before. I _____
(19)   (20)
always _____ near the Equator.
(21)

A: Don't worry. You'll be OK. You just need warm clothes for the winter.

B: I have class now. I've got to go.

A: I _____ _____ so much about your
(22)   (23)
country in such a short time.

B: It's easy to learn things fast using a computer and a search engine.

9.9 | The Present Perfect vs. the Simple Past

Do not confuse the present perfect with the simple past.	
Examples	Explanation
Compare: a. Sergey Brin **came** to the U.S. in 1979. b. Sergey Brin **has been** in the U.S. since 1979. a. Brin and Page **started** Google in 1998. b. Google **has been** popular since 1998.	Sentences (a) show a single action in the past. This action does not continue. Sentences (b) show the continuation of an action or state from the past to the present.
a. When **did** Brin **come** to the U.S.? b. How long **has** Brin **been** in the U.S.?	Question (a) with *when* uses the simple past tense. Question (b) with *how long* uses the present perfect tense.

EXERCISE 14 Fill in the blanks with the simple past or the present perfect of the verb in parentheses ( ).

A: Do you like to surf the Internet?

B: Of course, I do. I ____*have had*____ my Internet connection
(example: have)
since 1999, and I love it. A couple of months ago, I _____
(1 buy)
a new computer with lots of memory and speed. And last month I
_____ from a dial-up connection to a cable modem.
(2 change)
Now I can surf much faster.

A: What kind of things do you search for?

B: Lots of things. I _____ to learn about the
(3 always/want)
stock market, and with the Web, I can start to learn. Last week
I _____ my first investment in the stock market.
(4 make)

A: Do you ever buy products online?

B: Sometimes I do. Last month, I _____ a great Web
(5 find)
site where I can download music for 99¢. So far I _____
(6 download)
about a hundred songs, and I _____ several CDs.
(7 make)
My old computer _____ a CD burner, so I'm very
(8 not/have)
happy with my new one.

A: _____ your old computer?
(9 you/sell)

B: No. It was about eight years old. I just _____ it on
(10 leave)
top of the garbage dumpster. When I _____ by a
(11 pass)
few hours later, it was gone. Someone _____ it.
(12 take)

A: Was your new computer expensive?

B: Yes, but I _____ a great deal online.
(13 get)

A: I _____ my computer for three years, and it seems
(14 have)
so old by comparison to today's computers. But it's too expensive to
buy a new one every year.

B: There's a joke about computers: "When is a computer old?"

A: I don't know. When?

B: As soon as you get it out of the box!

The Present Perfect; The Present Perfect Continuous

9.10 The Present Perfect Continuous—An Overview

We use the present perfect continuous to talk about an action that started in the past and continues to the present.

Affirmative	I **have been using** the Internet for two hours.
Negative	You **haven't been working** on your computer all day.
Question	**Have** you **been surfing** the Web for great deals?

GENEALOGY

Before You Read

1. Do you think it's important to know your family's history? Why or why not?
2. What would you like to know about your ancestors?

 Read the following article. Pay special attention to the present perfect and the present perfect continuous tenses.

Did You Know?
Family history is the second most popular hobby in the U.S. after gardening.

In the last 30 years, genealogy **has become** one of America's most popular hobbies. If you type *genealogy* in a search engine, you can find about 16 million hits. If you type *family history*, you will get about 10 million hits. The percentage of the U.S. population interested in family history **has been increasing** steadily. Forty-five percent of Americans in 1996 stated they were interested in genealogy. In 2000, that number rose to 60 percent according to a national survey. This increase probably has to do with the ease of searching on the Internet.

The number of genealogy Web sites **has been growing** accordingly as people ask themselves: Where does my family come from? How long **has** my family **been** in the U.S.? Why did they come here? How did they come here? What kind of people were my ancestors?

Genealogy is a lifelong hobby for many. The average family historian **has been doing** genealogy for 14 years, according to a recent study. Most family historians are over 40. Cyndi Howells, from Washington State, quit her job in 1992 and **has been working** on her family history ever since. She **has created** a Web site to help others with their search. Her Web site has over 99,000 resources. Since its start in 1996, her Web site **has had** over 22 million visitors and more than 32 million page hits each month. Cyndi **has** also **been giving** lectures all over the country to genealogy groups. Cyndi's Web site **has won** an award three times for the best genealogy site on the Web.

While the Internet **has made** research easier for amateur genealogists, it is only the beginning for serious family historians. Researchers still need to go to courthouses and libraries to find public records, such as land deeds[5], obituaries[6], wedding notices, and tax records. Another good source of information is the U.S. Census. Early census records are not complete, but since the mid-1800s, the U.S. Census **has been keeping** detailed records of family members, their ages, occupations, and places of birth.

Are you interested in knowing more about your ancestors and their stories, their country or countries, and how you fit into the history of your family? Maybe genealogy is a good hobby for you.

9.11 | The Present Perfect Continuous—Forms

Subject	have/has	been	Present Participle	Complement
I	have	been	**using**	the Internet for two hours.
We	have	been	**reading**	about search engines.
You	have	been	**studying**	computers.
They	have	been	**living**	in California.
He	has	been	**writing**	since one o'clock.
She	has	been	**surfing**	the Internet all day.
It	has	been	**raining**	all day.

Language Notes:
1. To form the negative, put *not* between *have* or *has* and *been*.
   You **have** *not* **been** listening.
   She **hasn't been** working hard.
2. To form the question, reverse the subject and *have/has*.
   Has she been using her new computer?
   How long **have they** been living in the U.S.?

---

[5] A *land deed* is a document that shows who the owner of the land is.
[6] *Obituaries* are death notices posted in the newspaper.

The Present Perfect; The Present Perfect Continuous

9.12 The Present Perfect Continuous—Statements and Questions

Compare affirmative statements and questions

Wh- Word	have/ has	Subject	have/ has	Been + Verb -ing	Complement	Short Answer
		Cyndi	has	been working	on her family history.	
	Has	she		been working	on her Web site?	Yes, she has.
How long	has	she		been working	on her Web site?	Since 1992.

Compare negative statements and questions

Wh- Word	haven't/ hasn't	Subject	haven't/ hasn't	Been + Verb -ing	Complement
		They	haven't	been using	the public library.
Why	haven't	they		been using	the public library?

EXERCISE 15 Fill in the blanks with the present perfect continuous form of the verb in parentheses ( ).

EXAMPLE How long ___has___ Cyndi ___been managing___ a genealogy Web site?
(example: manage)

1. Interest in genealogy _____.
(grow)

2. Cyndi _____ on her family history since 1992.
(work)

3. Cyndi _____ all over the U.S. to
(lecture)
genealogy groups.

4. The number of genealogy Web sites _____.
(increase)

5. How long _____ the U.S. Census
(keep)
_____ records?

6. _____ you _____ a family tree
(make)
for your family?

7. People _____ the Internet to do
(use)
family research for about ten years.

8. My family _____ in the U.S. for
(not/live)
many generations.

294 Lesson 9

9.13 | The Present Perfect Continuous—Use

We use the present perfect continuous tense to show that an action or state started in the past and continues to the present.

Past ←———————————— Now ————————————→ Future

He **has been living** in the U.S. since 1979.

Examples	Explanation
Cyndi **has been working** on her family tree since 1992. Sergey Brin **has been living** in the U.S. for more than 25 years.	We use *for* and *since* to show the time spent at an activity.
He **has been living** in the U.S. since 1979. OR He **has lived** in the U.S. since 1979.	With some verbs (*live, work, study, teach,* and *wear*) we can use either the present perfect or the present perfect continuous with actions that began in the past and continue to the present. The meaning is the same.
My father *is working* on the family tree right now. He **has been working** on it since 9 o'clock this morning.	If the action is still happening, use the present perfect continuous, not the present perfect.
Google **has become** one of the most popular search engines. I **have had** my computer for three months.	We do not use the continuous form with nonaction verbs. See below for a list of nonaction verbs.
I **have** always **taken** computer courses. My grandmother **has** never **used** a computer.	Do not use the continuous form with *always* and *never*.

Action: I **have been thinking** about doing a family tree.
Nonaction: I **have** always **thought** that genealogy is an interesting hobby.
	Think can be an action or nonaction verb, depending on its meaning.
	   Think about = action verb
	   Think that = nonaction verb

Nonaction: Some people **have had** a lot of success in locating information. **Action:** We **have been having** a hard time locating information about our ancestors.	*Have* is usually a nonaction verb. However, *have* is an action verb in these expressions: *have experience, have a hard time, have a good time, have difficulty,* and *have trouble*.

Nonaction verbs:

like	know	see	cost
love	believe	smell	own
hate	think (that)	hear	have (for possession)
want	care (about)	taste	become
need	understand	feel	
prefer	remember	seem	

EXERCISE 16 ABOUT YOU Write **true** statements using the present perfect continuous with the words given and *for* or *since*. Share your sentences with the class.

EXAMPLE   work *My brother has been working as a waiter for six years.*

1. study English _____
2. work _____
3. live _____
4. use _____
5. study _____

EXERCISE 17 ABOUT YOU Read aloud each of the following present tense questions. Another student will answer. If the answer is *yes*, add a present perfect continuous question with *"How long have you . . . ?"*

EXAMPLE   Do you play a musical instrument?

A: Do you play a musical instrument?
B: Yes. I play the piano.
A: How long have you been playing the piano?
B: I've been playing the piano since I was a child.

1. Do you drive?
2. Do you work?
3. Do you use the Internet?
4. Do you wear glasses?
5. Do you play a musical instrument?

EXERCISE 18 Ask the teacher questions with *"How long . . . ?"* and the present perfect continuous form of the words given. The teacher will answer your questions.

EXAMPLE   speak English

A: How long have you been speaking English?
B: I've been speaking English all[7] my life.

1. teach English
2. work at this school
3. live in this city
4. use this book
5. live at your present address

---

[7] We do not use the preposition *for* before *all*.

EXERCISE 19 Fill in the blanks in the following conversations. Answers may vary.

EXAMPLE
A: Do you wear glasses?
B: Yes, I ____do____.
A: How long ___have___ you ___been wearing___ glasses?
B: I __'ve been wearing__ glasses since I ___was___ in high school.

1. A: Are you working on your family history?
   B: Yes, I am.
   A: How long _____ you _____ on your family history?
   B: I _____ on it for about ten years.

2. A: Is your sister surfing the Internet?
   B: Yes, she _____.
   A: How long _____ she _____ surfing the Internet?
   B: Since she woke up this morning!

3. A: Does your father live in the U.S.?
   B: Yes, he _____.
   A: How long _____ he been _____ in the U.S.?
   B: He _____ in the U.S. since he _____ 25 years old.

4. A: Are you studying for the test now?
   B: Yes, I _____.
   A: How long _____ for the test?
   B: For _____.

5. A: Is your teacher teaching you the present perfect lesson?
   B: Yes, he _____.
   A: _____ long _____ you this lesson?
   B: Since _____.

The Present Perfect; The Present Perfect Continuous

6. **A:** Are they using the computers now?
   B: Yes, _____.
   A: How long _____ them?
   B: _____ they started to write their compositions.

7. **A:** _____ you using the Internet?
   B: Yes, I _____.
   A: How _____?
   B: _____ for two hours.

8. **A:** _____ your grandparents live in the U.S.?
   B: Yes, they _____.
   A: How _____ in the U.S.?
   B: Since they _____ born.

9. **A:** Is she studying her family history?
   B: Yes, she _____.
   A: How long _____?
   B: Since she _____.

9.14 The Present Perfect with Repetition from Past to Present

We use the present perfect to talk about the repetition of an action in a time period that includes the present. There is a probability that this action will occur again.

Past ← Cyndi **has won** three awards so far. | Now → Future

Examples	Explanation
a. Cyndi **has won** three awards. b. Cyndi's Web site **has had** over 22 million visitors.	a. Cyndi may win another award. b. Cyndi's Web site will probably get more visitors.
So far, Brin and Page **haven't changed** their lifestyles. We **have completed** eight lessons in this book up to now.	Adding the words *so far* and *up to now* indicate that we are counting up to the present.
How many "hits" **has** Cyndi's Web site **had** this month? How much information **have** you **gotten** from her Web site so far?	We can ask a question about repetition with *how many* and *how much*.
How many times **have** you **checked** your e-mail today? I **haven't checked** my e-mail **at all** today.	To indicate zero times, we use a negative verb + *at all*. But there is a probability that this action may happen.
Compare: a. Google **had** 10,000 searches a day in 1998. b. Google **has had** billions of searches since 1998. a. Cyndi's list **appeared** for the first time in 1996. b. Many new genealogy Web sites **have appeared** in the last ten years.	a. We use the simple past with a time period that is finished or closed: *1998, 50 years ago,* etc. b. We use the present perfect in a time period that is open. There is a probability of more repetition.

Language Note:
Do not use the continuous form for repetition.
  Right: I **have checked** my e-mail three times today.
  Wrong: I *have been checking* my e-mail three times today.

EXERCISE 20 ABOUT YOU Ask a *yes / no* question with *so far* or *up to now* and the words given. Another student will answer.

EXAMPLE you / come to every class.
A: Have you come to every class so far?
B: Yes, I have.
   OR
B: No, I haven't. I've missed three classes.

1. we / have any tests
2. this lesson / be difficult
3. the teacher / give a lot of homework
4. you / understand all the explanations
5. you / have any questions about this lesson

EXERCISE 21 ABOUT YOU Ask a question with *"How many . . . ?"* and the words given. Talk about this month. Another student will answer.

EXAMPLE times / go to the post office
A: How many times have you gone to the post office this month?
B: I've gone to the post office once this month.
   OR
   I haven't gone to the post office at all this month.

1. letters / write
2. times / eat in a restaurant
3. times / get paid
4. long-distance calls / make
5. books / buy
6. times / go to the movies
7. movies / rent
8. times / cook

EXERCISE 22 ABOUT YOU Write four questions to ask another student or your teacher about repetition from the past to the present. Use *how much* or *how many*. The other person will answer.

EXAMPLES How many cities have you lived in?
How many English courses have you taken at this college?

1. _____
2. _____
3. _____
4. _____

300 Lesson 9

9.15 The Simple Past vs. the Present Perfect with Repetition

We use the present perfect with repetition in a present time period. There is probability of more repetition. We use the simple past with repetition in a past time period. There is no possibility of any more repetition during that period.

Examples	Explanation
How many hits **has** your Web site **had** today? It **has had** over 100 hits today. How many times **have** you **been** absent this semester? I**'ve been** absent twice so far.	To show that there is possibility for more repetition, use the present perfect. In the examples on the left, *today* and *this semester* are not finished. *So far* indicates that the number given may not be final.
Last month my Web site **had** 5,000 hits. How many times **were** you absent last semester?	To show that the number is final, use the simple past tense and a past time expression. *Yesterday, last week, last year, last semester,* etc. are finished. The number is final.
a. Brin and Page **have added** new features to Google over the years. b. Before she died, my grandmother **added** many details to our family tree.	a. Brin and Page are still alive. They can (and probably will) add new features to Google in the years to come. b. Grandmother is dead. The number of details she added is final.
Compare: a. I **have checked** my e-mail twice today. b. I **checked** my e-mail twice today. a. She **has gone** to the library to work on her family tree five times this month. b. She **went** to the library to work on her family tree five times this month.	With a present time expression (such as *today, this week, this month,* etc.), you may use either the present perfect or the simple past. In sentences (a), the number may not be final. In sentences (b), the number seems final.
Compare: a. In the U.S., I **have had** two jobs. b. In my native country, I **had** five jobs. a. In the U.S., I **have lived** in three apartments so far. b. In my native country, I **lived** in two apartments.	a. To talk about your experiences in this phase of your life, you can use the present perfect tense. b. To talk about a closed phase of your life, use the simple past tense. For example, if you do not plan to live in your native country again, use the simple past tense to talk about your experiences there.

EXERCISE 23 ABOUT YOU Fill in the blanks with the simple past or the present perfect to ask a question. A student from another country will answer.

EXAMPLES How many cars ___*have you owned*___ in the U.S.?
I've owned two cars in the U.S.

How many cars ___*did you own*___ in your country?
I owned only one car in my country.

1. How many apartments _____ in your country?
2. How many apartments _____ in the U.S.?
3. How many schools _____ in your country?
4. How many schools _____ in the U.S.?
5. How many jobs _____ in the U.S.?
6. How many jobs _____ in your country?

9.16 | The Present Perfect with Indefinite Past Time

We use the present perfect to refer to an action that occurred at an indefinite time in the past that still has importance to the present situation. Words that show indefinite time are: *ever*, *yet*, and *already*.

Past ←——————————————— Now ———————————————→ Future

Have you ever **used** Google?

Examples	Explanation

Have you *ever* **noticed** that Google doesn't have ads on its opening page?
   Yes, I **have**.
Have you *ever* **studied** your family history?
   No, I never **have**.
Have you *ever* **"googled"** your name?
   No, I haven't.
	A question with *ever* asks about any time between the past and the present. Put *ever* between the subject and the main verb.

Has Larry Page **gotten** his degree from Stanford University *yet*?
   No, not *yet*.
Have Larry and Sergey **become** billionaires *yet*?
   Yes, they have.
Have you **read** the story about genealogy *yet*?
   Yes, I *already* have.
	Yet and *already* refer to an indefinite time in the near past. There is an expectation that an activity took place a short time ago.

The success of Google over its rivals **has shown** that users don't want to see a lot of ads. Google **has added** many new features to its Web site. Cyndi Howells **has created** a very useful Web site for family historians.	We can use the present perfect to talk about the past without any reference to time. The time is not important or not known or imprecise. Using the present perfect, rather than the simple past, shows that the past is relevant to a present situation.

Lesson 9

EXERCISE 24 ABOUT YOU Answer the following questions with: *Yes, I have;* *No, I haven't;* or *No, I never have.*

1. Have you ever "googled" your own name?
2. Have you ever researched your family history?
3. Have you ever made a family tree?
4. Have you ever used the Web to look for a person you haven't seen in a long time?
5. Have you ever added hardware to your computer?
6. Have you ever downloaded music from the Internet?
7. Have you ever used a search engine in your native language?
8. Have you ever sent photos by e-mail?
9. Have you ever received a photo by e-mail?
10. Have you ever bought anything from a Web site?
11. Have you ever built a computer?
12. Has your computer ever had a virus?

EXERCISE 25 ABOUT YOU Answer the questions with: *Yes, I have;* *Yes, I already have;* or *Not yet.*

1. Have you eaten lunch yet?
2. Have you finished Lesson 8 yet?
3. Have you done today's homework yet?
4. Have you paid this month's rent yet?
5. Have you learned the names of all the other students yet?
6. Have you visited the teacher's office yet?
7. Have you done Exercise 22 yet?
8. Have you learned the present perfect yet?
9. Have you learned all the past participles yet?

9.17 Answering a Present Perfect Question

We can answer a present perfect question with the simple past tense when a specific time is introduced in the answer. If a specific time is not known or necessary, we answer with the present perfect.

Examples	Explanation
Have you ever **used** Google? **Answer A:** Yes. I'**ve used** Google many times. **Answer B:** Yes. I **used** Google a few hours ago.	Answer A, with *many times*, shows repetition at an indefinite time. Answer B, with *a few hours ago*, shows a specific time in the past.
Have you ever **heard** of Larry Page? **Answer A:** No. I'**ve never** heard of him. **Answer B:** Yes. We **read** about him yesterday.	Answer A, with *never*, shows continuation from past to present. Answer B, with *yesterday*, shows a specific time in the past.
Have you **done** your homework yet? **Answer A:** Yes. I'**ve done** it already. **Answer B:** Yes. I **did** it this morning.	Answer A, with *already*, is indefinite. Answer B, with *this morning*, shows a specific time.
Have Brin and Page **become** rich? **Answer A:** Yes, they have. **Answer B:** Yes. They **became** rich before they were 30 years old.	Answer A is indefinite. Answer B, with *before they were 30 years old*, is definite.

EXERCISE 26 ABOUT YOU Ask a question with *"Have you ever . . . ?"* and the present perfect tense of the verb in parentheses ( ). Another student will answer. To answer with a specific time, use the past tense. To answer with a frequency response, use the present perfect tense. You may work with a partner.

EXAMPLES (go) to the zoo

A: Have you ever gone to the zoo?
B: Yes. I've gone there many times.

(go) to Disneyland

A: Have you ever gone to Disneyland?
B: Yes. I went there last summer.

1. (work) in a factory
2. (lose) a glove
3. (run) out of gas[8]
4. (fall) out of bed

---

[8] *To run out of gas* means to use all the gas in your car while driving.

5. (make) a mistake in English grammar
6. (tell) a lie
7. (eat) raw[9] fish
8. (study) calculus
9. (meet) a famous person
10. (go) to an art museum
11. (stay) up all night
12. (break) a window
13. (get) locked out[10] of your house or car
14. (see) a French movie
15. (go) to Las Vegas
16. (travel) by ship
17. (be) in love
18. (write) a poem

EXERCISE 27 ABOUT YOU Write five questions with *ever* to ask your teacher. Your teacher will answer.

EXAMPLES *Have you ever gotten a ticket for speeding?*

Have you ever visited Poland?

1. _____
2. _____
3. _____
4. _____
5. _____

EXERCISE 28 ABOUT YOU Ask a student from another country questions using the words given. The other student will answer.

EXAMPLE your country / have a woman president

A: Has your country ever had a woman president?
B: Yes, it has. We had a woman president from 1975 to 1979.

1. your country / have a civil war
2. your country's leader / visit the U.S.
3. an American president / visit your country
4. your country / have a woman president
5. you / go back to visit your country
6. there / be an earthquake in your hometown

---

[9] *Raw* means not cooked.
[10] *To get locked out* of your house means that you can't get in because you do not have keys with you to get inside.

EXERCISE 29 ABOUT YOU Ask a student who has recently arrived in this country if he or she has done these things yet.

EXAMPLE buy a car

A: Have you bought a car yet?
B: Yes, I have.   OR   No, I haven't.   OR   I bought a car last month.

1. find a job
2. make any American friends
3. open a bank account
4. save any money
5. buy a car
6. write to your family
7. get a credit card
8. buy a computer
9. get a telephone

EXERCISE 30 *Combination Exercise.* Fill in the blanks with the correct tense of the verb in parentheses ( ). Also fill in other missing words.

A: Your Spanish is a little different from my Spanish. Where are you from?

B: I'm from Guatemala.

A: How ___long___ ___have you been___ here?
         (example)   (example: you/be)

B: I _____ here for about six months. Where are
      (1 only/be)
you from?

A: Miami. My family comes from Cuba. They _____
                                              (2 leave)
Cuba in 1962, after the revolution. I _____ born in
                                         (3 be)
the U.S. I'm starting to become interested in my family's history.
I _____ several magazine articles about genealogy
   (4 read)
so far. It's fascinating. Are you interested in your family's history?

B: Of course I am. I _____ interested in it _____
                      (5 be)   (6)
a long time. I _____ on a family tree for many years.
                 (7 work)

A: When _____?
                         (8 you/start)

B: I _____ when I _____ 16 years old.
     (9 start)   (10 be)
Over the years, I _____ a lot of interesting
                      (11 find)

306   Lesson 9

information about my family. Some of my ancestors were Mayans and some were from Spain and France. In fact, my great-great grandfather was a Spanish prince.

A: How _____ all that information?
          (12 you/find)

B: I _____ the Internet a lot. I _____
       (13 use)   *(14 also/go)*
to many libraries to get more information.

A: _____ to Spain or France to look at records
       (15 ever/go)
there?

B: Last summer I _____ to Spain, and I _____
                    (16 go)   *(17 find)*
a lot of information while I was there.

A: How many ancestors _____ so far?
                          (18 you/find)

B: So _____ I _____ about 50,
          (19)   *(20 find)*
but I'm still looking.

A: How can I get started?

B: There's a great Web site called "Cyndi's list." I'll give you the Web address, and you can get started there.

SUMMARY OF LESSON 9

1. Compare the present perfect and the simple past.

Present Perfect	Simple Past
A. The action of the sentence began in the past and includes the present: 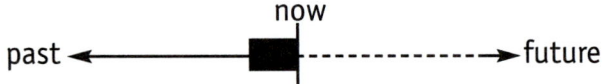 My father **has been** in the U.S. since 1992. My father **has had** his job in the U.S. for many years. How long **have** you **been** interested in genealogy? I've always **wanted** to learn more about my family's history.	A. The action of the sentence is completely past:  My father **came** to the U.S. in 1992. My father **was** in Canada for two years before he came to the U.S. When **did** you **start** your family tree? When I was a child, I always **wanted** to spend time with my grandparents.
B. Repetition from past to present:  We **have had** four tests so far. She **has used** the Internet three times today.	B. Repetition in a past time period.  We **had** two tests last semester. She **used** the Internet three times yesterday.
C. The action took place at an indefinite time between the past and the present. 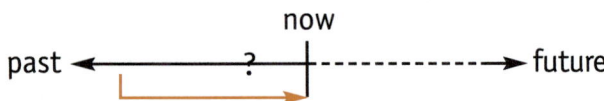 **Have** you ever **made** a family tree? I've **done** the homework already. **Have** you **visited** the art museum yet?	C. The action took place at a definite time in the past. 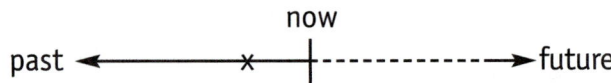 **Did** you **make** a family tree last month? I **did** the homework last night. **Did** you **visit** the art museum last month?

2. Compare the present perfect and the present perfect continuous.

Present Perfect	Present Perfect Continuous
A. A continuous action (nonaction verbs) I **have had** my car for five years.	A. A continuous action (action verbs) I**'ve been driving** a car for 20 years.
B. A repeated action Cyndi's Web site **has won** several awards.	B. A nonstop action The U.S. Census **has been keeping** records since the 1880s.
C. Question with *how many* How many times **have** you **gone** to New York?	C. Question with *how long* How long **has** he **been living** in New York?
D. An action that is at an indefinite time, completely in the past. Cyndi **has created** a Web site.	D. An action that started in the past and is still happening. Cyndi **has been working** on her family history since 1992.

EDITING ADVICE

1. Don't confuse the *-ing* form and the past participle.

          taking
   She has been ~~taken~~ a test for two hours.

         given
   She has ~~giving~~ him a present.

2. Use the present perfect, not the simple present, to describe an action or state that started in the past and continues to the present.

      had
   He has a car for two years.

          have   *ed*
   How long ~~do~~ you work in a factory?

3. Use *for*, not *since*, with the amount of time.

                  for
   I've been studying English ~~since~~ three months.

4. Use the simple past, not the present perfect, with a specific past time.

      came
   He ~~has come~~ to the U.S. five months ago.

       did
   When ~~have~~ you come to the U.S.?

5. Use the simple past, not the present perfect, in a *since* clause.

                                                  came
   He has learned a lot of English since he ~~has come~~ to the U.S.

6. Use correct word order. Put the adverb between the auxiliary and the main verb.

          never seen
He has ~~seen never~~ a French movie.

          ever gone
Have you ~~gone ever~~ to France?

7. Use correct word order in questions.

          have you
How long ~~you have~~ been a teacher?

8. Use *yet* for negative statements; use *already* for affirmative statements.

          yet
I haven't eaten dinner ~~already~~.

9. Don't forget the verb *have* in the present perfect (continuous).

     have
I ^ been living in New York for two years.

10. Don't forget the *-ed* of the past participle.

        ed
He's listen ^ to that CD many times.

11. Use the present perfect, not the continuous form, with *always, never, yet, already, ever,* and *how many*.

                  gone
How many times have you ~~been going~~ to Paris?

          visited
I've never ~~been visiting~~ Paris.

12. Don't use *time* after *how long*.

How long ~~time~~ have you had your job?

LESSON 9 TEST/REVIEW

PART 1 Find the mistakes with the underlined words, and correct them. Not every sentence has a mistake. If the sentence is correct, write *C*.

          had
EXAMPLES I <u>have</u> my car for six years.

We've <u>always wanted</u> to learn English.   *C*

1. Since <u>I've come</u> to the U.S., I've been studying English.
2. Have you ever <u>eating</u> Chinese food?
3. How long <u>you've</u> been in the U.S.?

4. Have you <u>gone ever</u> to Canada?
5. I've <u>know</u> my best friend since I was a child.
6. She's a teacher. She's been a teacher <u>since</u> ten years.
7. I <u>never gone</u> to Mexico.
8. How <u>long time</u> has your father been working as an engineer?
9. Has he ever gone to Paris? Yes, he <u>went</u> to Paris last year.
10. He works in a restaurant. <u>He been working</u> there since 1995.
11. Have you ever <u>study</u> biology?
12. Have they finished the test <u>yet</u>?
13. She's done the homework <u>yet</u>.

PART 2 Fill in the blanks with the simple past, the present perfect, or the present perfect continuous form of the verb in parentheses ( ). In some cases, more than one answer is possible.

Conversation 1

A: ___*Have*___ you ever ___*studied*___ computer programming?
(example: study)

B: Yes. I _____ it in college. And I _____
(1 study)   (2 work)

as a programmer for five years. But my job is boring.

A: _____ you ever _____ about changing jobs?
(3 think)

B: Yes. Since I _____ a child, I _____ to be an
(4 be)   (5 always/want)

actor. When I was in college, I _____ in a few plays, but
(6 be)

since I _____, I _____ time
(7 graduate)   (8 not/have)

to act.

Conversation 2

A: How long _____ in the U.S.?
(1 you/be)

B: For about two years.

A: _____ your life _____ a lot since
(2 change)

you _____ to the U.S.?
(3 come)

B: Oh, yes. Before I _____ (4 come) here, I _____ (5 live) with my family. Since I came here, I _____ (6 live) alone.

A: _____ (7 always/live) in the same apartment in this city?

B: No. I _____ (8 move) three times so far. And I plan to move again at the end of the year.

A: Do you plan to have a roommate?

B: Yes, but I _____ (9 not/find) one yet.

PART 3 Fill in the blanks with the simple present, the simple past, the present perfect, or the present perfect continuous form of the verb in parentheses ( ). In some cases, more than one answer is possible.

Paragraph 1

I _____ (1 use) the Internet every day. I _____ (2 use) it for three years. I _____ (3 start) to use it when I _____ (4 become) interested in genealogy. I _____ (5 work) on my family tree for three years. Last month, I _____ (6 find) information about my father's ancestors. My grandfather _____ (7 live) with us now and likes to tell us about his past. He _____ (8 be) born in Italy, but he _____ (9 come) here when he was very young, so he _____ (10 live) here most of his life. He doesn't remember much about Italy. I _____ (11 not/find) any information about my mother's ancestors yet.

Paragraph 2

I _____ to the U.S. when a war
(1 come)

_____ out in my country. I _____
(2 break)   (3 live)

in the U.S. for five years. At first, everything _____
(4 be)

very hard for me. I _____ any English when I
(5 not/know)

_____. But I _____ English for the
(6 arrive)   (7 study)

past five years, and now I _____ it pretty well.
(8 speak)

I _____ my college education yet, but I plan to
(9 not/start)

next semester.

EXPANSION ACTIVITIES

Classroom Activities

1. Form a group of between 4 and 6 students. Find out who in your group has done each of these things. Write that person's name in the blank.

   a. _____ has made a family tree.
   b. _____ has found a good job.
   c. _____ has been on a ship.
   d. _____ has never eaten Mexican food.
   e. _____ hasn't done today's homework yet.
   f. _____ has never seen a French movie.
   g. _____ has taken a trip to Canada.
   h. _____ has acted in a play.
   i. _____ has gone swimming in the Pacific Ocean.
   j. _____ has flown in a helicopter.
   k. _____ has served in the military.
   l. _____ has worked in a hotel.
   m. _____ has never studied chemistry.
   n. _____ has taken the TOEFL test.
   o. _____ has just gotten a "green card."

2. Draw your family tree for the past three generations, if you can. Why do you think so many people are interested in genealogy? What is valuable about finding your family's history?

Write About it

1. Write a composition about one of the following:

   How your life has changed (*choose one*):

   a. since you came to the U.S.
   b. since you got married
   c. since you had a baby
   d. since you started college
   e. since you graduated from high school

2. Write about an interesting member of your family. What has he or she done that you think is interesting?

Outside Activity

Interview an American who has relatives who have been in the U.S. for several generations. Does this person know the stories of his or her ancestors and their native countries? What is something interesting you discovered from this interview?

Internet Activities

1. On the Internet, find Cyndi Howell's genealogy Web site. Find out about people who have the same last name as yours.

2. Type the word *genealogy* at a search engine. How many Web sites did you find?

3. Go to a search engine and type in *Larry Page, Sergey Brin*. Find an interesting fact about one of them that you didn't know. Bring it to class.

Additional Activities at **http://elt.heinle.com/gic**

LESSON 10

GRAMMAR
Gerunds
Infinitives

CONTEXT: Finding a Job
Finding a Job
Tips on Writing a Résumé
Rita's Story

10.1 Gerunds—An Overview

To form a gerund, we use the *-ing* form of a verb *(finding, learning, eating, running)*. A *gerund phrase* is a gerund + a noun phrase *(finding a job, learning English)*. A gerund (phrase) can appear in several positions in a sentence.

Examples	Explanation
Finding a job is hard.	• The gerund is the subject.
I don't enjoy **talking** about myself.	• The gerund is the object.
I thought about **changing** my career.	• The gerund is the object of the preposition.
I got information **by talking** with my counselor.	• The gerund is part of an adverbial phrase.
I like to **go shopping**.	• The gerund is in many expressions with *go*.
Not having a job is frustrating. You can impress the boss by **not being** late.	We can put *not* in front of a gerund to make it negative.

FINDING A JOB

Before You Read

1. Have you ever had a job interview in this city?
2. What is your profession or job? What profession or job do you plan to have in the future?

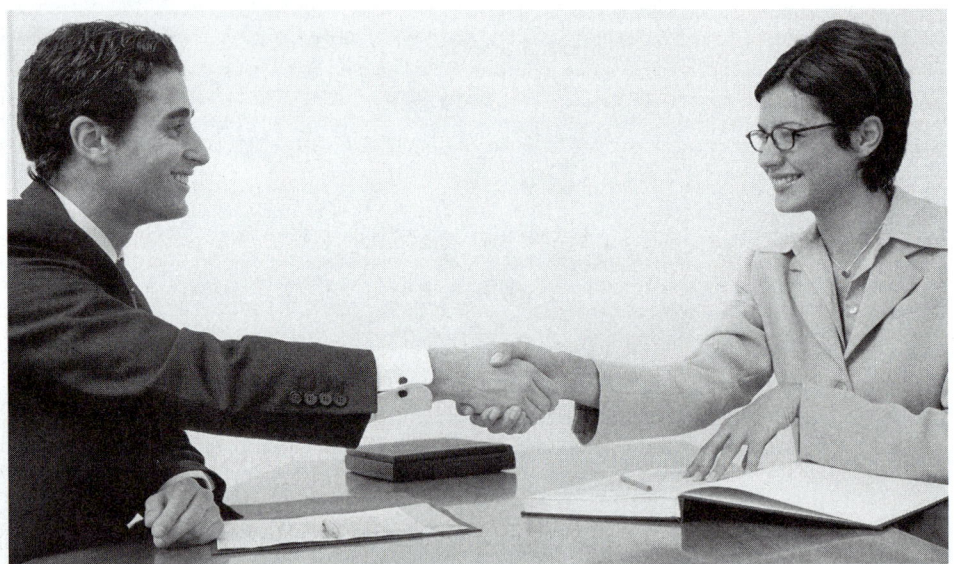

 Read the following article. Pay special attention to gerunds.

Finding a job in the United States takes specific skills. The following advice will help you find a job.

- Write a good résumé. Describe your accomplishments.[1] Avoid **including** unnecessary information. Your résumé should be one page, if possible.

---

[1] *Accomplishments* are the unusual good things you have done, such as awards you have won or projects you have successfully managed.

Did You Know?

According to the Bureau of Labor Statistics, the fastest growing field is for medical assistants. The growth for this career between 2002 and 2012 is expected to be 59 percent.

- Find out about available jobs. One way is by **looking** in the newspaper or on the Internet. Another way is by **networking. Networking** means **exchanging** information with anyone you know—family, friends, neighbors, classmates, former coworkers, professional groups—who might know of a job. These people might also be able to give you insider information about a company, such as who is in charge and what it is like to work at their company. According to an article in the *Wall Street Journal,* 94 percent of people who succeed in **finding** a job say that **networking** was a big help.
- Practice the interview. The more prepared you are, the more relaxed you will feel. If you are worried about **saying** or **doing** the wrong thing, practice will help.
- Learn something about the company. You can find information by **going** to the company's Web site. **Getting** information takes time, but it pays off.

You can get help in these skills—**writing** a résumé, **networking**, **preparing** for an interview, **researching** a company—by **seeing** a career counselor. Most high schools and colleges have one who can help you get started.

Finding a job is one of the most difficult jobs. Some people send out hundreds of résumés and go on dozens of interviews before **finding** a job. And it isn't something you do just once or twice in your lifetime. For most Americans, **changing** jobs many times in a lifetime is not uncommon.

Tips for Getting a Job

Preparation:
1. Learn about the organization and have a specific job or jobs in mind.
2. Review your résumé.
3. Practice an interview with a friend or relative.
4. Arrive at least 15 minutes before the scheduled time of your interview.

Personal appearance:
1. Be well-groomed[2] and dress appropriately.
2. Do not chew gum.

The interview:
1. Relax and answer each question concisely.
2. Use good manners. Shake hands and smile when you meet someone.
3. Be enthusiastic. Tell the interviewer why you are a good candidate for the job.
4. Ask questions about the position and the organization.
5. Thank the interviewer when you leave and in writing as a follow-up.

Information to bring to an interview:
1. Social Security card.
2. Government-issued identification (driver's license).
3. Résumé or application. Include information about your education, training, and previous employment.
4. References. Employers typically require three references. Get permission before using anyone as a reference. Make sure that each will give you a good reference. Avoid using relatives as references.

---

[2] When you are *well-groomed*, your appearance is neat and clean.

10.2 | Gerund as Subject

Examples	Explanation
Gerund Phrase **Finding a good job** takes time. **Writing a résumé** isn't easy.	We can use a gerund or gerund phrase as the subject of the sentence.
Exchanging ideas with friends **is** helpful. **Visiting** company Web sites **takes** time.	A gerund subject takes a singular verb.
Not preparing for an interview could have a bad result.	We can put *not* in front of a gerund to make it negative.

EXERCISE 1 The following things are important before a job interview. Make a sentence with each one, using a gerund phrase as the subject.

EXAMPLE get a good night's sleep
Getting a good night's sleep will help you feel rested and alert for an interview.

1. take a bath or shower

2. select serious-looking clothes

3. prepare a résumé

4. check your résumé carefully

5. get information about the company

6. prepare answers to possible questions

EXERCISE 2 Complete each statement with a gerund (phrase) as the subject.

EXAMPLE *Learning a foreign language* takes a long time.

1. _____ is one of the most difficult jobs.
2. _____ is one of the best ways to find a job.
3. _____ is not permitted in this classroom.
4. _____ is difficult for a foreign student.
5. _____ takes a long time.
6. _____ is not polite.

318   Lesson 10

7. _____ makes me feel good.
8. _____ makes me nervous.
9. _____ scares me.
10. _____ is against the law.

EXERCISE 3 ABOUT YOU In preparing for an interview, it is good to think about the following questions. Answer these questions. Use a gerund in some of your answers, but do NOT try to use a gerund in every answer. It won't work. Give a lot of thought to your answers and compare them with your classmates' answers.

EXAMPLES What are your strengths?
Working with others; learning quickly; thinking fast in difficult situations

What are your strong and weak subjects in school?
I'm strong in math. I'm weak in history.

1. What are your strengths?
   _____

2. What are some of your weaknesses?
   _____

3. List your accomplishments and achievements. (They can be achievements in jobs, sports, school, etc.)
   _____

4. What are your interests?
   _____

5. What are your short-term goals?
   _____

6. What are your long-term goals?
   _____

7. What are things you like? Think about personalities, tasks, environments, types of work, and structure.
   _____

8. What are some things you dislike? Think about personalities, tasks, environments, types of work, and structure.
   _____

9. Why should we hire you?
   _____

Gerunds; Infinitives

EXERCISE 4 Write a list of personal behaviors during an interview that would hurt your chances of getting a job. You may work with a partner or in a small group.

EXAMPLES *Chewing gum during the interview looks bad.*

Not looking directly at the interviewer can hurt your chances.

1. _____
2. _____
3. _____
4. _____
5. _____

10.3 | Gerund After Verb

Some verbs are commonly followed by a gerund (phrase). The gerund (phrase) is the object of the verb.

Examples	Explanation
Have you considered **going** to a job counselor? Do you appreciate **getting** advice? You can discuss **improving** your skills. You should practice **answering** interview questions.	The verbs below can be followed by a gerund: admit discuss mind put off appreciate dislike miss quit avoid enjoy permit recommend can't help finish postpone risk consider keep practice suggest
I have many hobbies. I like to **go fishing** in the summer. I **go skiing** in the winter. I like indoor sports too. I **go bowling** once a month.	*Go* + gerund is used in many idiomatic expressions. go boating go jogging go bowling go sailing go camping go shopping go dancing go sightseeing go fishing go skating go hiking go skiing go hunting go swimming
a. I don't **mind** wearing a suit to work. b. Don't **put off** writing your résumé. Do it now. c. I have an interview tomorrow morning. I **can't help** feeling nervous.	a. *I mind* means that something bothers me. *I don't mind* means that something is OK with me; it doesn't bother me. b. *Put off* means postpone. c. *Can't help* means to have no control over something.

320 Lesson 10

EXERCISE 5 ABOUT YOU Fill in the blanks with an appropriate gerund (or noun) to complete these statements. Share your answers with the class.

EXAMPLE I don't mind _shopping for food_, but I do[3] mind _cooking it_.

1. I usually enjoy _____ during the summer.
2. I don't enjoy _____.
3. I don't mind _____, but I do mind _____.
4. I appreciate _____ from my friends.
5. I need to practice _____ if I want to improve.
6. I often put off _____.
7. I need to keep _____ if I want to be successful.
8. I should avoid _____ if I want to improve my health.
9. I miss _____ from my hometown.

EXERCISE 6 ABOUT YOU Make a list of suggestions and recommendations for a tourist who is about to visit your hometown. Read your list to a partner, a small group, or the entire class.

EXAMPLES _I recommend taking warm clothes for the winter._
You should avoid drinking tap water.

1. I recommend:
   _____
   _____
   _____

2. You should avoid:
   _____
   _____
   _____

EXERCISE 7 ABOUT YOU Tell if you like or don't like the following activities. Explain why.

EXAMPLES go shopping
I like to go shopping for clothes because I like to try new styles.
go bowling
I don't like to go bowling because I don't think it's an interesting sport.

1. go fishing   3. go jogging   5. go hunting
2. go camping   4. go swimming   6. go shopping

[3] *Do* makes the verb more emphatic. In this sentence, it shows contrast with *don't mind*.

Gerunds; Infinitives **321**

10.4 Gerund After Preposition[4]

A gerund can follow a preposition. It is important to choose the correct preposition after a verb or adjective.

Preposition combinations		Common combinations	Examples
Verb + Preposition	verb + *about*	care about complain about dream about forget about talk about think about worry about	I **care about doing** well on an interview. My sister **dreams about becoming** a doctor.
	verb + *to*	adjust to look forward to object to	I am **looking forward to getting** a job and **saving** money.
	verb + *on*	depend on insist on plan on	I **plan on going** to a career counselor.
	verb + *in*	believe in succeed in	My father **succeeded in finding** a good job.
Adjective + Preposition	adjective + *of*	afraid of capable of guilty of proud of tired of	I'm **afraid of losing** my job.
	adjective + *about*	concerned about excited about upset about worried about sad about	He is **upset about not getting** the job.
	adjective + *for*	responsible for famous for grateful to . . . for	Who is **responsible for hiring** in this company?
	adjective + *at*	good at successful at	I'm not very **good at writing** a résumé.
	adjective + *to*	accustomed to used to	I'm not **accustomed to talking** about my strengths.
	adjective + *in*	interested in successful in	Are you **interested in getting** a better job?

[4] For a list of verbs and adjectives followed by a *preposition*, see Appendix H.

Language Notes:
1. *Plan, afraid,* and *proud* can be followed by an infinitive too.

   I plan **on seeing** a counselor./I plan **to see** a counselor.
   I'm afraid **of losing** my job./I'm afraid **to lose** my job.
   He's proud **of being** a college graduate./He's proud **to be** a college graduate.

2. Notice that in some expressions, *to* is a preposition followed by a gerund, not part of an infinitive.

   Compare:
   I need **to write** a résumé. (infinitive)
   I'm not accustomed **to writing** a résumé. (*to* + gerund)

EXERCISE 8 ABOUT YOU Complete the questions with a gerund (phrase). Then ask another student these questions.

EXAMPLE Are you lazy about _doing your homework?_

1. Do you ever worry about _____
2. Do you plan on _____
3. Do you ever think about _____
4. When you get tired of _____, what do you do?
5. Are you interested in _____

EXERCISE 9 ABOUT YOU Fill in the blanks with a preposition and a gerund (phrase) to make a **true** statement.

EXAMPLE I plan _on going back to Haiti soon._

1. I'm afraid _____
2. I'm not afraid _____
3. I'm interested _____
4. I'm not interested _____
5. I want to succeed _____
6. I'm not very good _____
7. I'm accustomed _____
8. I'm not accustomed _____
9. I plan _____
10. I don't care _____

Gerunds; Infinitives

EXERCISE 10 ABOUT YOU Fill in the blanks to complete each statement. Compare your experiences in the U.S. with your experiences in your native country. You may share your answers with a small group or with the entire class.

EXAMPLES   In the U.S., I'm afraid of _walking alone at night._

In my native country, I was afraid of _not being able to give my children a good future._

1. In the U.S., I'm interested in _____

   In my native country, I was interested in _____
   _____

2. In the U.S., I worry about _____

   In my native country, I worried about _____
   _____

3. In the U.S., I dream about _____

   In my native country, I dreamed about _____
   _____

4. In the U.S., I look forward to _____

   In my native country, I looked forward to _____
   _____

5. In the U.S., people often complain about _____

   In my native country, people often complain about _____
   _____

6. In the U.S., families often talk about _____

   In my native country, families often talk about _____
   _____

7. American students are accustomed to _____

   Students in my native country are accustomed to _____
   _____

10.5 Gerund in Adverbial Phrase

Examples	Explanation
You should practice interview questions **before going** on an interview. I found my job **by looking** in the newspaper. She took the test **without studying.**	We can use a gerund in an adverbial phrase that begins with a preposition: *before, by, after, without,* etc.

EXERCISE 11 Fill in the blanks to complete the sentences.

EXAMPLE The best way to improve your vocabulary is by _____*reading.*_____

1. One way to find a job is by _____
2. It is very difficult to find a job without _____
3. The best way to improve your pronunciation is by _____
4. The best way to quit a bad habit is by _____
5. One way to find an apartment is by _____
6. I can't speak English without _____
7. It's impossible to get a driver's license without _____
8. You should read the instructions of a test before _____

EXERCISE 12 Fill in the blanks in the conversation below with the gerund form. Where you see two blanks, use a preposition before the gerund. Answers may vary.

A: I need to find a job. I've had ten interviews, but so far no job.

B: Have you thought ___*about*___ ___*going*___ to a job counselor?
(example)

A: No. Where can I find one?

B: Our school office has a counseling department. I suggest _____ an appointment with a counselor.
(1)

A: What can a job counselor do for me?

B: Do you know anything about interviewing skills?

A: No.

B: Well, with the job counselor, you can talk _____(2)_____ _____(3)_____ a good impression during an interview. You can practice _____(4)_____ questions that the interviewer might ask you.

A: Really? How does the counselor know what questions the interviewer will ask me?

B: Many interviewers ask the same general questions. For example, the interviewer might ask you, "Do you enjoy _____(5)_____ with computers?" Or she might ask you, "Do you mind _____(6)_____ overtime and on weekends?" Or "Are you good _____(7)_____ _____(8)_____ with other people?"

A: I dislike _____(9)_____ about myself.

B: That's what you have to do in the U.S.

A: What else can the counselor help me with?

B: If your skills are low, you can talk about _____(10)_____ your skills. If you don't know much about computers, for example, she can recommend _____(11)_____ more classes.

A: It feels like I'm never going to find a job. I'm tired _____(12)_____ _____(13)_____ and not finding anything.

B: If you keep _____(14)_____, you will succeed _____(15)_____ _____(16)_____ a job. I'm sure. But it takes time and patience.

326   Lesson 10

10.6 Infinitives—An Overview

To form an infinitive, we use *to* + the base form of a verb (*to find, to help, to run, to be*).

Examples	Explanation
I want **to find** a job.	An infinitive is used after certain verbs.
I want you **to help** me.	An object can be added before an infinitive.
I'm happy **to help** you.	An infinitive can follow certain adjectives.
It's important **to write** a good résumé.	An infinitive follows certain expressions with *it*.
He went to a counselor **to get** advice.	An infinitive is used to show purpose.

TIPS[5] ON WRITING A RÉSUMÉ

Before You Read

1. Have you ever written a résumé? What is the hardest part about writing a résumé?
2. Do people in your native country have to write a résumé?

 Read the following article. Pay special attention to infinitives.

It's important **to write** a good, clear résumé. A résumé should be limited to one page. It is only necessary **to describe** your most relevant work.[6] Employers are busy people. Don't expect them **to read** long résumés.

You need **to present** your abilities in your résumé. Employers expect you **to use** action verbs **to describe** your experience. Don't begin your sentences with "I". Use past tense verbs like: *managed, designed, created,* and *developed*. It is not enough **to say** you improved something. Be specific. How did you improve it?

Before making copies of your résumé, it is important **to check** the grammar and spelling. Employers want **to see** if you have good communications skills. Ask a friend or teacher **to read** and **give** an opinion about your résumé.

It isn't necessary **to include** references. If the employer wants you **to provide** references, he or she will ask you **to do** so during or after the interview.

Don't include personal information such as marital status, age, race, family information, or hobbies.

Be honest in your résumé. Employers can check your information. No one wants **to hire** a liar.

[5] A *tip* is a small piece of advice.
[6] *Relevant work* is work that is related to this particular job opening.

TINA WHITE
1234 Anderson Avenue
West City, MA 01766
tina.white@met.com
617-123-1234 (home)
617-987-9876 (cellular)

EXPERIENCE

COMPUTER SALES MANAGER
Acme Computer Services, Inc., Concord, MA
March 2003–Present

- Manage computer services department, overseeing 20 sales representatives throughout New England.
- Exceeded annual sales goal by 20 percent in 2004.
- Created online customer database, enabling representatives and company to track and retain customers and improve service.
- Developed new training program and materials for all company sales representatives.

OFFICE MANAGER
West Marketing Services, West City, MA
June 1999–March 2003

- Implemented new system for improving accounting records and reports.
- Managed, trained, and oversaw five customer service representatives.
- Grew sales contracts for support services by 200 percent in first two years.

EDUCATION AND TRAINING
Northeastern Community College, Salem, MA
    Associates Degree Major: Accounting
Institute of Management, Boston, MA
    Certificate of Completion. Course: Sales Management

COMPUTER SKILLS
Proficient in use of MS Windows, PowerPoint, Excel, Access, Outlook, MAC OS, and several accounting and database systems

10.7 Infinitive as Subject

An infinitive can be the subject of a sentence. We begin the sentence with *it* and delay the infinitive.

Examples	Explanation
It is important **to write** a good résumé. It isn't necessary **to include** all your experience. It takes time **to find** a job.	We can use an infinitive after these adjectives: dangerous good necessary difficult great possible easy hard sad expensive important wrong fun impossible
It is necessary **for the manager** to choose the best candidate for the job. It isn't easy **for me** to talk about myself. It was hard **for her** to leave her last job.	Include *for* + noun or object pronoun to make a statement that is true of a specific person.
Compare Infinitive and Gerund Subjects: It's important **to arrive** on time. **Arriving** on time is important.	There is no difference in meaning between an infinitive subject and a gerund subject.

EXERCISE 13 Fill in the blanks with an appropriate infinitive to give information about résumés and interviews. Answers may vary.

EXAMPLE It is necessary _____*to have*_____ a Social Security card.

1. It isn't necessary _____ *all* your previous experience. Choose only the most relevant experience.

2. It's important _____ your spelling and grammar before sending a résumé.

3. It is a good idea _____ interview questions before going on an interview.

4. It is important _____ your best when you go on an interview, so choose your clothes carefully.

5. It isn't necessary _____ references on a résumé. You can simply write, "References available upon request."

6. It's important _____ your past work experience in detail, using words like *managed, designed, supervised,* and *built.*

Gerunds; Infinitives **329**

EXERCISE 14 Complete each statement with an infinitive phrase. You can add an object, if you like.

EXAMPLES It's easy _to shop in an American supermarket._

It's necessary _for me to pay my rent by the fifth of the month._

1. It's important _____
2. It's impossible _____
3. It's possible _____
4. It's necessary _____
5. It's dangerous _____
6. It isn't good _____
7. It's expensive _____
8. It's hard _____

EXERCISE 15 ABOUT YOU Tell if it's important or not important for you to do the following.

EXAMPLE own a house
It's (not) important for me to own a house.

1. get a college degree
2. find an interesting job
3. have a car
4. speak English well
5. read and write English well
6. study American history
7. become an American citizen
8. own a computer
9. have a cell phone
10. make a lot of money

EXERCISE 16 Write a sentence with each pair of words below. You may read your sentences to the class.

EXAMPLE hard / the teacher
It's hard for the teacher to pronounce the names of some students.

1. important / us (the students)
   _____

2. difficult / Americans
   _____

330   Lesson 10

3. easy / the teacher

_____

4. necessary / children

_____

5. difficult / a woman

_____

6. difficult / a man

_____

EXERCISE 17 Write a list of things that a foreign student or immigrant should know about life in the U.S. Use gerunds or infinitives as subjects. You may work with a partner.

EXAMPLES *It is possible for some students to get financial aid.*

Learning English is going to take longer than you expected.

1. _____
2. _____
3. _____
4. _____
5. _____
6. _____

10.8 | Infinitive After Adjective

Some adjectives can be followed by an infinitive.

Examples	Explanation
I would be happy **to help** you with your résumé. Are you prepared **to make** copies of your résumé?	Adjectives often followed by an infinitive are: afraid　　happy　　prepared　　ready glad　　　lucky　　　proud　　　　sad

Gerunds; Infinitives **331**

EXERCISE 18 Complete this conversation with appropriate infinitives. Answers may vary.

EXAMPLE **A:** I have my first interview tomorrow. I'm afraid __to go__ *(example)* alone. Would you go with me?

B: I'd be happy _____(1)_____ with you and wait in the car. But nobody can go with you on an interview. You have to do it alone. It sounds like you're not ready _____(2)_____ a job interview. You should see a job counselor and get some practice before you have an interview. I was lucky _____(3)_____ a great job counselor. She prepared me well.

A: I don't have time to make an appointment with a job counselor before tomorrow. Maybe you can help me.

B: I'd be happy _____(4)_____ you. Do you have some time this afternoon? We can go over some basic questions.

A: Thanks. I'm glad _____(5)_____ you as my friend.

B: That's what friends are for.

EXERCISE 19 ABOUT YOU Fill in the blanks.

EXAMPLE I'm lucky __to be in the U.S._____

1. I was lucky _____
2. I'm proud _____
3. I'm sometimes afraid _____ alone.
4. I'm not afraid _____
5. In the U.S., I'm afraid _____
6. Are we ready _____
7. I'm not prepared _____

10.9 | Infinitive After Verb

Some verbs are commonly followed by an infinitive (phrase).

Examples	Explanation
I need **to find** a new job. I decided **to quit** my old job. I prefer **to work** outdoors. I want **to make** more money.	We can use an infinitive after the following verbs: agree decide like promise ask expect love refuse attempt forget need remember begin hope plan start continue learn prefer try want

Pronunciation Note:
The *to* in infinitives is often pronounced "ta" or, after a *d* sound, "da." *Want to* is often pronounced "wanna." Listen to your teacher pronounce the sentences in the above box.

EXERCISE 20 ABOUT YOU Ask a question with the words given in the present tense. Another student will answer.

EXAMPLE   like / work with computers
       A: Do you like to work with computers?
       B: Yes, I do.   OR   No, I don't.

1. plan / look for a job
2. expect / make a lot of money at your next job
3. like / work with computers
4. prefer / work the second shift
5. need / see a job counselor
6. hope / become rich some day
7. like / work with people
8. try / keep up with changes in technology
9. want / learn another language
10. continue / speak your native language at home

EXERCISE 21 ABOUT YOU Write a sentence about yourself, using the words given, in any tense. You may share your sentences with the class.

EXAMPLES like / eat
I like to eat Chinese food.

try / find
I'm trying to find a job.

1. like / read
   _____

2. not like / eat
   _____

3. want / visit
   _____

4. decide / go
   _____

5. try / learn
   _____

6. begin / study
   _____

EXERCISE 22 ABOUT YOU Check (✓) the activities that you like to do. Tell the class why you like or don't like this activity.

1. _____ stay home on the weekends
2. _____ eat in a restaurant
3. _____ get up early
4. _____ talk on the phone

5. _____ go to museums
6. _____ dance
7. _____ write letters
8. _____ play chess

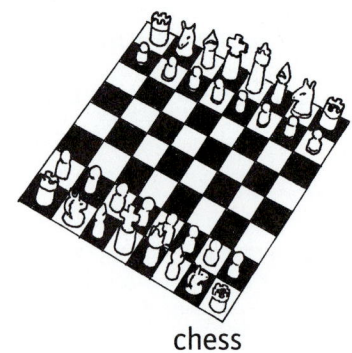
chess

10.10 Gerund or Infinitive After Verb

Some verbs can be followed by either a gerund or an infinitive with almost no difference in meaning.

Examples	Explanation
I started **looking** for a job a month ago. I started **to look** for a job a month ago. He continued **working** until he was 65 years old. He continued **to work** until he was 65 years old.	The verbs below can be followed by either a gerund or an infinitive with almost no difference in meaning: attempt deserve prefer begin hate start can't stand[7] like try continue love

Language Notes:
1. The meaning of *try* + infinitive is a little different from the meaning of *try* + gerund.
   Try + infinitive means to make an effort.
   > I'll **try to improve** my résumé.
   > You should **try to relax** during the interview.
2. *Try* + gerund means to use a different technique when one technique doesn't produce the result you want.
   > I wanted to reach you yesterday, but I couldn't. I **tried calling** your home phone, but I got your answering machine. I **tried calling** your cell phone, but it was turned off. I **tried e-mailing** you, but you didn't check your e-mail.

EXERCISE 23 ABOUT YOU Complete each statement using either a gerund (phrase) or an infinitive (phrase). Practice both ways.

EXAMPLES I started *to learn English four years ago.*
(learn)

I started *studying French when I was in high school.*
(study)

1. I started _____ (come) to this school in _____.

2. I began _____ (study) English _____.

3. I like _____ (watch) _____ on TV.

4. I like _____ (live).

5. I hate _____ (wear).

6. I love _____ (eat).

[7] *Can't stand* means hate or can't tolerate. I *can't stand* waiting in a long line.

10.11 Object Before Infinitive

We can use a noun or object pronoun (*me, you, him, her, it, us,* and *them*) before an infinitive.

Examples	Explanation
Don't **expect an employer to read** a long résumé. I **want you to look** at my résumé. My boss **wants me to work** overtime. I **expected him to give** me a raise.	We often use an object between the following verbs and an infinitive: advise invite want allow need would like ask permit expect tell
He helped me **find** a job. He helped me **to find** a job	*Help* can be followed by either an object + base form or an object + infinitive.

EXERCISE 24   Fill in the blanks with pronouns and infinitives to complete the conversation below.

A: I want to quit my job.

B: Why?

A: I don't like my supervisor. He expects __me__ __to work__
                                    (example) (example: work)
at night and on weekends.

B: But you get extra pay for that, don't you?

A: No. I asked _____ _____ me a raise,
                      (1)   (2 give)
but he said the company can't afford it.

B: Is that the only problem?

A: No. My co-workers and I like to go out for lunch. But he doesn't want _____ _____ out. He
          (3)   (4 go)
expects _____ _____ in the company
       (5)   (6 eat)
cafeteria. He says that if we go out, we might not get back on time.

B: That's awful. He should permit _____
                                    (7)
_____ wherever you want to.
(8 eat)

A: That's what I think. I also have a problem with my manager. She never gives anyone a compliment. When I do a good job, I expect _____ _____ something nice. But she
(9) (10 say)

only says something when we make a mistake.

B: It's important to get positive feedback too.

A: Do you know of any jobs in your company? I'd like

_____ _____ your boss if he
(11) (12 ask)

needs anyone.

B: I don't think there are any job openings in my company. My boss has two sons in their twenties. He wants _____
(13)

_____ for him on Saturdays. But they're so
(14 work)

lazy. The boss allows _____ _____
(15) (16 come)

late and _____ early. He would never permit
(17 leave)

_____ _____ that. We have to be
(18) (19 do)

on time exactly, or he'll take away some of our pay.

A: Maybe I should just stay at my job. I guess no job is perfect.

EXERCISE 25 Tell if the teacher wants or doesn't want the students to do the following.

EXAMPLES do the homework
The teacher wants us to do the homework.

use the textbook during a test
The teacher doesn't want us to use the textbook during a test.

1. talk to another student during a test
2. study before a test
3. copy another student's homework in class
4. learn English
5. speak our native languages
6. improve our pronunciation

Gerunds; Infinitives 337

EXERCISE 26 ABOUT YOU Tell if you expect or don't expect the teacher to do the following.

EXAMPLES give homework
I expect him / her to give homework.

give me private lessons
I don't expect him / her to give me private lessons.

1. correct the homework
2. give tests
3. speak my native language
4. help me after class
5. come to class on time
6. pass all the students
7. know a lot about my native country
8. answer my questions in class
9. teach us American history
10. pronounce my name correctly

EXERCISE 27 ABOUT YOU Write sentences to tell what one member of your family wants (or doesn't want) from another member of your family.

EXAMPLES *My father doesn't want my brother to watch so much TV.*

My brother wants me to help him with his math homework.

1. _____
2. _____
3. _____
4. _____

10.12 | Infinitive to Show Purpose

Examples	Explanation
You can use the Internet **to find** job information. I need a car **to get** to work. I'm saving my money **to buy** a car.	*To* is the short form of *in order to*.
You can use the Internet **in order to find** job information. I need a car **in order to get** to work. I'm saving my money **in order to buy** a car.	The long form is *in order to*.

EXERCISE 28 Fill in the blanks with an infinitive to show purpose. Answers will vary.

EXAMPLE I bought the Sunday newspaper ___*to look for a job*___.

1. I called the company _____ an appointment.
2. She wants to work overtime _____.

3. You should use the Internet _____ jobs.

4. You can use a résumé writing service _____ your résumé.

5. My interview is in a far suburb. I need a car _____ the interview.

6. Use express mail _____ faster.

7. In the U.S., you need experience _____ a job, and you need a job _____ experience.

8. I need two phone lines. I need one _____ on the phone with my friends and relatives. I need the other one _____ business calls.

9. I'm sending a letter that has a lot of papers in it. I need extra stamps _____ this letter.

10. You should go to the college admissions office _____ _____ a copy of your transcripts.

11. After an interview, you can call the employer _____ _____ that you're very interested in the position.

RITA'S STORY

Before You Read

1. What are some differences in the American workplace and the workplace in other countries?

2. In your native culture, is it a sign of respect or disrespect to look at someone directly?

Read the following story. Pay special attention to *used to, be used to,* and *get used to.*

I've been in the U.S. for two years. I **used to** study British English in India, so I had a hard time **getting used to** the American pronunciation. But little by little, I started to **get used to** it. Now I understand Americans well, and they understand me.

I **used to be** an elementary school teacher in India. But for the past two years in the U.S., I've been working in a hotel cleaning rooms. I have to work the second shift. I'**m not used to working** nights. I don't like it because I don't see my children very much. When I get home from work, they're asleep.

(continued)

My husband is home in the evening and cooks for them. In India, I **used to do** all the cooking, but now he has to help with household duties. He didn't like it at first, but now he**'s used to it.**

When I started looking for a job, I had to **get used to** a lot of new things. For example, I had to learn to talk about my abilities in an interview. In India, it is considered impolite to say how wonderful you are. But my job counselor told me that I had to **get used to** it because that's what Americans do. Another thing I**'m not used to** is wearing American clothes. In India, I **used to wear** traditional Indian clothes to work. But now I wear a uniform to work. I don't like to dress like this. I prefer traditional Indian clothes, but my job requires a uniform. There's one thing I **can't get used to:** everyone here calls each other by their first names. It's our native custom to use a term of respect with people we don't know.

It has been hard to **get used to** so many new things, but little by little, I'm doing it.

10.13 Used To vs. Be Used To

Used to + base form is different from *be used to* + gerund.

Examples	Explanation
Rita **used to be** an elementary school teacher. Now she cleans hotel rooms. She **used to wear** traditional Indian clothes. Now she wears a uniform to work. She **used to cook** dinner for her family in India. Now her husband cooks dinner.	*Used to* + base form tells about a past habit or custom. This activity has been discontinued.
Her husband **didn't use to cook** in India.	The negative is *didn't use to* + base form. (Remove the *d* at the end.)
I'm used to working in the day, not at night. Women in India **are used to wearing** traditional clothes.	*Be used to* + gerund or noun means *be accustomed to*. Something is a person's custom and is therefore not difficult to do.
People who studied British English **aren't used to the American pronunciation**.	The negative is *be* + *not* + *used to* + gerund or noun. (Do not remove the *d* of **used to**.)
If you emigrate to the U.S., you have to **get used to many new things**. Children from another country usually **get used to living** in the U.S. easily. But it takes their parents a long time to **get used to a new life**.	*Get used to* + gerund or noun means *become accustomed to*.
I **can't get used to** the cold winters here. She **can't get used to** calling people by their first names.	For the negative, we usually say *can't get used to*.

EXERCISE 29 ABOUT YOU Write four sentences comparing your former behaviors to your behaviors or customs now.

EXAMPLES *I used to live with my family. Now I live with a roommate.*

I used to worry a lot. Now I take it easy most of the time.

1. _____
2. _____
3. _____
4. _____

EXERCISE 30 ABOUT YOU Write sentences comparing the way you used to live in your country or in another city and the way you live now. Read your sentences to the class.

EXAMPLE I used to go everywhere by bus. Now I have a car.

1. _____
2. _____
3. _____
4. _____

EXERCISE 31 A student wrote about things that are new for her in an American classroom. Fill in the blanks with a gerund. Then tell if *you* are used to these things or not.

EXAMPLE I'm not used to _____*taking*_____ multiple-choice tests. In my native country, we have essay tests.

1. I'm not used to _____ at small desks. In my native country, we sit at large tables.

2. I'm not used to _____ the teacher by his / her first name. In my country, we say "Professor."

3. I'm not used to _____ in a textbook. In my native country, we don't write in the books because we borrow them from the school.

4. I'm not used to _____ jeans to class. In my native country, students wear a uniform.

5. I'm not used to _____ and studying at the same time. Students in my native country don't work. Their parents support them.

6. I'm not used to _____ a lot of money to attend college. In my native country, college is free.

7. I'm not used to _____ when a teacher asks me a question. In my native country, students stand to answer a question.

EXERCISE 32 ABOUT YOU Name four things that you had to get used to in the U.S. or in a new town or school. (These things were strange for you when you arrived.)

EXAMPLES I had to get used to *living in a small apartment.*
I had to get used to *American pronunciation.*

1. I had to get used to _____
2. I had to get used to _____
3. I had to get used to _____
4. I had to get used to _____

EXERCISE 33 ABOUT YOU Answer each question with a complete sentence. Practice *be used to* + gerund or noun.

EXAMPLE What are you used to drinking in the morning?
I'm used to drinking coffee in the morning.

1. What kind of work are you used to?
2. What kind of relationship are you used to having with co-workers?
3. What kind of food are you used to (eating)?
4. What kind of weather are you used to?
5. What time are you used to getting up?
6. What kinds of clothes are you used to wearing to work or class?
7. What kinds of things are you used to doing every day?
8. What kinds of classroom behaviors are you used to?
9. What kinds of things are you used to doing alone?

EXERCISE 34 Circle the correct words to complete this conversation.

A: How's your new job?

B: I don't like it at all. I have to work the night shift. I can't get used to *(sleep / sleeping)* during the day.
(1)

A: I know. That's hard. I used to *(work / working)* the night shift, and I
(2)
hated it. That's why I quit.

B: But the night shift pays more money.

A: I know it does, but I was never home for my children. Now my kids speak more English than Spanish. They used to *(speaking / speak)*
(3)
Spanish well, but now they mix Spanish and English. They play with their American friends all day or watch TV.

A: My kids are the same way. But *(I'm / I)* used to it. It doesn't bother me.
(4)

B: I can't *(get / be)* used to it. My parents came to live with us, and they
(5)
don't speak much English. So they can't communicate with their grandchildren anymore.

A: My parents used to *(living / live)* with us too. But they went back
(6)
to Mexico. They didn't like the winters here. They couldn't get *(use / used)* to the cold weather.
(7)

A: Do you think Americans are *(used to / use to)* cold weather?
(8)

B: I'm not sure. My coworker was born in the U.S., but she says she hates winter. She *(is used to / used to)* live in Texas, but now she
(9)
lives here in Minnesota.

A: Why did she move here if she hates the cold weather?

B: The company where she used to *(work / working)* closed down and
(10)
she had to find another job. Her cousin helped her find a job here.

A: Before I came to the U.S., I thought everything here would be perfect. I didn't *(use / used)* to *(think / thinking)* about the
(11) (12)
problems. But I guess life in every country has its problems.

SUMMARY OF LESSON 10

Gerunds

Examples	Explanation
Working all day is hard.	As the subject of the sentence
I don't enjoy **working** as a taxi driver.	After certain verbs
I **go shopping** after work.	In many idiomatic expressions with *go*
I'm worried about **finding** a job.	After prepositions
She found a job by **looking** in the newspaper.	In adverbial phrases

Infinitives

Examples	Explanation
I need **to find** a new job.	After certain verbs
My boss wants me **to work** overtime.	After an object
I'm ready **to quit**.	After certain adjectives
It's important **to have** some free time. It's impossible for me **to work** 80 hours a week.	After certain impersonal expressions beginning with *it*.
I work (in order) **to support** my family.	To show purpose

Gerund or Infinitive—No Difference in Meaning

Gerund	Infinitive
I like **working** with computers.	I like **to work** with computers.
I began **working** three months ago.	I began **to work** three months ago.
Writing a good résumé is important.	It's important **to write** a good résumé.

Gerund or Infinitive—Difference in Meaning

Infinitive (Past Habit)	Gerund (Custom)
Rita **used to be** a teacher in India. Now she works in a hotel.	She **isn't used to working** the night shift. It's hard for her.
Rita **used to wear** traditional Indian clothes to work. Now she wears a uniform.	Rita studied British English. She had to **get used to hearing** the American pronunciation.

EDITING ADVICE

1. Use a gerund after a preposition.

   He read the whole book without ~~use~~ *using* a dictionary.

2. Use the correct preposition.

   She insisted ~~in~~ *on* driving me home.

3. Use a gerund after certain verbs.

   I enjoy ~~to~~ walk*ing* in the park.

   He went ~~to~~ shop*ping* after work.

4. Use an infinitive after certain verbs.

   I decided *to* buy a new car.

5. Use a gerund, not a base form, as a subject.

   ~~Find~~ *Finding* a good job is important.

6. Don't forget to include *it* for a delayed infinitive subject.

   It i~~Is~~ important to find a good job.

7. Don't use the past form after *to*.

   I decided to ~~bought~~ *buy* a new car.

8. After *want, expect, need, advise,* and *ask*, use an object pronoun, not a subject pronoun, before the infinitive. Don't use *that* as a connector.

   He wants ~~that I~~ *me to* drive.

   The teacher expects ~~we~~ *us to* do the homework.

9. Use *for*, not *to*, when introducing an object after impersonal expressions beginning with *it*. Use the object pronoun after *for*.

   It's important ~~to~~ *for* me to find a job.

   It's necessary for ~~he~~ *him* to be on time.

10. Use *to* + base form, not *for*, to show purpose.

    I called the company ~~for~~ *to* make an appointment.

11. Don't put *be* before *used to* for the habitual past.

    I~~'m~~ used to live in Germany. Now I live in the U.S.

12. Don't use the *-ing* form after *used to* for the habitual past.

    We used to ~~having~~ *have* a dog, but he died.

13. Don't forget the *d* in *used to*.

    I use *d* to live with my parents. Now I live alone.

LESSON 10 TEST/REVIEW

PART 1 Find the mistakes with the underlined words, and correct them. Not every sentence has a mistake. If the sentence is correct, write *C*.

EXAMPLES He wrote the composition without ~~check~~ *checking* his spelling.

Do you like to play tennis?   **C**

1. Using the Internet is fun.
2. I recommend to see a job counselor.
3. Do you enjoy learning a new language?
4. Save your money is important for your future.
5. It's important to me to know English well.
6. It's impossible for she to work 60 hours a week.
7. Do you go fish with your brother every week?
8. Do you want the teacher to review modals?
9. He got rich by working hard and investing his money.
10. The teacher tried to explained the present perfect, but we didn't understand it.
11. Is necessary to come to class on time.
12. Do you want to watch TV?
13. She use to take the bus every day. Now she has a car and drives everywhere.
14. It's necessary for me have a good education.

Gerunds; Infinitives   347

15. She came to the U.S. for find a better job.

16. He's interested in becoming a nurse.

17. We're thinking to spend our vacation in Acapulco.

18. We've always lived in a big city. We're used to living in a big city.

19. I'm used to live with my family. Now I live alone.

20. She's from England. She can't get used to drive on the right side of the road.

21. My mother wants that I call her every day.

22. Are you worried about lose your job?

PART 2 Fill in the blanks in the conversation below. Use a gerund or an infinitive. In some cases, either the gerund or the infinitive is possible. Answers may vary.

A: Hi, Molly. I haven't seen you in ages. What's going on in your life?

B: I've made many changes. First, I quit ___working___ in a factory.
(example)

I disliked _____ (1) the same thing every day. And I wasn't used to _____ (2) on my feet all day. My boss often wanted me _____ (3) overtime on Saturdays. I need _____ (4) with my children on Saturdays. Sometimes they want me _____ (5) them to the zoo or to the museum. And I need _____ (6) them with their homework too.

A: So what do you plan on _____ (7) ?

B: I've started _____ (8) to college _____ (9) some general courses.

A: What career are you planning?

B: I'm not sure. I'm interested in _____ (10) with children. Maybe I'll become a teacher's aide. I've also thought about _____ (11) in a day care center. I care about _____ (12) people.

A: Yes, it's wonderful _____ (13) other people, especially children. It's important _____ (14) a job that you like. So you're starting a whole new career.

B: It's not new, really. Before I came to the U.S., I used _____ (15) a kindergarten teacher in my country. But my English wasn't so good when I came here, so I found a job in a factory. I look forward to _____ (16) to my former profession or doing something similar.

A: How did you learn English so fast?

B: By _____ (17) with people at work, by _____ (18) TV, and by _____ (19) the newspaper. It hasn't been easy for me _____ (20) American English. I studied British English in my country, but here I have to get used to _____ (21) things like "gonna" and "wanna." At first I didn't understand Americans, but now I'm used to their pronunciation. I've had to make a lot of changes.

A: You should be proud of _____ (22) so many changes in your life so quickly.

B: I am.

A: Let's get together some time and talk some more.

B: I'd love to. I love to dance. Maybe we can go _____ (23) together sometime.

A: That would be great. And I love _____ (24). Maybe we can go shopping together sometime.

Gerunds; Infinitives **349**

EXPANSION ACTIVITIES

Classroom Activities

1. If you have a job, write a list of five things you enjoy and don't enjoy about your job. If you don't have a job, you can write about what you enjoy and don't enjoy about this school or class. Share your answers with the class.

I enjoy:	I don't enjoy:
I enjoy talking to people.	I don't enjoy working at 6 a.m.

2. Compare the work environment in the U.S. to the work environment in another country. Discuss your answers in a small group or with the entire class. (If you have no experience with American jobs, ask an American to fill in his / her opinions about the U.S.)

	The U.S.	Another Country
1. Coworkers are friendly with each other at the job.		
2. Coworkers get together after work to socialize.		
3. Arriving on time for the job is very important.		
4. The boss is friendly with the employees.		
5. The employees are very serious about their jobs.		
6. The employees use the telephone for personal use.		
7. Everyone wears formal clothes.		
8. Employees get long lunch breaks.		
9. Employees get long vacations.		
10. Employees call the company if they are sick and can't work on a particular day.		
11. Employees are paid in cash.		
12. Employees often take work home.		

3. Find a partner. Pretend that one of you is the manager of a company and the other one is looking for a job in that company. First decide what kind of company it is. Then write the manager's questions and the applicant's answers. Perform your interview in front of the class.

Talk About it

1. Talk about your experiences in looking for a job in the U.S.
2. Talk about the environment where you work.
3. Talk about some professions that interest you.
4. Talk about some professions that you think are terrible.

Write About it

1. Write your résumé and a cover letter.
2. Write about a job you wouldn't want to have. Tell why.
3. Write about a profession you would like to have. Tell why.
4. Write about your current job or a job you had in the past. Tell what you like(d) or don't (didn't) like about this job.

Internet Activities

1. Type *career* in a search engine. See how many "hits" come up.
2. Find some career counseling Web sites. Find a sample résumé in your field or close to your field. Print it out and bring it to class.
3. From one of the Web sites you found, get information on one or more of the following topics:
   - how to write a cover letter
   - how to find a career counselor
   - how to plan for your interview
   - how to network
   - what questions to ask an interviewer
4. See if your local newspaper has a Web site. If it does, find the Help Wanted section of this newspaper. Bring job listings that interest you to class.

Additional Activities at http://elt.heinle.com/gic

LESSON 11

GRAMMAR
Adjective Clauses

CONTEXT: Making Connections—Old Friends and New
Finding Old Friends
Internet Matchmaking

11.1 Adjective Clauses—An Overview

An adjective is a word that describes a noun. An adjective clause is a group of words (with a subject and a verb) that describes a noun. Compare **adjectives** (ADJ.) and **adjective clauses** (AC) below.

Examples	Explanation
ADJ: Do you know your **new** neighbors? **AC:** Do you know the people **who live next door to you**?	An adjective (ADJ) precedes a noun. An adjective clause (AC) follows a noun.
ADJ: This is an **interesting** book. **AC:** This is a book **that has pictures of the high school graduates**.	
ADJ: I attended an **old** high school. **AC:** The high school **that I attended** was built in 1920.	Relative pronouns, such as *who* and *that*, introduce an adjective clause.

FINDING OLD FRIENDS

Before You Read
1. Do you keep in touch with old friends from elementary school or high school?
2. Have you ever thought about contacting someone you haven't seen in years?

High School Yearbook

Read the following article. Pay special attention to adjective clauses.

Americans move numerous times during their lives. As a result, they often lose touch with old friends. Usually, during their twenties and thirties, people are too busy building their careers and starting their families to think much about the past. But as people get older, they often start to wonder about the best friend **they had in high school,** the soldier **with whom they served in the military,** the person **who lived next door** when they were growing up, or their high school sweetheart. Many people want to connect with the past.

Before the Internet, finding a lost love or an old friend required searching through old phone books in libraries in different cities, a detective, and a lot of luck. It was especially hard to find married women **who changed their names.**

Now with the Internet, old friends can sometimes find each other in seconds. Several Web sites have emerged to meet people's growing desire to make connections with former classmates. There are Web sites **that list the students in high schools and colleges in the U.S.** People **who went to high school in the U.S.** can list themselves according to the school **they attended** and the year **they graduated.** A man might go to these Web sites looking for the guys **he played football with** or a long-lost friend—and find the name of a first love **whom he hasn't seen in years.**

One Web site, Classmates.com, claims that more than 30 million Americans have listed themselves on their site. Married women **who have changed their names** list themselves by their maiden names so that others can recognize them easily.

Another way **that people make connections with old classmates** is through reunions. Some high school graduating classes meet every ten years. They usually have dinner, remember the time **when they were young,** and exchange information about what they are doing today. They sometimes bring their high school yearbooks, **which have pictures of the graduates and other school memories.**

Some classes have their reunions in the schools **where they first met.** Others have their reunions in a nice restaurant. There are Web sites **that specialize in helping people find their former classmates and plan reunions.**

In America's highly mobile society, it takes some effort to connect with old friends. Looking back at fond memories, renewing old friendships, making new friends, and even starting a new romance with an old love can be the reward for a little work on the Internet.

EXERCISE 1 Tell if the statement is true or false based on the reading on page 355. Write *T* or *F*.

EXAMPLE People who graduate from high school have to attend their reunions.   F

1. A yearbook is a book that has the diplomas of the graduates.
2. Classmates.com is a Web site that has lists of graduates from various high schools in the U.S.
3. Americans move a lot and often lose touch with the friends that they had in high school.
4. Women who get married often change their last names.
5. People who attend reunions meet their old classmates.
6. There are several Web sites that help people make connections with old friends.
7. Some Web sites can help you find people with whom you served in the military.

EXERCISE 2 Underline the adjective clauses in the sentences in Exercise 1.

EXAMPLE People who graduate from high school have to attend their reunions.

11.2 | Relative Pronoun as Subject

The relative pronouns *who, that,* and *which* can be the subject of the adjective clause. Use *who* or *that* for people. Use *that* or *which* for things.

I found a Web site. *The Web site* (Subject) lists people by high school.

I found a Web site [that / which] lists people by high school.

Women .... often change their last names.

Women (Subject) get married.

Women [who / that] get married often change their last names.

Language Notes:
1. *Which* is less common than *that.*
2. A present tense verb in the adjective clause must agree in number with its subject.
   A woman who **gets** married usually changes her name.
   Women who **get** married usually change their names.

EXERCISE 3 Fill in the blanks with *who* or *that* + the correct form of the verb in parentheses ( ).

EXAMPLE A yearbook has photos ___that show___ the activities of the high school.
(show)

1. He has a yearbook _____ pictures of all his classmates.
(have)

2. People _____ to a reunion exchange information about their lives.
(go)

3. Classmates.com is a Web site _____ people make connections with old friends.
(help)

4. There are Web sites _____ in helping people plan a reunion.
(specialize)

5. People _____ a reunion have to contact former classmates.
(plan)

EXERCISE 4 Fill in the blanks with *who* or *that* + the correct form of the verb in parentheses ( ). Then complete the statement. Answers will vary.

EXAMPLE People ___who work___ hard ___are often successful.___
(work)

1. People _____ regularly _____
(exercise)

2. A person _____ a cell phone while driving _____
(use)

3. Students _____ absent a lot _____
(be)

4. Schools _____ computers _____
(not/have)

5. A computer _____ more than five years old _____
(be)

6. People _____ digital cameras _____
(have)

7. Colleges _____ evening classes _____
(have)

8. A college _____ a day-care center _____
(have)

9. Students _____ a full-time job _____
(have)

Adjective Clauses 357

EXERCISE 5 Complete each statement with an adjective clause. Answers will vary.

EXAMPLE I know some women *who don't want to get married.*

1. People _____ can make a lot of friends.
2. Men _____ have a busy social life.
3. I like people _____
4. I don't like people _____
5. Students like a teacher _____
6. People _____ are very fortunate.
7. People _____ aren't usually successful.
8. Parents _____ are good.
9. A college _____ is good for foreign students.
10. People _____ have a hard life.

11.3 | Relative Pronoun as Object

The relative pronouns *who(m)*, *that*, and *which* can be the object of the adjective clause.

Object
She attended *the high school*.
The high school . . . . is in New York City.

The high school | which / that / ∅ | she attended is in New York City.

Object
I knew *a friend* in high school.
A friend . . . . sent me an e-mail.

A friend | who(m) / that / ∅ | I knew in high school sent me an e-mail.

Language Notes:
1. The relative pronoun is usually omitted in conversation when it is the object of the adjective clause.

    The high school she attended is in New York City.

2. *Whom* is considered more correct or more formal than *who* when used as the object of the adjective clause. However, as seen in the above note, the relative pronoun is usually omitted altogether in conversation.

    Formal: A friend *whom* I knew in high school sent me an e-mail.

    Informal: A friend I knew in high school sent me an e-mail.

EXERCISE 6 In each sentence below, underline the adjective clause.

EXAMPLE I've lost touch with some of the friends <u>I had in high school</u>.

1. The high school <u>I attended</u> is in another city.
2. The teachers <u>I had in high school</u> are all old now.
3. We didn't have to buy the textbooks <u>we used in high school</u>.
4. She married a man <u>she met at her high school reunion</u>.
5. The friends <u>I've made in this country</u> don't know much about my country.

EXERCISE 7 A mother (M) is talking to her teenage daughter (D). Fill in the blanks to complete the conversation. Answers may vary.

M: I'd like to contact an old friend I ___*had*___ in high school.
    (example)

I wish I could find her. I'll never forget the good times _____(1)_____ in high school. When we graduated, we said we'd always stay in touch. But then we went to different colleges.

D: Didn't you keep in touch by e-mail?

M: When I was in college, e-mail didn't exist. At first we wrote letters. But little by little we wrote less and less until, eventually, we stopped writing.

D: Do you still have the letters she _____(2)_____ ?

M: Yes, I do. They're in a box in the basement.

D: Why don't you write to the address on the letters?

M: That doesn't make sense. The address she _____(3)_____ on the letters was of the college town where she lived. I don't know what happened to her after she left college.

D: Have you tried calling her parents?

M: The phone number _____(4)_____ is now disconnected. Maybe her parents have died.

D: Have you looked on Classmates.com?

M: What's that?

Adjective Clauses 359

D: It's a Web site that _____(5)_____ lists of people. The list is categorized by the high school you _____(6)_____ and the dates you _____(7)_____ there.

M: Is everyone in my high school class on the list?

D: Unfortunately, no. Only the people _____(8)_____ add their names are on the list.

M: But my friend probably got married. I don't know the name of the man _____(9)_____ married.

D: That's not a problem. You can search for her by her maiden name.

M: Will this Web site give me her address and phone number?

D: No. But for a fee, you can send her an e-mail through the Web site. Then if she wants to contact you, she can give you her personal information.

M: She'll probably think I'm crazy for contacting her almost 25 years later.

D: I'm sure she'll be happy to receive communication from a good friend _____(10)_____ hasn't seen in years. When I graduate from high school, I'm never going to lose contact with the friends _____(11)_____ made. We'll always stay in touch.

M: That's what you think. But as time passes and your lives become more complicated, you may lose touch.

D: But today we have e-mail.

M: Well, e-mail is a help. Even so, the direction you _____(12)_____ in life is different from the direction your friends choose.

EXERCISE 8 Fill in the blanks with appropriate words to complete the conversation. Answers may vary.

A: I'm lonely. I have a lot of friends in my native country, but I don't have enough friends here. The friends _**I have there**_ (example) send me e-mail all the time, but that's not enough. I need to make new friends here.

B: Haven't you met any people here?

A: Of course. But the people _____(1)_____ here don't have my interests.

B: What are you interested in?

A: I like reading, meditating, going for quiet walks. Americans seem to like parties, TV, sports, movies, going to restaurants.

B: You're never going to meet people with the interests _____(2)_____. Your interests don't include other people. You should find some interests _____(3)_____ other people, like tennis or dancing, to mention only a few.

A: The activities _____(4)_____ cost money, and I don't have a lot of money.

B: There are many parks in this city _____(5)_____ free tennis courts. If you like to dance, I know of a park district near here _____(6)_____ free dance classes. In fact, there are a lot of things _____(7)_____ or very low cost in this city. I can give you a list of free activities, if you want.

A: Thanks. I'd love to have the list. Thanks for all the suggestions _____(8)_____.

B: I'd be happy to give you more, but I don't have time now. Tomorrow I'll bring you a list of activities from the parks in this city. I'm sure you'll find something _____(9)_____ on that list.

A: Thanks.

EXERCISE 9 We often give a definition with an adjective clause. Work with a partner to give a definition of the following words by using an adjective clause.

EXAMPLES twins
Twins are brothers or sisters who are born at the same time.

an answering machine
An answering machine is a device that takes phone messages.

1. a babysitter
2. an immigrant
3. an adjective
4. a verb
5. a fax machine
6. a dictionary
7. a mouse
8. a coupon

mouse

Adjective Clauses **361**

11.4 Where and When

Examples	Explanation
Some classes have their reunion in the school **where they first met.** There are Web sites **where you can find lists of high schools and their students.** She attended the University of Washington, **where she met her best friend.**	*Where* means "in that place." *Where* cannot be omitted.
Do you remember the time **(when) you were in high school?** High school was a time **(when)** I had many good friends and few responsibilities. In 1984, **when I graduated from high school,** my best friend's family moved to another state.	*When* means "at that time." *When* can sometimes be omitted.

Punctuation Notes:

1. An adjective clause is sometimes separated from the sentence with a comma. This is true when the person or thing in the main clause is unique.

   Compare:
   I visited a Web site **where** I found the names of my classmates. (No Comma)
   I visited Classmates.com, **where** I found the names of my classmates. (Comma: Classmates.com is a unique Web site.)
   I remember the year **when** I graduated from high school. (No Comma)
   In 1984, **when** she graduated from high school, she got married. (Comma: 1984 is a unique year.)

2. *When* without a comma can be omitted.
   I remember the year I graduated from high school.

EXERCISE 10 This is a conversation between a son (S) and his dad (D). Fill in the blanks with *where* or *when* to complete this conversation.

S: How did you meet mom? Do you remember the place ___*where*___ you met?
                          (example)

D: We met in high school. I'll never forget the day _____(1)_____ I met your mother. She was such a pretty girl.

S: Did you go to the same school?

D: Yes. We were in a typing class together. She was sitting at the typewriter next to mine.

S: Dad, what's a typewriter?

D: There was a time _____(2)_____ we didn't have computers. We had to type our papers on typewriters.

S: Did you start dating right away?

362 Lesson 11

D: No. We were friends. There was a time _____(3)_____ people were friends before they started dating. There was a soda shop near school _____(4)_____ we used to meet.

S: What's a soda shop, Dad?

D: It's a store _____(5)_____ you could buy milk shakes, sodas, and hamburgers. We used to sit there after school drinking one soda with two straws.

S: That doesn't seem too romantic to me.

D: But it was.

S: So did you get married as soon as you graduated from high school?

D: No. I graduated from high school at a time _____(6)_____ there was a war going on in this country. Mom went to college and I went into the army. We wrote letters during that time. When I got out of the army, I started college. So we got married about seven years after we met.

11.5 Formal vs. Informal

Examples	Explanation
Informal: I lost touch with the friends I used to go to high school **with.** **Formal:** I lost touch with the friends **with whom** I used to go to high school.	Informally, most native speakers put the preposition at the end of the adjective clause. The relative pronoun is usually omitted.
Informal: I saved the yearbook my friends wrote **in.** **Formal:** I saved the yearbook **in which** my friends wrote.	In very formal English, the preposition comes before the relative pronoun, and only *whom* and *which* may be used. *That* is not used directly after a preposition.

EXERCISE 11 Change the sentences to formal English.

EXAMPLE What is the name of the high school you graduated from?
What is the name of the high school from which you graduated?

1. He found his friend that he served in the military with.

   _____

2. I can't find the friend I was looking for.

   _____

3. The high school she graduated from was torn down.

   _____

4. Do you remember the teacher I was talking about?
   _____

5. In high school, the activities I was interested in were baseball and band.
   _____

INTERNET MATCHMAKING

Before You Read
1. Where do you meet new people?
2. Do you know anyone who has tried an online dating service?

 Read the following article. Pay special attention to adjective clauses beginning with *whose*.

Did You Know?
Fifty-three percent of women 75 years old and older live alone. Twenty-one percent of men over 75 live alone.

Is it possible to find love on the Internet? About 40 million people a month visit an online dating service in hopes of finding true love. Some of these dating sites let you easily search the pictures and biographical descriptions of people who list themselves there. You can search by age and location. Other Web sites make you fill out lengthy questionnaires so that they can match you with people **whose interests** and **values** are similar to yours. Most of these sites charge a fee for this service.

Meg Olson, a 40-year-old woman from Michigan who wanted to get married, was simply not meeting men. She used an online dating site and met Don Trenton, 42, **whose wife** had recently died. After e-mailing, they started to talk on the phone and realized how many things they had in common. They met, started dating, and a year later, they were married. Don, **whose son** was six years old at the time, wanted to create a stable family for his son.

There are sites for all kinds of interests and connections. Some sites specialize in a specific religion or ethnic group. There are sites for senior citizens. Sadie Kaplan is a 75-year-old widow who wants to meet men **whose age** and **interests** are similar to her own. However, it's harder for women in this age group to meet men because women live longer than men. Because the life expectancy for women is much higher than it is for men (79 for women, 73 for men), many of the women in her age group are widows.

As people live busier and busier lives, they sometimes don't have the time to go out and meet new people. Dating Web sites provide a fast, easy way for people to find romance.

11.6 | Whose + Noun

Whose is the possessive form of *who*. It substitutes for *his, her, its, their,* or the possessive form of the noun.

He met a woman.
He met a woman | Her | values are similar to his own.
He met a woman | **whose** | values are similar to his own.

Don wanted to create a family.
| Don's | son was six years old.
Don, | **whose** | son was six years old, wanted to create a family.

Language Note:
Use *who* to substitute for a person. Use *whose* for possession or relationship.
Compare:
   She married a man **who** has a child.
   She married a man **whose interests** are similar to hers.

Punctuation Note:
An adjective clause is sometimes separated from the sentence with a comma. This is true when the person or thing in the main clause is unique.
Compare:
   Some dating Web sites match you with someone **whose values** are similar to your own.
   Sally met Harry, **whose values** were similar to her own. (Harry is unique.)

EXERCISE 12 This is a conversation between two friends. Fill in the blanks. Answers may vary.

A: I know you're trying to meet a man. I have a cousin whose ____*wife*____ died last year. He's your age. He's ready to start dating.
            (example)

B: Tell me more about him.

A: He likes sports and the outdoors.

B: You know I don't like sports. I prefer to stay home and read or watch movies. I want to meet someone whose _____
                                                                                            (1)
are the same as mine.

A: I'm sure you can become interested in football and fishing.

B: I'm not so sure about that. What kind of work does he do?

A: He's a traveling salesman. He's almost never home.

B: I prefer to meet a man whose _____ doesn't take him
                                        (2)
away from home all the time. What else can you tell me about him?

A: He has a three-year-old son and a five-year-old daughter.

B: I don't want to marry a man whose _____(3)_____ are small. My kids are grown up, and I don't want to start raising kids again.

A: It's okay. His mother lives with him now, and she helps take care of the kids.

B: I don't want to date a man whose _____(4)_____ lives with him.

A: But she's a nice woman. She's my aunt.

B: I'm sure she is, but I'm 45 and don't want to live with someone's mother.

A: You know my intentions are good.

B: I have a lot of friends whose _____(5)_____ are good, but then I meet the man and find we have nothing in common. I think it's better if I meet a man on my own.

EXERCISE 13 ABOUT YOU Fill in the blanks.

EXAMPLE I would like to own a car that _has enough room for my large family._

1. My mother is a woman who _____
2. My city is a place where _____
3. My childhood was a time when _____
4. My favorite kind of book is one that _____
5. A great teacher is a person who _____
6. I have a friend whose _____
7. I have a computer that _____
8. I like to shop at a time when _____
9. I don't like people who _____

EXERCISE 14 *Combination Exercise. Part A:* Some women were asked what kind of man they'd like to marry. Fill in the blanks with a response, using the words in parentheses ( ).

EXAMPLE I'd like to marry a man _whose values are the same as mine._
(His values are the same as mine.)

1. I'd like to marry a man _____
(I can trust him.)

2. I don't want a husband _____
(He doesn't put his family first.)

3. I want to marry a man _____
   (He makes a good living.)

4. I'd like to marry a man _____
   (His mother lives far away.)

5. I'd like to marry a man _____
   (He's older than I am.)

6. I'd like to marry a man _____
   (He wants to have children.)

7. (Women: Add your own sentence telling what kind of man you'd like to marry, or what kind of man you married.)

   _____

Part B: Some men were asked what kind of woman they'd like to marry. Fill in the blanks with a response, using the words in parentheses ( ).

EXAMPLE I'd like to marry a woman __*who knows how to cook.*__
(She knows how to cook.)

1. I'd like to marry a woman _____
   (She has a sense of humor.)

2. I'd like to marry a woman _____
   (I can admire her wisdom.)

3. I'd like to marry a woman _____
   (Her manners are good.)

4. I'd like to marry a woman _____
   (Her family is supportive.)

5. I'd like to marry a woman _____
   (I have known her for a long time.)

6. I'd like to marry a woman _____
   (She wants to have a lot of kids.)

7. (Men: Add your own sentence telling what kind of woman you'd like to marry, or what kind of woman you married.)

   _____

EXERCISE 15 *Combination Exercise.* Fill in the blanks with appropriate words to complete the conversation. Answers may vary.

A: I'm getting married in two months.

B: Congratulations. Are you marrying the woman __*you met*__
(example)
at Mark's party last year?

Adjective Clauses **367**

A: Oh, no. I broke up with that woman a long time ago. I'm going to marry a woman _____(1)_____ online about ten months ago.

B: What's your fiancée's name? Do I know her?

A: Sarah Liston.

B: I know someone whose _____(2)_____ is Liston. I wonder if they're from the same family.

A: I doubt it. Sarah comes from Canada.

B: Where are you going to live after you get married? Here or in Canada?

A: We're going to live here. Sarah's just finishing college and doesn't have a job yet. This is the place _____(3)_____ I have a good job, so we decided to live here.

B: Where are you going to get married?

A: At my parents' friend's house. They have a very big house and garden. The wedding's going to be in the garden.

B: My wife and I made plans to get married outside too, but we had to change our plans because it rained that day.

A: That's OK. The woman _____(4)_____ is more important than the place _____(5)_____ we get married. And the life _____(6)_____ together is more important than the wedding day.

B: You're right about that!

EXERCISE 16 *Combination Exercise.* Use the words in parentheses ( ) to form an adjective clause. Then read the sentences and tell if you agree or disagree. Give your reasons.

EXAMPLE A good friend is a person ____I can trust____.
(I can trust her.)

1. A good friend is a person _____ almost every day.
(I see him.)

2. A good friend is a person _____.
(She would lend me money.)

3. A good friend is a person _____.
(He knows everything about me.)

4. A person _____ cannot be my friend.
(He has different political opinions.)

5. A person _____ cannot
   (She doesn't speak my native language.)
   be my good friend.

6. A person _____ cannot
   (His religious beliefs are different from mine.)
   be my good friend.

7. A person _____ cannot be a good friend.
   (She lives far away.)

8. I would discuss the problems _____ with a
   (I have problems.)
   good friend.

9. This school is a place _____
   (I can make many new friends easily at this school.)

10. Childhood is the only time in one's life _____
    _____
    (It is easy to make friends at this time.)

SUMMARY OF LESSON 11

Adjective Clauses

1. **Pronoun as Subject**
   She likes men **who have self-confidence.**
   The man **that arrived late** took a seat in the back.

2. **Pronoun as Object**
   I'd like to meet the man **(who / m) (that) she married.**
   The book **(which) (that) I'm reading** is very exciting.

3. **Pronoun as Object of Preposition**
   FORMAL: The person **about whom** I'm talking is my cousin.
   INFORMAL: The person **(who)** I'm talking **about** is my cousin.
   FORMAL: The club **of which** I am a member meets at the community center.
   INFORMAL: The club **(that)** I am a member **of** meets at the community center.

4. **Whose** + Noun
   I have a friend **whose brother lives in Japan.**
   The students **whose last names begin with A or B** can register on Friday afternoon.

5. **Where**
   He moved to New Jersey, **where** he found a job.
   The apartment building **where** he lives has a lot of immigrant families.

6. **When**

She came to the U.S. at a time **when** she was young enough to learn English easily.

She came to the U.S. in 1995, **when** there was a war going on in her country.

EDITING ADVICE

1. Use *who*, *that*, or *which* to introduce an adjective clause. Don't use *what*.

   I know a woman ~~what~~ *who* has ten cats.

2. If the relative pronoun is the subject, don't omit it.

   I know a man *who* has been married four times.

3. Use *whose* to substitute for a possessive form.

   I live next door to a couple ~~their~~ *whose* children make a lot of noise.

4. If the relative pronoun is used as the object, don't put an object after the verb of the adjective clause.

   I had to pay for the library book that I lost ~~it~~.

5. Don't use *which* for people.

   The man ~~which~~ *who* bought my car paid me by check.

6. Use subject-verb agreement in all clauses.

   I have a friend who live*s* in Madrid.

   People who talk~~s~~ too much bother me.

7. Don't use an adjective clause when a simple adjective is enough.

   I don't like long movies.
   ~~I don't like movies that are long.~~

8. An adjective clause is a dependent clause. It is never a sentence.

   I sold my car to a man. ~~Who~~ *who* lives on the next block.

9. Put a noun before an adjective clause.

   A student w
   ~~W~~ho needs help should ask the teacher.

10. Put the adjective clause immediately after the noun it describes.

The car is beautiful ~~that you bought~~. *(that you bought moved after "car")*

11. Use *where*, not *that*, to mean "in a place."

The store ~~that~~ *where* I buy my textbooks is having a sale this week.

12. Use *whom* and *which*, not *that*, if the preposition precedes the relative pronoun.

She would never want to go back to the country from ~~that~~ *which* she came.

13. Use correct word order in an adjective clause (subject before verb).

The fish that ~~caught my father~~ *my father caught* was very big.

14. Don't confuse *whose* (possessive form) and *who's* (who is).

A woman ~~whose~~ *who's* in my math class is helping me study for the test.

LESSON 11 TEST/REVIEW

PART 1 Find the mistakes with the underlined words, and correct them. Not every sentence has a mistake. If the sentence is correct, write *C*.

EXAMPLES Do you know the man ~~whose~~ *who's* standing in the back of the theater?

Could you please return the book <u>I lent</u> you last week?   **C**

1. The wallet <u>which found my friend</u> has no identification.
2. The coat is too small <u>that I bought</u> last week.
3. I don't know the people <u>who lives</u> next door to me.
4. I have to return the books <u>that I borrowed</u> from the library.
5. I don't like neighbors <u>what make</u> a lot of noise.
6. I don't like the earrings <u>that I bought them</u>.
7. I have a <u>friend lives</u> in Houston.
8. <u>Who</u> speaks English well doesn't have to take this course.
9. I can't understand a word <u>you are saying</u>.
10. I prefer to have an English teacher <u>which speaks</u> my language.
11. Everyone <u>whose last name</u> begins with *A* should stand up.

Adjective Clauses

12. The store <u>that</u> I buy my groceries is open 24 hours a day.
13. I don't understand a thing <u>you are talking about</u>.
14. The woman <u>with whom he came to the party</u> was not his wife.
15. I don't know <u>anyone. Who</u> has a record player anymore.
16. We rented an apartment <u>that doesn't have</u> a refrigerator.
17. A couple <u>who's</u> children are small has a lot of responsibilities.
18. I have a friend <u>her</u> brother just graduated from medical school.

PART 2 Fill in the blanks to complete the adjective clause. Answers may vary.

EXAMPLE **A:** You lost a glove. Is this yours?

B: No. The glove ___*that I lost*___ is brown.

1. **A:** My neighbor's children make a lot of noise.

   B: That's too bad. I don't like to have neighbors _____
   _____

2. **A:** I have a new cat. Do you want to see him?

   B: What happened to the other cat _____

   A: She died last month.

3. **A:** Do you speak French?

   B: Yes, I do. Why?

   A: The teacher is looking for a student _____
   to help her translate a letter.

4. **A:** Did you meet your boyfriend on an Internet dating site?

   B: No. I didn't like any of the men _____
   on the Internet.

5. **A:** Does your last name begin with *A*?

   B: Yes, it does. Why?

   A: Registration is by alphabetical order. Students _____
   _____ can register after two o'clock today.

6. **A:** Did you go to your last high school reunion?

   B: No. I was out of town on the day _____.

   A: Do you usually go to your reunions?

   B: Yes. I love to keep in touch with the people _____.

7. **A:** Are you planning to marry Charles?

   B: No. He lives with his mother. I want to marry a man _____
   _____ lives far away.

EXPANSION ACTIVITIES

Classroom Activities

1. Tell if you agree or disagree with the statements below. Discuss your answers.

	I agree.	I disagree.
a. People who have different religions can have a good marriage.		
b. People who come from different countries or have different languages can have a good marriage.		
c. Women who marry younger men can be happy.		
d. It's possible to fall in love with someone you've just met.		
e. Young people who want to get married should get the approval of their parents.		
f. A man shouldn't marry a divorced woman who has children.		
g. Couples who have children shouldn't get divorced.		
h. Older women whose husbands have died should try to get married again.		
i. A man should always marry a woman who is shorter than he is.		
j. Couples who live with a mother-in-law usually have problems.		
k. A woman shouldn't marry a man who has a lower level of education.		

2. Write a short definition or description of an object or a person. Read your definition to a small group. The others will try to guess what it is. Continue to add to your definition until someone guesses it.

   EXAMPLE   It's an animal that lives in the water.
   Is it a fish?
   No, it isn't. It's an animal that needs to come up for air.
   Is it a dolphin?
   Yes, it is.

3. Write a word from your native language that has no English translation. It might be the name of a food or a traditional costume. Define the word. Read your definition to a small group or to a partner.

   EXAMPLE   A *sari* is a typical Indian dress for women. It is made of a cloth that a woman wraps around her. She wraps one end around her waist. She puts the other end over her shoulder.

4. Bring to class something typical from your country. Demonstrate how to use it.

   EXAMPLE   a samovar
   This is a pot that we use in Russia to make tea.

Adjective Clauses

5. Dictionary game. Form a small group. One student in the group will look for a hard word in the dictionary. (Choose a noun. Find a word that you think no one will know.) Other students will write definitions of the word. Students can think of funny definitions or serious ones. The student with the dictionary will write the real definition. Students put all the definitions in a box. The student with the dictionary will read the definitions. The others have to guess which is the real definition.

   EXAMPLE parapet
   Sample definition: A parapet is a small pet that has wings, like a parakeet.
   Real definition: A parapet is a low wall that runs along the edge of a roof or balcony.

(The teacher can provide a list of words and definitions beforehand, writing them on small pieces of paper. A student can choose one of the papers that the teacher has prepared.)

Talk About it

1. Do you think the Internet is a good way to meet a romantic partner? Why or why not?

2. How do people in your native culture find a spouse?

3. Talk about the kind of person who makes a good husband, wife, father, mother, or friend.

4. If you are married, tell where or how you met your spouse.

5. Are you surprised that there are Internet sites for seniors who are single and looking for a partner?

6. In your native culture, do people usually keep in touch with the friends they made in school?

7. Are there class reunions in your native country?

Write About it

1. Write a short composition describing your best friend from your school days.

2. Write a short composition describing the difference between dating customs in the U.S. and in your native culture.

Internet Activities

1. Visit an online dating service. Bring in a profile of a person that you think is interesting.

2. Visit an online dating service for senior citizens. Bring in a profile of a person that you think is interesting.

3. Visit a Web site that lists classmates. If you graduated from high school in the U.S., see if your high school is listed.

4. Visit a Web site that plans reunions. Find out some of the steps that are necessary in planning a reunion.

Additional Activities at **http://elt.heinle.com/gic**

LESSON 12

GRAMMAR
Superlatives
Comparatives

CONTEXT: Sports and Athletes
Michael Jordan
Americans' Attitude Toward Soccer
An Amazing Athlete
Football and Soccer

375

12.1 Superlatives and Comparatives—An Overview

Examples	Explanation
Baseball and basketball are **the most popular** sports in the U.S. Jack is **the tallest player** on the basketball team.	We use the superlative form to point out the number one item or items in a group of three or more.
Baseball is **more popular than** soccer in the U.S. Basketball players are **taller than** baseball players.	We use the comparative form to compare two items or groups of items.
He is **as tall as** a basketball player. Soccer is not **as popular as** baseball. Soccer players are not **the same height as** basketball players.	We can show equality or inequality.

MICHAEL JORDAN

Before You Read

1. Do you like sports? Which are your favorites?
2. Who are your favorite athletes?

376 Lesson 12

Read the following article. Pay special attention to superlative forms.

Michael Jordan is probably **the best known** basketball player in the world. His career started in the early 1980s, when he played college basketball with the University of North Carolina. Although he was not **the tallest** or **the strongest** player, he won the attention of his coach for being an excellent athlete. Probably his **most important** achievement[1] at that time was scoring the winning basket in the 1983–1984 college championship game.

Jordan left college early to join the Chicago Bulls, a professional basketball team. He led the Bulls to **the best** record in professional basketball history. He was voted **the most valuable** player five times. Jordan holds several records: **the highest** scoring average (31.7 points per game) and **the most** points in a playoff game (63). Many people think that Michael Jordan was **the most spectacular** basketball player of all time. A statue of Jordan in Chicago has these words, "**The best** there ever was. **The best** there ever will be." Jordan retired from the Chicago Bulls in 1999 at the age of 35.

Jordan came out of retirement in 2001 to play a few more seasons with another team, the Washington Wizards. When he announced his comeback, he said he would donate his $1 million salary the first year to the families of the victims of the September 11, 2001 terrorist attacks. He retired from basketball for good in 2003, at the age of 40. L.A. Laker superstar Magic Johnson said it well when he said, "There's Michael, then there's all the rest of us."

Jordan's popularity with his fans brought him to the attention of advertisers. Jordan is paid a lot of money to have his name appear on sports products and to appear in TV commercials. *Forbes Magazine* in 2004 ranked him the fourth **highest** paid athlete and the seventh **highest** paid celebrity.

In his retirement, Jordan works with charities. He created The Jordan Institute for Families, an organization that tries to help solve the problems facing poor families. He is hoping to help families accomplish their dreams.

Did You Know?

When Michael Jordan tried out for the basketball team in high school, he didn't make it on the first try.

[1] An *achievement* is something you attain through practice or hard work.

12.2 | The Superlative Form

We use the superlative form to point out the number one item of a group of three or more. The superlative has two forms, depending on the number of syllables in the adjective or adverb.

Examples	Explanation
Jordan was not **the tallest** player on his team. Jordan was not **the strongest** player on his team. Who runs **the fastest** on the team?	Use: *the* + [short adjective/adverb] + *-est* We often put a prepositional phrase after a superlative phrase: *in the world, on his team, in the U.S., of all time.*
Jordan was probably **the most spectacular** player of all time. He was **the most valuable** player on this team.	Use: *the most* + [long adjective/adverb]
Jordan is **one of the richest athletes** in the world. Jordan was **one of the oldest players** on his team.	We often say "one of the" before a superlative form. The noun that follows is plural.
Jordan is one of the best athletes **who has ever lived.** His last game with the Bulls was one of the most exciting games **I have ever seen.**	An adjective clause with *ever* and the present perfect tense often completes a superlative statement.
Who is **the best** athlete in the world?	Some superlatives are irregular. See 12.3 for more information.

Language Note:
Use *the* before a superlative form. Omit *the* if there is a possessive form before the superlative form.
   Jordan was **the team's most valuable** player. (*Not:* Jordan was the *team's the most* valuable player.)
   My oldest brother loves basketball. (*Not:* My *the oldest* brother loves basketball.)

EXERCISE 1 Tell if the statement is true (*T*) or false (*F*). Underline the superlative forms. Not every sentence has a superlative form.

EXAMPLE Michael Jordan is one of <u>the best</u> basketball players in the world.   **T**

1. Magic Johnson said, "Jordan is the best there ever was, the best there ever will be."
2. Jordan was voted the most valuable player more than one time.
3. Jordan is one of the richest athletes in the world.
4. Jordan scored the most points in a playoff game.
5. Jordan retired for good at the age of 35.
6. One year, Jordan donated his $1 million salary to the families of the victims of September 11.

12.3 Comparative and Superlative Forms of Adjectives and Adverbs

Explanation	Simple	Comparative	Superlative
One-syllable adjectives and adverbs*	tall fast	taller faster	the tallest the fastest
Two-syllable adjectives that end in -y	easy happy	easier happier	the easiest the happiest
Other two-syllable adjectives	frequent active	more frequent more active	the most frequent the most active
Some two-syllable adjectives have two forms. Other two-syllable adjectives that have two forms are *handsome, quiet, gentle, narrow, clever, friendly, angry, polite, stupid*.	simple common	simpler more simple commoner more common	the simplest the most simple the commonest the most common
Adjectives with three or more syllables	important difficult	more important more difficult	the most important the most difficult
-ly adverbs	quickly brightly	more quickly more brightly	the most quickly the most brightly
Irregular adjectives and adverbs	good/well bad/badly far little a lot	better worse farther less more	the best the worst the farthest the least the most

Spelling Rules for Short Adjectives and Adverbs

Rule	Simple	Comparative	Superlative
Add -er and -est to short adjectives and adverbs.	tall fast	taller faster	tallest fastest
For adjectives that end in *y*, change *y* to *i* and add -er and -est.	easy happy	easier happier	easiest happiest
For adjectives that end in *e*, add -r and -st.	nice late	nicer later	nicest latest
For words ending in consonant-vowel-consonant, double the final consonant, then add -er and -est.**	big sad	bigger sadder	biggest saddest

Language Notes:

*Exceptions: bored   more bored   the most bored
              tired   more tired   the most tired

**Exception: Do not double final *w*: new—newer—newest

Superlatives; Comparatives

EXERCISE 2 Give the comparative and superlative forms of each word.

EXAMPLES fat   _____fatter_____   _____the fattest_____

important   _____more important_____   _____the most important_____

1. interesting _____ _____
2. young _____ _____
3. beautiful _____ _____
4. good _____ _____
5. common _____ _____
6. thin _____ _____
7. carefully _____ _____
8. pretty _____ _____
9. bad _____ _____
10. famous _____ _____
11. lucky _____ _____
12. simple _____ _____
13. high _____ _____
14. delicious _____ _____
15. far _____ _____
16. foolishly _____ _____

EXERCISE 3 Many people have said that Jordan is or was the superlative in these categories. Write the superlative form in each blank.

EXAMPLE He was __the most elegant__ athlete.
(elegant)

1. He was _____ athlete.
   (popular)

2. He was _____ athlete.
   (great)

3. He was _____ athlete.
   (powerful)

4. He was _____ athlete.
   (graceful)

5. He is _____ -known American basketball
   (good)

   player in the world.

6. He was _____ player.
        (valuable)

7. He is one of _____ people in the world.
              (rich)

8. He is one of _____ -dressed people in the world.
              (good)

EXERCISE 4 Write the superlative form of the word in parentheses ( ).

1. Michael Schumacher is one of _____
                                  (fast)
   race car drivers in the world.

2. Training for the Olympics is one of _____
                                        (difficult)
   things for an athlete.

3. Soccer is _____ sport in the world.
             (popular)

4. Sumo wrestlers are _____ athletes.
                       (fat)

5. Michael Jordan was _____ player on the
                       (valuable)
   Chicago Bulls.

6. Swimming and gymnastics are _____ events
                                (watched)
   during the Summer Olympics.

Superlatives; Comparatives   **381**

7. Yao Ming is one of _____ (tall) basketball players in the world.

8. _____ (common) name for soccer in the world is "football."

9. Running a marathon was one of _____ (hard) things I've ever done.

10. In your opinion, what is _____ _____ (interesting) sport?

EXERCISE 5 ABOUT YOU Write a superlative sentence giving your opinion about each of the following items. You may find a partner and compare your answers to your partner's answers.

EXAMPLES big problem in the world today
I think the biggest problem in the world today is hunger.

big problem in the U.S. today
I think crime is one of the biggest problems in the U.S. today.

1. good way to make friends

2. quick way to learn a language

3. good thing about life in the U.S.

4. bad thing about life in the U.S.

5. terrible tragedy in the world

6. big problem in (*choose a country*)

EXERCISE 6 ABOUT YOU Write superlative sentences about your experience with the words given. Use the present perfect form after the superlative.

EXAMPLE big / city / visit
London is the biggest city I have ever visited.

1. tall / building / visit

2. beautiful / actress / see

3. difficult / subject / study

4. far / distant / travel

5. bad / food / eat

6. good / vacation / have

7. good / athlete / see

8. hard / job / have

9. interesting / sporting event / see

EXERCISE 7 ABOUT YOU Fill in the blanks.

EXAMPLE *Swimming across a lake alone at night*
was one of the most dangerous things I've ever done.

1. _____
is one of the most foolish things I've ever done.

2. _____
is one of the hardest decisions I've ever made.

3. _____
is one of the most dangerous things I've ever done.

12.4 Superlatives and Word Order

Examples	Explanation
Who is **the best basketball player**? (Superlative Adjective + Noun Phrase) Who is **the most popular player**? (Superlative Adjective + Noun)	A superlative adjective comes **before** a noun or noun phrase.
Football is **the most popular sport** in the U.S. OR **The most popular sport** in the U.S. is football.	When the verb *be* connects a noun to a superlative adjective + noun, there are two possible word orders.
Interest in soccer **is growing the most quickly** in the U.S. (Verb + Superlative Adverb) Michael Jordan **shot baskets the most gracefully**. (Verb Phrase + Superlative Adverb)	We put superlative adverbs **after** the verb (phrase).
Michael Jordan **played the best** with the Bulls. (Verb + Superlative) Fans **loved Michael Jordan the most**. (Verb Phrase + Superlative)	We put *the most, the least, the best,* and *the worst* **after** a verb (phrase).
Who scored **the most points**? (Superlative + Noun) The Bulls had **the best record**. (Superlative + Noun)	We put *the most, the least, the best,* and *the worst* **before** a noun.

EXERCISE 8 ABOUT YOU Name the person who is the superlative in your family in each of the following categories.

EXAMPLE works hard
My mother works the hardest in my family.

1. drives well
2. lives far from me
3. speaks English confidently
4. spends a lot of money
5. is well dressed
6. watches a lot of TV
7. worries a lot
8. lives well
9. works hard
10. is athletic
11. is a big sports fan
12. is learning English quickly

AMERICANS' ATTITUDE TOWARD SOCCER

Before You Read

1. Are you interested in soccer?
2. What's your favorite team?

Read the following article. Pay special attention to comparisons.

Soccer is by far the most popular sport in the world. Almost every country has a professional league. In many countries, top international soccer players are **as** well-known **as** rock stars or actors. However, in 1994 when the World Cup soccer competition was held in the U.S., there was not a lot of interest in soccer among Americans. Many people said that soccer was boring.

Recently, Americans' attitude toward soccer has been changing. In 1999, when the Women's World Cup was played in the U.S., there was **more** interest than ever before. Little by little, soccer is becoming **more popular** in the U.S. The number of children playing soccer is growing. In fact, soccer is growing **faster** than any other sport. For elementary school children, soccer is now the number two sport after basketball. **More** kids play soccer than baseball. Many coaches believe that soccer is **easier** to play than baseball or basketball, and that there aren't **as many** injuries **as** with sports such as hockey or football.

Interest in professional soccer in the U.S. is still much **lower** than in other countries. The number of Americans who watch professional basketball, football, or hockey is still much **higher** than the number who watch Major League Soccer. However, **the more** parents show interest in their children's soccer teams, **the more** they will become interested in professional soccer.

12.5 Comparatives

We use the comparative form to compare two items. The comparative has two forms, depending on the number of syllables in the adjective or adverb.

Examples	Explanation
Soccer players are **shorter than** basketball players. Interest in baseball is **higher than** interest in soccer in the U.S.	Use: short adjective/short adverb + -er + than
Basketball is **more popular than** soccer in the U.S. Interest in soccer is growing **more quickly than** interest in hockey.	Use: more + longer adjective + than more + -ly adverb + than
My brother plays soccer **better than** I do.	Some comparative forms are irregular. See 12.3 for more information.
Basketball is popular in the U.S., but football is **more popular.** Michael Jordan is tall, but other basketball players are **taller.**	Omit than if the second item of comparison is not included.
Interest in soccer is **much** lower in the U.S. than in other countries. I like soccer **a little** better than I like baseball.	Much or a little can come before a comparative form.
You are taller than **I am.** (FORMAL) You are taller than **me.** (INFORMAL) I can play soccer better than **he can.** (FORMAL) I can play soccer better than **him.** (INFORMAL)	When a pronoun follows than, the correct form is the subject pronoun (he, she, I, etc.). Usually an auxiliary verb follows (is, do, did, can, etc.). Informally, many Americans use the object pronoun (him, her, me, etc.) after than. An auxiliary verb does not follow.
The more they practice, **the better** they play. **The older** you are, **the harder** it is to learn a new sport.	We can use two comparisons in one sentence to show cause and result.

EXERCISE 9 Circle the correct word to complete each statement.

EXAMPLE In the U.S., soccer is *more /(less)* popular than basketball.

1. Football players have *more / fewer* injuries than soccer players.
2. In the U.S., soccer is growing *faster / slower* than any other sport.
3. In 1999, there was *more / less* interest in soccer than in 1994.

4. Professional soccer is *more / less* popular in the U.S. than in other countries.

5. In the U.S., soccer players are *more / less* famous than movie stars.

EXERCISE 10 Fill in the blanks with the comparative form of the word in parentheses ( ). Include *than* when necessary.

EXAMPLE In the U.S., basketball is _____more popular than_____ soccer.
(popular)

1. Tall people are often _____ basketball players _____ short people.
(good)

2. Do you think volleyball is _____ tennis?
(fun)

3. Which do you think is _____, skiing or surfing?
(difficult)

4. A soccer ball is _____ a tennis ball.
(large)

5. Children learn sports _____ adults.
(easily)

6. People who exercise a lot are in _____ shape _____ people who don't.
(good)

7. Do you think soccer is _____ football?
(interesting)

8. Do you think soccer is _____ than baseball?
(exciting)

EXERCISE 11 **ABOUT YOU** Compare the people of your native country (or a place you know well) to Americans (in general). Give your own opinion.

EXAMPLE tall
Americans are taller than Koreans.

1. polite
2. friendly
3. formal
4. tall
5. thin
6. serious
7. wealthy
8. educated
9. happy

EXERCISE 12 ABOUT YOU Compare the U.S. and your native country (or a place you know well). Explain your response.

EXAMPLES cars
Cars are cheaper in the U.S. Most people in my native country can't afford a car.

education
Education is better in my native country. Everyone must finish high school.

1. rent
2. housing
3. cars
4. education
5. medical care
6. food
7. gasoline
8. the government
9. clothes (or fashions)

12.6 Comparatives and Word Order

Examples	Explanation
Be (Linking Verb) **Comparative Adjective** Basketball **is more popular** than soccer in the U.S. Football **looks more dangerous** than soccer.	Put the comparative adjective after the verb *be* or other linking verbs: *seem, feel, look, sound,* etc.
Verb Phrase **Comparative Adverb** Jordan **played basketball more gracefully** than any other player. **Verb** **Comparative Adverb** Soccer **is growing faster** than any other sport.	Put the comparative adverb **after** the verb (phrase).
Comparative Noun There is **less interest** in hockey than there is in basketball. **Comparative Noun** Soccer players have **fewer injuries** than football players.	We can put *more, less, fewer, better,* and *worse* **before** a noun.
Verb Phrase **Comparative** My sister **likes soccer more** than I do. **Verb Phrase** **Comparative** I **play soccer worse** than my sister does.	You can put *more, less, better,* and *worse* **after** a verb (phrase).

EXERCISE 13 Find the mistakes with word order and correct them. Not every sentence has a mistake. If the sentence is correct, write *C*.

EXAMPLES A football team has players (more) than a baseball team.

A golf ball is smaller than a tennis ball.   *C*

1. A basketball player is taller than a gymnast.
2. A baseball game has action less than a soccer game.

388 Lesson 12

3. Football players use padding more than soccer players.
4. Michael Jordan more beautifully played basketball than other players.
5. I more like baseball than basketball.
6. Team A won more games than Team B.
7. Team A better played than Team B.

EXERCISE 14 ABOUT YOU Use a comparative adverb to compare the people of your native country (or a place you know well) to Americans (in general). Give your own opinion.

EXAMPLE drive well
Mexicans drive better than Americans.

1. dress stylishly
2. work hard
3. spend a lot
4. live long
5. worry a little
6. live comfortably
7. have freedom
8. have a good life
9. exercise a lot

EXERCISE 15 ABOUT YOU Compare this school to another school you attended. Use *better, worse, more, less,* or *fewer* before the noun.

EXAMPLE classroom / space
This classroom has more space than a classroom in my native country.

1. class / students
2. school / courses
3. teachers / experience
4. library / books
5. school / facilities[2]
6. school / teachers

EXERCISE 16 *Combination Exercise.* Fill in the blanks with the comparative or superlative form of the word in parentheses ( ). Include *than* or *the* when necessary.

EXAMPLES In the U.S., baseball is __more popular than__ soccer.
(popular)

Baseball is one of __the most popular__ sports in the U.S.
(popular)

1. A tennis ball is _____ a baseball.
(soft)

2. An athlete who wins the gold medal is _____ athlete
(good)
in his or her sport.

3. Who is _____ player on the Chicago Bulls today?
(tall)

4. I am _____ in baseball _____ in basketball.
(interested)

5. In my opinion, soccer is _____ sport.
(exciting)

6. Weightlifters are _____ than golfers.
(muscular)

[2] *Facilities* are things we use, such as a swimming pool, cafeteria, library, exercise room, or student union.

7. Golf is a _____ sport _____ soccer.
    (slow)

8. A basketball team has _____ players _____
    (few)
    a baseball team.

9. Even though January is _____ month of the year,
    (cold)
    football players play during this month.

10. My friend and I both jog. I run _____ than my friend.
    (far)

11. Who's a _____ soccer player—you or your brother?
    (good)

AN AMAZING ATHLETE

Before You Read

1. Can people with disabilities do well in sports?
2. Why do people want to climb the tallest mountain in the world?

 Read the following article. Pay special attention to comparisons.

Did You Know?
The oldest person to climb Mount Everest was 70 years old.

Erik Weihenmayer is **as tough as** any mountain climber. In 2001 he made his way to the top of the highest mountain in the world—Mount Everest—at the age of 33. But Erik is **different from** other mountain climbers in one important way—he is completely blind. He is the first sightless person to reach the top of the tallest mountain.

Erik was an athletic child who lost his vision in his early teens. At first he refused to use a cane or learn Braille, insisting he could do **as well as** any teenager. But he finally came to accept his disability and to excel within it. He couldn't play **the same** sports **as** he used to. He would never be able to play basketball or catch a football again. But then he discovered wrestling, a

Did You Know?

Almost 90 percent of Everest climbers fail to reach the top. At least 180 have died while trying.

sport where sight was not **as** important **as** feel and touch. Then, at 16, he discovered rock climbing, which **was like** wrestling in some ways; a wrestler and a rock climber get information through touch. Rock climbing led to mountain climbing, the greatest challenge of his life.

Teammates climbing with Erik say that he isn't **different from** a sighted mountaineer. He has **as much** training **as** the others. He is **as** strong **as** the rest. The major difference is he is not **as** thin **as** most climbers. But his strong upper body, flexibility, mental toughness, and ability to tolerate physical pain make him a perfect climber. The only accommodation for Erik's blindness is to place bells on the jackets of his teammates so that he can follow them easily.

Climbing Mount Everest was a challenge for every climber on Erik's team. The reaction to the mountain air for Erik was **the same as** it was for his teammates: lack of oxygen causes the heart to beat slower than usual and the brain does not function **as clearly as** normal. In some ways, Erik had an advantage over his teammates: as they got near the top, the vision of all climbers was restricted. So at a certain altitude, all his teammates **were like** Erik—nearly blind.

To climb Mount Everest is an achievement for any athlete. Erik Weihenmayer showed that his disability wasn't **as important as** his ability.

12.7 | As . . . As

Examples	Explanation
Erik is **as strong as** his teammates. At high altitudes, the brain doesn't function **as clearly as** normal. Erik can climb mountains **as well as** sighted climbers.	We can show that two things are equal or unequal in some way by using: *as* + adjective/adverb + *as*.
Erik is not **as thin as** most climbers. Skiing is not **as difficult as** mountain climbing.	When we make a comparison of unequal items, we put the lesser item first.
Baseball is popular in the U.S. Soccer is not **as popular.**	Omit the second *as* if the second item of comparison is omitted.

Usage Notes:

1. A very common expression is *as soon as possible*. Some people say *A.S.A.P* for short.
   I'd like to see you *as soon as possible*.
   I'd like to see you *A.S.A.P.*
2. These are some common expressions using *as . . . as*.

   as poor as a church mouse
   as old as the hills
   as quiet as a mouse
   as stubborn as a mule

   mule

   as sick as a dog
   as proud as a peacock
   as gentle as a lamb
   as happy as a lark

   peacock

EXERCISE 17 Write true (*T*) or false (*F*).

EXAMPLE In wrestling, the sense of sight is as important as the sense of touch.   F

1. Rock climbing is not as dangerous as mountain climbing.
2. At high altitudes, you can't think as clearly as you can at lower altitudes.
3. Erik was not as strong as his teammates.
4. When Erik became blind, he wanted to do as well as any other teenager.
5. Erik could not go as far as his teammates.
6. Erik was as prepared for the climb as his teammates.

EXERCISE 18 ABOUT YOU Compare yourself to another person. (Or compare two people you know.) Use the following adjectives and *as . . . as*. You may add a comparative statement if there is inequality.

EXAMPLES thin
I'm not as thin as my sister. (She's thinner than I am.)

old
My mother is not as old as my father. (My father is older than my mother.)

1. old
2. educated
3. intelligent
4. patient
5. lazy
6. tall
7. religious
8. friendly
9. strong
10. talkative
11. athletic
12. interested in sports

EXERCISE 19 ABOUT YOU Use the underlined word to compare yourself to the teacher.

EXAMPLE speak Spanish <u>well</u>
The teacher doesn't speak Spanish as well as I do. (I speak Spanish better.)

1. arrive at class <u>promptly</u>
2. work <u>hard</u> in class
3. understand American customs <u>well</u>
4. speak <u>quietly</u>
5. speak English <u>fluently</u>
6. understand a foreigner's problems <u>well</u>
7. write <u>neatly</u>
8. speak <u>fast</u>

12.8 As Many/Much . . . As

Examples	Explanation
Soccer players don't have **as many injuries as** football players. Erik had **as much training as** his teammates.	We can show that two things are equal or not equal in quantity by using *as many* + count noun + *as* or *as much* + noncount noun + *as*.
I don't play soccer **as much as** I used to. She doesn't like sports **as much as** her husband does.	We can use *as much as* after a verb phrase.

EXERCISE 20 ABOUT YOU *Part A:* Fill in the blanks.

EXAMPLE   I drive about ____30____ miles a week.
(number)

1. I'm _____ tall.
   (feet/inches)

2. The highest level of education that I completed is _____
   _____.
   (high school, bachelor's degree, master's degree, doctorate)

3. I work _____ hours a week.
   (number)

4. I study _____ hours a day.
   (number)

5. I exercise _____ days a week.
   (number)

6. I'm taking _____ courses now.
   (number)

7. I have _____ siblings.[3]
   (number)

8. I live _____ miles from this school.
   (number)

Part B: Find a partner and compare your answers to your partner's answers. Write statements with the words given and *(not) as . . . as* or *(not) as much / many as*.

EXAMPLE   drive *I don't drive as much as Lisa.*

1. tall _____
2. have education _____
3. work _____
4. study _____

[3] *Siblings* are a person's brothers and sisters.

Superlatives; Comparatives   393

5. exercise frequently _____

6. take courses _____

7. have siblings _____

8. live far from school _____

EXERCISE 21 Compare men and women (in general). Give your own opinion. Use *as many as* or *as much as*.

EXAMPLE show emotion
Men don't show as much emotion as women. (Women show more emotion than men.)

1. earn
2. spend money
3. talk
4. gossip
5. use bad words
6. have responsibilities
7. have freedom
8. have free time

EXERCISE 22 ABOUT YOU Compare this school and another school you attended. Use *as many as*.

EXAMPLE classrooms
This school doesn't have as many classrooms as King College. (King College has more classrooms.)

1. teachers
2. classrooms
3. floors (or stories)
4. English courses
5. exams
6. students

EXERCISE 23 Make a comparison between this city and another city you know well using the categories below.

EXAMPLE public transportation *The buses are cleaner in Boston than in this city.*
OR *The buses in this city are not as crowded as the buses in Boston.*

1. traffic _____
2. people _____
3. gardens and parks _____
4. public transportation _____
5. museums _____
6. universities _____
7. houses _____
8. buildings _____
9. stores or shopping _____

394   Lesson 12

12.9 | The Same . . . As

Examples	Explanation
Pattern A: Erik had **the same ability as** his teammates. A soccer ball isn't **the same shape as** a football.	We can show that two things are equal or not equal in some way by using *the same* + noun + *as*.
Pattern B: Erik and his teammates had **the same ability.** A soccer ball and a football aren't **the same shape.**	Omit *as* in Pattern B.

Language Note:
We can make statements of equality with many nouns, such as *size, shape, color, value, religion,* or *nationality*.

EXERCISE 24 Make statements with *the same . . . as* using the words given.

EXAMPLES a golf ball / a tennis ball (size)
A golf ball isn't the same size as a tennis ball.

1. a soccer ball / a volleyball (shape)

2. a soccer player / a basketball player (height)

3. an amateur athlete / a professional athlete (ability)

4. a soccer player / a football player (weight)

5. team A's uniforms / team B's uniforms (color)

EXERCISE 25 **ABOUT YOU** Talk about two relatives or friends of yours. Compare them using the words given.

EXAMPLE age
My mother and my father aren't the same age.
OR
My mother isn't the same age as my father. (My father is older than my mother.)

1. age
2. height
3. weight
4. nationality
5. religion
6. (have) level of education

EXERCISE 26 **ABOUT YOU** Work with a partner. Make a **true** affirmative or negative statement with the words given.

EXAMPLES the same nationality
I'm not the same nationality as Alex. I'm Colombian, and he's Russian.
the same color shoes
Martina's shoes are the same color as my shoes. They're brown.

Superlatives; Comparatives

1. the same hair color
2. the same eye color
3. (speak) the same language
4. (like) the same sports
5. (have) the same level of English
6. the same nationality

12.10 Equality with Nouns or Adjectives

For equality or inequality with nouns, use *the same . . . as*. For inequality with adjectives and adverbs, use the comparative form.

Noun	Adjective	Examples
height	tall, short	A soccer player is not **the same height as** a basketball player. A soccer player is **shorter**.
age	old, young	He's not **the same age as** his wife. His wife is **older**.
weight	fat, thin	Wrestler A is not **the same weight as** Wrestler B. Wrestler B is **fatter**.
length	long, short	This shelf is not **the same length as** that shelf. This shelf is **shorter**.
price	expensive, cheap	This car is not **the same price as** that car. This car is **cheaper**.
size	big, small	These shoes are not **the same size as** those shoes. These shoes are **smaller**.

EXERCISE 27 Change the following to use the comparative form. Answers may vary.

EXAMPLE Lesson 11 is not the same length as Lesson 12.

Lesson 11 is _____*shorter*_____.

1. I am not the same height as my brother.

   My brother is _____.

2. You are not the same age as your husband.

   You are _____.

3. I am not the same height as a basketball player.

   A basketball player is _____.

4. My left foot isn't the same size as my right foot.

   My right foot is _____.

5. My brother is not the same weight as I am.

   My brother is _____.

FOOTBALL AND SOCCER

Before You Read

1. Which do you like better, football or soccer?
2. How are soccer players different from football players?

 Read the following article. Pay special attention to similarities and differences.

tackle

It may seem strange that Americans give the name "football" to a game played mostly by throwing and carrying a ball with one's hands. But Americans give the name football to a sport that is very **different from** soccer.

Many of the rules in soccer and American football are the **same**. In both games, there are 11 players on each side, and a team scores its points by getting the ball past the goal of the other team. The playing fields for both teams are also very much **alike**.

When the action begins, the two games look very **different**. In addition to using their feet, soccer players are allowed to hit the ball with their heads. In football, the only person allowed to touch the ball with his feet is a special player known as the kicker. Also, in football, tackling the player who has the ball is not only allowed but encouraged, whereas tackling any player in soccer will get the tackler thrown out of the game.

(continued)

Football players and soccer players don't **dress alike** or even **look alike** in many ways. Since blocking and tackling are a big part of American football, the players are often very large and muscular and wear heavy padding and helmets. Soccer players, on the other hand, are usually thinner and wear shorts and polo shirts. This gives them more freedom of movement to show off the fancy footwork that makes soccer such a popular game around the world.

While both games are very **different,** both have a large number of fans that enjoy the exciting action.

12.11 | Similarity with *Like* and *Alike*

We can show that two things are similar (or not) with *like* and *alike*.

Examples	Explanation
Pattern A: A soccer player **looks like** a rugby player. A soccer player doesn't **dress like** a football player.	**Pattern A:** Noun 1 + verb + *like* + Noun 2
Pattern B: A soccer player and a rugby player **look alike.** A soccer player and a football player don't **dress alike.**	**Pattern B:** Noun 1 + Noun 2 + verb + *alike*
Language Note: We often use the sense perception verbs (*look, sound, smell, taste, feel,* and *seem*) with *like* and *alike*. We can also use other verbs with *like*: *act like, sing like, dress like,* etc.	

EXERCISE 28 Make a statement with the words given.

EXAMPLE taste / Pepsi / Coke
Pepsi tastes like Coke (to me).
OR
Pepsi and Coke taste alike (to me).

1. taste / diet cola / regular cola
2. taste / 2% milk / whole milk
3. look / an American classroom / a classroom in another country
4. sound / Asian music / American music
5. feel / polyester / silk
6. smell / cologne / perfume
7. look / salt / sugar
8. taste / salt / sugar
9. act / American teachers / teachers in other countries
10. dress / American teenagers / teenagers in other countries

EXERCISE 29 Fill in the blanks. In some cases, more than one answer is possible.

EXAMPLE Players on the same team dress _____alike_____.

1. Twins _____ alike.
2. Americans and people from England don't sound _____. They have different accents.
3. My daughter is only 15 years old, but she _____ an adult. She's very responsible and hard-working.
4. My son is only 16 years old, but he _____ an adult. He's tall and has a beard.
5. Teenagers often wear the same clothing as their friends. They like to _____.
6. Soccer players don't look _____ football players at all.
7. Do you think I'll ever _____ an American, or will I always have an accent?

8. Children in private schools usually wear a uniform. They _____ alike.

9. My children learned English very quickly. Now they sound _____ Americans. They have no accent at all.

10. Dogs don't _____ cats at all. Dogs are very friendly. Cats are more distant.

12.12 | Be Like

We can show that two things are similar (or not) in internal characteristics with *be like* and *be alike*.

Explanation	Examples
Pattern A: For Erik, mountain climbing **is like** wrestling in some ways. Touch is more important than sight. Erik **was like** his teammates in many ways—strong, well trained, mentally tough, and able to tolerate pain.	**Pattern A:** Noun 1 + *be* + *like* + Noun 2
Pattern B: For Erik, wrestling and mountain climbing **are alike** in some ways. Erik and his teammates **were alike** in many ways.	**Pattern B:** Noun 1 + Noun 2 + *be* + *alike*
Compare: a. Erik **looks like** an athlete. He's tall and strong. b. Erik **is like** his teammates. He has a lot of experience and training.	Use *look like* to describe physical appearance. Use *be like* to describe an internal characteristic.

EXERCISE 30 **ABOUT YOU** Work with a student from another country. Ask a question with the words given. Use *be like*. The other student will answer.

EXAMPLE families in the U.S. / families in your native country

A: Are families in the U.S. like families in your native country?
B: No, they aren't. Families in my native country are very big. Family members live close to each other.

1. an English class in the U.S. / an English class in your native country
2. your house (or apartment) in the U.S. / your house (or apartment) in your native country
3. the weather in this city / the weather in your hometown
4. food in your country / American food
5. women's clothes in your native country / women's clothes in the U.S.
6. a college in your native country / a college in the U.S.
7. American teachers / teachers in your native country
8. American athletes / athletes in your native country

12.13 | Same or Different

We show that two things are the same (or not) by using *the same as*. We show that two things are different by using *different from*.

Examples	Explanation
Pattern A: Football is not **the same as** soccer. Football is **different from** soccer.	**Pattern A:** Noun 1 is *the same as* Noun 2. Noun 1 is *different from* Noun 2.
Pattern B: Football and soccer are not **the same**. Football and soccer are **different**.	**Pattern B:** Noun 1 and Noun 2 are *the same*. Noun 1 and Noun 2 are *different*.
Language Note: You will hear some Americans say *different than*.	

EXERCISE 31 Tell if the two items are the same or different.

EXAMPLES boxing, wrestling
Boxing and wrestling are different.

fall, autumn
Fall is the same as autumn.

1. Michael Jordan, Michael Schumacher
2. baseball in Cuba, baseball in the U.S.
3. the Chicago Bulls, the Chicago Bears
4. a kilometer, 1,000 meters
5. L.A., Los Angeles
6. a mile, a kilometer
7. football, rugby
8. football rules, soccer rules

EXERCISE 32 *Combination Exercise.* Fill in the blanks in the following conversation.

A: I heard that you have a twin brother.

B: Yes, I do.

A: Do you and your brother look ____alike____? (example)

B: No. He _____(1)_____ look _____(2)_____ me at all.

A: But you're twins.

B: We're fraternal twins. That's different _____(3)_____ identical twins who have the _____(4)_____ genetic code. We're just brothers who were born at _____(5)_____ time. We're not even the same _____(6)_____. I'm much taller than he is.

A: But you're _____(7)_____ in many ways, aren't you?

B: No. We're completely _____(8)_____. I'm athletic and I'm on the high school football team, but David hates sports. He's a much _____(9)_____ student than I am. He's much more _____(10)_____ our mother, who loves to read and learn new things, and I _____(11)_____ our father, who's athletic and loves to build things.

A: What about your character?

B: I'm outgoing and he's very shy. Also we don't dress _____(12)_____ at all.

He likes to wear neat, conservative clothes, but I prefer torn jeans and T-shirts.

A: From your description, it _____ like you're not even from
(13)

the same family.

B: We have one thing in common. We were both interested in

_____ girl at school. We both asked her out, but she
(14)

didn't want to go out with either one of us!

EXERCISE 33 *Combination Exercise.* This is a conversation between two women. Fill in the blanks with an appropriate word to complete the comparisons.

A: In the winter months, my husband doesn't pay as ____much____
(example)

attention to me _____ he does to his football games.
(1)

B: Many women have the same problem _____ you do.
(2)

These women are called football "widows" because they lose their husbands during football season.

A: I feel _____ a widow. My husband is in front of the TV
(3)

all day on the weekends. In addition to the football games, there

are pre-game shows. These shows last _____ long as the
(4)

game itself.

B: I know what you mean. He's no different _____ my
(5)

husband. During football season, my husband is _____
(6)

interested in watching TV _____ he is in me. He looks
(7)

_____ a robot sitting in front of the TV. When I complain, he
(8)

tells me to sit down and join him.

A: It sounds _____ all men act _____ during football
(9)   (10)

season.

B: To tell the truth, I don't like football at all.

A: I don't either. I think soccer is much _____ interesting than
(11)

football.

Superlatives; Comparatives **403**

B: Soccer is very different _____(12)_____ football. I think the action is _____(13)_____ exciting. And it's more fun to watch the footwork of the soccer players. Football players look _____(14)_____ big monsters with their helmets and padded shoulders. They don't look handsome at all.

A: Soccer is not _____(15)_____ popular in the U.S. _____(16)_____ it is in other countries. I wonder why.

B: What's your favorite team?

A: I like the Chicago Fire.

B: In my opinion they're not _____(17)_____ good as the Los Angeles Galaxy. But to tell the truth, I'm not very interested in sports at all. When our husbands start watching football next season, let's do our favorite sport: shopping. We can spend _____(18)_____ time shopping as they spend in front of the TV.

A: I was just thinking the same thing! You and I think _____(19)_____. Instead of being football widows, they can be shopping "widowers."

SUMMARY OF LESSON 12

1. Simple, Comparative, and Superlative Forms

    SHORT WORDS
    Jacob is **tall.**
    Mark is **taller than** Jacob.
    Bart is **the tallest** member of the basketball team.

    LONG WORDS
    Golf is **popular** in the U.S.
    Baseball is **more popular than** golf.
    Soccer is **the most popular** game in the world.

2. Other Kinds of Comparisons
    She looks **as young as** her daughter.
    She speaks English **as fluently as** her husband.
    She is **the same age as** her husband.
    She and her husband are **the same age.**
    She works **as many hours as** her husband.
    She doesn't have **as much time as** her husband.
    She works **as much as** her husband.

Lesson 12

3. Comparisons with *Like*
    She**'s like** her mother. (She and her mother **are alike.**) They're both athletic.
    She **looks like** her sister. (She and her sister **look alike.**) They're identical twins.
    Coke **tastes like** Pepsi. (They taste **alike.**)
    Western music doesn't **sound like** Asian music. (They don't **sound alike.**)

4. Comparisons with *Same* and *Different*
    Football is **different from** soccer.
    My uniform is **the same as** my teammates' uniforms.

EDITING ADVICE

1. Don't use a comparison word when there is no comparison.

    New York is a ~~bigger~~ city.

2. Don't use *more* and *-er* together.

    He is ~~more~~ older than his teacher.

3. Use *than* before the second item of comparison.

            than
    He is younger ~~that~~ his wife.

4. Use *the* before a superlative form.

        the
    The Nile is ^longest river in the world.

5. Use a plural noun in the phrase "one of the [superlative] [nouns]."

                         cities
    Chicago is one of the biggest ~~city~~ in the U.S.

6. Use the correct word order.

       speaks more
    She ~~more speaks~~ than her husband.

          more time
    I have ~~time more~~ than you.

7. Use *be like* for similar character. Use *look like* for a physical similarity.

           s
    He ~~is~~ look^like his brother. They both have blue eyes and dark hair.

    He is ~~look~~ like his sister. They are both talented musicians.

Superlatives; Comparatives

8. Don't use *the* and a possessive form together.

   My ~~the~~ youngest son likes soccer.

9. Use the correct negative for *be like, look like, sound like, feel like,* etc.

   I'~~m not~~ *don't* look like my father.

   He ~~is~~ *does* not act like a professional athlete.

LESSON 12 TEST/REVIEW

PART 1 Find the mistakes with the underlined words, and correct them. Not every sentence has a mistake. If the sentence is correct, write *C*.

EXAMPLES She ~~is~~ look*s* like her sister. They both have curly hair.

A house in the suburbs is much more expensive than a house in the city. **C**

1. I am the same tall as my brother.
2. New York City is the larger city in the U.S.
3. That man is smarter that his wife.
4. The youngest student in the class has more better grades than you.
5. A big city has crime more than a small town.
6. I have three sons. My oldest son is married.
7. I visited many American cities, and I think that San Francisco is the more beautiful city in the U.S.
8. New York is one of the largest city in the world.
9. My uncle is the most intelligent person in my family.
10. She faster types than I do.
11. Texas is one of the biggest state in the U.S.
12. He more carefully drives than his wife.
13. Paul is one of the youngest students in this class.
14. She is richer than her best friend, but her friend is happier than.
15. My the best grade this semester was A–.
16. She isn't look like her sister at all. She's short and her sister is tall.

PART 2 Fill in the blanks.

EXAMPLE A tangerine is __the same__ color __as__ a clementine.

1. She's 35 years old. Her husband is 35 years old. She and her husband are _____ age.

2. She earns $30,000 a year. Her husband earns $35,000. She doesn't earn as _____ her husband.

3. The little girl _____ like her mother. They both have brown eyes and curly black hair.

4. My name is Sophia Weiss. My teacher's name is Judy Weiss. We have _____ last name.

5. Chinese food is different _____ American food.

6. A dime isn't the same _____ a nickel. A dime is smaller.

7. She is as tall as her husband. They are the same _____.

8. I ate a tangerine and a clementine, and I don't know which is which. They have the same flavor. To me, a tangerine _____ like a clementine.

9. She _____ like her husband in many ways. They're both intelligent and hard-working. They both like sports.

10. **A:** Are you like your mother?
    B: Oh, no. We're not _____ at all! We're completely different.

11. Please finish this test _____ possible!

12. *Borrow* and *lend* don't have _____ meaning. *Borrow* means take. *Lend* means give.

13. My two sisters look _____. In fact, some people think they're twins.

Superlatives; Comparatives **407**

EXPANSION ACTIVITIES

Classroom Activities

1. Work with a partner. Find some differences between the two of you. Then write five sentences that compare you and your partner. Share your answers in a small group or with the whole class.

   EXAMPLES I'm taller than Alex.
   Alex is taking more classes than I am.

2. Form a small group (about 3–5 people) with students from different native countries, if possible. Make comparisons about your native countries. Include a superlative statement. (If all the students in your class are from the same native country, compare cities in your native country.)

   EXAMPLES Cuba is closer to the U.S. than Peru is.
   China has the largest population.
   Cuba doesn't have as many resources as China.

3. Work with a partner. Choose one of the categories below, and compare two examples from this category. Use any type of comparative method. Write four sentences. Share your answers with the class.

   a. countries
   b. cars
   c. restaurants
   d. teachers
   e. cities
   f. animals
   g. types of transportation
   h. schools
   i. sports
   j. athletes

   EXAMPLE animals
   A dog is different from a cat in many ways.
   A dog can't jump as high as a cat.
   A dog is a better pet than a cat, in my opinion.
   A cat is not as friendly as a dog.

408 Lesson 12

4. Compare the U.S. to another country you know. Tell if the statement is true in the U.S. or in the other country. Form a small group and explain your answers to the others in the group.

	Country _____	The U.S.
People have more free time.		
People have more political freedom.		
Families are smaller.		
Children are more polite.		
Teenagers have more freedom.		
People are friendlier.		
The government is more stable.		
Health care is better.		
There is more crime.		
There are more poor people.		
People are generally happier.		
People are more open about their problems.		
Friendship is more important.		
Women have more freedom.		
Schools are better.		
Job opportunities are better.		
Athletes make more money.		
Children have more fun.		
People dress more stylishly.		
Families are closer.		
People are healthier.		

5. Game—Test your knowledge of world facts.
   Form a small group. Answer the questions below with other group members. When you're finished, check your answers. (Answers are at the bottom of the next page.) Which group in the class has the most correct answers?

   1. Which athlete said, "I'm the greatest"?
      Michael Jordan   Pelé   Muhammad Ali   Serena Williams

   2. Where is the tallest building in the world?
      New York City   Chicago   Tokyo   Taipei

Superlatives; Comparatives

3. What country has the largest population?
   the U.S.   India   China   Russia

4. Which country has the largest area?
   the U.S.   China   Canada   Russia

5. What is the tallest mountain in the world?
   Mount McKinley   Mount Everest
   Mount Kanchenjunga   Mount Lhotse

6. Which state in the U.S. has the smallest population?
   Alaska   Wyoming   Rhode Island   Vermont

7. What is the longest river in the world?
   the Mississippi   the Missouri   the Nile   the Amazon

8. What is the biggest animal?
   the elephant   the rhinoceros   the giraffe   the whale

9. What is the world's largest island?
   Greenland   New Guinea   Borneo   Madagascar

10. What country has the most time zones?
    China   Russia   the U.S.   Canada

11. What is the world's largest lake?
    Lake Superior   Lake Victoria
    the Caspian Sea   the Aral Sea

12. Which planet is the closest to the Earth?
    Mercury   Venus   Mars   Saturn

13. Where is the world's busiest airport?
    Chicago   New York   Los Angeles   London

14. Which is the most popular magazine in the U.S.?
    Time   *Sports Illustrated*   *TV Guide*   *People Weekly*

15. What language has the largest number of speakers?
    English   Chinese   Spanish   Russian

16. Which country has the most neighboring countries?
    China   Russia   Saudi Arabia   Brazil

The answers are: 1. Muhammad Ali 2. Taipei 3. China 4. Russia 5. Mount Everest 6. Wyoming 7. the Nile 8. the whale 9. Greenland 10. Russia 11. the Caspian Sea 12. Mars 13. Chicago 14. *TV Guide* 15. Chinese 16. China (It has 16 neighboring countries.)

6. Look at the list of jobs below. Use the superlative form to name a job that matches each description. You may discuss your answers in a small group or with the entire class.

EXAMPLE interesting
In my opinion, a psychologist has the most interesting job.

coach
psychologist
computer programmer
high school teacher
factory worker
doctor
police officer
engineer

referee
letter carrier
athlete
actress
photojournalist
firefighter
politician
nurse

(*you may add other professions*)

a. interesting _____
b. dangerous _____
c. easy _____
d. tiring _____
e. dirty _____
f. boring _____
g. exciting _____
h. important _____
i. challenging _____
j. difficult _____

Write a short composition comparing one of the sets of items below:

- two stores where you shop for groceries
- watching a movie at home and at a movie theater
- two friends of yours
- you and your parents
- football and soccer (or any two sports)
- clothing styles in the U.S. and your native country
- life in the U.S. (in general) and life in your native country
- your life in the U.S. and your life in your native country
- the American political system and the political system in your native country
- schools (including teachers, students, classes, etc.) in the U.S. and schools in your native country
- American families and families in your native country

Talk About it

1. Do athletes in other countries make a lot of money?
2. Do children in most countries participate in sports? Which sports?

Outside Activity

Interview someone who was born in the U.S. Get his or her opinion about the superlative of each of the following items. Share your findings with the class.

- prestigious job in the U.S.
- beautiful city in the U.S.
- popular TV program
- terrible tragedy in American history
- big problem in the U.S.
- handsome or beautiful actor
- good athlete
- good sports team

Internet Activities

1. Find an article about Michael Jordan on the Internet. Print the article and circle some interesting facts.

2. Find an article about an athlete that you admire. Print the article and circle some interesting facts.

3. Find an article about Enrique Oliu. Summarize the article. What makes Oliu so special?

4. Visit the Olympics Web site or a Web site with sports statistics and information. Find out which country has won the most medals in a particular sport. Which sport is the newest to be an Olympic event? Which athlete has the most Olympic medals?

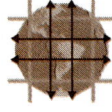

Additional Activities at www.http://elt.heinle.com/gic

LESSON 13

GRAMMAR
Passive Voice and Active Voice

CONTEXT: The Law
Jury Duty
Unusual Lawsuits

13.1 The Passive Voice and the Active Voice—An Overview

	Examples			Explanation
Active	Subject The thief The police	Active Verb **stole** **arrested**	Object the bicycle. the thief.	The **active voice** focuses on the person who performs the action. The subject is active.
Passive	Subject The bicycle The thief	Passive Verb **was stolen** **was arrested**	*By* Phrase by the thief. by the police.	The **passive voice** focuses on the receiver or the result of the action. The subject is passive. The person who does the action is in the *by* phrase.
Passive	Subject The thief The bicycle	Passive Verb **was taken** **will be returned**.	to jail.	Many passive sentences do not contain a *by* phrase.

JURY DUTY

Before You Read

1. Have you ever been to court?
2. Have you ever seen a courtroom in a movie or TV show?

Read the following article. Pay special attention to the passive voice.

All Americans **are protected** by the Constitution. No one person can decide if a person is guilty of a crime. Every citizen has the right to a trial by jury. When a person **is charged** with a crime, he **is considered** innocent until the jury decides he is guilty.

Most American citizens **are chosen** for jury duty at some time in their lives. How **are** jurors **chosen?** The court gets the names of citizens from lists of taxpayers, licensed drivers, and voters. Many people **are called** to the courthouse for the selection of a jury. From this large number, 12 people **are chosen.** The lawyers and the judge ask each person questions to see if the person is going to be fair. If the person has made any judgment about the case before hearing the facts presented in the trial, he **is** not **selected.** If the juror doesn't understand enough English, he **is** not **selected.** The court needs jurors who can understand the facts and be open-minded. When the final jury selection **is made,** the jurors must raise their right hands and promise to be fair in deciding the case.

Sometimes a trial goes on for several days or more. Jurors **are** not **permitted** to talk with family members and friends about the case. In some cases, jurors **are** not **permitted** to go home until the case is over. They stay in a hotel and **are** not **permitted** to watch TV or read newspapers that give information about the case.

After the jurors hear the case, they have to make a decision. They go to a separate room and talk about what they heard and saw in the courtroom. When they are finished discussing the case, they take a vote.

Jurors **are paid** for their work. They receive a small amount of money per day. Employers must give a worker permission to be on a jury. Being on a jury **is considered** a very serious job.

13.2 | The Passive Voice

Examples			Explanation
	Be	**Past Participle**	The passive voice uses a form of *be* (any tense) + the past participle.
The jurors	**are**	**chosen** from lists.	
My sister	**was**	**selected** to be on a jury.	
The jurors	**will be**	**paid** for jury duty.	
Compare Active (A) and Passive (P): (A) Ms. Smith *paid* her employees at the end of the week. (P) Ms. Smith *was paid* for being a juror.			The verb in active voice (A) shows that the subject (Ms. Smith) performed the action of the verb. The verb in passive voice (P) shows that the subject (Ms. Smith) did not perform the action of the verb.
I was helped **by the lawyer.** My sister was helped **by him** too.			When a performer is included after a passive verb, use *by* + noun or object pronoun.

Passive Voice and Active Voice

EXERCISE 1 Read the following sentences. Decide if the underlined verb is active (A) or passive (P).

EXAMPLES I received a letter from the court. A

I was told to go to court on May 10. P

1. The jury voted at the end of the trial.
2. The jurors received $20 a day.
3. Some jurors were told to go home.
4. Not every juror will be needed.
5. Twelve people were selected for the jury.
6. The judge told the jurors about their responsibilities.
7. My sister has been selected for jury duty three times.
8. You will be paid for jury duty.
9. A juror must be at least 18 years old and an American citizen.
10. The judge and the lawyers ask a lot of questions.

13.3 | Passive Voice—Form and Use

Form: The passive voice can be used with different tenses and with modals. The tense of the sentence is shown by the verb *be*. Use the past participle with every tense.

Tense	Active	Passive (*Be* + Past Participle)
Simple Present	They **take** a vote.	A vote **is taken**.
Simple Past	They **took** a vote.	A vote **was taken**.
Future	They **will take** a vote. They **are going to take** a vote.	A vote **will be taken**. A vote **is going to be taken**.
Present Perfect	They **have taken** a vote.	A vote **has been taken**.
Modal	They **must take** a vote.	A vote **must be taken**.

Language Notes:
1. An adverb can be placed between the auxiliary verb and the main verb.
    The jurors **are** *always* **paid**.
    Noncitizens **are** *never* **selected** for jury duty.
2. If two verbs in the passive voice are connected with *and*, do not repeat *be*.
    The jurors **are taken** to a room and **shown** a film about the court system.

Use: The passive voice is used more frequently **without** a performer than with a performer.	
Examples	Explanation
English **is spoken** in the U.S. Independence Day **is celebrated** in July.	The passive voice is used when the action is done by people in general.
The jurors **are given** a lunch break. The jurors **will be paid** at the end of the day. Jurors **are** not **permitted** to talk with family members about the case.	The passive voice is used when the actual person who performs the action is of little or no importance.
a. The criminal **was arrested.** b. The students **will be given** a test on the passive voice.	The passive voice is used when it is obvious who performed the action. In (a), it is obvious that the police arrested the criminal. In (b), it is obvious that the teacher will give a test.
Active: The lawyers **presented** the case yesterday. Passive: The case **was presented** in two hours. Active: The judge and the lawyers **choose** jurors. Passive: People who don't understand English **are not chosen.**	The passive voice is used to shift the emphasis from the performer to the receiver of the action.

EXERCISE 2 Change to the passive voice. (Do not include a *by* phrase.)

ACTIVE　　　　　　　　　　　　　　　PASSIVE

EXAMPLE　They chose him.　　　　　　　*He was chosen.*

1. They will choose him.　　　　　　　_____
2. They always choose him.　　　　　　_____
3. They can't choose him.　　　　　　 _____
4. They have never chosen us.　　　　 _____
5. They didn't choose her.　　　　　　_____
6. They shouldn't choose her.　　　　 _____

EXERCISE 3 Fill in the blanks with the passive voice of the verb in parentheses ( ). Use the present tense.

EXAMPLE Jurors ____are chosen____ from lists.
(choose)

1. Only people over 18 years old _____ for jury duty.
(select)

2. Questionnaires _____ to American citizens.
(send)

3. The questionnaire _____ out and _____.
(fill) (return)

4. Many people _____ to the courthouse.
(call)

5. Not everyone _____.
(choose)

6. The jurors _____ a lot of questions.
(ask)

7. Jurors _____ to discuss the case with outsiders.
(not/permit)

8. Jurors _____ a paycheck at the end of the day for their work.
(give)

EXERCISE 4 Fill in the blanks with the passive voice of the verb in parentheses ( ). Use the past tense.

EXAMPLE I ____was sent____ a letter.
(send)

1. I _____ to go to the courthouse on Fifth Street.
(tell)

2. My name _____.
(call)

3. I _____ a form to fill out.
(give)

4. A video about jury duty _____ on a large TV.
(show)

5. The jurors _____ to the third floor of the building.
(take)

6. I _____ a lot of questions by the lawyers.
(ask)

7. I _____.
(not/choose)

8. I _____ home before noon.
(send)

EXERCISE 5 Fill in the blanks with the passive voice of the verb in parentheses ( ). Use the present perfect tense.

EXAMPLE The jurors ___have been given___ a lot of information.
(give)

1. Many articles _____ about the courts.
(write)

2. Many movies _____ about the courts.
(make)

3. Many people _____ for jury duty.
(choose)

4. Your name _____ for jury duty.
(select)

5. The jurors _____ for their work.
(pay)

6. The check _____ at the door.
(leave)

7. The money _____ in an envelope.
(put)

EXERCISE 6 The people called to jury duty are getting instructions about what to expect. Fill in the blanks with the passive voice of the verb in parentheses ( ). Use the future tense.

EXAMPLE You ___will be taken___ to a courtroom.
(take)

1. You _____ to stand up when the judge enters the room.
(tell)

2. Each of you _____ a lot of questions.
(ask)

3. The lawyers _____.
(introduce)

4. Information about the case _____ to you.
(give)

5. You _____ to eat in the courtroom.
(not/allow)

Passive Voice and Active Voice   419

6. Twelve of you _____.
   (select)

7. If you do not speak and understand English well, you _____.
   (not/pick)

8. Besides the 12 jurors, two alternates[1] _____.
   (choose)

9. The rest of you _____ home.
   (send)

10. All of you _____.
    (pay)

EXERCISE 7 Fill in the blanks with the passive voice of the underlined verbs. Use the same tense.

EXAMPLE The jury took a vote. The vote __was taken__ after three hours.

1. The lawyers asked a lot of questions. The questions _____ to find facts.

2. The court will pay us. We _____ $20 a day.

3. They told us to wait. We _____ to wait on the second floor.

4. They gave us instructions. We _____ information about the law.

5. People pay for the services of a lawyer. Lawyers _____ a lot of money for their services.

6. You should use a pen to fill out the form. A pen _____ for all legal documents.

7. They showed us a film about the court system. We _____ the film before we went to the courtroom.

---

[1] An *alternate* takes the place of a juror who cannot serve for some reason (such as illness).

13.4 | Negatives and Questions with Passive Voice

Compare affirmative statements to negative statements and questions with the passive voice.

Simple Past	Present Perfect
The jurors **were paid**.	I **have been chosen** for jury duty several times.
They **weren't paid** a lot.	I **haven't been chosen** this year.
Were they **paid** in cash?	**Have** you ever **been chosen**?
No, they **weren't**.	No, I **haven't**.
How much **were** they **paid**?	How many times **have** you **been chosen**?
Why **weren't** they **paid** in cash?	Why **haven't** you **been chosen**?

Language Note:
Never use *do, does,* or *did* with the passive voice.
   Wrong: The juror **didn't** paid.

EXERCISE 8 Change to the negative form of the underlined words.

EXAMPLE I <u>was selected</u> for jury duty last year. I _wasn't selected_ this year.

1. The jurors <u>are paid</u>. They _____ a lot of money.

2. Twelve people <u>were chosen</u>. People who don't speak English well _____.

3. Jurors <u>are allowed</u> to talk with other jurors about the case. They _____ to talk to friends and family about the case.

4. We <u>were told</u> to keep an open mind. We _____ how to vote.

5. We <u>have been given</u> instructions. We _____ our checks yet.

EXERCISE 9 Change the statements to questions using the words in parentheses ( ).

EXAMPLE The jurors are paid. (how much)
How much are the jurors paid?

1. Some people aren't selected. (why)
_____

2. The jurors are given a lunch break. (when)
_____

3. I wasn't chosen for the jury. (why)

4. You were given information about the case. (what kind of information)

5. A film will be shown. (when)

6. Several jurors have been sent home. (why)

7. The jurors should be paid more money. (why)

8. We were told to go to the courtroom. (when)

9. The jury has been instructed by the judge. (why)

UNUSUAL LAWSUITS

Before You Read

1. Are drivers permitted to use cell phones in the area where you live?
2. Have you read about any unusual court cases in the newspaper or heard about any on TV?

Read the following article. Pay special attention to the active and passive voice.

When a person **is injured** or **harmed**, it is the court's job to determine who is at fault. Most of these cases never **make** the news. But a few of them **appear** in the newspapers and on the evening news because they are so unusual.

In 1992, a fast-food restaurant **was sued** by a 79-year-old woman in New Mexico who **spilled** hot coffee on herself while driving. She **suffered** third-degree burns on her body. At first the woman **asked** for $11,000 to cover her medical expenses. When the restaurant **refused,** the case **went** to court and the woman **was awarded** nearly $3 million.

In 2002, a group of teenagers **sued** several fast-food chains for serving food that **made** them fat. The case **was thrown** out of court. According to Congressman Ric Keller, Americans **have to** "get away from this new culture where people always **try** to play the victim and **blame** others for their problems." Mr. Keller, who is overweight and **eats** at fast-food chains once every two weeks, **said** that suing "the food industry is not going to make a single individual any skinnier. It **will** only **make** the trial attorneys' bank accounts fatter."

In June 2004, an Indiana woman **sued** a cell phone company for causing an auto accident in which she **was involved.** The court **decided** that the manufacturer of a cell phone cannot **be held** responsible for an auto accident involving a driver using its product. In March 2000, a teenage girl in Virginia **was struck** and **killed** by a driver conducting business on a cell phone. The girl's family **sued** the driver's employer for $30 million for wrongful death. They **said** that it was the company's fault because employees **are expected** to conduct business while driving. The family **lost** its case.

We **are protected** by the law. But as individuals we **need to take** personal responsibility and not blame others for our mistakes. The court system **is designed** to protect us; it **is** up to us to make sure that trials remain serious.

Did You Know?

In the United States about 148 million people used cell phones in 2003, compared with approximately 4.3 million in 1990.

Source: The Cellular Telecommunications & Internet Association

13.5 | Choosing Active Voice or Passive Voice

Examples	Explanation
(A) A driver using a cell phone **caused** the accident. (P) The accident **was caused** by a driver using a cell phone. (A) A driver **struck** and **killed** a teenager. (P) A teenager **was struck** and **killed** by a driver.	When the sentence has a specific performer, we can use either the active (A) or passive (P) voice. The active voice puts more emphasis on the person who performs the action. The passive voice puts more emphasis on the action or the result. The performer is mentioned in a *by* phrase (*by the driver, by a woman, by the court*). The active voice is more common than the passive voice when there is a specific performer.
(P) The obesity case **was thrown** out of court. (P) The manufacturer of a cell phone **cannot be held** responsible for a car accident. (P) Some employees **are expected** to conduct business while driving.	When there is no specific performer or the performer is obvious, the passive voice is usually used.
(P) It **was found** that six percent of accidents are the result of driver distraction. (P) It **is believed** that cell phone use distracts drivers.	Often the passive voice is used after *it* when talking about findings, discoveries, or general beliefs.
(A) The woman **went** to court. (A) The accident **happened** in Virginia. (A) Unusual court cases **appear** in the newspaper. (A) The teenager **died**.	Some verbs have no object. We cannot make these verbs passive. Some verbs with no object are: happen go fall become live sleep come look die seem work recover be remain arrive stay appear seem run sound grow depend wake up leave (a place)
(A) **She** sued **them.** (P) **They** were sued by **her.** (A) **He** helps **us.** (P) **We** are helped by **him.**	Notice the difference in pronouns in an active sentence and a passive sentence. After *by*, the object pronoun is used.

Language Note:
Even though *have* and *want* are followed by an object, these verbs are not usually used in the passive voice.

He **has** a cell phone. (*Not:* A cell phone is had by him.)
She **wants** a new car. (*Not:* A new car is wanted by her.)

EXERCISE 10 Change these sentences from active to passive voice. Mention the performer in a *by* phrase. Use the same tense.

EXAMPLE An Indiana woman sued the cell phone company.
The cell phone company was sued by an Indiana woman.

1. Employees use cell phones.

2. A driver hit a pedestrian.

3. The court threw out the case.

4. Distracted drivers cause accidents.

5. Congress makes the laws.

6. Should the government control cell phone use?

7. The president signs a new law.

8. The court has decided the case.

9. The judge will make a decision.

10. Fast-food restaurants sell hamburgers and fries.

EXERCISE 11 The following sentences would be better in passive voice without a performer. Change them. Use the same tense.

EXAMPLE They paid me for jury duty.
I was paid for jury duty.

1. They sent me a questionnaire.

2. They have taken us to a separate room.

3. They told us not to discuss the case.

4. They will choose 12 people.

5. Has someone selected your name?

6. They didn't permit us to read any newspapers.

7. They will not select him again for jury duty.

8. Will they pay you?

9. They don't allow us to eat in the courtroom.

10. Someone has called my name.

EXERCISE 12 The following sentences would be better in active voice. Change them to active voice. Use the same tense.

EXAMPLE Fast food is eaten by Mr. Keller.
Mr. Keller eats fast food.

1. A cell phone was had by the driver.

2. Hot coffee was spilled by the driver.

3. Is a cell phone used by you?

4. The car has been driven by me.

5. A lot of money is made by lawyers.

6. A headset should be used by drivers with cell phones.

7. Business is conducted by me from my car.

8. The news is watched by us every night.

9. Fast food is eaten by a lot of teenagers.
_____

10. The accident will be reported by them.
_____

EXERCISE 13 Fill in the blanks with the active or passive voice of the verb in parentheses ( ). Use the tense or modal given.

In about 40 countries, laws __have been passed__ that
(example: present perfect: pass)
prohibit drivers from using cell phones. In the U.S., the law

_____ on the place where you
(1 present: depend)

_____. In New York, for example, the use of
(2 present: live)

hand-held cell phones while driving _____, but
(3 present: prohibit)

the use of hands-free units _____. A driver who
(4 present: permit)

_____ this law can be fined $100 for a first
(5 present: not/obey)

offense, $200 for a second, and $500 after that. Other states

_____ to become tougher on drivers who use
(6 present perfect: start)

cell phones.

However, even when drivers _____
(7 present: use)

hands-free cell phones, they still _____ accidents.
(8 present: cause)

Drivers _____ their hands off the wheel to make
(9 must/take)

or end a call. The problem _____ if drivers
(10 can/reduce)

_____ voice-activated cell phones.
(11 present: use)

But the problem of driver distraction is not only a result of cell phones. According to one study conducted, it was found that six percent of accidents _____ by drivers who are not
(12 present: cause)

paying attention. But the distractions were not just from cell phones.

This study _____ that drivers
(13 past: determine)

_____ by many things: eating, putting on makeup,
(14 present: distract)

Passive Voice and Active Voice

reading, reaching for things, changing stations on the radio—as well as by cell phone use. It is clear that all drivers _____ (15 present: need) to give driving their full attention.

EXERCISE 14 Fill in the blanks with the passive or active voice of the verb in parentheses ( ), using the past tense.

A: Why weren't you at work last week? Were you sick?

B: No. I __was chosen__ (example: choose) to be on a jury.

A: How was it?

B: It was very interesting. A man _____ (1 arrest) for fighting with a police officer.

A: Oh. How was the jury selection process?

B: The jury selection was interesting too. But it took half a day to choose 12 people.

A: Why?

B: The judge and lawyers _____ (2 interview) more than 50 people.

A: Why so many people?

B: Well, several people _____ (3 not/understand) the judge's questions. They _____ (4 not/speak) English very well. And a woman _____ (5 tell) the judge that she was very sick. The judge _____ (6 give) her permission to leave. I don't know why the other people _____ (7 not/choose).

A: What kind of questions _____ (8 you/ask) by the judge and lawyers?

B: First the lawyers _____ (9 want) to see if we could be fair. Some jurors _____ (10 say) that they had a bad experience with a police officer. Those jurors _____ (11 not/select).

A: Why not?

B: Because the judge probably thought they couldn't be fair in this case.

A: How long did the trial last?

B: Only two days.

A: _____ about the case with your family when you _____ home the first night?
(12 you/talk)   (13 go)

B: Oh, no. We _____ not to talk to anyone about the case. When it was over, I _____ my wife and kids about it.
(14 tell)   (15 tell)

A: How long did it take the jurors to make a decision?

B: About two hours. One of the jurors _____ with the other 11 jurors. We _____ about the evidence until she changed her mind.
(16 not/agree)   (17 talk)

A: _____ you for the days you missed work?
(18 your boss/pay)

B: Of course. He had to pay me. That's the law.

A: Now that you've done it once, you won't have to do it again. Right?

B: That's not true. This was the second time I _____ .
(19 choose)

SUMMARY OF LESSON 13

1. Active and Passive Voice

Active	Passive
He **drove** the car.	The car **was driven** by him.
He **didn't drive** the car.	The car **wasn't driven** by him.
He **will drive** the car.	The car **will be driven** by him.
He **has driven** the car.	The car **has been driven** by him.
He often **drives** the car.	The car **is** often **driven** by him.
He **should drive** the car.	The car **should be driven** by him.
Did he **drive** the car?	**Was** the car **driven** by him?
When **did** he **drive** the car?	When **was** the car **driven** by him?

2. The Active Voice

Examples	Explanation
I **bought** a new cell phone. He **eats** fast food. We **will drive** the car.	In most cases, the active voice is used when there is a choice between active and passive.
The accident **happened** last month. She **went** to court.	When there is no object, the active voice must be used. There is no choice.

3. The Passive Voice

Examples	Explanation
I **was chosen** for jury duty. My cell phone **was made** in Japan.	Use the passive voice when the performer is not known or is not important.
The criminal **was taken** to jail. Some employees **are expected** to conduct business while driving.	Use the passive voice when the performer is obvious.
Cell phones **are used** all over the world. Jury duty **is considered** a responsibility of every citizen.	Use the passive voice when the performer is everybody or people in general.
The court paid me. I **was paid** at the end of the day. The coffee was very hot. The coffee **was bought** at a fast-food restaurant.	Use the passive voice when the emphasis is shifted from the performer to the receiver of the action.
It **was discovered** that many accidents are the result of driver distraction. It **is believed** that a person can get a fair trial in the U.S.	Use the passive voice with *it* when talking about findings, discoveries, or beliefs.
Accidents **are caused** by distracted drivers. A fast-food company **was sued** by a woman in New Mexico.	Use the passive voice when we want to emphasize the receiver of the action more than the performer. (In this case, the performer is included in a *by* phrase.)

EDITING ADVICE

1. Never use *do, does,* or *did* with the passive voice.

   The money ~~didn't find~~ **wasn't found**.

   Where ~~did~~ **were** the jurors taken?

2. Don't use the passive voice with *happen, die, sleep, work, live, fall,* or *seem.*

   My grandfather ~~was~~ died four years ago.

3. Don't confuse the *-ing* form with the past participle.

   The criminal was ~~taking~~ **taken** to jail.

4. Don't forget the *-ed* ending for a regular past participle.

   My cousin was select**ed** to be on a jury.

5. Don't forget to use *be* with a passive sentence.

   The books **were** found on the floor by the janitor.

6. Use the correct word order with adverbs.

   I was told (never) about the problem.

LESSON 13 TEST/REVIEW

PART 1 Find the mistakes with the underlined words, and correct them. Not every sentence has a mistake. If the sentence is correct, write *C*.

EXAMPLES The same mistake <u>has made</u> many times. **been**

We <u>were told</u> not to say anything.   **C**

1. Children <u>should taught</u> good behavior.
2. Parents <u>should teach</u> children good behavior.
3. I <u>never was given</u> any information about the test.
4. I <u>have been had</u> my car for three years.

Passive Voice and Active Voice   **431**

5. The driver <u>was given</u> a ticket for driving without a seatbelt.
6. Where <u>did</u> your gloves <u>find</u>?
7. They <u>were find</u> in the back seat of a taxi.
8. Something <u>was happened</u> to my bicycle.
9. This carpet <u>has been cleaned</u> many times.
10. The answers <u>don't written</u> in my book.

PART 2 Change sentences from active to passive voice. Do not mention the performer. (The performer is in parentheses.) Use the same tense as the underlined verb.

EXAMPLE (Someone) <u>took</u> my dictionary.
My dictionary was taken.

1. (People) <u>speak</u> English in the U.S.

2. (You) <u>can use</u> a dictionary during the test.

3. (The police) <u>took</u> the criminal to jail.

4. (People) <u>have seen</u> the president on TV many times.

5. (Someone) <u>will take</u> you to the courtroom.

6. (Someone) <u>has broken</u> the mirror into small pieces.

7. (People) <u>expect</u> you to learn English in the U.S.

8. (They) <u>don't allow</u> cameras in the courtroom.

PART 3 Change the sentences from passive to active voice. Use the same tense.

EXAMPLE You <u>were told</u> by me to bring your books.
I told you to bring your books.

1. You <u>have been told</u> by the teacher to write a composition.

2. Your phone bill must be paid.
   _____

3. You are not allowed by the teacher to use your books during a test.
   _____

4. The tests will be returned by the teacher.
   _____

5. When are wedding gifts opened by the bride and groom?
   _____

6. Your missing car was not found by the police.
   _____

PART 4 Fill in the blanks with the passive or active form of the verb in parentheses ( ). Use an appropriate tense.

EXAMPLES The tests ___will be returned___ tomorrow.
(will/return)

The teacher ___will return___ the tests.
(will/return)

1. My neighbor had a heart attack and _____ to the
   (take)
   hospital in an ambulance yesterday.

2. I _____ my neighbor in the hospital tomorrow.
   (will/visit)

3. I _____ the movie *Star Wars* five times.
   (see)

4. This movie _____ by millions of people.
   (see)

5. I _____ a lot of friends.
   (have)

6. I _____ many times by my friends.
   (help)

7. Ten people _____ in the fire last night.
   (die)

8. Five people _____ by the fire department in
   (rescue)
   yesterday's fire.

9. Her husband _____ home from work at six o'clock
   (come)
   every day.

Passive Voice and Active Voice 433

10. He _____ home by his coworker last night.
   (drive)

11. The answer to your question _____ by anyone.
   (not/know)

12. Even the teacher _____ the answer to your question.
   (not/know)

EXPANSION ACTIVITIES

Classroom Activities

1. Form a small group and talk about the legal system in another country. Use the chart below to get ideas.

   Country: _____

	Yes	No
People are treated fairly in court.		
Citizens are selected to be on a jury.		
People are represented by lawyers in court.		
Lawyers make a lot of money.		
Famous trials are shown on TV.		
Punishment is severe for certain crimes.		
The death penalty is used in some cases.		
The laws are fair.		

2. Form a small group and tell about how a holiday is celebrated in your native culture. Use the chart below to get ideas.

	Yes	No
Gifts are given.		
The house is cleaned.		
Special clothing is worn.		
The house is decorated with special symbols of the holiday.		
Special food is prepared.		
Stores and businesses are closed.		
Special programs are shown on TV.		
Candles are used.		

3. Form two groups. One group should make a presentation telling why cell phone use should be permitted in cars. One group should make a presentation telling why cell phone use should *not* be permitted in cars.

Talk About it

1. Would you like to be on a jury? Why or why not?
2. In a small group, discuss your impressions of the American legal system from what you've seen on TV, from what you've read, or from your own experience.
3. Do you think drivers who use cell phones while driving cause accidents?
4. What laws should be changed in the U.S.? What laws should be added?
5. Do you think fast-food restaurants are responsible for obesity in the U.S.?

Write About it

1. Write about an experience you have had with the court system in the U.S. or your native country.
2. Write about a famous court case that you know of. Do you agree with the decision of the jury?
3. Write about the advantages of owning a cell phone.

Outside Activities

1. Watch a court movie, such as *The Firm, Witness to the Prosecution, Inherit the Wind, A Time to Kill, To Kill a Mockingbird, Presumed Innocent, Twelve Angry Men, A Civil Action,* or *The Client*. Write about your impressions of the American court system after watching one of these movies.
2. Watch a court TV show, such as *People's Court* or *Judge Judy*. What do you think of the judges' decisions on these shows?
3. Ask an American if he or she has ever been selected for a jury. Ask him or her to tell you about this experience.

Internet Activities

1. At a search engine, type in *Insurance Information Institute* and *cell phones*. Find some statistics about drivers who use cell phones. Bring the information to class. Is there anything that surprises you?
2. Look for information about one of these famous American trials:
   a. the O.J. Simpson trial
   b. the Leopold and Loeb trial
   c. the Sacco and Vanzetti trial
   d. the Amistad trials
   e. the Scopes trial
   f. the Rosenberg trial
   g. the Bruno Hauptmann trial

(continued)

Answer these questions about one of the trials:

- What was the defendant accused of?
- When did the trial take place?
- How long did the trial last?
- Was the defendant found guilty?

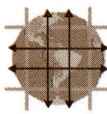 Additional Activities at **http://elt.heinle.com/gic**

LESSON 14

GRAMMAR

Articles
Other / Another
Indefinite Pronouns

CONTEXT: Money

Kids and Money
Changing the American Dollar
The High Cost of a College Education

14.1 Articles—An Overview

Articles precede nouns and tell whether a noun is definite or indefinite.

Examples	Explanation
Do you have **a credit card**? I bought **an old house**.	The indefinite articles are *a* and *an*.
It's a holiday today. **The banks** are closed. There are many poor people in **the world**.	The definite article is *the*.
Money is important for everyone. **Children** like to spend money.	Sometimes a noun is used without an article.

KIDS AND MONEY

Before You Read

1. Do you think parents should give money to their children? At what age?
2. Do you think teenagers should work while they're in high school?

 Read the following article. Pay special attention to nouns and the articles that precede them. (Some nouns have no article.)

Kids in the U.S. like to spend **money.** In 2001, kids between the ages of 12 and 19 spent an average of $104 a week. Much of today's **advertising** is directed at kids. When you go into **a store,** you often hear **toddlers,**[1] who are just learning to talk, saying to their parents, "Buy me **a toy.** Buy me **some candy.**" Some kids feel **gratitude** when they receive **a dollar** or **a toy** from

[1] A *toddler* is a child between the ages of one and three.

Did You Know?

In a study of young people aged 12 to 17, 58 percent said they wouldn't bother to pick up off the sidewalk anything less than a dollar.

a grandparent. But some kids feel a sense of entitlement[2]. Even during **the** hard economic **times** of the early 1990s, sales of **soft drinks, designer blue jeans, fast food, sneakers, gum,** and **dolls** remained high. One factor in parents' **generosity** is **guilt**. As **parents** become busier in their **jobs,** they often feel guilty about not spending **time** with their **kids**. Often they deal with their **guilt** by giving their kids **money** and **gifts**.

To help children understand **the value** of **money, parents** often give their **children an allowance. The child's spending** is limited to **the money** he or she receives each week. How much should parents give **a child** as **an allowance?** Some parents give **the child a dollar** for each year of his or her age. **A five-year-old** would get five dollars. **A fifteen-year-old** would get fifteen dollars. Some parents pay their kids extra for **chores,** such as taking out **the garbage** or shoveling **snow.** Other parents believe kids should do chores as part of their family responsibilities.

When is **the right time** to start talking to **kids** about **money?** According to Nathan Dungan, **a financial expert,** the right time is as soon as **kids** can say, "I want." By **the time** they start **school,** they must know there are **limits.**

14.2 The Indefinite Article—Classifying or Identifying the Subject

Examples	Explanation
A doll is **a toy.** A toddler is **a small child.** An allowance is **a weekly payment** to children. A penny is **a one-cent coin.** "Big" is **an adjective.** "Inflation" is **an economic term.**	After the verb *be*, we use the indefinite articles *a* or *an* + singular count noun to define or classify the subject of the sentence. We are telling who or what the subject is. Singular subject + *is* + *a(n)* + (adjective) + noun
Jeans are **popular clothes.** Teenagers are **young adults.** Chores are **everyday jobs.**	When we classify or define a plural subject, we don't use an article. Plural subject + *are* + (adjective) + noun

Language Note:
We can also use *be* in the past tense to give a definition.
  The Depression **was** a difficult time in American history.
  Abraham Lincoln **was** an American president.

---

[2] A sense of *entitlement* is a feeling that you have the right to receive something.

EXERCISE 1 Define the following words. Answers may vary.

EXAMPLE A toddler _is a small child._

1. A teenager _____
2. A quarter _____
3. A dime _____
4. A credit card _____
5. A wallet _____
6. Gold _____
7. Silver and gold _____

EXERCISE 2 Tell who these people are or were by classifying them. These people were mentioned in previous lessons in this book. Answers will vary.

EXAMPLE Martin Luther King, Jr. _was an African-American leader._

1. Albert Einstein _____
2. Michael Jordan _____
3. Erik Weihenmayer _____
4. Oprah Winfrey _____
5. George Dawson _____
6. Navajos _____
7. George Washington and Abraham Lincoln _____

14.3 | The Indefinite Article—Introducing a Noun

Examples	Explanation
She has **a son.** Her son has **a job.** Her son has **a checking account.**	Use *a* or *an* to introduce a singular noun.
He has **(some)** toys. He doesn't have **(any)** video games. Does he have **(any)** CDs?	Use *some* and *any* to introduce a plural noun. Use *any* for negatives and questions. *Some* and *any* can be omitted.
He has **(some)** money. He doesn't have **(any)** cash. Does he have **(any)** time?	Use *some* and *any* to introduce a noncount noun. Use *any* for negatives and questions. *Some* and *any* can be omitted.

EXERCISE 3 Fill in the blanks with the correct word: *a, an, some,* or *any.*

EXAMPLE There are ___some___ symbols on the back of a credit card.

1. Do you have _____ account with the bank?
2. Do you have _____ money in your savings account?
3. I have _____ twenty-dollar bill in my pocket.
4. I have _____ quarters in my pocket.
5. I have _____ money with me.
6. Do you have _____ credit cards?
7. I don't have _____ change.
8. Buy me _____ toy.
9. Buy me _____ candy.
10. I need _____ dollar.
11. Many teenagers want to have _____ job.
12. Does your little brother get _____ allowance?

EXERCISE 4 A mother (M) and a son (S) are talking. Fill in the blanks with *a, an, some,* or *any.*

S: I want to get ___a___ job.
     (example)

M: But you're only 16 years old.

S: I'm old enough to work. I need to make _____ money.
                                                    (1)

M: But we give you _____ allowance each week. Isn't
                          (2)
that enough money for you?

S: You only give me $15 a week. That's not even enough to buy

_____ CD or take _____ girl to
     (3)   (4)

_____ movie.
     (5)

M: If you work, what are you going to do about school? You won't have

_____ time to study. Do you know how hard it is to
     (6)
work and do well in school?

S: Of course, I do. You know I'm _____ good student.
                                          (7)

I'm sure I won't have _____ problems working part-time.
                            (8)

M: Well, I'm worried about your grades falling. Maybe we should raise your allowance. That way you won't have to work.

S: I want to have my own money. I want to buy _____(9)_____ new clothes. And I'm going to save money to buy _____(10)_____ car someday.

M: Why do you want a car? You have _____(11)_____ bike.

S: Bikes are great for exercise, but if my job is far away, I'll need a car for transportation.

M: So, you need _____(12)_____ job to buy _____(13)_____ car, and you need _____(14)_____ car to get work.

S: Yes. You know, a lot of my friends work, and they're good students.

M: Well, let me think about it.

S: Mom, I'm not _____(15)_____ baby anymore. I need _____(16)_____ job.

14.4 The Definite Article

We use *the* to talk about a specific person or thing or a unique person or thing.

Examples	Explanation
The book talks about kids and money. **The author** wants to teach kids to be responsible with money.	The sentences to the left refer to a specific object or person that is present. There is no other book or author present, so the listener knows which noun is referred to.
Many kids in **the world** are poor. **The first** chapter talks about small children. **The back** of the book has information about the author. When is **the right** time to talk to kids about money?	Sometimes there is only one of something. There is only one world, only one first chapter, only one back of a book. We use *the* with the following words: *first, second, next, last, only, same,* and *right*.
Where's **the** teacher? I have a question about **the** homework.	When students in the same class talk about **the** teacher, **the** textbook, **the** homework, **the** chalkboard, they are talking about a specific one that they share.
Did you read **the article about money?** Children often spend **the money they get from their grandparents.**	The sentences to the left refer to a specific noun that is defined in the phrase or clause after the noun: *the article* **about money;** *the money* **they get from their grandparents.**
I'm going to **the** store after work. Do you need anything? **The** bank is closed. I'll go tomorrow. You should make an appointment with **the** doctor.	We often use *the* with certain familiar places and people when we refer to the one that we usually use: the bank the beach the bus the zoo the post office the train the park the doctor the movies the store
a. I saw **a child** in the supermarket with her mother. b. **The child** kept saying, "Buy me this, buy me that." a. She used **a credit card.** b. She put **the credit card** back in her purse.	a. A noun is first introduced as an indefinite noun (with *a* or *an*). b. When referring to the same noun again, the definite article *the* is used.

My grandparents gave me lots of presents.
Kim's kids have lots of toys.
	Don't use the definite article with a possessive form.
	   Wrong: My the grandparents
	   Wrong: Kim's the kids

Articles; *Other/Another*; Indefinite Pronouns

EXERCISE 5 Fill in the blanks with the definite article *the*, the indefinite article *a* or *an*, or quantity words *any* or *some*.

Conversation 1: between two friends

A: Where are you going?

B: To __*the*__ bank. I want
        (example)
to deposit _____ check.
              (1)

A: _____ bank is
      (2)
probably closed now.

B: No problem. I have

_____ ATM card.
    (3)

There's _____
              (4)
ATM on _____
              (5)
corner of Wilson and Sheridan.

A: I'll go with you. I want to get _____ cash.
                                          (6)

Later, at the ATM . . .

B: Oh, no. _____ ATM is out of order.
              (7)

A: Don't worry. There's _____ ATM in _____
                              (8)   (9)
supermarket near my house.

Conversation 2: between two students at the same school

A: Is there _____ cafeteria at this school?
                (1)

B: Yes, there is. It's on _____ first floor of this building.
                              (2)

A: I want to buy _____ cup of coffee.
                      (3)

B: You don't have to go to _____ cafeteria. There's
                                (4)

_____ coffee machine on this floor.
    (5)

A: I only have a one-dollar bill. Do you have _____ change?
                                                      (6)

B: There's _____ dollar-bill changer next to _____
              (7)   (8)
coffee machine.

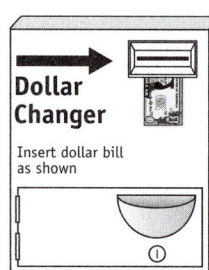

444   Lesson 14

Conversation 3: between two students (A and B) in the same class

A: Where's _____(1)_____ teacher? It's already 7:00.

B: Maybe she's absent today.

A: I'll go to _____(2)_____ English office and ask if anyone knows where she is.

B: That's _____(3)_____ good idea.

A few minutes later . . .

A: I talked to _____(4)_____ secretary in _____(5)_____ English office. She said that _____(6)_____ teacher just called. She's going to be about 15 minutes late. She had _____(7)_____ problem with her car.

14.5 | Making Generalizations

When we make a generalization, we say that something is true of ALL members of a group.

Examples	Explanation
a. **Children** like to copy their friends. b. **A child** likes to copy his or her friends. a. **Video games** are expensive. b. **A video game** is expensive.	There are two ways to make a generalization about a countable subject: a. Use *a* or *an* + singular noun OR b. Use no article + plural noun.
Money doesn't buy happiness. **Love** is more important than money. **Honesty** is a good quality.	To make a generalization about a noncount subject, don't use an article.
a. Children like **toys**. a. People like to use **credit cards**. b. Everyone needs **money**. b. No one has enough **time**.	Don't use an article to make a generalization about the object of the sentence. a. Use the plural form for count nouns. b. Noncount nouns are always singular.
Language Note: Do not use *some* or *any* with generalizations. **Compare:** 　I need **some money** to buy a new bike. 　Everyone needs **money**.	

EXERCISE 6 Decide if the statement is general (true of all examples of the subject), or specific (true of the pictures on this page or of specific objects that everyone in the class can agree on). Fill in the blanks with *a, an, the,* or Ø (for no article).

EXAMPLES
     Ø children like Ø toys.
     The toys are broken.

1. _____ American teenager likes to have a job.
2. _____ teenager is shoveling snow to make money.
3. _____ teenagers like _____ cars.
4. _____ blue jeans are popular.
5. _____ blue jeans are torn.
6. _____ money is important for everyone.
7. _____ money on the table is mine.
8. Do you like _____ kids?
9. _____ American kids like to spend money.
10. _____ child is saying to her mother, "I want."
11. _____ coffee is hot.
12. _____ coffee contains sugar.
13. _____ cows give milk.
14. _____ cows are eating grass.
15. _____ children are playing.
16. _____ children can generally learn a foreign language faster than adults.

EXERCISE 7 ABOUT YOU Tell if you like the following or not. For count nouns (C), use the plural form. For noncount nouns (NC), use the singular form.

EXAMPLES coffee (NC)   apple (C)
I like coffee.   I don't like apples.

1. tea (NC)
2. corn (NC)
3. peach (C)
4. potato chip (C)
5. milk (NC)
6. orange (C)
7. cookie (C)
8. pizza (NC)
9. potato (C)

EXERCISE 8 Fill in the blanks with *the, a, an, some, any,* or Ø (for no article). In some cases, more than one answer is possible.

A: Where are you going?

B: I'm going to __the__ (example) post office. I need to buy _____ (1) stamps.

A: I'll go with you. I want to mail _____ (2) package to my parents.

B: What's in _____ (3) package?

A: _____ (4) shirts for my father, _____ (5) coat for my sister, and _____ (6) money for my mother.

B: You should never send _____ (7) money by mail.

A: I know. My mother never received _____ (8) money that I sent in my last letter. But what can I do? I don't have _____ (9) checking account.

B: You can buy _____ (10) money order at _____ (11) bank.

A: How much does it cost?

B: Well, if you have _____ (12) account in _____ (13) bank, it's usually free. If not, you'll probably have to pay a fee.

A: What about _____ (14) currency exchange on Wright Street? Do they sell _____ (15) money orders?

B: Yes.

A: Why don't we go there? We can save _____ (16) time. It's on _____ (17) same street as _____ (18) post office.

EXERCISE 9 Two women are talking. Fill in the blanks with *the, a, an, some, any,* or Ø (for no article). Answers may vary.

A: I bought my daughter __a__ (example) new doll for her birthday. She's been asking me to buy it for her for two months. But she played with _____(1) doll for about three days and then lost interest.

B: That's how _____(2) kids are. They don't understand _____(3) value of money.

A: You're right. They think that _____(4) money grows on _____(5) trees.

B: I suppose it's our fault. We have to set _____(6) good example. We buy a lot of things we don't really need. We use _____(7) credit cards instead of _____(8) cash and worry about paying the bill later.

A: I suppose you're right. Last month we bought _____(9) new flat screen TV. We were at the store looking for a DVD player when we saw it. It's so much nicer than our old TV, so we decided to get it and put our _____(10) old TV in _____(11) basement. I suppose we didn't really need it.

B: Last weekend my husband bought _____(12) new CD player. And he bought _____(13) new CDs. I asked him what was wrong with our old CD player, and he said that it only played two CDs at a time. _____(14) new CD player has room for 10 CDs.

A: Well, when we complain about our kids, we should realize that they are imitating us.

B: We need to make _____ changes in our own behavior. I'm
(15)
going to start _____ budget tonight. I'm going to start saving
(16)
_____ money each month.
(17)

A: Me too.

14.6 | General or Specific with Quantity Words

> If we put *of the* after a quantity word (*all, most, some,* etc.), we are making something specific. Without *of the,* the sentence is general.

Examples	Explanation
General: **All** children like toys. **Most** American homes have a television. **Many** teenagers have jobs. **Some** people are very rich. **Very few** people are billionaires.	We use *all, most, many, some, (a) few,* and *(a) little* before general nouns.

Specific:
a. **All (of) the students** in this class have a textbook.
b. **Most of the students** in my art class have talent.
c. **Many of the topics** in this book are about life in America.
d. **Some of the people** in my building come from Haiti.
e. **Very few of the students** in this class are American citizens.
f. **Very little of the time** spent in this class is for reading.
g. **None of the classrooms** at this school has a telephone.
	We use *all of the, most of the, many of the, some of the, (a) few of the, (a) little of the,* and *none of the* before specific nouns.
	
	After *all, of* is often omitted.
	    All the students in this class have a textbook.
	
	After *none of the* + plural noun, a singular verb is correct. However, you will often hear a plural verb used.
	    None of the classrooms **have** a telephone.

Language Note:
Remember the difference between *a few* and *(very) few, a little* and *(very) little.* When we omit *a,* the emphasis is on the negative. We are saying the quantity is not enough. (See Lesson 5, Section 5.14 for more information.)

    Few people wanted to have a party. The party was canceled.
    A few people came to the meeting. We discussed our plans.

EXERCISE 10 Fill in the blanks with *all, most, some,* or *(very) few* to make a general statement about Americans. Discuss your answers.

EXAMPLE _____Most_____ Americans have a car.

1. _____ Americans have educational opportunities.
2. _____ Americans have a TV.
3. _____ American families have more than eight children.
4. _____ Americans know where my native country is.
5. _____ Americans shake hands when they meet.
6. _____ Americans use credit cards.
7. _____ Americans are natives of America.
8. _____ American citizens can vote.
9. _____ Americans speak my native language.
10. _____ Americans are unfriendly to me.

EXERCISE 11 **ABOUT YOU** Fill in the blanks with a quantity word to make a **true** statement about specific nouns. If you use *none,* change the verb to the singular form.

EXAMPLES _____All of the_____ students in this class want to learn English.

None of the students in this class come*s* from Australia.

1. _____ students in this class speak Spanish.
2. _____ students brought their books to class today.
3. _____ students are absent today.
4. _____ students want to learn English.
5. _____ students have jobs.
6. _____ students are married.
7. _____ students are going to return to their native countries.
8. _____ lessons in this book end with a review.
9. _____ pages in this book have pictures.
10. _____ tests in this class are hard.

CHANGING THE AMERICAN DOLLAR

Before You Read

1. Does American money look different from money in another country (size, color, etc.)?
2. Compare a one-dollar bill to a twenty-dollar bill. Do you see differences in design?

 Read the following article. Pay special attention to *other* and *another*.

The appearance of the American dollar did not change for a long time—from 1928 to 1996. But with advances in technology in recent years, it has become easier for counterfeiters[3] to copy dollar bills, making frequent changes necessary.

Look at the two twenty-dollar bills above. (Or see if you and your classmates have old and new bills.) You can see that on one twenty-dollar bill, the picture of Andrew Jackson is in an oval. On **the other** one, the picture is not in an oval. One bill has no background. **The other** bill has an eagle on the left and the words "Twenty USA" on the right. **Another** important change is in the color. The old bills are green. The new ones have some color. In the lower right corner of the old bill, the number "20" is in green. On the new bill, the "20" changes from gold to green, depending on how the light hits it. There are **other** changes too. If you have an old and a new bill, try to find **the other** differences.

The latest change to the U.S. bills began in 2003. The government decided to change the appearance of the twenty-dollar bill first, then the fifty- and one hundred-dollar bills. It has not been decided if the five- and ten-dollar bills will be changed. **The other** two bills ($1 and $2) will not be changed. Counterfeiters are not interested in small amounts of money. As new bills come into use, the old ones are "retired."

Some aspects of the bills remain the same: size, paper, the pictures on the front and back, and the motto "In God We Trust." In order to stay ahead of counterfeiters, the U.S. Treasury plans to redesign new bills every seven to ten years.

(*continued*)

Did You Know?

Before 1928, the U.S. dollar was much bigger than the dollars we use today. The size of the dollar was reduced to save money on paper.

---

[3] A *counterfeiter* is a person who makes copies of bills illegally.

U.S. Dollar Bills		
Denomination	**Front Side**	**Back Side**
$1	George Washington	Great Seal of the United States
$2	Thomas Jefferson	Declaration of Independence
$5	Abraham Lincoln	Lincoln Memorial
$10	Alexander Hamilton	Treasury Building
$20	Andrew Jackson	White House
$50	Ulysses S. Grant	U.S. Capitol
$100	Benjamin Franklin	Independence Hall

14.7 | *Another* and *Other*

The use of *other* and *another* depends on whether a noun is singular or plural, definite or indefinite.

The other + a singular noun is definite. It means the only one remaining.

One side has a picture of Washington.
The other side has the American seal.

The other + a plural noun is definite. It means all the remaining ones.

The $100 bill was changed first.
The other bills are being changed too.

Another + a singular noun is indefinite. It means one of several.

One bill has a picture of Lincoln.
Another bill has a picture of Washington.

Other + a plural noun is indefinite. It means some, but not all, of the remaining ones.

One American president was Lincoln.
Other American presidents were Kennedy and Clinton.

14.8 More About *Another* and *Other*

Examples	Explanation
One change is the color. Another **one** is the frame around the face. The two-dollar bill is not common. The other **ones** are common.	We can use pronouns, *one* or *ones*, in place of the noun.
The two-dollar bill is not common. The **others** are common.	When the plural noun or pronoun (*ones*) is omitted, change *other* to *others*.
I have two bank accounts. One is for savings. **My other** account is for checking.	*The* is omitted when we use a possessive form. *Wrong:* My *the* other account is for checking.
I'm busy now. Can you come **another** time? Can you come **any other** time? Can you come **some other** time?	After *some* or *any, another* is changed to *other*. *Wrong:* Can you come *any another* time?
This dollar bill is old. You can't put it in the vending machine. You have to use **another** one.	*Another* is sometimes used to mean a different one.

EXERCISE 12 Fill in the blanks with *the other, another, the others, others,* or *other*.

EXAMPLE One side of the one-dollar bill has a picture of George Washington. _____*The other*_____ side has a picture of the American seal.

1. Some bills were changed in 2003. _____ bills were changed in 2004. Not all bills were changed.

2. Franklin, on the $100 bill, and Hamilton, on the $10 bill, were not American presidents. All _____ bills have pictures of American presidents.

3. Franklin was an important person in American history. _____ important people were Thomas Jefferson and John Hancock.

4. One bill has a picture of Lincoln. _____ one has a picture of George Washington.

5. George Washington was an American president. _____ presidents were Lincoln, Roosevelt, and Truman.

6. There were two presidents named Roosevelt. One was Theodore Roosevelt. _____ was Franklin Roosevelt.

7. The child has a lot of toys, but he wants _____ one.

8. New York is one big city in the U.S. _____ big cities are Philadelphia, Houston, and Detroit.

9. Many cities in the U.S. have warm weather. One city is Miami. _____ one is San Diego.

10. Do you know the capital of this state? Do you know _____ 49 state capitals?

11. Johnson is a common last name in the U.S. _____ common last names are Smith, Wilson, and Jones.

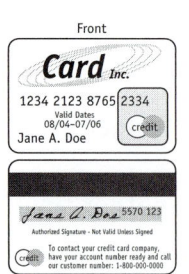

12. One side of the credit card has a name and number. _____ side has a place to sign your name.

13. If I use the ATM at my bank, I don't have to pay a fee. If I use it at any _____ bank, I have to pay a fee.

14. The bank is going to close now. Please come back some _____ time.

15. *Money* is a noncount noun. _____ ones are *love, freedom,* and *time.*

16. Some kids get an allowance for doing nothing. _____ kids have to do chores to get an allowance. But not all kids get an allowance.

17. We celebrate two presidents' birthdays in February. One is Lincoln's birthday. _____ is Washington's birthday.

18. The child gets presents from his grandparents. One grandparent is dead, but _____ three are alive.

EXERCISE 13 A grandson (GS) and grandfather (GF) are talking. Fill in the blanks with *the other, another, the others,* or *others*.

GS: I want to buy ___*another*___ pair of sneakers.
                    (example)

GF: What?! You already have about six pairs of sneakers. In fact, I bought you a new pair last month for your birthday.

GS: The new pair is fine, but _____ five are too small
                                      (1)
for me. You know I'm growing very fast, so I threw them away.

GF: Why did you throw them away? _____ boys in your
                                         (2)
neighborhood could use them.

GS: They wouldn't like them. They're out of style.

454   Lesson 14

GF: You kids are so wasteful today. What's wrong with the sneakers I bought you last month? If they fit you, why do you need _____ pair?
(3)

GS: Everybody in my class at school has red sneakers with the laces tied backward. The sneakers you gave me are not in style anymore.

GF: Do you always have to have what all _____ kids in
(4)
school have? Can't you think for yourself?

GS: Didn't you ask your parents for stuff when you were in junior high?

GF: My parents were poor, and my two brothers and I worked to help them. When we couldn't wear our clothes anymore because we outgrew them, we gave them to _____ families
(5)
nearby. And our neighbors gave us the things that their children outgrew. One neighbor had two sons. One son was a year older than me. _____ one was two years younger. So we
(6)
were constantly passing clothes back and forth.

GS: What about style? When clothes went out of style, didn't you throw them out?

GF: No. We never threw things out. Styles were not as important to us then. We didn't waste our parents' money thinking of styles. In fact, my oldest brother worked in a factory and gave all his salary to our parents. My _____ brother and I helped our father
(7)
in his business. My dad didn't give us a salary or an allowance. It was our duty to help him.

GS: You don't understand how important it is to look like all _____ kids.
(8)

GF: I guess I don't. I'm old-fashioned. Every generation has _____ way of looking at things.
(9)

THE HIGH COST OF A COLLEGE EDUCATION

Before You Read

1. Have you received any financial aid to take this course?
2. Do you know how much it costs to get a college degree in the U.S.?

  Read the following conversation between a son (S) and a dad (D). Pay attention to *one, some, any* (indefinite pronouns) and *it* and *them* (definite pronouns).

Did You Know?

In 2002, about 60 percent of undergraduates received some form of financial aid: grants, loans, and scholarships.

S: I decided not to go to college, Dad.

D: What? Do you know how important a college education is?

S: College is expensive. Besides, if I don't go to college now, I can start making money immediately. As soon as I earn **some,** I'd like to buy a car. Besides, my friends aren't going to college.

D: I'm not concerned about **them.** I'm interested in you and your future. I was just reading an article in a magazine about how much more money a college graduate earns than a high school graduate. Here's the article. Look at **it.** It says, "According to U.S. Census Bureau statistics, people with a bachelor's degree earn over 60 percent more than those with only a high school diploma. Over a lifetime, the gap in earning potential between a high school diploma and a B.A. (or higher) is more than $1,000,000."

S: Wow. I never realized that I could earn much more with a college degree than without **one.** Look. But the article also says, "In the 2003–2004 school year, the average tuition at a four-year private college was $27,000, and at a four-year public college, it was $10,000**.**" How can you afford to send me to college?

456 Lesson 14

D: I didn't just start to think about your college education today. I started to think about **it** when you were born. We saved money each month to buy a house, and we bought **one**. And we saved **some** each month for your college tuition.

S: That's great, Dad.

D: I also want you to apply for financial aid. There are grants, loans, and scholarships you should also look into. Your grades are good. I think you should apply for a scholarship.

S: I'll need to get an application.

D: I already thought of that. I brought **one** home today. Let's fill **it** out together.

S: Dad, if a college degree is so important to you, why didn't you get **one**?

D: When I was your age, we didn't live in the U.S. We were very poor and had to help our parents. You have a lot of opportunities for grants and scholarships, but we didn't have **any** when I was young.

S: Thanks for thinking about this from the day I was born.

Grants and Scholarships
Grants and scholarships provide aid that does not have to be repaid. However, some require that recipients maintain good grades or take certain courses.

Loans
Loans are another type of financial aid and are available to both students and parents. Like a car loan or a mortgage for a house, an education loan must eventually be repaid. Often, payments do not begin until the student finishes school. The interest rate on education loans is commonly lower than for other types of loans.

Source: http://www.ed.gov/pubs

Amount You Would Need to Save to Have $10,000 Available When Your Child Begins College
(Assuming a 5 percent interest rate.)

If you start saving when your child is	Number of years of saving	Approximate monthly savings	Amount Available When Child Begins College		
			Principal	Interest earned	Total savings
Newborn	18	$29	$6,197	$3,803	$10,000
Age 4	14	41	6,935	3,065	10,000
Age 8	10	64	7,736	2,264	10,000
Age 12	6	119	8,601	1,399	10,000
Age 16	2	397	9,531	469	10,000

Source of chart: http://www.ed.gov/pubs/Prepare/pt4.html

14.9 Definite and Indefinite Pronouns

Examples	Explanation
I've always thought about your education. I started to think about **it** when you were born. I received two college applications. I have to fill **them** out. The father wants his son to go to college. The father is going to help **him.**	We use definite pronouns *him, her, them,* and *it* to refer to definite count nouns.
A college degree is important. It's hard to make a lot of money without **one.** I don't have a scholarship. I hope I can get **one.**	We use the indefinite pronoun *one* to refer to an indefinite singular count noun.
a. The father knew it was important to save money. He saved **some** every month. b. You received five brochures for colleges. Did you read **any?** c. You have a lot of opportunities today. When I was your age, we didn't have **any.**	We use *some* (for affirmative statements) and *any* (for negative statements and questions) to refer to an indefinite noncount noun (a) or an indefinite plural count noun (b) and (c).

Language Note:
We often use *any* and *some* before *more*.
   Dad, I don't have enough money. I need **some more.**
   Son, I'm not going to give you **any more.**

EXERCISE 14 A mother (M) is talking to her teenage daughter (D) about art school. Fill in the blanks with *one* or *it*.

M: I have some information about the state university. Do you want to look at ___*it*___ with me?
               (example)

D: I don't know, Mom. I don't know if I'm ready to go to college when I graduate.

M: Why not? We've been planning for _____(1)_____ since the day you were born.

D: College is not for everyone. I want to be an artist.

M: You can go to college and major in art. I checked out information about the art curriculum at the state university. It seems to have a very good program. Do you want to see information about _____(2)_____?

D: I'm not really interested in college. To be an artist, I don't need a college degree.

M: But it's good to have _____ anyway.
(3)

D: I don't know why. In college, I'll have to study general courses, too, like math and biology. You know I hate math. I'm not good at _____.
(4)

M: Well, maybe we should look at art schools. There's one downtown. Do you want to visit _____?
(5)

D: Yes, I'd like to. We can probably find information about _____ on the Web too.
(6)

(*looking at the art school's Web site*)

D: This school sounds great. Let's call and ask for an application.

M: I think you can get _____ online. Oh, yes, here it is.
(7)

D: Let's make a copy of _____.
(8)

M: You can fill _____ out online and submit _____ electronically.
(9) (10)

EXERCISE 15 ABOUT YOU Answer each question. Substitute the underlined words with an indefinite pronoun (*one, some, any*) or a definite pronoun (*it, them*).

EXAMPLES Do you have a pen with you?
Yes, I have one.

Are you using your pen now?
No. I'm not using it now.

1. Does this school have a library?
2. How often do you use the library?
3. Do you have a dictionary?
4. When do you use your dictionary?
5. Did you buy any textbooks this semester?
6. How much did you pay for your textbooks?
7. Did the teacher give any homework last week?
8. Where did you do the homework?
9. Do you have any American neighbors?
10. Do you know your neighbors?
11. Does this college have a president?
12. Do you know the college president?
13. Did you receive any mail today?
14. What time does your letter carrier deliver your mail?

EXERCISE 16 *Combination Exercise.* This is a conversation between a teenage girl (A) and her mother (B). Fill in the blanks with *one, some, any, it, them, a, an, the,* or Ø (for no article).

A: Can I have 15 dollars?

B: What for?

A: I have to buy ____*a*____ poster of my favorite singer.
(example)

B: I gave you _____ money last week. What did you do with
(1)

_____?
(2)

A: I spent _____ on a CD.
(3)

B: No, you can't have _____ more money until next week.
(4)

A: Please, please, please. All of my friends have _____. I'll
(5)

die if I don't get _____.
(6)

B: What happened to all _____ money Grandpa gave you for
(7)

your birthday?

460 Lesson 14

A: I spent _____(8)_____.

B: What about _____(9)_____ money you put in the bank after your graduation?

A: I don't have _____(10)_____ more money in the bank.

B: You have to learn that _____(11)_____ money doesn't grow on trees. If you want me to give you _____(12)_____, you'll have to work for it. You can start by cleaning your room.

A: But I cleaned _____(13)_____ two weeks ago.

B: Two weeks ago was two weeks ago. It's dirty again.

A: I don't have _____(14)_____ time. I have to meet my friends.

B: You can't go out. You need to do your homework.

A: I don't have _____(15)_____. Please let me have 15 dollars.

B: When I was your age, I had _____(16)_____ job. And I gave my parents half of _____(17)_____ money I earned. You kids today have _____(18)_____ easy life.

A: Why do _____(19)_____ parents always say that to _____(20)_____ kids?

B: Because it's true. It's time you learn that _____(21)_____ life is hard.

A: I bet Grandpa said that to you when you were _____(22)_____ child.

B: And I bet you'll say it to your kids when you're _____(23)_____ adult.

Articles; *Other/Another*; Indefinite Pronouns

SUMMARY OF LESSON 14

1. Articles

	Count—Singular	Count—Plural	Noncount
General	*A/An* **A child** likes toys.	Ø Article **Children** like toys. I love **children**.	Ø Article **Money** can't buy happiness. Everyone needs **money**.
Indefinite	*A/An* I bought **a toy**.	*Some/Any* I bought **some toys**. I didn't buy **any games**.	*Some/Any* I spent **some money**. I didn't buy **any candy**.
Specific	*The* **The toy** on the floor is for the baby.	*The* **The toys** on the table are for you.	*The* **The money** on the table is mine.
Classification	*A/An* A toddler is **a young child**.	Ø Article Teenagers are **young adults**.	———

2. *Other / Another*

	Definite	Indefinite
Singular	the other book my other book the other one the other	another book some/any other book another one another
Plural	the other books my other books the other ones the others	other books some/any other books other ones others

3. **Indefinite Pronouns**—Use *one / some / any* to substitute for indefinite nouns.

   I need a quarter. Do you have **one**?
   I need some pennies. You have **some**.
   I don't have any change. Do you have **any**?

EDITING ADVICE

1. Use *the* after a quantity word when the noun is definite.

   Most of ^the students in my class are from Romania.

2. Be careful with *most* and *almost*.

   ~~Almost~~ Most of my teachers are very patient.

3. Use a plural count noun after a quantity expression.

   A few of my friend^s live in Canada.

4. *Another* is always singular.

   Some teachers are strict. ~~Another~~ Other teachers are easy.

5. Use an indefinite pronoun to substitute for an indefinite noun.

   I need to borrow a pen. I didn't bring ~~it~~ one today.

6. *A* and *an* are always singular.

   She has ~~a~~ beautiful eyes.

7. Don't use *there* to introduce a unique, definite noun.

   ~~There's t~~T he Statue of Liberty ^is in New York.

8. Use *a* or *an* for a definition or a classification of a singular count noun.

   The Statue of Liberty is ^a monument.

9. Don't use *the* with a possessive form.

   One of my sisters lives in New York. My ~~the~~ other sister lives in New Jersey.

LESSON 14 TEST/REVIEW

PART 1 Find the mistakes with the underlined words, and correct them. Not every sentence has a mistake. If the sentence is correct, write *C*.

EXAMPLES One of her classmates is from Mexico. ~~Other~~ *Another* one is from Spain.

Most Americans own a TV. *C*

1. All of teachers at this college have a master's degree.
2. Some of the animals eat only meat. They are called "carnivores."
3. The students in this class come from many countries. Some of the students are from Poland. Another students are from Hungary.
4. A battery has two terminals. One is positive; another is negative.
5. I'm taking two classes. One is English. The other is math.
6. I lost my dictionary. I need to buy another one.
7. I lost my textbook. I think I lost it in the library.
8. I don't have a computer. Do you have it?
9. Most my teachers have a lot of experience.
10. Cuba is country.
11. Most women want to have children.
12. I have some money with me. Do you have any?
13. Very few of the students in this class have financial aid. Most of us pay tuition.
14. I have two brothers. One of my brothers is an engineer. The other my brother is a physical therapist.
15. Almost my friends come from South America.
16. There's the Golden Gate Bridge in San Francisco.

PART 2 Fill in the blanks with *the, a, an, some, any,* or Ø (for no article). In some cases, more than one answer is possible.

A: Do you want to come to my house tonight? I rented ___*some*___ (example) movies. We can make ___(1)___ popcorn and watch ___(2)___ movies together.

464 Lesson 14

B: Thanks, but I'm going to _____(3)_____ party. Do you want to go with me?

A: Where's it going to be?

B: It's going to be at Michael's apartment.

A: Who's going to be at _____(4)_____ party?

B: Most of _____(5)_____ students in my English class will be there. Each student is going to bring _____(6)_____ food.

A: _____(7)_____ life in the U.S. is strange. In my country, _____(8)_____ people don't have to bring _____(9)_____ food to a party.

B: That's the way it is in my country, too. But we're in _____(10)_____ U.S. now. I'm going to bake _____(11)_____ cake. You can make _____(12)_____ special dish from your country.

A: You know I'm _____(13)_____ terrible cook.

B: Don't worry. You can buy something. My friend Max is going to buy _____(14)_____ crackers and cheese. Why don't you bring _____(15)_____ salami or roast beef?

A: But I don't eat _____(16)_____ meat. I'm _____(17)_____ vegetarian.

B: Well, you can bring _____(18)_____ bowl of fruit.

A: That's _____(19)_____ good idea. What time does _____(20)_____ party start?

B: At 8 o'clock.

A: I have to take my brother to _____(21)_____ airport at 6:30. I don't know if I'll be back on time.

B: You don't have to arrive at 8 o'clock exactly. I'll give you _____(22)_____ address, and you can arrive any time you want.

PART 3 Fill in the blanks with *other, others, another, the other,* or *the others.*

A: I don't like my apartment.

B: Why not?

A: It's very small. It only has two closets. One is big, but ____the other____ is very small.
                                                                   (example)

B: That's not very serious. Is that the only problem? Are there _____ problems?
                                                                         (1)

A: There are many _____.
                            (2)

B: Such as?

A: Well, the landlord doesn't provide enough heat in the winter.

B: Hmm. That's a real problem. Did you complain to him?

A: I did, but he says that all _____ tenants are happy.
                                       (3)

B: Why don't you look for _____ apartment?
                                   (4)

A: I have two roommates. One wants to move, but _____ likes it here.
                                                           (5)

B: Well, if one wants to stay and _____ two want to move, why don't you move and look for _____ roommate?
                                            (6)   (7)

PART 4 Fill in the blanks with *one, some, any, it,* or *them.*

EXAMPLE I have a computer, but my roommate doesn't have ____one____.

1. Do you want to use my bicycle? I won't need _____ this afternoon.

2. I rented a movie. We can watch _____ tonight.

3. My English teacher gives some homework every day, but she doesn't give _____ on the weekends.

4. My class has a lot of Mexican students. Does your class have _____?

5. I wrote two compositions last week, but I got bad grades because I wrote _____ very quickly.

6. I don't have any problems with English, but my roommate has _____.

7. I can't remember the teacher's name. Do you remember _____?

8. You won't need any paper for the test, but you'll need _____ for the composition.

9. I went to the library to find some books in my language, but I couldn't find _____.

EXPANSION ACTIVITIES

Classroom Activities

1. Fill in the blanks with *all*, *most*, *some*, *a few*, or *very few* to make a general statement about your native country or another country you know well. Find a partner from a different country, if possible, and compare your answers.

   a. _____ banks are safe places to put your money.
   b. _____ doctors make a lot of money.
   c. _____ teenagers work.
   d. _____ children work.
   e. _____ teachers are rich.
   f. _____ government officials are rich.
   g. _____ children get an allowance.
   h. _____ people work on Saturdays.
   i. _____ businesses are closed on Sundays.
   j. _____ families own a car.
   k. _____ women work outside the home.
   l. _____ people have a college education.
   m. _____ people have servants.
   n. _____ married couples have their own apartment.
   o. _____ old people live with their grown children.
   p. _____ people speak English.
   q. _____ children study English in school.
   r. _____ parents have more than five children.

s. _____ people live in an apartment.

t. _____ young men serve in the military.

u. _____ people are happy with the political situation.

2. Bring in coins and bills from your native country or another country you've visited. Form a small group of students from different countries, and show this money to the other students in your group.

Talk About it

1. The following sayings and proverbs are about money. Discuss the meaning of each one. Do you have a similar saying in your native language?
   - All that glitters isn't gold.
   - Money is the root of all evil.
   - Friendship and money don't mix.
   - Another day, another dollar.
   - Money talks.

2. Discuss ways to save money. Discuss difficulties in saving money.

3. Discuss this saying: The difference between men and boys is the price of their toys.

Write About it

Do you think kids should get an allowance from their parents? How much? Does it depend on the child's age? Should the child have to work for the money? Write a few paragraphs.

Internet Activities

1. Look for bank rates on the Internet. Compare the interest on a one-year CD (certificate of deposit) at two banks.

2. Find a currency converter on the Web. Convert the American dollar to the currency of another country.

3. Go online to find an application for financial aid. Do you have any questions on how to fill it out?

4. Find the Web site of a college or university you are interested in. Find out the cost of tuition.

Additional Activities at **http://elt.heinle.com/gic**

Appendices

APPENDIX A

Spelling and Pronunciation of Verbs

Spelling of the -s Form of Verbs

Rule	Base Form	-s Form
Add s to most verbs to make the -s form.	hope eat	hopes eats
When the base form ends in s, z, sh, ch, or x, add es and pronounce an extra syllable, /əz/.	miss buzz wash catch fix	misses buzzes washes catches fixes
When the base form ends in a consonant + y, change the y to i and add es.	carry worry	carries worries
When the base form ends in a vowel + y, do not change the y.	pay obey	pays obeys
Add es to go and do.	go do	goes does

Three Pronunciations of the -s Form

Rule		
We pronounce /s/ if the verb ends in these voiceless sounds: /p t k f/.	hope—hopes eat—eats	pick—picks laugh—laughs
We pronounce /z/ if the verb ends in most voiced sounds.	live—lives grab—grabs read—reads	run—runs sing—sings borrow—borrows
When the base form ends in s, z, sh, ch, x, se, ge, or ce, we pronounce an extra syllable, /əz/.	miss—misses buzz—buzzes wash—washes watch—watches	fix—fixes use—uses change—changes dance—dances
These verbs have a change in the vowel sound.	do/**du**/—does/**dəz**/	say/**sei**/—says/**sez**/

Spelling of the -ing Form of Verbs

Rule	Base Form	-ing Form
Add -ing to most verbs. **Note:** Do not remove the y for the -ing form.	eat go study	eating going studying
For a one-syllable verb that ends in a consonant + vowel + consonant (CVC), double the final consonant and add -ing.	p l a n | | | C V C s t o p | | | C V C s i t | | | C V C	planning stopping sitting
Do not double the final w, x, or y.	show mix stay	showing mixing staying
For a two-syllable word that ends in CVC, double the final consonant only if the last syllable is stressed.	refér admít begín	referring admitting beginning
When the last syllable of a two-syllable word is not stressed, do not double the final consonant.	lísten ópen óffer	listening opening offering
If the word ends in a consonant + e, drop the e before adding -ing.	live take write	living taking writing

Spelling of the Past Tense of Regular Verbs

Rule	Base Form	-ed Form
Add *ed* to the base form to make the past tense of most regular verbs.	start kick	started kicked
When the base form ends in *e*, add *d* only.	die live	died lived
When the base form ends in a consonant + *y*, change the *y* to *i* and add *ed*.	carry worry	carried worried
When the base form ends in a vowel + *y*, do not change the *y*.	destroy stay	destroyed stayed
For a one-syllable word that ends in a consonant + vowel + consonant (CVC), double the final consonant and add *ed*.	s t o p | | | C V C p l u g | | | C V C	stopped plugged
Do not double the final *w* or *x*.	sew fix	sewed fixed
For a two-syllable word that ends in CVC, double the final consonant only if the last syllable is stressed.	occúr permít	occurred permitted
When the last syllable of a two-syllable word is not stressed, do not double the final consonant.	ópen háppen	opened happened

Pronunciation of Past Forms that End in -ed

The past tense with -ed has three pronunciations.

We pronounce a /**t**/ if the base form ends in these voiceless sounds: /**p, k, f, s, š, č**/.	jump—jumped cook—cooked	cough—coughed kiss—kissed	wash—washed watch—watched
We pronounce a /**d**/ if the base form ends in most voiced sounds.	rub—rubbed drag—dragged love—loved bathe—bathed use—used	charge—charged glue—glued massage—massaged name—named learn—learned	bang—banged call—called fear—feared free—freed
We pronounce an extra syllable /**əd**/ if the base form ends in a /**t**/ or /**d**/ sound.	wait—waited hate—hated	want—wanted add—added	need—needed decide—decided

APPENDIX B

Irregular Noun Plurals

Singular	Plural	Explanation
man woman mouse tooth foot goose	men women mice teeth feet geese	Vowel change (**Note:** The first vowel in *women* is pronounced /I/.)
sheep fish deer	sheep fish deer	No change
child person	children people (OR persons)	Different word form
	(eye)glasses belongings clothes goods groceries jeans pajamas pants/slacks scissors shorts	No singular form
alumnus cactus radius stimulus syllabus	alumni cacti OR cactuses radii stimuli syllabi OR syllabuses	us → i
analysis crisis hypothesis oasis parenthesis thesis	analyses crises hypotheses oases parentheses theses	is → es

Continued

Singular	Plural	Explanation
appendix index	appendices OR appendixes indices OR indexes	ix → ices OR → ixes ex → ices OR → exes
bacterium curriculum datum medium memorandum criterion phenomenon	bacteria curricula data media memoranda criteria phenomena	um → a ion → a on → a
alga formula vertebra	algae formulae OR formulas vertebrae	a → ae

APPENDIX C

Spelling Rules for Adverbs Ending in -ly

Adjective Ending	Examples	Adverb Ending	Adverb
Most endings	careful quiet serious	Add -ly.	carefully quietly seriously
-y	easy happy lucky	Change y to i and add -ly.	easily happily luckily
-e	nice free	Keep the e and add -ly.*	nicely freely
consonant + le	simple comfortable double	Drop the e and add -ly.	simply comfortably doubly
-ic	basic enthusiastic	Add -ally.**	basically enthusiastically

Exceptions:
    *true—truly
    **public—publicly			

APPENDIX D

Metric Conversion Chart

LENGTH

When You Know	Symbol	Multiply by	To Find	Symbol
inches	in	2.54	centimeters	cm
feet	ft	30.5	centimeters	cm
feet	ft	0.3	meters	m
yards	yd	0.91	meters	m
miles	mi	1.6	kilometers	km
Metric:				
centimeters	cm	0.39	inches	in
centimeters	cm	0.03	feet	ft
meters	m	3.28	feet	ft
meters	m	1.09	yards	yd
kilometers	km	0.62	miles	mi

Note:
1 foot = 12 inches; 1 yard = 3 feet or 36 inches

AREA

When You Know	Symbol	Multiply by	To Find	Symbol
square inches	in^2	6.5	square centimeters	cm^2
square feet	ft^2	0.09	square meters	m^2
square yards	yd^2	0.8	square meters	m^2
square miles	mi^2	2.6	square kilometers	km^2
Metric:				
square centimeters	cm^2	0.16	square inches	in^2
square meters	m^2	10.76	square feet	ft^2
square meters	m^2	1.2	square yards	yd^2
square kilometers	km^2	0.39	square miles	mi^2

WEIGHT (Mass)

When You Know	Symbol	Multiply by	To Find	Symbol
ounces	oz	28.35	grams	g
pounds	lb	0.45	kilograms	kg

Metric:

grams	g	0.04	ounces	oz
kilograms	kg	2.2	pounds	lb

Note:
16 ounces = 1 pound

VOLUME

When You Know	Symbol	Multiply by	To Find	Symbol
fluid ounces	fl oz	30.0	milliliters	mL
pints	pt	0.47	liters	L
quarts	qt	0.95	liters	L
gallons	gal	3.8	liters	L

Metric:

milliliters	mL	0.03	fluid ounces	fl oz
liters	L	2.11	pints	pt
liters	L	1.05	quarts	qt
liters	L	0.26	gallons	gal

TEMPERATURE

When You Know	Symbol	Do This	To Find	Symbol
degrees Fahrenheit	°F	Subtract 32, then multiply by 5/9	degrees Celsius	°C

Metric:

degrees Celsius	°C	Multiply by 9/5, then add 32	degrees Fahrenheit	°F

Sample temperatures:

Fahrenheit	Celsius	Fahrenheit	Celsius
0	−18	60	16
10	−12	70	21
20	−7	80	27
30	−1	90	32
40	4	100	38
50	10	212	100

APPENDIX E

The Verb *Get*

Get **has many meanings. Here is a list of the most common ones:**

- get something = receive

  I got a letter from my father.

- get + (to) place = arrive

  I got home at six. What time do you get to school?

- get + object + infinitive = persuade

  She got him to wash the dishes.

- get + past participle = become

get acquainted	get worried	get hurt
get engaged	get lost	get bored
get married	get accustomed to	get confused
get divorced	get used to	get scared
get tired	get dressed	

  They got married in 1989.

- get + adjective = become

get hungry	get upset	get dark
get rich	get sleepy	get angry
get nervous	get fat	get old
get well		

  It gets dark at 6:30.

- get an illness = catch

  While she was traveling, she got malaria.

- get a joke or an idea = understand

  Everybody except Tom laughed at the joke. He didn't get it.

  The boss explained the project to us, but I didn't get it.

- get ahead = advance

  He works very hard because he wants to get ahead in his job.

- get along (well) (with someone) = have a good relationship

  She doesn't get along with her mother-in-law.

  Do you and your roommate get along well?

- get around to something = find the time to do something

  I wanted to write my brother a letter yesterday, but I didn't get around to it.

- get away = escape

  The police chased the thief, but he got away.

- get away with something = escape punishment
    He cheated on his taxes and got away with it.
- get back = return
    He got back from his vacation last Saturday.
- get back at someone = get revenge
    My brother wants to get back at me for stealing his girlfriend.
- get back to someone = communicate with someone at a later time
    The boss can't talk to you today. Can she get back to you tomorrow?
- get by = have just enough but nothing more
    On her salary, she's just getting by. She can't afford a car or a vacation.
- get in trouble = be caught and punished for doing something wrong
    They got in trouble for cheating on the test.
- get in(to) = enter a car
    She got in the car and drove away quickly.
- get out (of) = leave a car
    When the taxi arrived at the theater, everyone got out.
- get on = seat oneself on a bicycle, motorcycle, horse
    She got on the motorcycle and left.
- get on = enter a train, bus, airplane
    She got on the bus and took a seat in the back.
- get off = leave a bicycle, motorcycle, horse, train, bus, airplane
    They will get off the train at the next stop.
- get out of something = escape responsibility
    My boss wants me to help him on Saturday, but I'm going to try to get out of it.
- get over something = recover from an illness or disappointment
    She has the flu this week. I hope she gets over it soon.
- get rid of someone or something = free oneself of someone or something undesirable
    My apartment has roaches, and I can't get rid of them.
- get through (to someone) = communicate, often by telephone
    She tried to explain the harm of eating fast food to her son, but she couldn't get through to him.
    I tried to call my mother many times, but her line was busy. I couldn't get through.
- get through with something = finish
    I can meet you after I get through with my homework.
- get together = meet with another person
    I'd like to see you again. When can we get together?
- get up = arise from bed
    He woke up at 6 o'clock, but he didn't get up until 6:30.

APPENDIX F

Make and *Do*

Some expressions use *make*. Others use *do*.	
Make	**Do**
make a date/an appointment	do (the) homework
make a plan	do an exercise
make a decision	do the dishes
make a telephone call	do the cleaning, laundry, ironing, washing, etc.
make a reservation	do the shopping
make a mistake	do one's best
make an effort	do a favor
make an improvement	do the right/wrong thing
make a promise	do a job
make money	do business
make noise	What do you do for a living? (asks about a job)
make the bed	How do you do? (said when you meet someone for the first time)

APPENDIX G

Nouns That Can Be Both Count or Noncount

In the following cases, the same word can be a count or a noncount noun. The meaning is different, however.

Noncount	Count
I spent a lot of *time* on my project.	I go shopping two *times* a month.
I have a lot of *experience* with computers.	I had a lot of interesting *experiences* on my trip to Europe.

In the following cases, there is a small difference in meaning. We see a noncount noun as a whole unit. We see a count noun as something that can be divided into parts.

Noncount	Count
There is a lot of *crime* in a big city.	A lot of *crimes* are never solved.
There is a lot of *opportunity* to make money in the U.S.	There are a lot of job *opportunities* in my field.
She bought a lot of *fruit*.	Oranges and lemons are *fruits* that have a lot of Vitamin C.
I don't have much *food* in my refrigerator.	Milk and butter are *foods* that contain cholesterol.
I have a lot of *trouble* with my car.	He has many *troubles* in his life.

APPENDIX H

Verbs and Adjectives Followed by a Preposition

Many verbs and adjectives are followed by a preposition.

accuse someone of
(be) accustomed to
adjust to
(be) afraid of
agree with
(be) amazed at/by
(be) angry about
(be) angry at/with
apologize for
approve of
argue about
argue with
(be) ashamed of
(be) aware of
believe in
blame someone for
(be) bored with/by
(be) capable of
care about/for
compare to/with
complain about
(be) concerned about
concentrate on
consist of
count on
deal with
decide on
depend on/upon
(be) different from
disapprove of
(be) divorced from
dream about/of
(be) engaged to
(be) excited about
(be) familiar with

(be) famous for
feel like
(be) fond of
forget about
forgive someone for
(be) glad about
(be) good at
(be) grateful to someone for
(be) guilty of
(be) happy about
hear about
hear of
hope for
(be) incapable of
insist on/upon
(be) interested in
(be) involved in
(be) jealous of
(be) known for
(be) lazy about
listen to
look at
look for
look forward to
(be) mad about
(be) mad at
(be) made from/of
(be) married to
object to
(be) opposed to
participate in
plan on
pray to
pray for
(be) prepared for/to

prevent (someone) from
prohibit (someone) from
protect (someone) from
(be) proud of
recover from
(be) related to
rely on/upon
(be) responsible for
(be) sad about
(be) satisfied with
(be) scared of
(be) sick of
(be) sorry about
(be) sorry for
speak about
speak to/with
succeed in
(be) sure of/about
(be) surprised at
take care of
talk about
talk to/with
thank (someone) for
(be) thankful (to someone) for
think about/of
(be) tired of
(be) upset about
(be) upset with
(be) used to
wait for
warn (someone) about
(be) worried about
worry about

APPENDIX I

Direct and Indirect Objects

Word order with direct and indirect objects:

The order of direct and indirect objects depends on the verb you use.

          IO   DO
He told his friend the answer.

             DO   IO
He explained the answer to his friend.

The order of the objects sometimes depends on whether you use a noun or a pronoun object.

S V   IO   DO
He gave the woman the keys.

S V   DO   IO
He gave them to her.

In some cases, the connecting preposition is *to;* in some cases, *for*. In some cases, there is no connecting preposition.

    She'll serve lunch *to* her guests.
    She reserved a seat *for* you.
    I asked him a question.

The order of direct and indirect objects depends on the verb you use. It also can depend on whether you use a noun or a pronoun as the object.

Group 1 Pronouns affect word order. The preposition used is *to*.

Patterns: He gave a present to his wife. (DO to IO)
He gave his wife a present. (IO/DO)
He gave it to his wife. (DO to IO)
He gave her a present. (IO/DO)
He gave it to her. (DO to IO)

Verbs:

bring	lend	pass	sell	show	teach
give	offer	pay	send	sing	tell
hand	owe	read	serve	take	write

Group 2 Pronouns affect word order. The preposition used is *for*.

Patterns: He bought a car for his daughter. (DO for IO)
He bought his daughter a car. (IO/DO)
He bought it for his daughter. (DO for IO)
He bought her a car. (IO/DO)
He bought it for her. (DO for IO)

Verbs:

bake	buy	draw	get	make
build	do	find	knit	reserve

Group 3 Pronouns don't affect word order. The preposition used is *to*.

Patterns: He explained the problem to his friend. (DO to IO)
He explained it to her. (DO to IO)

Verbs:

admit	introduce	recommend	say
announce	mention	repeat	speak
describe	prove	report	suggest
explain			

Group 4 Pronouns don't affect word order. The preposition used is *for*.

Patterns: He cashed a check for his friend. (DO for IO)
He cashed it for her. (DO for IO)

Verbs:

answer	change	design	open	prescribe
cash	close	fix	prepare	pronounce

Group 5 Pronouns don't affect word order. No preposition is used.

Patterns: She asked the teacher a question. (IO/DO)
She asked him a question. (IO/DO)
It took me five minutes to answer the question. (IO/DO)

Verbs:

ask	charge	cost	wish	take (with time)

APPENDIX J

Capitalization Rules

- The first word in a sentence: **M**y friends are helpful.
- The word "I": My sister and **I** took a trip together.
- Names of people: **M**ichael **J**ordan; **G**eorge **W**ashington
- Titles preceding names of people: **D**octor (**D**r.) **S**mith; **P**resident **L**incoln; **Q**ueen **E**lizabeth; **M**r. **R**ogers; **M**rs. **C**arter
- Geographic names: the **U**nited **S**tates; **L**ake **S**uperior; **C**alifornia; the **R**ocky **M**ountains; the **M**ississippi **R**iver

    NOTE: The word "the" in a geographic name is not capitalized.

- Street names: **P**ennsylvania **A**venue (**A**ve.); **W**all **S**treet (**S**t.); **A**bbey **R**oad (**R**d.)
- Names of organizations, companies, colleges, buildings, stores, hotels: the **R**epublican **P**arty; **T**homson **H**einle; **D**artmouth **C**ollege; the **U**niversity of **W**isconsin; the **W**hite **H**ouse; **B**loomingdale's; the **H**ilton **H**otel
- Nationalities and ethnic groups: **M**exicans; **C**anadians; **S**paniards; **A**mericans; **J**ews; **K**urds; **E**skimos
- Languages: **E**nglish; **S**panish; **P**olish; **V**ietnamese; **R**ussian
- Months: **J**anuary; **F**ebruary
- Days: **S**unday; **M**onday
- Holidays: **C**hristmas; **I**ndependence **D**ay
- Important words in a title: **G**rammar in **C**ontext; **T**he **O**ld **M**an and the **S**ea; **R**omeo and **J**uliet; **T**he **S**ound of **M**usic

    NOTE: Capitalize "the" as the first word of a title.

APPENDIX K

Glossary of Grammatical Terms

- **Adjective** An adjective gives a description of a noun.

    It's a *tall* tree.   He's an *old* man.   My neighbors are *nice*.

- **Adverb** An adverb describes the action of a sentence or an adjective or another adverb.

    She speaks English *fluently*.   I drive *carefully*.
    She speaks English *extremely* well.   She is *very* intelligent.

- **Adverb of Frequency** An adverb of frequency tells how often the action happens.

    I *never* drink coffee.   They *usually* take the bus.

- **Affirmative** means *yes*.
- **Apostrophe** ' We use the apostrophe for possession and contractions.
    My *sister's* friend is beautiful.　　Today *isn't* Sunday.
- **Article** The definite article is *the*. The indefinite articles are *a* and *an*.
    I have *a* cat.　　I ate *an* apple.　　*The* president was late.
- **Auxiliary Verb** Some verbs have two parts: an auxiliary verb and a main verb.
    He *can't* study.　　We *will* return.
- **Base Form** The base form, sometimes called the "simple" form of the verb, has no tense. It has no ending (*-s* or *-ed*): *be, go, eat, take, write*.
    He doesn't *know* the answer.　　I didn't *go* out.
    You shouldn't *talk* loudly.
- **Capital Letter** A B C D E F G . . .
- **Clause** A clause is a group of words that has a subject and a verb. Some sentences have only one clause.
    She found a good job.

    Some sentences have a **main clause** and a **dependent clause.**

MAIN CLAUSE	DEPENDENT CLAUSE (**reason clause**)
She found a good job	because she has computer skills.
MAIN CLAUSE	DEPENDENT CLAUSE (**time clause**)
She'll turn off the light	before she goes to bed.
MAIN CLAUSE	DEPENDENT CLAUSE (***if* clause**)
I'll take you to the doctor	if you don't have your car on Saturday.

- **Colon :**
- **Comma ,**
- **Comparative Form** A comparative form of an adjective or adverb is used to compare two things.
    My house is *bigger* than your house.
    Her husband drives *faster* than she does.
- **Complement** The complement of the sentence is the information after the verb. It completes the verb phrase.
    He works *hard*.　　I slept *for five hours*.　　They are *late*.
- **Consonant** The following letters are consonants: *b, c, d, f, g, h, j, k, l, m, n, p, q, r, s, t, v, w, x, y, z*.
    NOTE: *y* is sometimes considered a vowel, as in the word *syllable*.
- **Contraction** A contraction is made up of two words put together with an apostrophe.
    He's my brother.　　*You're* late.　　They *won't* talk to me.
    (*He's = he is*)　　(*You're = you are*)　　(*won't = will not*)

- **Count Noun** Count nouns are nouns that we can count. They have a singular and a plural form.

    1 pen — 3 pens   1 table — 4 tables

- **Dependent Clause** See **Clause**.
- **Direct Object** A direct object is a noun (phrase) or pronoun that receives the action of the verb.

    We saw *the movie*.   You have *a nice car*.   I love *you*.

- **Exclamation Mark !**
- **Frequency Words** Frequency words are *always, usually, often, sometimes, rarely, seldom,* and *never.*

    I *never* drink coffee.   We *always* do our homework.

- **Hyphen** -
- **Imperative** An imperative sentence gives a command or instructions. An imperative sentence omits the word *you*.

    Come here.   *Don't be* late.   Please *sit* down.

- **Indefinite Pronoun** An indefinite pronoun (*one, some, any*) takes the place of an indefinite noun.

    I have a cell phone. Do you have *one?*

    I didn't drink any coffee, but you drank *some.* Did he drink *any?*

- **Infinitive** An infinitive is *to* + base form.

    I want *to leave*.   You need *to be* here on time.

- **Linking Verb** A linking verb is a verb that links the subject to the noun or adjective after it. Linking verbs include *be, seem, feel, smell, sound, look, appear, taste*.

    She *is* a doctor.   She *seems* very intelligent.   She *looks* tired.

- **Modal** The modal verbs are *can, could, shall, should, will, would, may, might,* and *must*.

    They *should* leave.   I *must* go.

- **Negative** means *no*.
- **Nonaction Verb** A nonaction verb has no action. We do not use a continuous tense (*be* + verb *-ing*) with a nonaction verb. The nonaction verbs are: *believe, cost, care, have, hear, know, like, love, matter, mean, need, own, prefer, remember, see, seem, think, understand,* and *want*.

    She *has* a laptop.   We *love* our mother.

- **Noncount Noun** A noncount noun is a noun that we don't count. It has no plural form.

    She drank some *water*.   He prepared some *rice*.

    Do you need any *money?*

- **Noun** A noun is a person (*brother*), a place (*kitchen*), or a thing (*table*). Nouns can be either count (*1 table, 2 tables*) or noncount (*money, water*).

    My *brother* lives in California.   My *sisters* live in New York.
    I get *mail* from my family.

- **Noun Modifier** A noun modifier makes a noun more specific.

    fire department   *Independence* Day   *can* opener

- **Noun Phrase** A noun phrase is a group of words that form the subject or object of the sentence.

    A very nice woman helped me at registration.
    I bought *a big box of candy*.

- **Object** The object of the sentence follows a verb. It receives the action of the verb.

    He bought *a car*.   I saw *a movie*.   I met *your brother*.

- **Object Pronoun** Use object pronouns (*me, you, him, her, it, us, them*) after the verb or preposition.

    He likes *her*.   I saw the movie. Let's talk about *it*.

- **Paragraph** A paragraph is a group of sentences about one topic.

- **Parentheses ( )**

- **Participle, Past** The past participle is verb + *-d* or *-ed*.

    They have *worked*.

- **Participle, Present** The present participle is verb + *-ing*.

    She is *sleeping*.   They were *laughing*.

- **Period .**

- **Phrase** A group of words that go together.

    Last month my sister came to visit.
    There is a strange car *in front of my house*.

- **Plural** Plural means more than one. A plural noun usually ends with *-s*.

    She has beautiful *eyes*.

- **Possessive Form** Possessive forms show ownership or relationship.

    Mary's coat is in the closet.   *My* brother lives in Miami.

- **Preposition** A preposition is a short connecting word: *about, above, across, after, around, as, at, away, back, before, behind, below, by, down, for, from, in, into, like, of, off, on, out, over, to, under, up, with*.

    The book is *on* the table.

- **Pronoun** A pronoun takes the place of a noun.

    I have a new car. I bought *it* last week.
    John likes Mary, but *she* doesn't like *him*.

- **Punctuation** Period . Comma , Colon : Semicolon ; Question Mark ? Exclamation Mark !

- **Question Mark ?**

- **Quotation Marks " "**
- **Regular Verb** A regular verb forms its past tense with *-ed*.
    He *worked* yesterday.   I *laughed* at the joke.
- **s Form** A present tense verb that ends in *-s* or *-es*.
    He *lives* in New York.   She *watches* TV a lot.
- **Sense-Perception Verb** A sense-perception verb has no action. It describes a sense.
    She *feels* fine.   The coffee *smells* fresh.   The milk *tastes* sour.
- **Sentence** A sentence is a group of words that contains a subject[1] and a verb (at least) and gives a complete thought.
    SENTENCE: She came home.
    NOT A SENTENCE: When she came home
- **Simple Form of Verb** The simple form of the verb, also called the base form, has no tense; it never has an *-s*, *-ed*, or *-ing* ending.
    Did you *see* the movie?   I couldn't *find* your phone number.
- **Singular** Singular means one.
    She ate a *sandwich*.   I have one *television*.
- **Subject** The subject of the sentence tells who or what the sentence is about.
    My sister got married last April. *The wedding* was beautiful.
- **Subject Pronouns** Use subject pronouns (*I, you, he, she, it, we, you, they*) before a verb.
    They speak Japanese.   *We* speak Spanish.
- **Superlative Form** A superlative form of an adjective or adverb shows the number one item in a group of three or more.
    January is the *coldest* month of the year.
    My brother speaks English the *best* in my family.
- **Syllable** A syllable is a part of a word that has only one vowel sound. (Some words have only one syllable.)
    change (one syllable)   after (af·ter = two syllables)
    look (one syllable)   responsible (re·spon·si·ble = four syllables)
- **Tag Question** A tag question is a short question at the end of a sentence. It is used in conversation.
    You speak Spanish, *don't you*?   He's not happy, *is he*?
- **Tense** A verb has tense. Tense shows when the action of the sentence happened.
    SIMPLE PRESENT: She usually *works* hard.
    FUTURE: She *will work* tomorrow.
    PRESENT CONTINUOUS: She *is working* now.
    SIMPLE PAST: She *worked* yesterday.

[1] In an imperative sentence, the subject *you* is omitted: *Sit down. Come here.*

- **Verb** A verb is the action of the sentence.
    He *runs* fast.   I *speak* English.

    Some verbs have no action. They are linking verbs. They connect the subject to the rest of the sentence.
    He *is* tall.   She *looks* beautiful.   You *seem* tired.

- **Vowel** The following letters are vowels: *a, e, i, o, u*. *Y* is sometimes considered a vowel (for example, in the word *syllable*).

APPENDIX L

Special Uses of Articles

No Article	Article
Personal names: 　John Kennedy 　Michael Jordan	The whole family: 　the Kennedys 　the Jordans
Title and name: 　Queen Elizabeth 　Pope John Paul	Title without name: 　the Queen 　the Pope
Cities, states, countries, continents: 　Cleveland 　Ohio 　Mexico 　South America	Places that are considered a union: 　the United States 　the former Soviet Union 　the United Kingdom Place names: the _____ of _____ 　the Republic of China 　the District of Columbia
Mountains: 　Mount Everest 　Mount McKinley	Mountain ranges: 　the Himalayas 　the Rocky Mountains
Islands: 　Coney Island 　Staten Island	Collectives of islands: 　the Hawaiian Islands 　the Virgin Islands 　the Philippines
Lakes: 　Lake Superior 　Lake Michigan	Collectives of lakes: 　the Great Lakes 　the Finger Lakes

Continued

Beaches: 　Palm Beach 　Pebble Beach	**Rivers, oceans, seas, canals:** 　the Mississippi River 　the Atlantic Ocean 　the Dead Sea 　the Panama Canal
Streets and avenues: 　Madison Avenue 　Wall Street	**Well-known buildings:** 　the Sears Tower 　the Empire State Building
Parks: 　Central Park 　Hyde Park	**Zoos:** 　the San Diego Zoo 　the Milwaukee Zoo
Seasons: 　summer　　fall 　spring　　winter 　Summer is my favorite season. NOTE: After a preposition, *the* may be used. 　In (the) winter, my car runs badly.	**Deserts:** 　the Mojave Desert 　the Sahara Desert
Directions: 　north　　south 　east　　west	**Sections of a piece of land:** 　the Southwest (of the U.S.) 　the West Side (of New York)
School subjects: 　history 　math	**Unique geographical points:** 　the North Pole 　the Vatican
Name + *college* or *university*: 　Northwestern University 　Bradford College	**The University (College) of _____:** 　the University of Michigan 　the College of DuPage County
Magazines: 　*Time* 　*Sports Illustrated*	**Newspapers:** 　the *Tribune* 　the *Wall Street Journal*
Months and days: 　September 　Monday	**Ships:** 　the *Titanic* 　the *Queen Elizabeth*
Holidays and dates **(Month + Day):** 　Thanksgiving 　Mother's Day 　July 4	**The day of (month):** 　the Fourth of July 　the fifth of May
Diseases: 　cancer　　AIDS 　polio　　malaria	**Ailments:** 　a cold　　a toothache 　a headache　　the flu

Games and sports: 　poker 　soccer	Musical instruments, after *play*: 　the drums 　the piano NOTE: Sometimes *the* is omitted. 　She plays (the) drums.
Languages: 　French 　English	The _____ language: 　the French language 　the English language
Last month, year, week, etc. = the one before this one: 　I forgot to pay my rent last month. 　The teacher gave us a test last week.	The last month, the last year, the last week, etc. = the last in a series: 　December is the last month of the year. 　Summer vacation begins the last week in May.
In office = in an elected position: 　The president is in office for four years.	In the office = in a specific room: 　The teacher is in the office.
In back/front: 　She's in back of the car.	In the back/the front: 　He's in the back of the bus.

APPENDIX M

Alphabetical List of Irregular Verb Forms

Base Form	Past Form	Past Participle	Base Form	Past Form	Past Participle
be	was/were	been	bite	bit	bitten
bear	bore	born/borne	bleed	bled	bled
beat	beat	beaten	blow	blew	blown
become	became	become	break	broke	broken
begin	began	begun	breed	bred	bred
bend	bent	bent	bring	brought	brought
bet	bet	bet	broadcast	broadcast	broadcast
bid	bid	bid	build	built	built
bind	bound	bound	burst	burst	burst

Continued

Base Form	Past Form	Past Participle	Base Form	Past Form	Past Participle
buy	bought	bought	hide	hid	hidden
cast	cast	cast	hit	hit	hit
catch	caught	caught	hold	held	held
choose	chose	chosen	hurt	hurt	hurt
cling	clung	clung	keep	kept	kept
come	came	come	know	knew	known
cost	cost	cost	lay	laid	laid
creep	crept	crept	lead	led	led
cut	cut	cut	leave	left	left
deal	dealt	dealt	lend	loaned/lent	loaned/lent
dig	dug	dug	let	let	let
dive	dove/dived	dove/dived	lie	lay	lain
do	did	done	light	lit/lighted	lit/lighted
draw	drew	drawn	lose	lost	lost
drink	drank	drunk	make	made	made
drive	drove	driven	mean	meant	meant
eat	ate	eaten	meet	met	met
fall	fell	fallen	mistake	mistook	mistaken
feed	fed	fed	overcome	overcame	overcome
feel	felt	felt	overdo	overdid	overdone
fight	fought	fought	overtake	overtook	overtaken
find	found	found	overthrow	overthrew	overthrown
fit	fit	fit	pay	paid	paid
flee	fled	fled	plead	pled/pleaded	pled/pleaded
fly	flew	flown	prove	proved	proven/proved
forbid	forbade	forbidden	put	put	put
forget	forgot	forgotten	quit	quit	quit
forgive	forgave	forgiven	read	read	read
freeze	froze	frozen	ride	rode	ridden
get	got	gotten	ring	rang	rung
give	gave	given	rise	rose	risen
go	went	gone	run	ran	run
grind	ground	ground	say	said	said
grow	grew	grown	see	saw	seen
hang	hung	hung[2]	seek	sought	sought
have	had	had	sell	sold	sold
hear	heard	heard	send	sent	sent

[2] *Hanged* is used as the past form to refer to punishment by death. *Hung* is used in other situations: She *hung* the picture on the wall.

Base Form	Past Form	Past Participle	Base Form	Past Form	Past Participle
set	set	set	swing	swung	swung
sew	sewed	sewed/sown	take	took	taken
shake	shook	shaken	teach	taught	taught
shed	shed	shed	tear	tore	torn
shine	shone/shined	shone	tell	told	told
shoot	shot	shot	think	thought	thought
show	showed	shown/showed	throw	threw	thrown
shrink	shrank/shrunk	shrunk/shrunked	understand	understood	understood
shut	shut	shut	uphold	upheld	upheld
sing	sang	sung	upset	upset	upset
sink	sank	sunk	wake	woke	woken
sit	sat	sat	wear	wore	worn
sleep	slept	slept	weave	wove	woven
slide	slid	slid	wed	wedded/wed	wedded/wed
slit	slit	slit	weep	wept	wept
speak	spoke	spoken	win	won	won
speed	sped	sped	wind	wound	wound
spend	spent	spent	withhold	withheld	withheld
spin	spun	spun	withdraw	withdrew	withdrawn
spit	spit	spit	withstand	withstood	withstood
split	split	split	wring	wrung	wrung
spread	spread	spread	write	wrote	written
spring	sprang	sprung			
stand	stood	stood			
steal	stole	stolen			
stick	stuck	stuck			
sting	stung	stung			
stink	stank	stunk			
strike	struck	struck/stricken			
strive	strove	striven			
swear	swore	sworn			
sweep	swept	swept			
swell	swelled	swelled/swollen			
swim	swam	swum			

Note:
The past and past participle of some verbs can end in *-ed* or *-t*.

burn	burned or burnt
dream	dreamed or dreamt
kneel	kneeled or knelt
learn	learned or learnt
leap	leaped or leapt
spill	spilled or spilt
spoil	spoiled or spoilt

APPENDIX N

The United States of America: Major Cities

AL Alabama	HI Hawaii	MA Massachusetts	NM New Mexico	SD South Dakota
AK Alaska	ID Idaho	MI Michigan	NY New York	TN Tennessee
AZ Arizona	IL Illinois	MN Minnesota	NC North Carolina	TX Texas
AR Arkansas	IN Indiana	MS Mississippi	ND North Dakota	UT Utah
CA California	IA Iowa	MO Missouri	OH Ohio	VT Vermont
CO Colorado	KS Kansas	MT Montana	OK Oklahoma	VA Virginia
CT Connecticut	KY Kentucky	NE Nebraska	OR Oregon	WA Washington
DE Delaware	LA Louisiana	NV Nevada	PA Pennsylvania	WV West Virginia
FL Florida	ME Maine	NH New Hampshire	RI Rhode Island	WI Wisconsin
GA Georgia	MD Maryland	NJ New Jersey	SC South Carolina	WY Wyoming
				DC* District of Columbia

*The District of Columbia is not a state. Washington, D.C. is the capital of the United States.
Note: Washinton, D.C., and Washington state are not the same.

North America

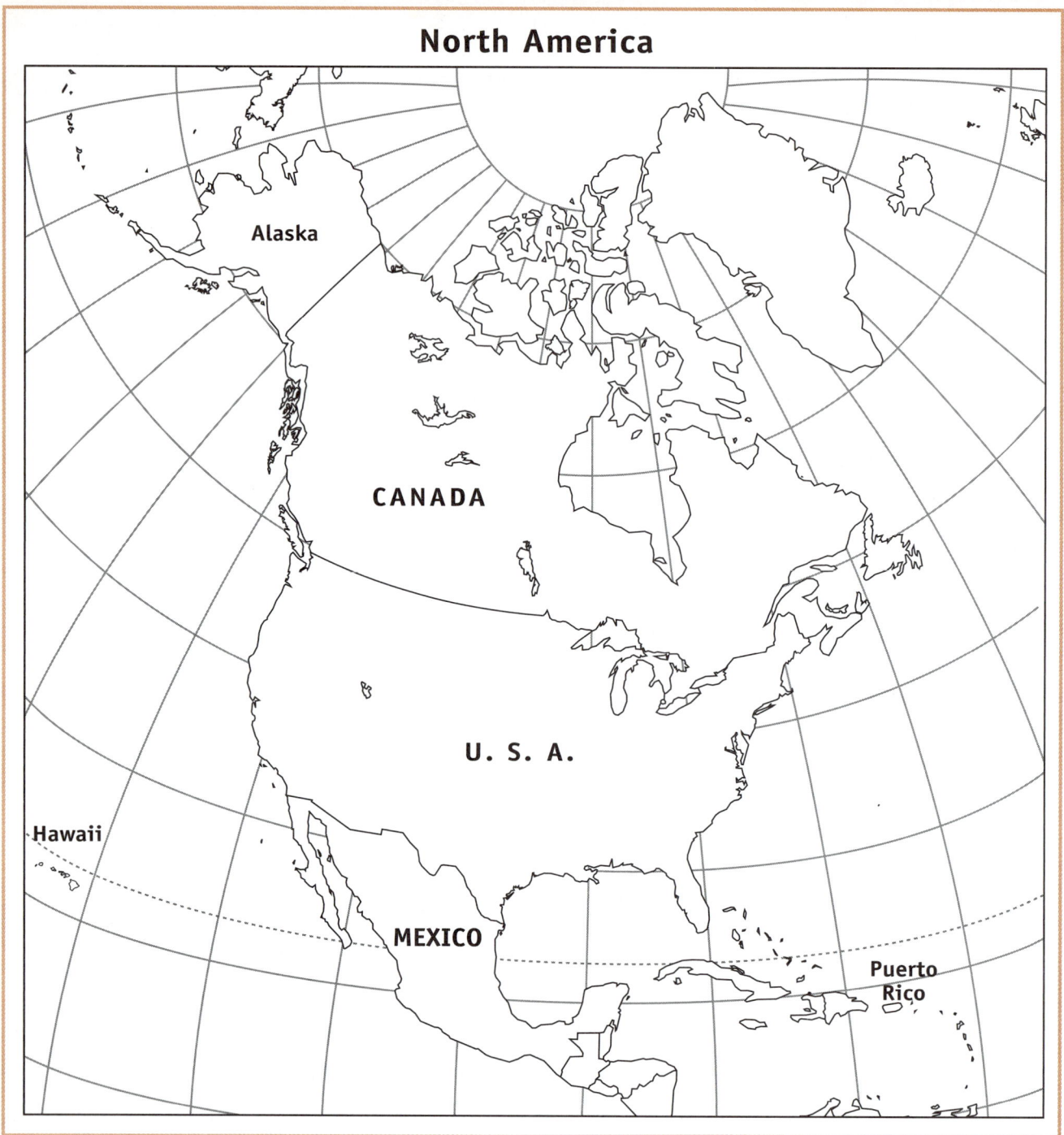

Index

A

A, 169–170, 438–442. *See also* Articles; Quantity words/expressions
Abstract nouns, 158
Action verbs, 59–64
Active voice, 414
  vs. passive voice, 424–429
Adjective(s), 190–192
  comparative, 379, 386–404
  definition of, 354
  editing advice for, 205–206
  equality with, 396
  infinitives after, 331–333
  -ly ending for, 196
  possessive, 119–120
  prepositions after, 322–323, AP12
  as subjects, 329–331
  superlative, 376–385, 379
  vs. adverbs, 198
Adjective clauses, 354–369
  definition of, 354
  editing advice for, 370–371
  formal vs. informal, 363–364
  prepositions in, 363–364
  punctuation of, 362, 365
  relative clause as subject of, 356–358
  superlative, 376–403
  vs. adjectives, 354
  when/where in, 362–363
  whose + noun in, 365–369

Adverb(s)
  comparative, 379, 386–404
  editing advice for, 205–206
  -ly ending for, 196
  in comparative/superlative form, 379, 386
  spelling rules for, AP5
  of manner, 196–198
  in passive voice, 416
  with past participles, 283–284
  spelling of, AP5
  superlative, 376–385, 379
  vs. adjectives, 198
Adverbial phrases, gerunds in, 325–326
A few, 174–179
  vs. *few*, 175, 449
After, 216
Ago, 216–217
Alike, 398–400
A little, 174–179
  vs. *little*, 175, 449
All, plural nouns with, 155
A lot of, 171–172
  vs. *enough*, 203–204
  vs. *too much/too many*, 172–174, 203
Already, 283
  in present perfect tense with indefinite past time, 302
Always, 285. *See also* Frequency words
Am, 3, 46. *See also Be*

An, 438–442. *See also* Articles
And
  between adjectives, 190
  in present continuous tense, 46
Another, 452–455
Any, 440–442
Apostrophe, for possessive nouns, 117
Are, 3, 46. *See also Be*
Articles
  definite, 438, 442–445
  editing advice for, 463
  in generalizations, 154, 445–449
  indefinite, 438–442
  before nouns, 440–442
  overview of, 438–439
  with quantity words, 169, 449–450
  with *there* + form of *be*, 164
  uses of, AP20–22
A.S.A.P., 391
As . . . as, 391–392
  for equality, 396
As many/much . . . as, 393–394
As soon as possible (A.S.A.P.), 391
As usual, 198
At all, 299
Auxiliary verbs
  in comparatives, 386
  with past participles, 278
  with present participles, 293

Index   **I1**

B

Base form, of verbs, 15
Be
   adjectives after, 190
   in definitions, 439
   with frequency words, 29
   in passive voice, 415
   in present continuous tense, 46–48
      contractions with, 46
   in present perfect tense, 278
      contractions with, 282
   in questions with *ever*, 31
   in simple past tense, 94–95
   in simple present tense
      contractions with, 5, 9
      forms of, 3
      questions with, 8–9, 19
      uses of, 3–4
   with superlatives, 384
   with *there*, 164–166
Before, 216
Be going to
   future tense with, 69–74
   prepositions with, 69
   vs. *will*, 72–74
Be like, 400–401
Be not supposed to, 253
Be supposed to
   obligation with, 244–246
   vs. *must*, 244
Better/better not, 250
Be used to, vs. *used to*, 341–344
British form, of *have*, 17
By
   in passive voice, 414, 415, 424
   with reflexive pronouns, 131
   in time expressions, 216

C

Can, 246–248
   for politeness, 265
   pronunciation of, 246
Cannot, 253
   contraction of, 240, 246, 253

Can't, 240, 246, 253
   pronunciation of, 246
Capitalization, AP15
Cities, major U.S., AP25
Classification, indefinite article for, 438–439
Commas
   for adjective clauses, 362
   between adjectives, 190
   for past continuous tense, 221
   for time/*if* clause, 75
Comparatives, 376, 386–404
   with *as . . . as*, 391–392
   with *be like*, 400–401
   with *different from*, 401–404
   editing advice for, 405–406
   for equality, 396–398
   forms of, 386–404
   irregular, 379
   with *as many/much . . . as*, 393–394
   with *same as*, 401–404
   with *the same . . . as*, 395–396
   for similarity, 398–404
   spelling rules for, 379
   word order for, 388–390
Complement
   questions about, 135
   with *there* + form of *be*, 164
Compound subjects/objects, pronouns for, 141–142
Conclusions, *must* for, 259–261
Connectors
   between adjectives, 190
   in present continuous tense, 46
Contractions
   of *be*, 5, 9, 46
   of *cannot*, 240, 246, 253
   of *do not*, 17, 253, 265
   of *had better*, 250
   of *has/have*, 17, 282–283
   of *have got to*, 242
   of *must not*, 240

   negative modal, 240, 246, 250
   in present perfect tense, 282–283
   of *should not*, 240, 250
   of *there is*, 164
   of *was not*, 218
   of *were not*, 218
   of *will not*, 66, 240, 261
Cost, questions about, 23
Could, 246–248
   for politeness, 265
Could not, contraction of, 240, 246
Count nouns, 158, 159–162, AP11
   quantities with, 162. *See also* Quantity words/expressions
Courtesy, modals and questions for, 265–268

D

Deductions, *must* for, 259–261
Definite articles, 438, 442–445. *See also* Articles
Definite nouns, 452–455
Definite pronouns, 458–461
Definitions, articles in, 439
Did. See Do
Different from, 401–404
Direct objects, 127–128, AP13–14
Do, AP10
   with continuous present tense, 56
   in questions, 51
   negative contractions of, 17, 253, 265
   in questions about complement, 135–139
   in questions with *ever*, 31
   in simple past tense, in questions, 103–104
   in simple present tense
      in affirmative statements, 15

in negative statements, 17
in questions, 19, 56
Don't have to, 253
During, 216

E

-ed ending
  for adjectives, 190
  for verbs
    in past participle, 280
    in present perfect tense, 280
    pronunciation of, AP3
    in simple past tense, 96–97
    spelling of, AP3
Editing advice
  for adjective clauses, 370–371
  for adjectives, 205–206
  for adverbs, 205–206
  for count/noncount words, 180–181
  for future tense, 80–81
  for gerunds, 346–347
  for habitual past tense, 107
  for infinitives, 346–347
  for modals and related expressions, 270–271
  for noun modifiers, 205
  for passive voice, 431
  for past continuous tense, 232
  for present continuous perfect tense, 309–310
  for present continuous tense, 80–81
  for present perfect tense, 309–310
  for quantity expressions, 180–181
  for simple past tense, 106–107
  for simple present tense, 33–36
  for singular and plural forms, 180
for *there* + form of *be*, 180–181
for time words/expressions, 232
Enough
  vs. *a lot of*, 203–204
  vs. *too*, 201–202
  vs. *very*, 203–204
Equality, comparatives for, 396–398
-er, in comparatives, 378, 379
+es form, of plural nouns, 151–154
-est, in superlatives, 378, 379
Ever
  in present perfect tense with indefinite past time, 302
  questions with, 31
  with superlatives, 378
Every, singular nouns with, 155

F

Few, vs. *a few*, 175, 449
For
  with infinitives as subjects, 329
  in time expressions, 216, 285, 295
Frequency words
  in *how often* questions, 32
  position of, 29
  simple present tense with, 27–33
  with *will*, 66
From, in time expressions, 216
Future tense
  with *be going to*, 69–74
  editing advice for, 80–81
  with time/*if* clause, 75–79
  uses of, 80
  with *will*, 66–68

G

Generalizations, 445–449
Gerunds, 316–326
  in adverbial phrases, 325–326
  after prepositions, 322–326
  after verbs, 320–321, 335
  with *be used to*, 341–344
  editing advice for, 346–347
  negative, 316, 318
  as noun modifiers, 192
  overview of, 316–317
  as subjects, 318–320, 329
Get
  adjectives vs. adverbs with, 198
  uses of, AP8–9
Glossary of grammatical terms, AP15–20
Go
  with gerunds, 320
  in simple present tense, 15
Going to, with *be*, 69–74
"*Gonna*," 69
Good/well, 196, 198
"*Gotta*," 242
Got to, pronunciation of, 242
Grammatical terms, AP15–20

H

Habitual past tense, 90–93
  editing advice for, 107
Had better, 250–253
Had better not, 253
Had to, 242
"*Hafta*," 242
Hard vs. *hardly*, 196
Has/have
  as action verb, 59, 295
  in active vs. passive voice, 424
  contractions of, 17, 282–283
  as nonaction verb, 59, 295
  with past participles, 278
  with present participles, 293
  in present perfect continuous tense, 293
  in simple present tense
    in affirmative statements, 15

Has/have (continued)
   in negative statements, 17
   in questions, 19
   vs. *must*, 253
"*Hasta*," 242
Has to/have to, 242–243
   pronunciation of, 242
Have. See Has/have
Have got to, 242–243
   contraction of, 242
Help, verb vs. infinitive after, 336
How long, 285, 290
How often, 32

I

Identification, indefinite article for, 438–439
+ies form, of plural nouns, 151–154
In
   with *be going to*, 69
   in time expressions, 216
Indefinite articles, 438–442. *See also* Articles
   in classification/identification, 438–439
   in generalizations, 445–449
Indefinite nouns, 452–455
Indefinite pronouns, 458–461
Indirect objects, 127–128, AP13–14
Infinitives, 327–344
   after adjectives, 331–332
   after verbs, 323, 333–335
   editing advice for, 346–347
   forms of, 327
   objects before, 336–338
   to show purpose, 338–339
   as subjects, 329–331
-ing ending
   for adjectives, 190
   for gerunds, 316
   for verbs
      in past continuous tense, 218, 220, 230
      in present continuous tense, 46
      in present perfect continuous tense, 293
   spelling of, AP2
In order to, 338
Irregular comparatives, 379
Irregular noun plurals, 152, AP4
Irregular superlatives, 379
Irregular verbs, 282, AP22–24
   past participles of, 280–282
   -s form of, 15
   simple past tense of, 98–101
Is, 3, 46. *See also Be*
It
   with infinitives as subjects, 329
   passive voice after, 424

L

Late vs. *lately*, 196
Like, for similarity, 398–400
Little, vs. *a little*, 175, 449
Live, 56
-ly ending
   for adjectives, 196
   for adverbs, 196
      in comparative/superlative form, 379, 386
   spelling rules for, AP5

M

Make, AP10
Many, 171–172
Maps
   of major U.S. cities, AP26
   of North America, AP26
May, 246–248, 261–263
   for politeness, 265
Maybe, 261
May/might, 261–263
May not, 240, 253
Meaning, questions about, 23
Metric conversion charts, AP6–7
Might, 261–263
Modals and related expressions, 238–269
   can/may/could, 246–248
   contractions of, 240, 246, 250
   definition of, 238
   editing advice for, 270–271
   list of, 238
   must/be supposed to, 244–245
   must for conclusions, 259–261
   must for obligation, 244–246
   must/have to/have got to, 242–243
   negatives of, 240, 253–257
   for politeness, 265–268
   questions with, 241
   should/had better, 250–253
   statements with, 241
   verb form with, 238
   will and *may/might*, 261–263
More than, 386
Much, 171–172
Must, 242–243
   for conclusions, 259–261
   for obligation, 244–246
   vs. *be supposed to*, 244
   vs. *had better*, 250
   vs. *have*, 253
   vs. *should*, 250
Must not, 253, 259
   contraction of, 240

N

Names, possessive form of, 117
Negative contractions. *See* Contractions
Negative forms, of modals, 240
Negative questions
   with *be going to*, 69
   with modals, 241
   in past continuous tense, 220

in present continuous tense, 51
in present perfect continuous tense, 294
in present perfect tense, 284–285
in simple past tense, 103–105
with *was/were*, 94
with *will*, 66
Negative statements
with *be going to*, 69
with *do*, 17
in habitual past tense, 90
with modals, 241
in passive voice, 421–422
in past continuous tense, 220
in present continuous tense, 51
in present perfect continuous tense, 292, 294
in present perfect tense, 284–285
in simple past tense, 101–102
in simple present tense, 17
with *there* + form of *be*, 164
with *was/were*, 94
with *will*, 66
Never. See also Frequency words
verb with, 31
No, 169–170
Nonaction verbs, 59–64
examples of, 295
Noncount nouns, 158–162, AP11
quantities with, 162. *See also* Quantity words/expressions
North America, map of, AP26
Not have to, 253
Noun(s)
abstract, 158
articles before, 440–442
comparatives before, 388
count, 158, 159–162, AP11
definite, 452–455
equality with, 396
indefinite, 452–455
noncount, 158–162, AP11
plural, 151–154
editing advice for, 180
generalizations about, 154–155
irregular, 152, AP4
possessive forms of, 117–118
special cases of, 155–156
possessive forms of, 117–118
singular
editing advice for, 180
generalizations about, 154–155
special cases of, 155–156
superlatives before, 384
with *there*, 164–166
Noun modifiers, 192–193
editing advice for, 205
n't, for contractions, 282

O

Object(s)
compound, pronouns for, 142
direct, 127–128, AP13–14
indirect, 127–128, AP13–14
before infinitive, 336–338
position of, 127–128
Object pronouns, 124–125
Obligation, *must* for, 244–246
Often. See Frequency words
On, in time expressions, 216
One of the, with superlatives, 378
Or, in present continuous tense, 46
Other, 452–455

P

Participles. *See* Past participles; Present participles
Passive voice, 414–429
editing advice for, 431
forms of, 416
negative statements in, 421–422
overview of, 414–416
questions in, 421–422
uses of, 417
vs. active voice, 424–429
Past continuous tense, 218–230
editing advice for, 232
forms of, 220
overview of, 218–220
time clause in, 221–225, 228–231
uses of, 221–225
vs. simple past tense, 229–230
with *was/were going to*, 226–227
with *when*, 228–229
Past participles, 278–282
adverbs with, 283–284
of irregular verbs, 281–282, AP22–24
in passive voice, 415
Past tense
of *be*, 94–95
continuous, 218–230. *See also* Past continuous tense
habitual, 90–93
simple, 94–107. *See also* Simple past tense
People, vs. *persons*, 152
Plural nouns, 151–154
editing advice for, 180
generalizations about, 154–155
possessive forms of, 117–118
special cases of, 155–156
Politeness, modals and questions for, 265–268

Possessive form, 120–123
  for adjectives, 119–120
  editing advice for, 141–142
  noun modifiers and, 192
  for nouns, 117–118, 192
  for pronouns, 120–123
Prepositions
  in adjective clauses, 363–364
  in adverbial phrases, gerunds after, 325–326
  after adjectives, 322–323, AP12
  after verbs, 322–323, AP12
  with *be going to*, 69
  gerunds after, 322–326
  object pronouns after, 124
  with questions, 21, 51
  in time expressions, 216–217, 295
Present continuous tense, 43–64
  connectors in, 46
  editing advice for, 80–81
  with future meaning, 72
  for longer actions, 49–51
  questions with, 51–55
  for trends, 49–51
  uses of, 46–51, 56, 79
  vs. simple present tense, 56–58
Present participles
  in present continuous tense, 46
  in present perfect continuous tense, 293
Present perfect continuous tense, 292–298
  editing advice for, 309–310
  forms of, 293
  overview of, 292
  questions in, 292, 294
  statements in, 292, 294
  uses of, 295–298
  vs. present perfect tense, 309
Present perfect tense, 278–314

  for continuation from past to present, 285–288
  contractions in, 282–283
  editing advice for, 309–310
  forms of, 278
  with indefinite past time, 302–303
  overview of, 278–280
  past participle in, 278–282
  questions in, 284–285, 304–307
  with repetition from past to present, 299–300
    vs. simple past tense, 301–302
  statements in, 284–285
  vs. present perfect continuous tense, 309
  vs. simple past tense, 290–291, 308
  vs. simple present tense, 288–290
Present tense, simple, 1–42. *See also* Simple present tense
Pronouns
  definite, 458–461
  editing advice for, 141–142
  indefinite, 458–461
  object, 124–125, 358–361
  possessive, 120–123
  reflexive, 131–133
  relative
    as objects of adjective clause, 358–361
    as subject of adjective clause, 356–358
  subject, 121, 124–125, 356–358
Pronunciation
  of *to*, 333
  of *can* vs. *can't*, 246
  of *going to*, 69
  of *got to*, 242
  of *had better*, 250
  of *has to*, 242
  of *have to*, 242

  of modals and related expressions, 242
  of noun modifiers, 192
  of plural nouns, 151
  of *supposed to*, 244
  of verbs, AP1, AP3
  of *want to*, 333
  of *yes/no* questions, 8
Proper names, possessive form of, 117
Punctuation
  for adjective clauses, 362, 365
  for adjectives, 190
  for past continuous tense, 221
  for time/*if* clauses, 75
Purpose, infinitives for, 338

Q

Quantity words/expressions, 167–179
  articles with, 169, 449–450
  editing advice for, 180–181
  few, 175
  a few/several/a little, 174–179
  little, 175
  a lot of/ much/ many, 171–174
  some/any/ a/ no, 169–170
  too much/too many, 171–174
Questions
  about meaning, spelling, and cost, 23
  about subject or complement, 135–139
  with *be*, 8–9
  with *be going to*, 69
  with modals, 241
  in passive voice, 421–422
  in past continuous tense, 220
  for politeness, 265–268
  with prepositions, 21, 51
  in present continuous tense, 51–55

in present perfect continuous tense, 292, 294
in present perfect tense, 284–285, 304–307
in simple past tense, 103–105
in simple present tense, 19–21
with *was/were*, 94
with *whose*, 123
with *will*, 66

R

Rarely. See Frequency words
Reflexive pronouns, 131–133
Relative pronouns
  as objects of adjective clause, 358–361
  as subjects of adjective clause, 356–358
Requests, modals and questions for, 265–268

S

's, for contractions, 283
Same as, 401–404
Say, vs. *tell*, 128–129
Seldom. See Frequency words
Sense perception verbs
  action vs. nonaction, 59–64
  adjectives after, 190
  adjectives vs. adverbs with, 198
  with *like/alike*, 398
Several, 174–179
+*s* form
  of plural nouns, 151–154
  of possessive nouns, 117
-*s* form, of verbs, 15
  pronunciation of, AP1
  spelling of, AP1
Should, 250–253
Should not, 253
  contraction of, 240, 250, 253

Similarity, comparatives for, 398–404
Simple past tense, 94–107
  with *be*, 94–95
  editing advice for, 106–107
  of irregular verbs, 98–101
  with negative statements, 101–102
  with questions, 103–104
  of regular verbs, 96–97
  vs. continuous past tense, 229–230
  vs. present perfect tense, 290–291, 308
  vs. present perfect tense with repetition, 301–302
  with *when*, 228–229
Simple present tense, 1–42
  with action vs. nonaction verbs, 59–64
  with affirmative statements, 15–16
  with *be*, 3–13
  editing advice for, 33–36
  with frequency words, 27–33
  with negative statements, 17–19
  with questions, 19–21
  with time/*if* clause, 75–79
  uses of, 56, 79
  vs. present continuous tense, 56–58
  vs. present perfect tense, 288–290
Since, 285, 295
Singular nouns
  editing advice for, 180
  generalizations about, 154–155
  special cases of, 155–156
So far, 299, 301
Some, 169–170, 440–442
Sometimes. See Frequency words

Spelling
  of comparatives and superlatives, 379
  of -*ly* verbs, AP5
  questions about, 23
  of verbs, AP1–3
Subject
  of adjective clause, relative clause as, 356–358
  compound, pronouns for, 141
  gerund as, 318–320, 329
  infinitive as, 329–331
  questions about, 135
Subject pronouns, 121–125
Subject-verb agreement, in adjective clauses, 356
Superlatives, 376–385
  editing advice for, 405–406
  forms of, 378
  irregular, 379
  spelling rules for, 379
  word order for, 384

T

Tell, vs. *say*, 128–129
Tense
  future, 66–81, 69–81. *See also* Future tense
  habitual past, 90–93
  past continuous, 218–230. *See also* Past continuous tense
  present continuous, 43–64. *See also* Present continuous tense
  present perfect, 278–314. *See also* Present perfect tense
  present perfect continuous, 292–298. *See also* Present perfect continuous tense
  simple past, 94–107. *See also* Simple past tense
  simple present, 1–42. *See also* Simple present tense

Than, with comparatives, 386
That
  as object of adjective clause, 358–361
  as subject of adjective clause, 356–358
  vs. *which*, 356
The, 438, 442–445. *See also* Articles
  with quantity words, 449–450
There + form of *be*, 164–166
  editing advice for, 180–181
The same . . . as, 395–396
  for equality, 396
The/the most, with superlatives, 378
Think, as action vs. nonaction verb, 295
Till, 216–217
Time/*if* clause
  with future tense, 75–79
  punctuation for, 75
Time words/expressions, 213–217
  editing advice for, 232
  -ing verb endings after, 230–231
  in past continuous tense, 221–225, 228–231
  in present perfect tense, 285–287, 301
  in simple past tense, 301
To
  gerunds after, 323
  in infinitives, 327, 333. *See also* Infinitives
  pronunciation of, 333
  in time expressions, 216
  vs. *in order to*, 338
Too, 201
  vs. *enough*, 201–202
  vs. *very*, 203–204
Too much/too many, vs. *a lot of*, 172–174, 203–204
Trends, present continuous tense for, 49

Try, with gerund vs. infinitive, 335

U

United States
  major cities of, AP25
  maps of, AP25, AP26
Until, 213, 216–217
Up to now, 299
Used to, 90–93
  vs. *be used to*, 341–344
Usually. *See* Frequency words

V

Verbs
  action vs. nonaction, 59–64
  in active voice, 414, 424–430
  auxiliary
    in comparatives, 386
    with past participles, 278
    with present participles, 293
  base form of, 15
  comparatives after, 388
  direct objects of, 127–128
  -ed ending for
    in past participles, 280
    in present perfect tense, 280
    pronunciation of, AP3
    in simple past tense, 96–97
    spelling of, AP3
  gerunds after, 320–321, 335
  indirect objects of, 127–128
  infinitives after, 323, 333–335
  -ing ending for
    in past continuous tense, 218, 220, 230
    in present continuous tense, 46

    in present perfect continuous tense, 293
    spelling of, AP2
  irregular, 282, AP22–24
    past participles of, 280–282
    -s form of, 15
    in simple past tense, 98–101
  with modals, 238
  nonaction, 59–64
    examples of, 295
  with no object, 424
  in passive voice, 414–430
  prepositions after, 322–323, AP12
  pronunciation of, AP1, AP3
  sense perception. *See* Sense perception verbs
  -s form of, 15
    pronunciation of, AP1
    spelling of, AP1
  spelling of, AP1–3
  superlatives after, 384
  tense of. *See* Tense
  with *used to*, 90
  with *will*, 69–74
Verb-subject agreement, in adjective clauses, 356
Very
  before adverbs, 196
  in quantity expressions, 175
  vs. *too*, 203
Very few, 175
+*ves* form, of plural nouns, 151–154
Voice. *See* Active voice; Passive voice

W

"*Wanna*," 333
Want, in active vs. passive voice, 424
Want to, pronunciation of, 333

Was
   in past continuous tense, 218, 220
   in simple past tense, 94–95
Was not, contraction of, 218, 246
Was/were going to, 226–227
Well, 196, 198
Were
   in past continuous tense, 218, 220
   in simple past tense, 94–95
Were not, contraction of, 218
When, 213
   in adjective clauses, 362–363
   in past continuous tense, 221, 228–230
   in simple past tense, 228–230
   vs. *whenever*, 213
Whenever, 213. *See also* Frequency words
Where, in adjective clauses, 362–363
Which
   as object of adjective clause, 358–361, 363
   as subject of adjective clause, 356–358
   vs. *that*, 356
While, 213
   in past continuous tense, 221, 229–230
   in simple past tense, 229–230
Who
   as object of adjective clause, 358–361
   as subject of adjective clause, 356–358
   vs. *whose*, 365
Whom, 135
   as object of adjective clause, 358–361, 363
Whose, questions with, 123
Whose + noun, 365–369
Wh- questions. *See also* Questions
   with *be*, 8–9
   with *be going to*, 69
   with prepositions, 21
   with present continuous tense, 51
   with simple present tense, 19
Why don't, 265
Will, 261–263
   frequency words with, 66
   future tense with, 66–74
   for politeness, 265
   vs. *be going to*, 72–74
Will not, contraction of, 66, 240, 261
Won't, 66, 240
Would, for politeness, 265
Would not, contraction of, 240

Y

Yes/no questions. *See also* Questions
   be with, 8–9
   pronunciation of, 8
   with simple present tense, 19
Yet, in present perfect tense with indefinite past time, 302

Photo Credits

2, left LWA-Dan Tardif/CORIBS, *right* Bill Truslow/Image Bank/Getty Images; *4,* Mary Kate Denny/Stone/Getty Images; *6,* Ann Marie Weber/Taxi/Getty Images; *14,* Stephen McBrady/PhotoEdit; *18,* Syracuse/Newspaper/David Lassman/The Image Works; *24,* Pam Gardner/Frank Lane Picture Agency/CORBIS; *25,* Michael Simpson/Taxi/Getty Images; *26,* Tim MacPherson/Stone/Getty Images; *43,* Tom and Dee Ann McCarthy/CORBIS; *44,* Ariel Skelley/CORBIS; *45,* Marty Heitner/The Image Works; *49,* Robin Sachs/PhotoEdit; *57,* Bonnie Kaufmann/CORBIS; *64,* Sandra Elbaum; *65,* Ariel Skelley/CORBIS; *68,* David Houser/CORBIS; *70,* Bonnie Kaufmann/CORBIS; *87, top,* Flip Schulke/CORBIS, *bottom,* William Philpott/Reuters/CORBIS; *88,* Bettmann/CORBIS; *89, left,* Duomo/CORBIS, *right,* Frank Trapper/CORBIS; *93,* Thomas Gilbert/AP/Wide World Photos; *97,* Bettmann/CORBIS; *100,* CORBIS; *115,* Rick Gomez/CORBIS; *126,* Steven Rothfeld/Stone/Getty Images; *127,* Brand X Pictures/Getty Images; *129,* Chuck Savage/CORBIS; *134,* Susan van Etten/PhotoEdit; *138,* Tony Freeman/PhotoEdit; *149,* Bob Daemmrich/The Image Works; *150,* Kelley Mooney Photography/CORBIS; *157,* Bruce Ayres/Stone/Getty Images; *166,* Ron Sachs/CORBIS; *168,* Tom Bean/CORBIS; *170,* Marty Heitner/The Image Works; *173,* Sandra Elbaum; *184,* Peter Turnley/CORBIS; *187, left,* Eric K.K. Yu/CORBIS, *right,* Royalty Free/CORBIS; *188,* Robert E. Daemmrich/Stone/Getty Images; *189,* ANA/The Image Works; *194,* Michael Newman/PhotoEdit; *195,* Dana White/PhotoEdit; *211,* CORBIS; *212,* Gail Mooney/CORBIS; *213,* Sandra Elbaum; *218,* Hulton Archive/Getty Images; *227,* Nancy Kaszerman/Zuma/CORBIS; *237,* Michael Newman/PhotoEdit; *239,* Shelley Gazin/The Image Works; *246,* David Young Wolff/PhotoEdit; *249,* Dwayne Newton/PhotoEdit; *252,* Bonnie Kamin/PhotoEdit; *257,* James Marshall/The Image Works; *262,* Willie Hill, Jr./The Image Works; *277,* Dex Images/CORBIS; *278,* Kim Kulshi/CORBIS; *289,* Aleata Evans; *292,* Images.com/CORBIS; *298,* Richard Lord/The Image Works; *315,* Ralf-Finn Hestoft/CORBIS; *316,* Royalty Free/CORBIS; *353,* Randy M. Ury/CORBIS; *354,* Tony Freeman/PhotoEdit; *361,* Aleata Evans; *364,* David Young Wolff/PhotoEdit; *375,* Duomo/CORBIS; *375,* Mike Segar/Reuters/CORBIS; *376,* Reuters/CORBIS; *377,* Reuters/CORBIS; *381,* Reuters/CORBIS; *382,* Reuters/CORBIS; *385,* Bob Daemmrich/The Image Works; *390,* Didrik Johnck/CORBIS; *397, left,* Albert Gea/Reuters/CORBIS, *right,* Robert Galbraith/Reuters/CORBIS; *413,* Jose Luis Pelaez, Inc./CORBIS; *414,* Billy E. Barnes/PhotoEdit; *422,* Michael Newman/PhotoEdit; *423,* Billy Aron/PhotoEdit; *437,* Susan van Etten/PhotoEdit; *438,* David Young Wolff/PhotoEdit; *442,* Mary Kate Denny/PhotoEdit; *444,* Jeff Greenberg/The Image Works; *451,* Michael Newman/PhotoEdit; *451,* Joseph Sohm/Visions of America/CORBIS; *456,* Dana White/PhotoEdit; *459,* David Young Wolff/PhotoEdit; *461,* Michele Birdwell/PhotoEdit.